INNOCENT
BYSTANDERS

INNOCENT
BYSTANDERS

Developing Countries and the War on Drugs

PHILIP KEEFER
AND
NORMAN LOAYZA
Editors

A COPUBLICATION OF PALGRAVE MACMILLAN AND
THE WORLD BANK

1818 H Street NW
Washington, DC 20433
Telephone: 202-473-1000
Internet: www.worldbank.org
E-mail: feedback@worldbank.org

1 2 3 4 13 12 11 10

A copublication of The World Bank and Palgrave Macmillan.

PALGRAVE MACMILLAN
Palgrave Macmillan in the United Kingdom is an imprint of Macmillan Publishers Limited, registered in England, company number 785998, of Houndmills, Basingstoke, Hampshire, RG21 6XS.

Palgrave Macmillan in the United States is a division of St. Martin's Press LLC, 175 Fifth Avenue, New York, NY 10010.

Palgrave Macmillan is the global academic imprint of the above companies and has companies and representatives throughout the world.

Palgrave® and Macmillan® are registered trademarks in the United States, the United Kingdom, Europe, and other countries.

ISBN: 978-0-8213-8034-5 (softcover) ISBN: 978-0-8213-8036-9 (hardcover)
DOI: 10.1596/978-0-8213-8034-5 (softcover) DOI: 10.1596/978-0-8213-8036-9 (hardcover)
eISBN: 978-0-8213-8035-2

Library of Congress Cataloging-in-Publication Data has been applied for.
Printed in the United States.

Contents

Foreword by Fernando Henrique Cardoso   *xi*

About the Editors and Authors   *xv*

Abbreviations   *xxi*

Introduction   **1**
Philip Keefer and Norman Loayza

1   **Drug Prohibition and Developing Countries:**
    Uncertain Benefits, Certain Costs   **9**
    Philip Keefer, Norman Loayza, and Rodrigo R. Soares

2   **The Historical Foundations of the Narcotic**
    Drug Control Regime   **61**
    Julia Buxton

3   **Can Production and Trafficking of Illicit**
    Drugs Be Reduced or Only Shifted?   **95**
    Peter Reuter

4   **Evaluating Plan Colombia**   **135**
    Daniel Mejía

5   **Evo, Pablo, Tony, Diego, and Sonny:**
    General Equilibrium Analysis of the
    Market for Illegal Drugs   **165**
    Rómulo A. Chumacero

6 Competitive Advantages in the Production and Trafficking of Coca-Cocaine and Opium-Heroin in Afghanistan and the Andean Countries   195
Francisco E. Thoumi

7 Cocaine Production and Trafficking: What Do We Know?   253
Daniel Mejía and Carlos Esteban Posada

8 Responding to the Challenge of Afghanistan's Opium Economy: Development Lessons and Policy Implications   301
William A. Byrd

Index   341

Box

8.1. National Drug Control Strategy—Objective, Priorities, Pillars   320

Figures

1.1. Number of Adults Incarcerated for Drug Law Violations in the United States, 1972–2002   14
1.2. (a) Potential Opium Production, 1990–2007; (b) Potential Cocaine Production, 1990–2007   30
1.3. (a) Retail Cocaine Price, 1990–2006; (b) Retail Opiate Price, 1990–2006   32
1.4. Real Prices for Cocaine, Heroin, and Marijuana, 1975–2003   33
1.5. Annual Prevalence of Marijuana, Cocaine, and Heroin Use among U.S. High School Seniors, 1975–2008   33
1.6. Rate of U.S. Hospital Emergency Room Mentions for Marijuana, Cocaine, and Heroin, 1978–2002 per 100,000 Population   34
1.7. (a) Cocaine Retail Price and GDP per capita; (b) Heroin Retail Price and GDP per capita, 1997–2005   38

1.8.   (a) Prevalence of Cocaine Consumption and
       GDP per Capita in Population Age 15–64;
       (b) Prevalence of Heroin Consumption and GDP
       per Capita in Population Age 15–64, 1997–2005   43
4.1.   Trends in Cocaine Use in Consumer Countries,
       1999–2006   137
4.2.   Trends in Cocaine Prices, 1999–2006   138
4.3.   Number of Hectares Cultivated with Coca Crops
       and Potential Cocaine Production in Colombia,
       1999–2006   139
4.4.   Productivity of Coca per Hectare per Year in
       Colombia, 1999–2006   139
4.5.   Potential Cocaine Production in Bolivia, Colombia,
       and Peru, 1999–2006   140
4.6.   Interdiction in Producer and Transit Countries,
       Since 2000   141
4.7.   Amount of Cocaine Interdicted and Disrupted from
       Flows toward the United States, 2000–06   142
4.8.   Estimated Quantity of Export-Quality Cocaine
       Flowing toward the United States, 2000–06   143
4.9.   The Model in a Nutshell   148
5.1.   Fitted Probabilities and Expenditures   178
7.1.   Estimates of Coca Bush Cultivation in Bolivia,
       Colombia, and Peru, 1987–2005   259
7.2.   Estimates of Coca Bush Cultivation in Bolivia,
       Colombia, and Peru by UNODC and ONDCP, 2000–08   260
7.3.   UNODC and ONDCP Estimates of Coca Bush
       Cultivation in Colombia, 1999–2005   262
7.4.   Potential Dried Coca Leaf Production and Prices
       in Bolivia and Peru, 1990–2007   263
7.5.   Coca Base Production and Prices in Colombia,
       2000–07   264
7.6.   UNODC and ONDCP Estimates of Potential Cocaine
       Production in Bolivia, Colombia, and Peru,
       1996–2006   266
7.7.   Average Expected Purity of Powder Cocaine in
       the United States, 1981–2007   268

7.8.   Average Purity of Powder Cocaine in the
       United States, 1981–2007   269
7.9.   Percentage of U. S. Population Age 12 and
       Older Reporting Use of Cocaine, 1985–2007   271
7.10. Cocaine Use in the Past 30 Days among 12th
       Graders in the United States, 1991–2006   271
7.11. Average Price of 1 Gram of Pure Powder
       Cocaine in the United States, 1981–2007   272
7.12. Price of Cocaine in the United States and
       Europe at Street Purity, 1990–2007   273
7.13. The Market for Cocaine (1980–2008) and
       the Stability of Cocaine Supply (2000–08)   274
7.14. Coca Bush Cultivation and Eradication in
       Bolivia, Colombia, and Peru, 1993–2008   281
7.15. Seizures of Coca Base and Cocaine in Bolivia
       and Colombia, 1997–2007   283
7.16. Destroyed Illegal Cocaine Laboratories in Bolivia
       and Colombia, 1997–2007   284
7.17. Seizures of Cocaine in the United States, 1989–2007   285
8.1.   Dry Opium Prices in Kandahar and Nangarhar,
       1997–2006   309
8.2.   Opium Poppy Cultivation in Selected Provinces,
       2003–07   309
8.3.   The Vicious Circle of the Drug Industry in
       Afghanistan   318
8.4.   Consolidation of the Drug Industry in Afghanistan   319

Tables

1.1.   Price Structure of 1 Kilo of Pure Cocaine and
       1 Kilo of Pure Heroin, Selected Countries and Cities,
       Mid-1990s and 2000   18
1.2.   Cross-Country Evidence on the Determinants of
       Retail Cocaine Prices, 1997–2005   36
1.3.   Cross-Country Evidence on the Determinants of
       Retail Heroin Prices, 1997–2005   37

1.4. Cross-Country Evidence on the Prevalence of
      Cocaine Consumption in Population Age 15–64,
      1997–2005   44
1.5. Cross-Country Evidence on the Prevalence of
      Heroin Consumption in Population Age 15–64,
      1997–2005   45
2.1. Pre–World War II Drug Conventions   74
2.2. Post–World War II Drug Conventions   82
2.3. The International Drug Control Apparatus   89
3.1. Estimated Prevalence Estimates of Opiate Abuse
      Worldwide, 2007   97
3.2. Estimated Prevalence of Cocaine Use
      Worldwide, 2007   98
3.3. Production of Dry Leaf Coca in Bolivia, Colombia,
      and Peru, Selected Years 1990–2007   99
3.4. Global Production of Opium, Selected Years
      1990–2006   100
3.5. Highest-Ranking Countries for Seizures of Cocaine
      and Opiates, 2006   102
3.6. Price and Purity Estimates for 1 Kilogram
      of Cocaine and Heroin, 2007   105
3.7. World Trade in Selected Agricultural and Industrial
      Commodities, 1999   117
4.1. U.S. Assistance for Plan Colombia by Program
      Objective   136
5.1. Functional Forms   176
5.2. Parameter Values   177
5.3. Probabilities   178
5.4. The Effects of Increased Risks   181
5.5. The Effects of Stiffer Penalties   183
5.6. The Effects of Legalization   185
A5.1. Distribution of the Expenditures of the U.S.
      Government on Control of Marijuana, Cocaine,
      Crack, Stimulants, LSD, PCP, and Heroin, 1986–2003 189
A5.2. Relative Prices, 1981–98   190
A5.3. Risks   191

6.1. Number of Neutralized Drug-Running Planes in Peru,
      1991–2001   237
8.1. Summary Statistics on Afghanistan's Opium Economy,
      1995 and 2000–09   308

Foreword

Fernando Henrique Cardoso
34th President of the Federative Republic of Brazil

Drug use/abuse is one of the most difficult challenges facing the contemporary world. If it is true that there has always been consumption of different types of drugs in different societies—although not in all of them—it is no less true that it generally took place in restricted, socially regulated realms, especially in ritualistic ceremonies. This is not the case today. Drug use has spread to all segments of society, with hedonistic motivations; although it is often not socially sanctioned, users are at times, depending on the drug, treated with leniency.

It is well-established that all drugs are harmful to our health, even the legal ones, such as alcohol and tobacco, and that some drugs are more harmful, such as heroin and crack. The discussion of "gateway drugs" is a medical issue on which there is no consensus. For the purposes of public policy design, the important thing to keep in mind is that drugs produce negative consequences for both users and societies in general, and that minimizing their consumption should be the main goal. The salient discussion, therefore, is about choosing among different strategies to achieve the same goal.

The dominant strategy to date has been called the "war on drugs." Under the auspices of this war, the United Nations, supported primarily by the United States, has signed successive agreements to broaden the criminalization of drug use and facilitate the reduction of production and drug trafficking.

Ten years after the last United Nations convention on the matter, and exactly one century after the first international effort to ban the trade of narcotic substances—the International Opium Commission—the United Nations Commission on Narcotic Drugs met in Vienna in March 2009 to assess the results achieved by the "war on drugs" strategy. Simultaneously in Europe and Latin America, committees of independent members did the same, relying on analyses prepared by experts. I co-chaired, with former presidents of Colombia and Mexico, César Gaviria and Ernesto Zedillo, respectively, the Latin American Commission on Drugs and Democracy.

Our conclusion was straightforward: We are losing the war on drugs. If we continue with the same strategy, we will be merely relocating agricultural plots and drug cartels to other areas, without necessarily reducing violence and corruption generated by the drug industry. Thus, instead of insisting on a strategy that has repeatedly failed to reduce the profitability and hence the power of the drug industry, why not change the approach? Why not focus our efforts on reducing consumption and the damage caused by the personal and social scourge of drugs? Such an approach would not overlook repression but would target policies to fight organized crime and corruption, rather than to jail thousands of drug users.

Throughout the world, we begin to see a departure from the purely coercive model, even in some American states. In Portugal, which since 2001 has had a model based on prevention, health care, and rehabilitation, critics strongly believed that drug consumption would explode. This was not the case. Instead, Portugal had a reduction in use, especially among young people aged 15 to 19 years. It would be simplistic, however, to propose that we simply replicate here and there the experiences of other countries without further consideration.

In Brazil, there is no large-scale production of drugs, except for marijuana. What exists is the territorial control by traffickers supplied mainly from abroad. Given poverty and unemployment in urban areas, the traffickers form extensive networks of dealers, distributors, and consumers, who recruit their members with ease. The country became a large consumer market, driven mainly by the middle- and high-income classes, and it is no longer only a transit route for drug trafficking. As long as demand and profitability remain high, it will be difficult to withhold the attraction that trafficking carries to a young mass of people, including children, coming from the poorest populations.

The situation is appalling. Fear reigns in the *favelas* (slums) of Rio. Drug lords impose their own rules and "sentence"—even to death—those who breach them. The police force, with some exceptions, is divided between those who assent to traffickers and those who enter the *favelas* to kill. To the mother of the often innocent victim, it makes no difference if the "stray bullet" left the gun of a criminal or a policeman.

Change is more than necessary: it is urgent. But there are no recipes or easy answers.

Innocent Bystanders: Developing Countries and the War on Drugs makes a valuable contribution to the debate. First, it recognizes that developed countries—the major consumers—have imposed harmful policies on the drug-producing countries. These policies have had dire consequences—corruption of the police forces and judiciary and traffic-related violence—for the economic development and political stability of the producer countries. Second, this book provides evidence that the "war on drugs" strategy did not have a significant impact on its goals to increase the street price of drugs and to reduce its consumption. Instead, the book presents us with examples of the "law of unintended consequences"—prohibition created economic incentives for traffickers to emerge and prosper; crop eradication in the Andean region helped increase the productivity of the remaining crops; and the fight against illegal heroin trade in Afghanistan mostly hurt the poor farmers and benefited the Taliban.

Most of all, this book contributes to the debate by shedding light on our understanding of the economics and logistics of the drug market. In proposing alternatives to the problem of drug consumption, passionate defenses of this or that model abound. But it is only through evidence-based knowledge and broad political coalition building that we will be best prepared to win one of the biggest challenges of our times.

About the Editors and Authors

Julia Buxton is senior research fellow in the Department of Peace Studies, University of Bradford, United Kingdom, where she is a specialist on conflict issues and policy responses, with a regional focus on South America. Her previous publications include *The Political Economy of Narcotics* and *The Failure of Political Reform in Venezuela*. She was part of the working party sponsored by the Andean Investment Fund that analyzed the impact of the United Nations General Assembly Special Session on Drugs, to which she contributed research on alternative development in counternarcotics strategies.

William A. Byrd serves in the World Bank's headquarters in Washington, D.C., as economic adviser in the Fragile and Conflict Affected Countries Group, where he is responsible for research, knowledge, and learning activities related to fragility and conflict. Previously, he was adviser in the Poverty Reduction and Economic Management Unit of the South Asia Region of the World Bank. In 2002, he established the World Bank's office in Kabul and helped develop the Bank's strategy for support to Afghanistan's reconstruction effort. Until late 2006, he was the World Bank's senior economic adviser in Afghanistan.

He has been with the World Bank for more than 20 years and has carried out a number of multiyear assignments based in developing countries, including Afghanistan, India, and Pakistan. He has published six books on China, other books, and numerous articles. He has been responsible for studies on Afghanistan's economic development, public finance management, economic cooperation in Central Asia, and the country's drug industry. More recently, he was coauthor of a joint report of the World Bank and the U.K. Department for International Development entitled "Afghanistan: Economic

Incentives and Development Initiatives to Reduce Opium Production" and also of a World Bank report, "Fighting Corruption in Afghanistan: Summaries of Vulnerabilities to Corruption Assessments." He has a Ph.D. in economics from Harvard University and an M.A. in East Asian regional studies from the same institution.

Rómulo A. Chumacero is an associate professor in the Department of Economics of the University of Chile and a senior economist in the Research Department of the Central Bank of Chile. He holds a B.A. in economics from the Catholic University of Bolivia, an M.A. in economics from ILADES/ Georgetown University, and a Ph.D. in economics from Duke University. His principal research interests are econometrics and macroeconomics.

Philip Keefer is a lead research economist in the Development Research Group of the World Bank. Since receiving his Ph.D. in economics from Washington University at St. Louis, he has worked continuously on the interaction of institutions, political economy, and economic development. His research has included investigations of the impact of insecure property rights on economic growth, the effect of political credibility on the policy choices of governments, and the sources of political credibility in democracies and autocracies. He has published the results of his research in journals that span economics and political science, ranging from the *Quarterly Journal of Economics* to the *American Review of Political Science*; his research has been influenced by his experience in a wide range of countries, including Bangladesh, Brazil, the Dominican Republic, Indonesia, México, Perú, Pakistan, and the Philippines.

Norman Loayza is lead economist in the research department of the World Bank. He was born in Arequipa, Peru, and completed his high school and general university studies in Lima. He obtained a B.A. from Brigham Young University in economics and sociology. He received a Ph.D. in economics from Harvard University in 1994. He has conducted research at the World Bank, with an interruption of two years (1999–2000) when he worked as senior economist at the Central Bank of Chile. He has taught postgraduate courses and seminars at the University of the Pacific in Lima, the Catholic University of Chile, and the University of São Paulo. He has presented seminars and conferences in places as diverse as Buenos Aires, Cairo, Helsinki, Madrid, Mexico City, Nairobi, and Rio de Janeiro. In his professional life, he has focused on several areas related to economic and social development, including economic growth, private saving, financial depth, monetary policy, openness to trade, poverty alleviation, and crime prevention. He has edited five books and published more than 30 articles in professional journals.

Daniel Mejía is professor of economics at the Universidad de los Andes in Bogotá, Colombia, where he has taught since 2006. He received a B.A. and M.A. in economics from the Universidad de los Andes and an M.A. and Ph.D. in economics from Brown University. Before joining the Universidad de los Andes, he worked as a researcher at the Central Bank of Colombia and at Fedesarrollo. His research includes studies on the political economy of conflict in Colombia; on the relationship among human capital formation, inequality, and economic growth; and on the relationship between the informal economy and aggregate economic activity. During the past few years, he has been actively involved in a research agenda whose main objective is to provide an independent economic evaluation of antidrug policies under Plan Colombia. The BBC, *Newsweek, El Espectador, Gazeta Wyborcza, Revista Semana, Foreign Policy,* and Stephen Walt's blog, among others, have discussed his research on this topic. His work has been published in the *Journal of Development Economics,* the *European Journal of Political Economy,* and the *Economics of Governance.* In 2008, he was awarded Fedesarrollo's German Botero de los Ríos prize for economic research and two grants from the Open Society Institute for the study of antidrug policies in Colombia.

Carlos Esteban Posada has a B.A. in economics from the Universidad de Medellín and is a Ph.D. candidate in economics at the Université de Paris 1. He has taught economics in several Colombian universities. In addition, he has been a researcher in three Colombian institutions (including Banco de la República, the Colombian Central Bank) and an economic policy officer in the Colombian Council of International Commerce and in the National Planning Department. He is now lecturing at the Universidad Nacional. Mr. Posada is author and coauthor of many academic papers on macroeconomics, labor economics, and the economics of crime and violence, several of them published in refereed journals and books.

Peter Reuter is a professor in the School of Public Policy and in the Department of Criminology at the University of Maryland. He is director of the

Program on the Economics of Crime and Justice Policy at the university and also senior economist at RAND. In 1989, he founded and then directed RAND's Drug Policy Research Center until 1993; the center is a multidisciplinary research program begun with funding from a number of foundations. His early research focused on the organization of illegal markets and resulted in the publication of *Disorganized Crime: The Economics of the Visible Hand,* which won the Leslie Wilkins award as outstanding book of the year in criminology and criminal justice. Since 1985, most of his research has dealt with alternative approaches to controlling drug problems, both in the United States and in Western Europe. He is coauthor (with Letizia Paoli and Victoria Greenfield) of *The World Heroin Market: Can Supply Be Cut?* His other books are (with Robert MacCoun) *Drug War Heresies: Learning from Other Places, Times and Vices* and (with Edwin Truman) *Chasing Dirty Money: The Fight against Money Laundering.* From 1999 to 2004, he was editor of the *Journal of Policy Analysis and Management.* In 2007, he was elected the first president of the International Society for the Study of Drug Policy.

Rodrigo Soares is associate professor of economics at the Pontifical Catholic University of Rio de Janeiro. He received his Ph.D. in economics from the University of Chicago in 2002. His research centers on development economics, ranging from health, human capital, and population to corruption, institutions, and crime. His work has appeared in various scientific journals, including the *American Economic Review, Journal of Political Economy, Journal of Public Economics,* and *Journal of Development Economics,* among others. His dissertation—"Life Expectancy, Educational Attainment, and Fertility Choice: The Economic Impacts of Mortality Reductions"—earned him the 2003 Brazilian National Award for best Ph.D. dissertation in economics. In 2006, he was awarded the Kenneth J. Arrow Award from the International Health Economics Association for the best paper published internationally in the field of health economics and also the Haralambos Simeonidis Award for the best paper published by an economist affiliated with a Brazilian institution. He is an affiliated fellow at the Brazilian Academy of Sciences, a faculty research fellow at the National Bureau of Economic Research, and a research fellow at the Institute for the Study of Labor (IZA, Germany).

Francisco E. Thoumi is Tinker Visiting Professor of Latin American studies at the University of Texas in Austin. He holds a Ph.D. in economics from the University of Minnesota. During the past 15 years, his research has focused on the political economy of illegal drugs, mainly in the Andean countries. His principal works on the subject include *Illegal Drugs, Economy and Society in the Andes* and *Political Economy and Illegal Drugs in Colombia*, in addition to the edited volumes *Drugs, Crime and Armed Conflict in Colombia*, the winter 2005 issue of the *Journal of Drug Issues*, and *Drogas Ilícitas en Colombia: su Impacto Económico, Político y Social*, Dirección Nacional de Estupefacientes and UNDP, Bogotá: Editorial Planeta, 1997. Mr. Thoumi was also research coordinator of the United Nations Global Programme against Money Laundering.

Abbreviations

ADAM	Arrestee Drug Abuse Monitoring
AD	alternative development
ADB	Asian Development Bank
ADP	alternative development program
AKDN	Aga Khan Development Network
AREU	Afghanistan Research and Evaluation Unit
CIA	Central Intelligence Agency (United States)
CICAD	Inter-American Drug Abuse Control Commission
CIP	Center for International Policy
CNC	Crime and Narcotics Center (United States)
CORAH	Special Coca Control and Eradication Project in the Upper Huallaga (Peru)
CPEF	Central Poppy Eradication Force (Afghanistan)
CPI	consumer price index
CV	Red Command (Brazil)
DARE	Drug Abuse Resistance Education
DEA	Drug Enforcement Administration (United States)
DEVIDA	voluntary eradication program (Peru)
DIRAN	antinarcotics police (Colombia)
DIRECO	Dirección de Reconversión de la Coca
DNE	Dirección Nacional de Estupefacientes (Colombia)
DNP	National Planning Department (Colombia)
ELN	Ejército de Liberación Nacional
ENACO	Empresa Nacional de la Coca (Peru)
FARC	Fuerzas Armadas Revolucionarias de Colombia (Revolutionary Armed Forces of Colombia)

g	gram
GAO	Government Accountability Office (United States)
GDP	gross domestic product
GNP	gross national product
GTZ	German Technical Corporation
INCB	International Narcotics Control Board
INCSR	International Narcotics Control Strategy Report
ISI	Inter Services Intelligence (Pakistan)
kg	kilogram
LSD	lysergic acid diethylamide
MAS	Movement toward Socialism (Bolivia)
MRTA	Tupac Amaru Revolutionary Movement (Peru)
mt	metric tons
NATO	North Atlantic Treaty Organization
NDCS	National Drug Control Strategy (Afghanistan)
NIDA	National Institute of Drug Abuse
OAS	Organization of American States
OEA	Organización de los Estados Americanos
OECD	Organization for Economic Co-operation and Development
ONDCP	White House Office of National Drug Control Policy
PCC	First Command of the Capital (Brazil)
PDPA	People's Democratic Party of Afghanistan
PEAH	Special Upper Huallaga Project (Peru)
PPP	purchasing power parity
PREM	Poverty Reduction and Economic Management network of the World Bank
SAMHSA	Substance Abuse and Mental Health Services Administration (United States)
SIN	National Intelligence Service (Peru)
SPY	Bolivian coca lobby
STRIDE	System to Retrieve Information from Drug Evidence
TNI	Transnational Institute
UDP	Popular Democratic Unity (Bolivia)
U.K.	United Kingdom (adjective)
UN	United Nations
UNHCR	United Nations High Commissioner for Refugees
UNIDIR	United Nations Institute for Disarmament Research

UNODC	United Nations Office on Drugs and Crime
UNODCCP	United Nations Office for Drug Control and Crime Prevention
USAID	U.S. Agency for International Development
VOC	Vereenigde Oost-Indische Compagnie
WHO	World Health Organization

Note: All dollar amounts are U.S. dollars, unless otherwise indicated.

Introduction

Philip Keefer and Norman Loayza

Societies have long grappled with how best to respond to the production, consumption, and distribution of psychoactive drugs. Unfortunately, they have not typically conducted a sober evaluation of the costs and benefits of different policy responses. More so than with other public policy issues, the interplay of deep-seated ideological stances and entrenched economic interests seem to have dictated government responses to the drug trade. MacCoun and Reuter (2001: 3) describe the debate in the United States as "essentially ideological, with bitter denunciations of motivation on both sides." To a large extent, this ideological standoff is the same now as it has been in the past. The British response to Chinese efforts to *restrict* the import of opium from colonial India resulted in the Opium Wars. The Spanish government relied on revenues from the taxation of the monopoly supplier of opium in its Philippines colony. After the Spanish-American War of 1898, the U.S. government tried to

---

We are grateful to the World Bank Presidential Contingency Fund, at that time under the stewardship of James Wolfensohn, for providing the resources to finance this effort. However, the views expressed here and the following chapters are those of the authors and do not necessarily reflect the views of the World Bank, its board of directors, or the countries it represents.

continue that monopoly, but religious opposition within the United States undercut those efforts (MacCoun and Reuter, 2001). A century later, the actors are different, but the confrontation between ideology and profit has continued to yield stubborn rates of drug consumption and violence.

Despite a policy-making environment that offers little encouragement to the analysis of the social costs and benefits of alternative policy proposals, efforts continue to evaluate the effects of decriminalization, different approaches to education and treatment, and unconventional enforcement strategies. Most such efforts are domestic in their focus: what are the internal, domestic consequences of different policies? Moreover, studies typically consider the issues from the perspective and interests of developed countries. Such studies, for example, point to the distributional consequences within wealthy consuming countries of changes in drug policy (such as the prospect that legalization could increase consumption and related costs in wealthier neighborhoods but reduce violence in poorer ones). Drug markets are international, however, and domestic drug policies in wealthy countries can have profound effects on economic development and political stability in less wealthy, more vulnerable ones. Those effects, which are not often analyzed or taken into account, are the focus of this volume.

Developing countries are heavily affected by current antidrug policies, but their interests are not weighted heavily in the decisions of wealthy consuming countries. Of course, countries always tend to place the greatest weight on the interests of their own citizens. It is not clear, though, that even domestic citizens benefit from current drug policies in the consuming countries with the harshest legal stances against drugs. It is a perverse calculation of social welfare that could support slight (if any) improvements in the welfare of domestic interests at the expense of dramatic declines in the welfare of foreign interests—although history is filled with examples of such calculations. Moreover, ignoring the effects on the larger international community is inconsistent with the goals of wealthy countries themselves, which invest heavily in promoting political stability and economic development throughout the world.

Three questions shape this volume and the efforts of contributors to achieve a better understanding of the development effects of drug policy choices.

- First, what does the evidence say about the effects of current antidrug policies imposed by wealthy nations on the economic development and political stability of developing countries?
- Second, what are the mechanisms through which those policy choices influence development?
- Third, what is the range of estimates of the domestic costs and benefits in wealthy countries of particular policy alternatives, against which development consequences can be compared?

Taking the contributions together, three conclusions emerge: current drug policies impose large costs on developing countries with little evidence of offsetting benefits to those countries; the aspects of prohibition most strongly associated with high costs in developing countries—interdiction and particularly crop eradication—have little or no impact on drug use in consuming countries; and alternatives to prohibition, such as those associated with education, prevention, and treatment of drug users, should be considered and more systematically implemented and evaluated.

Consequences of Drug Prohibition and Enforcement

In chapter 1, Philip Keefer, Norman Loayza, and Rodrigo Soares offer an overview of the consequences of drug prohibition and its enforcement. Those effects are controversial and not as well understood as one would expect. Several results seem to emerge clearly, however. First, while policy choices do affect drug consumption, significant drug consumption is a persistent phenomenon across dramatically different policy regimes. Second, the greatest impact of drug policies may be in their distributional effects: who in society bears the costs? Third, drug prohibition has important unintended consequences for developing countries, particularly when it emphasizes crop eradication and interdiction efforts in those countries. Poor farmers, in particular, bear heavy costs from eradication efforts relative to their own incomes and relative to the costs imposed on drug traffickers. Moreover, prohibition induces organized crime and undermines security and political stability in poor countries where drugs are produced.

The authors conclude that available evidence is entirely insufficient to make any claims about whether the social benefits of drug prohibition exceed its high social costs. The greater problem, though, is that available evidence about the efficacy of alternative policies to curb drug consumption and its consequences is deficient. The evidence leaves key questions essentially unanswered: how much do current policies reduce consumption and what would the welfare costs of higher consumption be? They argue that in the face of deep uncertainty about the benefits of different drug policies, greater weight should be placed on their social costs, which are much better understood. Policy makers who take into account the great uncertainty surrounding policy benefits would adopt a substantially different set of drug policies from those in force today: they would place much more emphasis on policies with low social cost, such as harm reduction, and invest much more in understanding the effects of diverse policies.

Ineffectiveness of Drug Policies That Target Production and Trafficking

Although prohibition policies could be confined to local markets and policies that penalize only domestic consumption and drug trafficking, in practice, consuming countries bolster prohibition with policies aimed at disrupting the supply of drugs from producer countries. The international focus of drug prohibition efforts has a long history. In chapter 2, Julia Buxton provides a historical account of how antidrug policies have evolved in the past century. She shows how particular interests in the United States promoted and eventually dominated the policy stance toward psychoactive drugs within the United States and around the world. Despite the lack of success of international efforts to control the production and trafficking of narcotics, Julia Buxton observes that "the drug control system has evolved over a one-hundred-year period, and during this time the prohibition model has become institutionalized, consolidated, and global." It is "accepted by all national governments regardless of regime type, religion, ideological orientation, or level of national development." Her chapter explores this remarkable cohesion, and the almost unprecedented *formal* unanimity of the world community regarding a policy choice that, within countries, continues to be hotly debated. She notes with special irony the persistence of that policy, given that when it was initially agreed, at a summit meeting of global powers in Shanghai in 1909, the incentives of the major actors to extract resources from their colonies rather than improve the welfare of citizens of poor countries were stronger than they are today.

Of course, drug prohibition in wealthy countries imposes costs on developing countries in large measure because of the policies used to suppress drug trafficking and production. In chapter 3, Peter Reuter describes the general lack of efficacy of all such policies aimed at reducing drug production and trafficking, ranging from many varieties of "sticks" (interdiction, crop eradication, and local law enforcement efforts to combat the drug trade) to, almost literally, "carrots" (alternative development strategies meant to wean farmers away from drug crop production and to encourage the cultivation of legal crops). He points to many reasons for the lack of efficacy, but chief among them is the wide range of conditions in which drug crops can be produced, the great mobility of illegal drug traders, and the large economic rewards of drug production in the face of persistent high demand. In fact, given that the raw material costs of heroin and cocaine are approximately 1 percent of their retail price in rich countries, it is hardly surprising that the effects of carrots and sticks on source-country drug prices have almost no effect on demand in consuming countries.

Daniel Mejía's detailed case study in chapter 4 on the effects of the antidrug policies implemented in Colombia between 2000 and 2006, an effort known as Plan Colombia, illustrates many of the obstacles to successful eradication outlined in the previous chapter. He reports a jump in the productivity of coca cultivation, as drug producers reacted to more vigorous eradication efforts with stronger plants, better planting techniques, and the use of molasses to insulate plants from the aerial spraying of herbicides. These improvements and the shift of production to neighboring countries more than offset the large increase in drug seizures, which rose from 140 tons in 2000 to 220 tons in 2006. He argues that the limited efficacy of Plan Colombia can be explained by the mixed motivations of the key actors. The Colombian government, for example, is far more efficient in interdicting drugs than in eradicating them. It invests significantly more resources in eradication, however, because that investment harms rebel forces, than in interdiction, which harms drug traffickers.

Chapter 5, by Rómulo Chumacero, focuses in greater detail on the economics of drug markets. He starts with the contention that assessing the effects of alternative policies should take into account the incentives and price signals that they imply for all economic agents. Chumacero's chapter develops a general equilibrium model that considers the full chain of the illegal drug trade, from production to trafficking to final consumption. The model is calibrated to characterize the market for cocaine and then is used to analyze the effects of either making enforcement stricter or legalizing the drug trade. Among the many insights that his model yields is that eradication efforts increase the risk of coca production, lowering the incentives to crop cultivators, but raise the potential profits from cocaine trade, inviting either more drug traffickers or stronger drug cartels. In contrast, legalization benefits coca farmers, who can command higher prices for their crop, and is generally disliked by drug producers and traffickers. Legalization can also lead to higher cocaine consumption, but even this effect can be controlled if resources are invested in diminishing the probability of addiction.

The Political and Social Consequences of the War on Drugs in Developing Countries

The last three chapters are case studies that explore the economic, political, and social consequences of international efforts to curb drug production and trafficking in specific countries. In chapter 6, Francisco Thoumi confronts the social and political consequences of the war on drugs in Afghanistan and the Andean countries. His point of departure is that, as Reuter also notes, drug production and trafficking can happen virtually anywhere: coca plants or opium poppies can be successfully cultivated in many countries, but extensive production is found in only a few. Why? Thoumi argues that specific social and political conditions and historical legacies favor the organization of illegal activity over others; and it is these that most heavily influence the locus of drug production and trafficking. The illegality of drug markets, in turn, reinforces country characteristics that are themselves detrimental to economic and political development. Illegality provides rents to criminal enterprises that they would not otherwise enjoy and gives them the wherewithal and incentives to intervene in the political and institutional processes of their countries.

In chapter 7, Daniel Mejía and Carlos Posada carefully review the difficulties of analyzing illegal drug markets, focusing on the cocaine trade and the three countries that produce most of it—the Plurinational State of Bolivia, Colombia, and Peru. A mystery that has bedeviled analysts is that cocaine prices appeared to fall between 2000 and 2004, although demand was seemingly flat and production apparently fell. Officials had lauded measured production declines as evidence of the effectiveness of eradication strategies. More accurate analysis, however, solved the puzzle: earlier production estimates were typically calculated by multiplying crude productivity estimates by estimates of the extent of cultivation, based on satellite photos. Those dramatically underestimated actual production quantities. More precise estimates of productivity, which are based on field research in Colombia, found a 40 percent increase in yields: although the extent of cultivation in Colombia fell by 30 percent, productivity increases more than compensated for the decline, and supply did not fall as previously thought.

Substantively, Mejía and Posada's chapter reveals in great detail one of the most daunting obstacles to a successful eradication policy: the wide array of countermeasures that producers have devised. Those measures include not only advances in productivity but also specific steps to avoid detection by intermingling coca and food crops and to mitigate the effects of aerial spraying of herbicides by spreading molasses over coca plants. They also point to the unintended effects of eradication, including income effects on poor farmers, social unrest, and environmental consequences of spraying (noting that coca cultivation is itself environmentally damaging but mostly because of efforts to avoid detection).

Finally, in chapter 8, William Byrd focuses on the economic implications of the illegal heroin trade for Afghanistan. His work highlights the dilemma that confronts wealthy countries intent on supply-side strategies for curbing domestic drug consumption. On the one hand, the economic development and political stability of Afghanistan are an international priority. On the other hand, the drive to eradicate opium poppy cultivation in Afghanistan has led to dramatic fluctuations in farmer incomes, has driven up the economic returns to illegal trafficking to the benefit of criminal organizations, has financed the operations of the Taliban insurgency, imperiling the political stability of the country, and has raised enormously the returns to corrupt behavior by those who should be agents of law and order in the country.

Byrd's straightforward account of the different options that have been tried to reduce poppy cultivation in Afghanistan is sobering. Ironically, only the Taliban enjoyed dramatic success but used means that most nations would abjure. Even there, production came back with a vengeance after short-lived success. Nevertheless, if the reduction of poppy cultivation is a "must," Byrd proposes an agenda for incremental "smart strategy" consisting of a selective application of eradication (for example, to better-off and new opium-producing areas), an emphasis on interdiction against medium and larger drug traffickers, and a comprehensive approach to supporting alternative livelihoods. This eradication strategy fully internalizes the costs of eradication in the target country.

Governments confront no easy policy choices with regard to psychoactive drugs. On the one hand, apart from the most draconian interventions, supply-centered approaches have been found ineffective in preventing the extensive, persistent drug trade and consumption. On the other hand, ideological (cultural, religious) imperatives render some otherwise worthwhile policy choices politically infeasible in many developed countries. In the long run, ideological convictions evolve only when the costs of those convictions are made clear. The contributions to this volume identify some of those costs. They point to the limited efficacy of efforts to curb drug production and trafficking in poor countries and the negative political and economic development consequences of those efforts. These costs are not very different, in principle, from those imposed by enforcing drug prohibition on the inner cities of wealthy countries. Consideration of the detrimental effects of "the war on drugs" on the poor and their potential development should play a more prominent role in drug policy debates in the future.

Reference

MacCoun, Robert J., and Peter Reuter. 2001. *Drug War Heresies: Learning from Other Vices, Times, and Places.* New York: Cambridge University Press.

1

Drug Prohibition and Developing Countries: Uncertain Benefits, Certain Costs

Philip Keefer, Norman Loayza, and
Rodrigo R. Soares

Motivated by the pernicious effects of narcotic drugs on individuals and society, most governments have proscribed their trade and consumption. Some have invested enormous resources in enforcing those prohibitions. Despite such efforts, drug consumption has grown and its trade has flourished. The efforts themselves have triggered a long train of unintended consequences, thus raising the possibility that policies focused on prohibition and interdiction cause more damage than the drugs themselves. The consequences, particularly for social stability, may be greatest in those developing countries in which drug production and transit occur. The costs are rarely recognized in drug policy discussions in wealthy consuming nations. This chapter discusses those costs, puts them in the context of the broader debate on drug policy, and reviews existing evidence of the costs and benefits of current policies for reducing drug consumption.

Naotaka Sugawara and Tomoko Wada provided excellent research assistance. For insightful comments and discussions, we are grateful to Ximena Del Carpio, Gabriel Demombynes, Daniel Mejía, Claudio Raddatz, Peter Reuter, Luis Servén, participants of the 2008 Latin America and Caribbean Economic Association Meetings, and three anonymous referees.

As argued in this chapter, we know more about the costs than the benefits of different policy approaches to limiting drug consumption. We know, for example, that such costs are much higher for prohibition, interdiction, and eradication than they are for policies loosely termed "harm reduction," such as treatment and education. The relative social benefits of these different policy options, however, are entirely uncertain. Given that the costs of current policies are so much higher than those of alternative policies, we conclude that the great uncertainty about relative benefits in and of itself justifies a fundamental review of current drug policies.

In this chapter, we first evaluate the social costs of prohibition. Some of them are well known and exist in both consuming and producing countries. Those costs include the opportunity costs of financial resources diverted to the police, judiciary, and prison systems and the human resources lost through prohibition-induced violence and incarceration. Other social costs, which we describe as the unintended or neglected consequences of prohibition, arise primarily in developing countries:

- First, the illegality of drug use can exacerbate some of its negative effects on individual and public health.
- Second, eradication and interdiction policies may result in losses to farmers who traditionally cultivate crops associated with the production of drugs.
- Third—and most important—in the face of high demand for drugs, current prohibition policies create the potential for massive profits, leading to high levels of violence and organized crime. When organized crime groups pursue those profits, their efforts produce not only violence but also corruption and political instability.

We then place the costs that current drug policies impose on producing and transit countries in the context of the broader debate on the costs and benefits of policies to curb drug use within consuming countries. We first examine what we know about the social benefits of suppressing drug use: that is, the degree to which suppression reduces the costs that drug use imposes on nondrug users (negative externalities) and the private costs that drug users unintentionally impose on themselves (for example, by underestimating the risks of addiction). We find, first, that the most serious tangible costs imposed by drug users are likely to be borne by themselves and their own families. Second, to an extent largely unknown, the private costs of at least some types of drug consumption may be anticipated and accepted by at least some users. And third, the private and social costs of drug consumption vary significantly across types of drugs (typically higher for the most addictive ones) and across demographic groups (with young people usually being the most vulnerable).

We then examine the evidence of how well different policy options—particularly those related to criminalization of the drug trade, eradication, and interdiction—reduce consumption. Evidence on eradication and interdiction generally shows that such strategies do not significantly curtail the supply of drugs to consuming countries, mainly because of the wide range of conditions in which drug crops can be produced and the great mobility of illegal drug traders. Large potential profits to drug traders lead them to innovate in the face of stronger enforcement: whenever necessary, they shift the areas of cultivation, the inputs of production, and the method of transportation. Evidence of the effects of prohibition within consuming countries is both sparse and, by the standards of evidence used in other policy debates, unreliable. It is difficult even to conclude whether the efficacy of any particular intervention is likely to be high or low, either absolutely or relative to other interventions. Existing analyses, as well as the new cross-country comparisons that we present, suggest that significant relaxation of current prohibitions on the sale of cocaine and heroin would double consumption.

Calling attention to the limitations and disadvantages of prohibition and to the war on drugs should not be interpreted as either a defense of unrestricted drug trade or a justification for a hands-off policy approach toward drug consumption.[1] Rather, we call for a drug policy that is guided by the principles of public intervention in the face of uncertainty: first, aggressive responses are justified only when the potential for error and large welfare losses is small; and, second, all policies should be constantly evaluated on the merits of their outcomes. In this framework, there seem to be grounds for regulatory intervention and for public programs that emphasize education and treatment.

In the following sections, the chapter addresses five specific topics:

- the negative consequences of the war on drugs as we highlight its effects on public health, distribution of wealth, and institutional stability in producing and trading countries

- the economic case for prohibition as we outline the basic economic framework that justifies intervention in any market and the limitations of its application to the case of drugs
- the efficacy of current policies in reducing drug trafficking
- the response of drug consumption to changes in prices and regulatory regimes
- the policy implications of those findings and conclusions.

The Negative Consequences of Illegality and Repression

The merits of any public policy depend crucially on the costs that the policy imposes. Drug policies range from those related to harm reduction, such as treatment and education, to the current dominant strategy of suppressing drug consumption through the eradication of supplies, the interdiction of drug shipments, and the criminalization of the drug trade—a set of policy responses that we loosely term "prohibition." The social costs of *harm reduction* policies arise largely from the opportunity costs of their budgetary allocations. In contrast, the social costs of *prohibition*, well documented and widely recognized by policy makers, go well beyond its financial costs in both developed and developing countries. The opportunity costs of prohibition spending (such as outlays on policing, courts, and prisons) are substantial. Federal, state, and local governments in the United States, for example, are currently spending roughly $40 billion annually on the war on drugs, up substantially from $10 billion in the mid-1980s (Reuter 2001). MacCoun and Reuter (2001, 28) and Pacula (2008) conclude that at least three-fourths of U.S. national expenditures on drugs are spent on apprehending and punishing dealers and users. Treatment expenditures account for, at most, one-sixth of total federal expenditures.

While the budgetary costs of prohibition to consuming countries appear to be quite high, one unintended effect of prohibition is to impose even higher budgetary costs (at least relatively) on some developing countries involved in the international war on drugs. The Mexican government, for example, is currently spending $9 billion per year to fight drug trafficking, more than three times the amount the United States spends relative to gross domestic product (GDP). This expenditure has financed the expansion of the federal police from 9,000 officers in 2006 to 26,000 in 2009, as well as the mobilization of 45,000 military troops to fight drug-trafficking gangs.

In another example, the Colombian government committed to increasing defense expenditures from 3.6 percent of GDP in 2003 to 6 percent by 2006, increasing security forces from 250,000 (150,000 military plus 100,000 police) to 850,000 over four years (Colombian Government 2003). These expenditures are intended to combat insurgency in the country, including drug trafficking as the most important source of financing and arms to both right-wing paramilitaries and left-wing guerrilla movements. In contrast, public expenditures on health in Colombia were around 5 percent of GDP in 2000 (World Development Indicators). The opportunity cost of these resources for developing countries, for investments in health, education, or infrastructure, is almost surely larger than that in richer countries and represents a substantial but generally neglected cost of prohibition strategy.

The social costs of prohibition policies go far beyond the budgetary, however. Two well-known costs associated with prohibition policies in the United States are the violence associated with drug trafficking and the productivity losses resulting from incarceration. In the United States, one in every four prisoners is in jail for drug-related, mostly nonviolent offenses (Caulkins and Chandler 2006). The imprisonment rate for drug-related offenses in the United States is above the overall imprisonment rate of most Western European countries (*The Economist* 2001; MacCoun and Reuter 2001). Figure 1.1 shows that the number of adults incarcerated for drug law violations in the United States increased more than tenfold between 1982 and 2002. Although it is unlikely that incarcerated drug offenders would be highly productive were they employed outside the drug sector, even estimates reported by proponents of these policies put production losses from the 660,000 incarcerated drug offenders at approximately $40 billion annually (Executive Office of the President, the White House, 2004).

Other significant social costs of prohibition have received less attention, as they are particularly relevant for developing countries:

- Prohibition damages public health, exacerbating the social costs of any given level of drug consumption.
- Prohibition exposes farmers to substantial losses.

Figure 1.1. Number of Adults Incarcerated for Drug Law Violations in the United States, 1972–2002

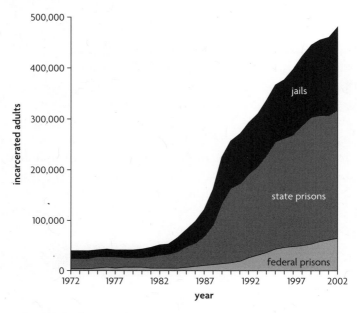

Source: Caulkins and Chandler (2006).

- Prohibition encourages organized crime and undermines public safety, security, and institutions.

Public Health

Prohibition has serious public health consequences as well. One is to drive drug traffickers to countries where drug consumption would otherwise be less prevalent and where governments are significantly less able to curb consumption and treat drug users. This phenomenon arises as drug traffickers seek friendlier countries through which they can export their product to rich consuming countries. Drug consumption grows in transit countries because the marginal cost of distribution is low and the supply abundant.

To expand their presence in European markets, for example, drug traffickers have opened a beachhead in Guinea-Bissau, where large shipments of cocaine are bundled into small packages that can be brought into Europe with a lower risk of detection. Anecdotal evidence indicates that cocaine use is now significant in the country.[2] Better known is the case of Central Asia. Drug traffickers have long preferred an overland route through Central Asia to bring opiates from Afghanistan to Europe. As a consequence, Central Asian countries have experienced a dramatic increase in rates of drug consumption. Some—Kazakhstan and the Kyrgyz Republic, among others—that had almost no drug dependency problems in 1990 now have addiction rates higher than those of many Western European nations (Reuter and others 2004).

According to the International Narcotics Control Strategy Report (2006) released by the Bureau for International Narcotics and Law Enforcement Affairs, U.S. Department of State,[3] around 60 percent of opiate exports smuggled out of Afghanistan bound for Europe, the Persian Gulf, Russia, and Turkey passes through Iran. Iran now has an estimated 3 million opiate abusers, as many as 60 percent of whom are reported as addicted. Iran is thus one of the countries with the highest prevalence of heroin consumption in the world. Iran is vigorous in its efforts to prevent drugs from reaching its citizens: more than 3,400 Iranian law enforcement personnel have died in clashes with drug traffickers in the past 20 years.

Second, illegality undermines the usual vehicles of product-quality assurance upon which legal markets rely. To various degrees in consuming countries, the quality of drugs is low and uncertain because illegality impedes consumer protection regulation and discourages retailers from building reputations for quality. Although reputational investments in illegal retail drug markets exist, they are limited: there is no open advertising or investment in the vertical supply chain to ensure quality, and distributors have low returns to reputational capital because of the probability of future incarceration and loss of control of their business. In this context, overdoses caused by uncertain strength and poisoning caused by adulteration are both likely to be more frequent among drug users than they otherwise would be (see Bernardo and others 2003; Miron and Zwiebel 1995; and Cameron and Collins 2006).

Third, illegality hinders efforts to treat drug users and to prevent the spread of disease. Drug users are seen primarily as criminal offenders rather than as patients needing help. Their treatment is often prescribed and perceived as a punishment rather than as an effective cure (indeed, it is a customary element of court sentencing for drug offenders in the

United States). As a consequence, governments invest little in treatment programs, which are often quite expensive and beyond what (often unemployed) problem drug users can afford. Furthermore, since drug consumption tends to take place in hidden and unsanitary conditions, the transmission of contagious diseases becomes more likely.

The spread of HIV/AIDS among intravenous drug consumers in recent decades is a case in point. Public health efforts to distribute free syringes for drug users and, in some circumstances, to make services available to check the purity of drugs may lessen these problems. However, users are reluctant to take advantage of these opportunities when consumption itself is criminalized (Godinho and Veen 2005). In addition, governments often refuse to implement these services because of fears that they increase the total demand for drugs.

Of course, as we discuss in greater detail later, a reduction in the costs of drug use that flows from relaxing prohibition would result in an increase in consumption and in the corresponding negative health effects of drug use. The negative health consequences related to prohibition, therefore, need to be set against the health costs of increased use and addiction if prohibition were replaced by a less aggressive drug policy.

Farmer Losses and Rents to Traffickers
Even if eradication efforts are unsuccessful in reducing consumption in rich countries, they still impose losses on farmers who cultivate poppies or coca. Those farmers do not have access to insurance against losses resulting from eradication, and they are too poor to self-insure. Moreover, eradication tends to target entire areas, so that any informal safety-net arrangements between farmers break down. For "eradicated" farmers, such losses could, therefore, be catastrophic.

Farmer welfare losses are usually considered irrelevant to evaluations of prohibition, precisely because their farming activity is regarded as either criminal in and of itself or because it contributes to criminal activity in other countries. These welfare losses should be taken more seriously, however. First, the farmers do not see themselves as criminals, nor do others in their societies view them as such, because criminalization of the cultivation of poppy seeds and coca is seen as an imposition of the drug policies of rich consuming countries. Second, given that these farmers are generally poor, their economic setbacks have a proportionally larger impact on their welfare.

In the cases of the Plurinational State of Bolivia and Peru, coca culti-vation has become a symbol of the indigenous population and of its lack of access to political representation. In those countries, coca has a long history of cultivation and use among the indigenous population and is closely related to their cultural identity. In the past few years, policies to limit coca cultivation have been used as a catalyst for organizing nation-wide protests against the political elites and the wealth expropriation perceived by the poorer indigenous population (see *The Economist* 2004 and 2007b). In the recent experience of Bolivia, President Sánchez de Lozada was removed from office after protests over natural gas and coca production rights. Evo Morales, a coca-grower (*cocalero*) organizer, was the leader of those protests and is the current president of the country. Politically active *cocalero* organizations are also present in Peru, where they have gained parliamentary representation and have demanded that Congress legalize coca cultivation (Thoumi 2009).

Prohibition also affects the generation and distribution of profits along the production and distribution chain of the illegal drug. The organized criminal network required for trafficking the goods funnels gains from farmers, upstream, and from consumers, downstream, to those criminal organizations. Because of the high barriers to entry to links in the distribution chain—barriers imposed by violence and offi-cial corruption—the criminal organizations can demand high prices from consumers and offer low prices to producers or farm-gate traders.

The extreme concentration of profits at the top of the distribution network, particularly in its last stages, is clear in all the estimates avail-able. For example, Wilson and Zambrano (1994) estimate that 87 percent of the profit of the cocaine trade remains in drug-consuming countries. More recently, Reuter and Greenfield (2001), Smith (2005), and Reuter (2010) estimate the price structure for 1 kilo of pure cocaine and heroin at different stages of the production and distribution chain. The num-bers are presented in table 1.1. The results indicate that a major part of the profits end up in the hands of those who control the later stages of the traffic and distribution process. Proportionally, the highest jump in price is observed as the drug leaves the producing country and reaches the wholesale market in the destination country, where it increases 25–30 times. That price structure supports the conclusion that most profits are appropriated by intermediaries with large market power. This role is the one traditionally played by the international drug cartels.

Table 1.1. Price Structure of 1 Kilo of Pure Cocaine and 1 Kilo of Pure Heroin, Selected Countries and Cities, Mid-1990s and 2000
(*dollars*)

Stage	Cocaine (mid-1990s)	Cocaine (2000)	Heroin (2000)
Farm-gate	370 (Leaf in Peru)	650 (Leaf in Colombia)	550 (Opium in Afghanistan)
Export	1,200 (Colombia)	1,050 (Colombia)	2,000–4,000 (Afghanistan)
Import	20,500 (Miami)	23,000 (Miami)	10,000 (Turkey export)
Wholesale (kilo)	31,000 (Chicago)	33,000 (Chicago)	50,000 (London)
Wholesale (oz.)	62,000 (Chicago)	52,000 (Chicago)	65,000 (London)
Final retail value	148,000 (Chicago)	120,000 (Chicago)	135,000 (London)

Source: Reuter (2010); Smith (2005).

If policies were relaxed, current drug traffickers would lose their comparative advantage and be replaced by regular businessmen. It is less clear what would happen to farmers in countries that currently produce cocaine, heroin, and marijuana. They would have to compete with other farmers in an open market and could lose from the increased competition (in a way similar to coffee, cotton, or fruit farmers in most developing countries who face potential losses from lower-cost or higher-quality competitors). If their expertise, labor resources, and especially natural endowments were sufficiently valuable, however, they would win a share of the market and appropriate its normal rents under less risky, potentially insurable conditions.

Organized Crime: Violence, Insurgency, and Corruption

It is not surprising that drug traffickers could overwhelm the institutions of a small, poor country such as Guinea-Bissau, with only 63 federal police officers.[4] However, the influence of organized drug traffickers is great even in far larger and wealthier countries. A recent detailed report by the International Crisis Group (2008) on cocaine trafficking concludes that "despite the expenditures of great efforts and resources, the counter-drug policies of the U.S., the European Union and its member states, and Latin American governments have proved ineffective and, in part, counterproductive, severely jeopardizing democracy and stability in Latin America." These conclusions are predictable. Whenever there are high rents from criminal activities and the costs of bribing are low, intensified sanctions and policing may actually generate the perverse consequences of promoting organized crime and its ensuing violence, widespread corruption, and higher crime rates (Kugler, Verdier, and Zenou 2005). The consequences, in turn, may threaten the institutional environment even further, leading to an increase in the very activity that prevention efforts initially intended to reduce.

The comparative advantage of organized crime resides in its use of violence and corruption for enforcing contracts, setting up distribution networks, and establishing trade routes. In conducting their business, criminal organizations use their own mechanisms to substitute for the state and other formal institutions. One immediate consequence of the usefulness of violence in drug markets is adverse selection into the drug business itself: individuals prone to or skilled in violence are more likely to enter the drug business than to become managers of, for instance, beer and tobacco companies. Violent individuals are disruptive in any society, but legal interventions that motivate them to organize have the unintended effect of exacerbating their negative influence (see Thoumi 2009).

The escalation of violence in areas that have become strongholds of illegal drug production and trade highlights the harmful effects. For example, 27,000 people died on average in Colombia in each year of the 1990s as a result of violence. This death toll implied a reduction of more than two years in Colombian life expectancy at birth (Soares 2006). Similar numbers have been observed in Brazil in recent years, where organized crime has reached a level not previously seen in the country. Linking the phenomenon of high crime with illegal drug trafficking, Sérgio Cabral, the governor of the Brazilian state of Rio de Janeiro, has declared that a lot of crime in his state and city "comes from [drug] prohibition. . . . [M]any young people die in wars over drug-selling spots," calling then for a debate on drug legalization in Brazil and internationally (Drug War Chronicle 2007).

Violence is not universally associated with drug trafficking, but it is intense and epidemic in settings where drug markets are heavily contested between competing gangs. Paradoxically, violence often intensifies as governments attempt to disrupt the drug trade by killing or arresting the heads of the criminal organizations: their semi-stable oligopoly is replaced by a multitude of warring factions.

Although much violence results from traffickers' competition for market share, state efforts to fight traffickers also unleash substantial violence. Large-scale police and army operations have resulted in high numbers of deaths throughout the world, from Brazil and Mexico to Colombia and Thailand. In Mexico, the army has recently been deployed to combat drug gangs, and they have responded in kind. Since President Felipe Calderón launched a major offensive against drug-trafficking gangs in December 2006, 10,000 people have died in drug-related violence (twice as many in 2008 as in 2007), including 800 police and soldiers (*The Economist* 2009a). The drug trade, though, continues unabated as drug traffickers have proved to be exceptionally resilient in their ability to pursue their highly profitable activities.

In Thailand, the 2003 government campaign against drug trafficking continues to be controversial. In only three months, more than 2,500 people died. Although initially the police blamed gang violence for the killings, a recent report found that they were the result of a government "shoot-to-kill" policy and that more than half of those killed had no links to drug trafficking (*The Economist* 2008). Adding to the multitude of concrete examples, the academic literature on the subject has found a clear and systematic causal link between drug prohibition and violence (see Dills, Miron, Summers 2008; Fajnzylber, Lederman, and Loayza 2002).

Organized crime groups link with other opponents of state institutions, magnifying the negative effects of drug traffickers on social and political stability. This connection is clear in the association among drug trafficking, guerrilla activities, and terrorism that has become common in South America, South Asia, and other drug-producing regions. In the past two decades, drug traffickers and guerrilla movements in Colombia (the Revolutionary Armed Forces of Colombia, or FARC) and Peru (the Shining Path) have exchanged money and arms for protection until they have eventually become undistinguishable from each other. In Colombia, guerrillas became involved in the drug business in the 1990s to such an extent that about half the FARC resources were estimated to have come from drug production and trade (Reuter and others 2004).

A similar coincidence between terrorist or guerrilla groups and drug production and trafficking has been documented in other areas of the world, including the Middle East and South Asia (Reuter and others 2004). Most notably, in present-day Afghanistan, the Taliban-led insurgency relies on the production of poppy-related drugs to finance its operations, a remarkable irony since the Taliban had successfully banned poppy cultivation during its last year in power (Byrd 2010). The commanders of NATO's International Security Assistance Force recognize that Taliban insurgents and drug traffickers function symbiotically, leading *The Economist* (2007a) to conclude that "arguably the biggest danger to the future of Afghanistan comes not from the external Taliban enemy but from two interconnected internal ones: corruption and opium."

Together, violence and insurgency generate social unrest and political instability that are tantamount to a frontal challenge to the state by organized crime. In the case of the guerrilla movements, this is obviously true, since the motivation for the existence of the movements themselves is typically to challenge the established political order. But that challenge is also present when organized drug traffickers defy the state purely in pursuit of their economic interests. Probably the most widely cited example goes back to Colombia and Pablo Escobar, the leader of the once powerful Medellín cartel who publicly declared that the cartel would pay $50 for each policeofficer killed. The cartel was responsible for the murder of a minister of justice, a Supreme Court judge, an attorney general, a chief of the Narcotics Police, and the front-running presidential candidate, to cite only a few.

In Mexico, *Los Zetas*, a hit squad that works for the Gulf of Mexico drug trafficking cartel and is composed of elite army deserters, is openly recruiting throughout Nuevo Laredo, which is near the border with the United States. There, public advertisements like the following proliferate: "Important Announcement: Operative Group Los Zetas is offering you, military or ex-military personnel, some dirty work. We offer: good salary: 5,000 pesos/week [about $500], stipends, and very good food. Interested people, call (044 867) 168 74 23. Deserters need not abstain."[5]

The two most powerful organized crime groups with clear links to drug trafficking in Brazil—the Red Command (CV) and the First Command of the Capital (PCC)—have coordinated simultaneous rebellions in as many as 29 different prisons and maintained effective control of certain slums and poorer areas. Assassinations of police officers, members of the judicial system, and authorities of the prison system are regular tactics of these groups.

Drug-trafficking organizations also threaten public institutions in more subtle ways. Corruption, though less violent and not explicitly challenging the established order, may be organized crime's most effective weapon. In some Central Asian countries (such as Kazakhstan, the Kyrgyz Republic, Tajikistan, Turkmenistan, and Uzbekistan), organized crime associated with the drug trade has become politically and economically influential (Reuter and others 2004). In Colombia, paramilitaries involved in trafficking have exercised significant political power in vast areas of the country (Thoumi 2009). In November 2008, Noe Ramírez, Mexico's drug policy czar and chief liaison with U.S. antidrug officials, was arrested and charged with taking bribes of $450,000 a month from the Sinaloa drug cartel. Another Mexican drug czar, General José Gutiérrez Rebollo, had followed the same path in the mid-1990s: only three months after U.S. officials had greeted his appointment enthusiastically, he was confined to a maximum-security prison and was charged with receiving bribes and protecting the Juarez cartel, the nation's largest drug trafficker at the time. The general had built a reputation of being "tough on drug trafficking—tough, that is, on organizations that competed with his patron's cartel" (Carpenter 2009).

In those countries, officials and politicians often face the choice of taking a bribe or risking their lives. Not surprisingly, many choose the bribe. Grand corruption involving the financing of political campaigns and bribing of high-ranking officials—as well as petty corruption of police, judicial, and customs officials—undermines the institutional stability of a country and can be very damaging in the long run (Thoumi 2009). A widespread culture of corruption, arbitrariness, and lawlessness weakens the legitimacy of the state and other institutions and severely restricts their capacity to provide basic public goods.[6]

Despite the large nonbudgetary social costs of policies associated with prohibition, if their benefits were similarly large, they could still be preferable to alternative policies. However, conclusive research on the efficacy of either prohibition-related policies or harm-reduction policies is surprisingly thin. It is safe to say that no evidence-based justification supports the policy conclusion implicit in the budget decisions of the United States, for example, that enforcement expenditures have a far more positive impact on social welfare than do expenditures on treatment and prevention. On the contrary, the following sections demonstrate that tremendous uncertainty surrounds the benefits of most drug policies and that what evidence there is offers little support for the current mix of policies.

Why Prohibit Drugs? The Uncertain Costs of Drug Consumption

The choice among regulatory alternatives in any policy arena depends on the relative financial and social costs and benefits of implementing them. Although the social *costs* of alternative drug policies are fairly well understood, the social *benefits* of alternative policies are highly uncertain: even probability distributions of the effects of each are not well defined. This type of uncertainty is the subject of a small literature, inspired in part by debates on climate change. Analyses by Ben-Haim (2006) and Bewley (1987), for example, imply that, confronted with large uncertainty about policy benefits, only policy makers with a high tolerance for welfare losses should prefer an aggressive policy response that seeks large short-term changes in outcomes; less tolerance for welfare losses implies less aggressive policy choices that promote more gradual change.

A key element in those analyses is the possibility that future learning can resolve uncertainty. Gollier, Jullien, and Treich (2000) conclude that, under some circumstances, the more information one expects in the future about toxicity (for example, the negative future climate effects of current emissions), the lower should be current consumption of the potentially toxic substance. This might seem, in the context of drugs, to justify more aggressive efforts to curb drug consumption. Their analysis, however, assumes that policies to curb consumption have known efficacy and no costs. With drugs, the greatest uncertainties concern the efficacy of strategies for curbing drug consumption or reducing the harm of drug consumption. When the benefits of policy are uncertain, though, less aggressive policy stances are called for, as in Akram, Ben-Haim, and Eitrheim (2006).

All analyses, though, emphasize that public policy should aim to resolve uncertainty, regardless of which policy is pursued. This view implies that the implementation (and evaluation) of multiple policies should be preferred, so that alternative policy approaches can be compared. Unfortunately, as the following discussion of the evidence regarding the benefits and efficacy of drug policies concludes, efforts to learn from different policy approaches are plagued by underinvestment in rigorous evaluation. The evidence reviewed next about the social benefits and efficacy of current drug policies documents not only the considerable uncertainty about the efficacy of policies that seek to reduce drug consumption and harm but also the absence of serious effort to resolve that uncertainty.

One significant area of uncertainty concerns the social costs of drug consumption. Prohibition of a specific good can be justified economically only when the negative externalities associated with its consumption or production outweigh the social costs imposed by its prohibition. Given the enormous costs of prohibition, even in consuming countries, one might expect, first, that the externalities associated with drug consumption would be particularly high and, second, that prohibition would be particularly effective in suppressing consumption. The evidence on both assumptions is far from conclusive.

We have few estimates of the tangible externalities that drug users impose on society and none regarding the intangible effects—that is, the welfare costs of drug use for those morally opposed to it. The existing estimates adopt extremely divergent methodologies and are often aimed at calculating costs other than pure externalities. For example, the White House estimates of the economic costs of drug abuse yield a total of $181 billion (1.7 percent of GDP) in 2002 (Executive Office of the President 2004). Of these, however, productivity losses account for 71.2 percent, partly because of drug users' own lost productivity (most of which are private to the drug user and not an externality) but mostly because of the incarceration of 660,000 drug offenders (whose lost productivity does not result from drug use, per se, but from drug criminalization). The remaining 28.8 percent is attributed mostly to crime-related costs. Most of those costs, however, relate to the budgetary costs of arresting and incarcerating individuals for drug offenses. The White House report concludes that the victim costs of property crimes committed *because* of drug use are on the order of $200 million. The victim costs of crime can be regarded as an authentic externality, to the extent that they are driven by drug use.

A study undertaken for the British Home Office (Godfrey and others. 2002) reached similar conclusions about the total cost of drug use in the

United Kingdom (approximately £15 billion in 2000, or 1.6 percent of GDP). However, productivity losses play little or no role in this estimate; by far its largest component is the victim costs of crime committed by problem drug users, amounting to £12.3 billion, far larger than the estimate for the United States. Why the difference? In their report, Godfrey and others. assume that all property crime associated with problem users is caused by drug use. Problem users are defined as all users of opiates or crack cocaine (as opposed to only addicted users). The crime attributed to problem users is based on a longitudinal study of patients in drug treatment programs (reported in Gossop, Marsden, and Stewart 2001) and is the amount by which those patients reported reducing their criminal activity from the three months prior to intake to the period 9–12 months after entering treatment. Godfrey and others conclude that the entire reduction can be attributable to the reduction in drug use and can assume that reductions would be similar if all nontreated problem drug users were also to reduce their consumption.

This estimate of victim costs is likely to be biased upward, however. First, both crime and drug use are the product of unobserved individual proclivities, which drug treatment seeks to address. Therefore, the observed association between drug use and crime is to some extent likely to be spurious, driven by the direct effect of treatment on crime rather than by its indirect effect on crime through reduced drug use. Second, users who enter treatment are more likely than other users to have committed crimes in the first place, again biasing upward the amount of crime that can be attributed to *all* drug users.

The victim costs of crime by addicted drug users are probably higher than the $200 million estimated by the White House (also taking into account the costs from reckless driving or intrafamily abuse committed by drug users, for example) but are also likely to be only a fraction of the more than £12 billion estimated for the British Home Office. The calculations leave out the intangible social costs of drug use—the costs that, in fact, may actually be driving drug policies in some countries. In some places, social and cultural norms are so strong and social opprobrium regarding drug use so great that the tangible social and private costs of drug production may be irrelevant in the evaluation of drug policies. Instead, policy debate is driven by the disutility that nonusers feel from having certain drug users in their midst.[7] Indeed, public policy mirrors the inconsistency of social views on drugs: some drugs are prohibited while others with significant externalities and addictive properties of their own, such as alcohol or nicotine, are much more lightly regulated.

Social opprobrium may determine why private interests of market participants are ignored in policy debates on drugs, in contrast to regulatory debates on legal markets. Levels of social opprobrium vary widely, however, and can change significantly: several U.S. states have decriminalized the medical use of marijuana, where before none had. Even within political parties, there is substantial divergence in views on decriminalization: decriminalization in New Mexico was signed into law by Republican governor Gary Johnson but was vigorously opposed by members of his own party. Much larger differences regarding the disapproval of certain drugs and addiction are present across countries, as evidenced in the way that they penalize possession and consumption (see *The Economist* 2009b). The differences are significant even between otherwise similar or neighboring countries: the Netherlands and Spain are more tolerant than England and France, Norway is more lenient than Sweden, Canada is more tolerant than the United States, and India is more relaxed than Indonesia or Malaysia.

Most of the public debate on drug use focuses on the social costs of drug consumption, such as criminal behavior, reckless driving, aggressive behavior, and other types of potentially irresponsible and dangerous actions by drug users. Little attention is given to the private costs and benefits of drug use, although these affect a very large fraction of the population. The U.S. Department of Health and Human Services estimates that, despite stringent policies and severe punishments, more than 35 million Americans age 12 or over used an illicit drug in 2004, consuming, in sharply decreasing order of importance, marijuana, cocaine, heroin, and other drugs. A complete economic evaluation of drug use policies should also take into account private costs and benefits of these drug users: the welfare gain or loss to them from consuming the good and the monetary gain to producers from being able to sell it above its average cost.

In general, there are three scenarios under which individuals might decide that the private benefits of drug use exceed their private costs. First, for many individuals, the private costs of drug use are low: such people are less vulnerable to addiction, they prefer to consume low enough quantities that the risks of addiction are manageable, or they prefer drugs that are less addictive. Second, more controversially, consumers might actually choose addiction and derive utility from the consumption plan that addiction entails. Economic theories of rational addiction have been developed (see, for example, Becker and Murphy 1988; Lee 1993) that clarify the plausibility and characteristics of this scenario. Third, more worrisome, individuals may underestimate the future consequences of drug use, leading to decisions that may be subsequently regretted but difficult to correct, given that drug addictiveness and its effects on physical and mental health limit the ability and willingness to recover.[8] In the first two scenarios, the justification for policies that suppress consumption depends entirely on the magnitude of the externalities that drug users impose. In the third scenario, however, public (though not necessarily government-driven) intervention may be required to guarantee an efficient allocation, even from the strictly individual perspective and in the absence of externalities.[9]

There is very limited evidence on the relative importance of controlled and planned drug use against unmanageable and undesirable drug consumption (Gruber and Köszegi 2001). Such information should be a key piece of information in the design of drug policies, but the illegality of consumption prevents any serious evaluation. Notwithstanding considerable uncertainty, some observations appear to be uncontroversial and should be taken into account. First, drugs differ significantly in their degrees of "problem" use, that is, the type of consumption that requires treatment for self-incapacitation and potential harm to others. Although a large fraction of chronic heroin users are viewed as "problem" users and in need of treatment, roughly one-half to two-thirds of chronic cocaine users and the large majority of chronic marijuana users do not fall into this category (Executive Office of the President 2001).

Second, most people realize the different effects and addictive power of various drugs and limit their exposure to them accordingly. This response is consistent with the far larger prevalence of consumption of drugs perceived as less harmful (such as legal alcohol and tobacco and illegal marijuana) than of those regarded as dangerous but not highly addictive (such as ecstasy and cocaine) and, in turn, larger than those perceived as highly addictive (such as heroin). People's ability to adjust their behavior to knowledge of harm from drugs is also evident in the considerable decrease in tobacco consumption (and to some extent cocaine consumption) in the mid-1980s when public campaigns alerted people to their health consequences.

Third, some demographic groups, such as teenagers and children, are more likely to fail to anticipate the negative consequences of drug use. Their immature social and physical skills make them more prone to take unreasonable risks, excessively discount their future, and fall under peer pressure. They are correspondingly more vulnerable to cheaper, more harmful drugs, such as crack cocaine and methamphetamines, although public policy devotes enormous effort to less harmful drugs like marijuana.

Drug policies should take into account the negative externalities that drug consumption imposes on others and the unwelcome personal effects of drug addiction. Those policies should, however, consider that drugs vary widely in their effects and that not all people respond similarly to them. Much of the violence associated with Mexican drug cartels and the militarization of drug policy in Mexico, for example, concerns marijuana—not heroin or methamphetamine—production and trafficking.

The Uncertain Efficacy of Policies to Curb Drug Trafficking

The foregoing discussion points to the high social costs of aggressive efforts to combat drug trafficking and consumption—costs that considerably exceed both the purely budgetary requirements and the social costs of alternative drug policies. Although this conclusion is not novel, the discussion diverges from the usual debates about costs to highlight the impact on developing countries of aggressive policies. It leads to the second issue addressed earlier, the extent to which curbing drug consumption improves social welfare. There is general agreement that drug consumption entails social losses, although debate surrounds the question of how high they are. Uncertainty is more extreme, however, when it comes to the design and efficacy of efforts to curb drug trafficking.

The central policy focus in combating drug trafficking is eradication, interdiction, and criminalization. Evidence on the efficacy of those policies exhibits significant uncertainty, thus reflecting the difficulties of collecting evidence on changes in the size of illegal markets, the lack of resources invested in assessing efficacy, and the differences across drug types in their susceptibility to policy intervention. Most estimates of policy efficacy rely on simple calculations of changes in supply and demand; analysts are hard-pressed to justify causal interpretations of such calculations.

With these serious caveats in mind, evidence from drug-producing countries offers little support for the thesis that interdiction and eradication reduce consumption. International efforts to reduce the supply of illicit drugs, a particular focus of this book, show ambiguous results. Drug production and trafficking can change significantly from year to year in a particular country, depending on interdiction efforts. Although international efforts dedicated to suppressing drug production and trafficking have increased substantially, production shows no sign of significant decline. Opium cultivation in Afghanistan, which is responsible for 80 percent of world production, reached one of its highest points historically in 2004 and has almost doubled since then (see figure 1.2a). In the case of coca, aggregate cultivation in Bolivia, Colombia, and Peru in 2007 was higher than the level observed at the end of the 1990s (see figure 1.2b), despite the fact that reported eradication is supposed to have risen substantially in all three countries (which are together responsible for virtually all the world production).

Although one could always argue that retail drug prices in consuming countries would have been much lower and consumption much higher if not for significant investments in eradication and interdiction, there are serious reasons to doubt this claim. Drug crops can be produced in a wide range of conditions, illegal drug traders are highly mobile, and producers and traders are quick to respond to the relatively large economic rewards of drug production in the face of persistent high demand (Reuter 2010). Even if eradication succeeded in raising the costs of raw materials to drug traffickers, the raw material costs of heroin and cocaine are approximately 1 percent of their retail price in rich countries. Even if the raw material costs in producing countries increase several-fold as a result of stronger eradication and interdiction, the drug prices in rich consuming countries are likely to be unaffected.

The large potential profits to drug traders induce them to innovate constantly in the face of stronger enforcement. They shift the areas of cultivation, the inputs of production, and the method of transportation to fulfill their business goals. Opium production, for instance, shifted from Thailand and Turkey to Myanmar and then to Afghanistan in

Figure 1.2. (a) Potential Opium Production, 1990–2007; (b) Potential Cocaine Production, 1990–2007

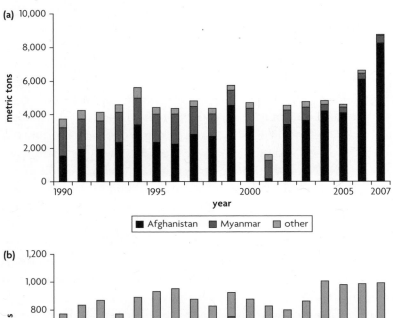

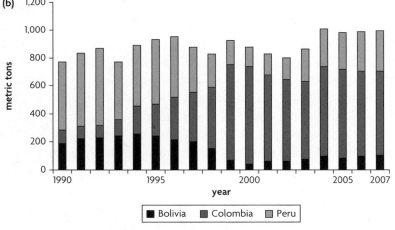

Source: U.N. World Drug Report (2008).
Note: "Potential" is the term used by the World Drug Report and is an estimate.

reaction to changes in enforcement conditions (see figure 1.2a). Likewise, coca production moved from Peru to Colombia in the 1990s as Colombia became weak from civil war; in the 2000s, production partly came back to Peru as Colombia implemented its plan to strengthen security in the country (Mejía and Posada 2010). The cocaine trade routes from South America to the United States have moved from the

Caribbean to Mexico as U.S. forces shut down aerial smuggling from South America. Similarly, the cocaine trade to Europe has involved a shifting variety of routes, directly from the Caribbean to the Iberian Peninsula and the United Kingdom, and more recently through western Africa and even the Balkans. There is much uncertainty about what drives total drug trade, but one thing seems quite clear: it is the countries and regions with weak governments and institutions that are chosen as sources of production and as conduits of drug smuggling (Thoumi 2009).

Uncertainty pervades analyses of the effects of criminalization on drug trafficking and consumption in consuming countries. What evidence there is does not point to high levels of efficacy, however. In the U.S. and European drug markets, although the intensity of prohibition enforcement has grown over time, prices have been stable or declining. The price of cocaine in the United States and Europe declined to its lowest historical levels in the mid 2000s (see figure 1.3a), while purity seemed to have stayed roughly unchanged (Mejía and Posada 2010; Grossman 2004). Heroin prices have followed a similarly declining trend in the United States and Europe (see figures 1.3b and 1.4), not even reflecting the sharp contraction in poppy cultivation during the Taliban regime (Byrd and Ward 2004; Byrd 2010; and Thoumi 2009).

Declining prices may be a sign of success if they reflect reduced demand or a sign of failure if they entail increased supply. The latter interpretation is arguably more likely, since self-reported consumption has changed little and drug-related hospitalizations (a rough indicator of actual drug use) have actually increased (Grossman 2004). As figure 1.5 shows, marijuana and cocaine use among high school seniors in the United States declined between the 1970s and the early 1990s, but since then it has either remained stable or increased slightly. Although drug use seems to have dropped significantly in the United States from the mid-1970s to the mid-1980s, figures reported by the White House confirm that self-reported use of drugs was essentially unchanged from 1988 to 2001.[10] For example, 7.7 percent of respondents reported having used drugs in the past 30 days in a 1988 survey; 7.1 percent reported the same in a (noncomparable) 2001 survey. The data indicate that the proportion of users is likely to have been fairly constant. Harm per dose may have increased, however, consistent with the earlier discussion about the

Figure 1.3. (a) Retail Cocaine Price, 1990–2006; (b) Retail Opiate Price, 1990–2006

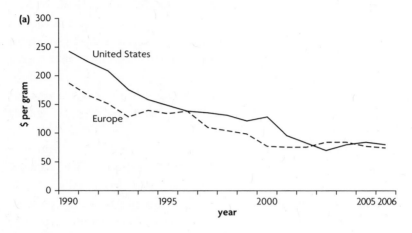

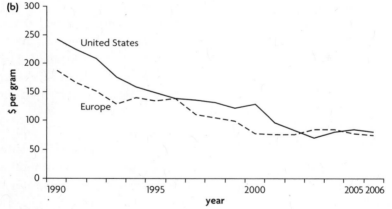

Source: U.N. World Drug Report (2008).
Note: Per gram price is in real terms.

public health consequences of prohibition. Figure 1.6 indicates that drug-related admissions experienced a sustained increase between 1978 and 2002 and more than doubled—for marijuana, cocaine, and heroin—in the shorter time interval between 1990 and 2002.

Evidence from other countries is consistent with the U.S. experience. The significant decline in cocaine prices in Europe throughout the 1990s was not accompanied by a reduction in demand. On the contrary, in

Figure 1.4. Real Prices for Cocaine, Heroin, and Marijuana, 1975–2003

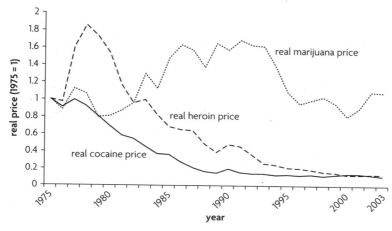

Source: Grossman (2004).

Figure 1.5. Annual Prevalence of Marijuana, Cocaine, and Heroin Use among U.S. High School Seniors, 1975–2008

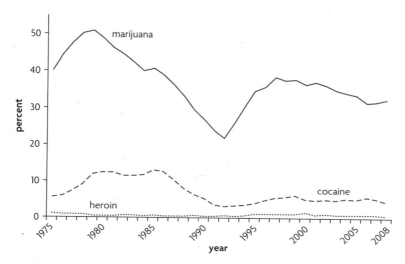

Source: Monitoring the Future (2008).

Figure 1.6. Rate of U.S. Hospital Emergency Room Mentions for Marijuana, Cocaine, and Heroin, 1978–2002 per 100,000 Population

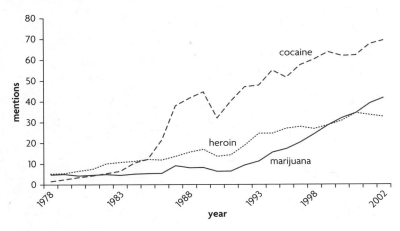

Source: Grossman (2004).

Britain, for instance, cocaine use has doubled since the mid-1990s, with 7.6 percent of young adults (age 15–34) now claiming to have tried it over the past year. And this increase has occurred despite stronger interdiction efforts: cocaine seizures by European forces increased from 20 tons in 1995 to 120 in 2006, a six-fold increase over the course of a decade.

Evidence from significant regime changes is also illustrative, although far from conclusive. Following the legalization of marijuana in the Netherlands, usage appears to have increased, in part due to the significant retailing and marketing efforts that legalization permitted (MacCoun and Reuter 2001). Increased marijuana consumption, however, was not associated either with any significant increase in marijuana-related health problems or with an increase in hard-drug use or drug-related crime. The Netherlands has one of the lowest rates of "problem" drug use in Europe, with only 1 percent of the young adult population reporting to have consumed cocaine over the past year, less than half the European average and less than one-fifth the U.S. average. After Italy relaxed penalties on drug consumption, it saw an increase in heroin deaths (MacCoun and Reuter 2001: 306). However, similar patterns of mortality were observed in both Spain (where policy was consistently permissive) and

Germany (where drug use was consistently penalized). None of the estimates allows us to make conclusive statements about causal relationships between policy changes, consumption shifts, and changes in the harm from drug use. They suffer from data reliability issues and do not permit causal inferences to be made about the effects of policy change. Still, none of the examples is consistent with the claim that the social benefits of prohibition outweigh its social costs.

Historical evidence from other episodes of prohibition, such as the American alcohol prohibition during the interwar period, also raises questions about its ability to deter consumption significantly. Miron and co-authors (Dills and Miron 2004; Dills, Jacobson, and Miron 2005) find that alcohol prohibition reduced consumption by no more than 10–20 percent in the medium run and that it may have had no impact whatsoever over the long run. The effects of prohibition on substances such as cocaine, heroin, and methamphetamines are not comparable to those of alcohol prohibition. The alcohol prohibition regime was less punitive than current enforcement efforts against illegal narcotics, and the physical effects and risks of addiction of substances such as methamphetamines are more pernicious than those of alcohol. Still, the failure of alcohol prohibition underlines the potentially low social benefits of hard policies aimed at preventing people from consuming substances they strongly prefer.

To complement this evidence from case studies, we present new evidence on the efficacy of national enforcement to affect drug retail prices. Clearly, drug prices are not the only cost that potential consumers face when deciding whether or not to use drugs—criminal charges and possible addiction are two important risks that are also taken into account. To the extent that raising drug prices, however, is an important objective of official strategy to combat drug trafficking, it is useful to analyze what drives them. Tables 1.2 and 1.3 present new cross-country evidence on the determinants of cocaine and heroin retail prices. Cross-country comparisons are particularly useful, despite difficult issues of endogeneity, omitted variables, and data quality, because they allow us to examine the effects of large differences in enforcement effort. Prices, qualities, and quantities of drugs vary much more *across* countries than they do *within* countries. A larger variation across countries conveys more information, because it considers a greater number, diversity, and range of

Table 1.2. Cross-Country Evidence on the Determinants of Retail Cocaine Prices, 1997–2005 (*constant 2000 US$ per gram*)

	[1]	[2]	[3]	[4]
Cocaine producer countries (dummy: 1 if cocaine cultivation is reported)	−29.56***	86.17	−29.00**	−28.46***
	−2.75	1.39	−2.41	−2.70
Cocaine seizures (base and salts; kg per 1,000 population)	−17.76***	−60.13**	−16.49***	−17.53***
	−3.66	−2.47	−3.39	−3.78
GDP per capita (PPP, 2000 $, in logs)	26.12***	21.81**	28.85***	22.08***
	6.39	2.55	4.36	3.17
People prosecuted for drug offenses (per 100,000 population, in logs)		0.33		
		0.06		
Police personnel (per 100,000 population, in logs)			1.4132	
			0.14	
Outlays for public order and safety (per capita, PPP, 2000 $, in logs)				1.8510
				0.60
Constant	−160.65***	−111.96	−193.65***	−127.69**
	−4.52	−1.50	−3.41	−2.14
Number of observations	102	57	69	70
R-squared	0.35	0.29	0.35	0.27

Source: Authors' estimation.

Note: Method of estimation: ordinary least squares with robust standard errors; *t*-statistics are presented below the corresponding coefficients; ** and *** denote significance at the 5 percent and 1 percent levels, respectively; variables are an average of 1997–2005 by country, except for a dummy variable for cocaine producer countries. See annex for their definitions and sources. PPP = purchasing power parity.

experiences. (In the next section, we continue this analysis by looking at the determinants of drug consumption prevalence.)

Our purpose for this empirical exercise, we should emphasize, is to analyze the relationship between country-specific retail drug prices and country-specific enforcement measures, not to assess the efficacy of international enforcement efforts. Finding that a country's enforcement strength does not affect its drug prices does not preclude an important price effect if countries jointly change their enforcement stance. This situation would occur, for instance, if the prohibition regime is relaxed internationally, which in all likelihood would reduce prices considerably in some countries. Therefore, our purpose for the following exercise is to ask if, given the current international prohibition regime, the same modest

Table 1.3. Cross-Country Evidence on the Determinants of Retail Heroin Prices, 1997–2005 (*constant 2000 US$ per gram*)

	[1]	[2]	[3]	[4]
Opium producer countries (dummy: 1 if opium cultivation is reported)	−24.07***	−12.28	−36.39***	−17.90
	−2.71	−0.75	−3.26	−1.37
Heroin seizures (kg per 1,000 population)	−1,256.87***	−1,556.16***	−2,271.87***	−1,298.97***
	−4.11	−3.31	−3.75	−3.61
GDP per capita (PPP, 2000 $, in logs)	41.01***	41.61***	45.71***	48.05***
	6.66	3.76	4.19	5.37
People prosecuted for drug offenses (per 100,000 population, in logs)		7.28		
		0.85		
Police personnel (per 100,000 population, in logs)			3.50	
			0.18	
Outlays for public order and safety (per capita, PPP, 2000 $, in logs)				3.13
				0.65
Constant	−272.06***	−299.71***	−320.73***	−350.47***
	−5.65	−3.41	−3.54	−4.40
Number of observations	110	66	70	76
R-squared	0.32	0.29	0.30	0.31

Source: Authors' estimation.

Note: Method of estimation: ordinary least squares with robust standard errors; *t*-statistics are presented below the corresponding coefficients; *** denotes significance at the 1 percent level; variables are an average of 1997–2005 by country, except for a dummy variable for opium producer countries. See annex for their definitions and sources. PPP = purchasing power parity.

effects of drug criminalization on retail prices that are observed in national-level data are also evident in cross-national data.

Our basic data source is the national-level information on drug prices and qualities obtained from United Nations Office on Drugs and Crime (UNODC). Although the data have been criticized for inaccuracy, we have found no evidence that they are systematically biased against the hypothesis that governs current policy choices—that enforcement increases prices. To the degree that they are significantly inaccurate and devoid of information, we would expect nothing to explain them, which is not the case. We focus on the markets for cocaine and heroin, the two drugs that are most traded internationally and that are most relevant to developing countries. Figures 1.7a and 1.7b show the world distribution

Figure 1.7. (a) Cocaine Retail Price and GDP per capita; (b) Heroin Retail Price and GDP per capita, 1997–2005

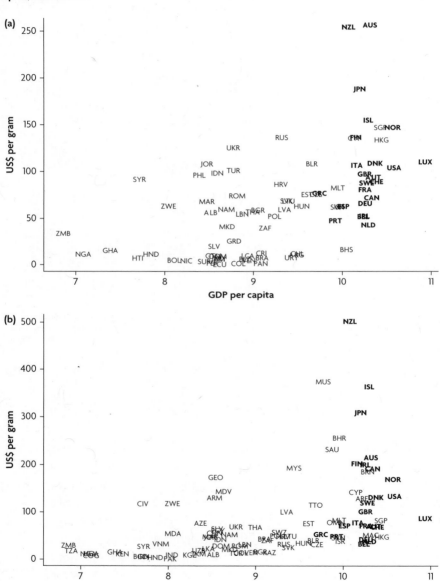

Sources: World Bank World Development Indicators; U.N. World Drug Report (various years).
Notes: Organisation for Economic Co-operation and Development (OECD) countries are presented in bold; prices are in constant 2000 US$; GDP per capita = PPP, 2000 dollars, in logs.

of cocaine and heroin retail prices (in constant 2000 U.S. dollars per gram) by country and corresponding per capita income.

Enforcement of laws prohibiting drug consumption can have two effects on drug prices, depending on the particular enforcement strategy. On the one hand, effective enforcement strategies that emphasize penalties on users suppress demand and *reduce* prices. On the other hand, enforcement strategies that emphasize penalties on suppliers *increase* prices. In fact, actual enforcement strategies are much more strongly focused on the supply side, thereby attacking supply networks, interdicting supplies, and arresting dealers.[11] Consequently, if enforcement is effective, we should observe significantly higher retail prices for cocaine and heroin when enforcement is stronger.[12]

The first challenge is to measure enforcement. Ideally, we would use variables that directly track a country's drug enforcement effort, but such variables are not available for a large sample of countries. We employ several proxies instead. The first is the number of people prosecuted for drug offenses, weighted by population. This proxy, though, is imperfect because more "law-abiding" countries that criminalize drug use will exhibit both lower drug demand (and therefore prices) and lower rates of prosecution. However, this problem would create a spurious bias *in favor* of finding that greater prosecutorial effort is associated with higher drug prices, consistent with the hypothesis that enforcement strategies can succeed in curbing supply and raising prices.[13] As additional proxies for drug enforcement effort, we also control for the number of police personnel in a country (also weighted by population) and the per capita outlays for public order and safety. These are good proxies to the extent that the resources devoted specifically to drug enforcement are systematically related to the overall resources invested in public security.

To limit the biases that result from relevant but omitted explanatory variables, we include per capita GDP and two measures of drug availability in the country as controls. Supply availability is proxied by a binary variable indicating whether the country is a major cocaine or heroin producer and by the intensity of drug seizures in the country.[14] Including per capita GDP controls for the possibility of a spurious correlation between prices and enforcement stemming from the fact that richer countries may have both better drug enforcement (because of more abundant public resources) and higher prices (because of higher demand). Including the measures of drug availability, in contrast, controls for the possibility of a *negative* spurious correlation between prices and enforcement: more drug availability causes prices to fall and, independently, induces larger policing efforts.

The results on the correlates of retail prices for cocaine and heroin are presented in tables 1.2 and 1.3. The R-squared for cocaine and heroin retail prices is around 0.30, and the same variables turn out to be significant in both regressions. For both, as we expect, retail prices are lower when supply is more abundant. The coefficients on the cocaine and heroin producer-country indicators are significantly negative in most regressions. The coefficients on drug seizures are always negative and statistically significant: more drug seizures are associated with lower prices, suggesting that seizures are a reasonable proxy for the supply of drugs in a country. At face value, drug seizures could be regarded as a measure of enforcement. Its negative coefficient would discredit the role of enforcement and of interdiction in particular. We recognize, however, that this interpretation would be extreme. The safest one is to relate drug seizures with availability.

What about the main measures of enforcement effort? The estimated effects of drug offense prosecution, police personnel, and public order budget are all statistically insignificant. That insignificance could be explained because the enforcement effort against drugs is better captured by income per capita, which is positive and significant in all regressions: drug prices are higher in richer countries. Even when income per capita is omitted, however, enforcement variables remain insignificant.[15] This pattern of results may suggest, as well, that income has a positive effect on prices, not because it is correlated with unobserved enforcement effort but rather because significant barriers to entry in drug distribution networks allow price discrimination to persist between richer and poorer countries.

None of the evidence presented in this section is sufficient to conclude that policies aimed at enforcing drug prohibition have failed. The possibility that unobserved factors might be driving the observed unsuccessful outcomes is, despite some attention to the problem, still present. And it may still be the case that the counterfactual situation—what would have happened under a more relaxed stance toward drug trafficking— could have been worse. Moreover, the evidence should not be interpreted as suggesting that a significant international regime shift would have no effect. For instance, a relaxation of the prohibition regime would in all likelihood result in lower prices in consuming countries and a smaller dispersion of prices across all countries. If anything, the lesson to be drawn from this section is that the efficacy of the costly strategies for reducing drug trafficking *in the current context of prohibition* is not evident and that significant uncertainty about its effects persists.

The Uncertain Response of the Demand for Drugs

Several reasons might explain why the evidence of a strong market response to drug prohibition is weak. One is that the necessary data have simply not been collected to estimate the effects correctly. Another is that drug enforcement is, in and of itself, not effective, which is an issue reviewed in the previous section and about which there is considerable uncertainty. It is also possible that the demand for drugs is highly inelastic and, therefore, insensitive to interventions that increase the cost of consumption. As Becker, Murphy, and Grossman (2006) argue, it is difficult to enforce a prohibition on the consumption of goods with inelastic demand. In this case, even interventions that significantly increase the price have a small effect on demand. As with other aspects of the policy debate, however, evidence on the elasticity of drug demand is highly uncertain.

We would expect elasticity to vary with the type of drug, given their different effects and levels of addictiveness. MacCoun and Reuter (2001, 76) report a very low elasticity of demand for highly addictive heroin (−0.2 to −0.3 percent), slightly less elastic than cigarettes (around −0.4 percent). There is more uncertainty in the case of cocaine. MacCoun and Reuter report estimates ranging from −0.7 and −2.0 percent. Most studies find price elasticities below 1 percent in absolute value in the short run, while others have estimated higher price responses in the long run and, in some cases, also in the short run (see the discussion in Mejía and Posada 2010).

The elasticity estimates are based on studies in which the price changes are relatively small; they may not apply to cases where the price change under consideration is large. A better evaluation of "arc" elasticities (that is, elasticities over large price changes) may be obtained through cross-country comparisons, to which we turn next. They reinforce the conclusion that more addictive heroin exhibits very low price elasticity and that cocaine use is more price sensitive than heroin use.

Figures 1.8a and 1.8b show the world distribution of the prevalence of consumption of cocaine and heroin (in percentage of the population aged 15–64) by country and corresponding per capita income. In tables 1.4 and 1.5, we present two empirical models to explain the prevalence of cocaine and heroin consumption across countries. They are formulated in the spirit of demand functions, with the caveats that consumption prevalence is more an indicator of number of users than quantity demanded and that we do not deal explicitly with the simultaneous determination of prices and quantities. The working assumption for this analysis (that is, estimation of a quasi-demand function) is that cross-country variations in the price of drugs have an important component that is orthogonal to the determinants of local demand. Therefore, if we control for GDP per capita and other demand determinants, price differences across countries would arise from supply conditions related to the natural availability of different types of drugs in various regions of the world (according to geographic patterns of production and trade routes) and government policies toward supply (although the evidence for policy effects is weak).

Each table first presents a basic model in which the drug's retail price and the country's per capita income are the sole explanatory variables. The second regression in each table is an extended model, in which the retail prices of alternative illicit drugs and other socioeconomic characteristics are included. The main advantage of the first model is that, because it imposes few data requirements, the sample of countries is quite large (82 for cocaine prevalence and 98 for heroin prevalence). The advantage of the extended model is that it takes into account a fuller array of relevant determinants (at the cost of a smaller sample, 39 countries for both cocaine and heroin).

The results indicate a striking difference in the extent to which similar factors explain the prevalence of the two drugs. Whereas for cocaine prevalence the simple and extended models do reasonably well (with R-squared coefficients of 0.17 and 0.53, respectively), the models have poor explanatory power for heroin prevalence (with corresponding R-squared coefficients of 0 and 0.28). Moreover, for cocaine prevalence, the basic and even some of the additional variables have significant

Figure 1.8. (a) Prevalence of Cocaine Consumption and GDP per Capita in Population Age 15–64; (b) Prevalence of Heroin Consumption and GDP per Capita in Population Age 15–64, 1997–2005

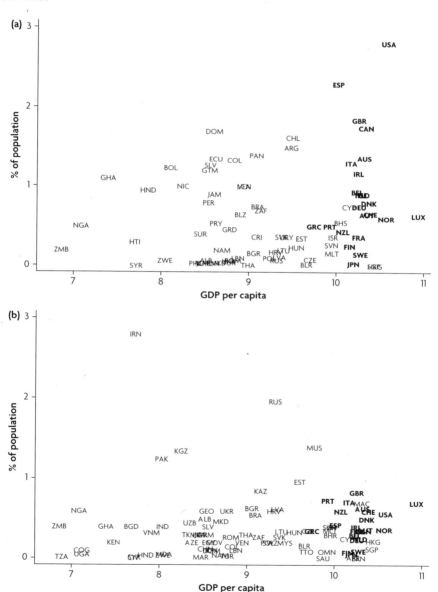

Sources: World Bank World Development Indicators; U.N. World Drug Report (various years).
Notes: OECD countries are presented in bold; prices are in constant 2000 US$; GDP per capita = PPP, 2000 dollars, in logs.

Table 1.4. Cross-Country Evidence on the Prevalence of Cocaine Consumption in Population Age 15–64, 1997–2005

	[1]	[2]
Cocaine retail prices (constant 2000 US$ per gram)	−0.0048*** −2.97	−0.0083*** −2.88
GDP per capita (PPP, 2000 $, in logs)	0.2725*** 3.52	0.3939* 1.76
Cocaine retail purity (%)		0.0119*** 3.11
Heroin retail prices (constant 2000 US$ per gram)		−0.0009 −0.74
Marijuana retail prices (constant 2000 US$ per gram)		0.0694** 2.30
Ecstasy retail prices (constant 2000 US$ per gram)		0.0332* 2.04
Urban population (% of total population)		0.0088 1.41
Youth population (age 10–24, % of total population)		0.0740** 2.25
Alcohol consumption (liters of pure alcohol per capita)		0.0296 0.91
Constant	−1.5589** −2.41	−6.2923** −2.21
Number of observations	82	39
R-squared	0.17	0.53

Source: Authors' estimation.

Note: Method of estimation: ordinary least squares with robust standard errors; t-statistics are presented below the corresponding coefficients; *, ** and *** denote significance at the 10 percent, 5 percent, and 1 percent levels, respectively; variables are an average of 1997–2005 by country. See annex for their definitions and sources.

coefficients, while for heroin consumption only one of the additional variables appears to be significant.

The prevalence of cocaine consumption (table 1.4) is larger in countries with lower cocaine retail prices and higher per capita income. The price and income effects are familiar from the demand functions for regular legal goods. The prevalence of cocaine consumption increases with cocaine purity, which suggests that potential consumers are aware of the deleterious health consequences of contaminated cocaine. The retail prices of marijuana and ecstasy carry significantly positive coefficients, thus suggesting that both drugs are substitutes for cocaine (or an underlying

Table 1.5. Cross-Country Evidence on the Prevalence of Heroin Consumption in Population Age 15–64, 1997–2005

	[1]	[2]
Heroin retail prices	−0.0002	−0.0013
(constant 2000 US$ per gram)	−0.57	−0.88
GDP per capita	−0.0042	−0.1979
(PPP, 2000 $, in logs)	−0.10	−1.55
Heroin retail purity		−0.0037
(%)		−1.05
Cocaine retail prices		0.0006
(constant 2000 US$ per gram)		0.64
Marijuana retail prices		0.0062
(constant 2000 US$ per gram)		0.61
Ecstasy retail prices		0.0166
(constant 2000 US$ per gram)		1.05
Urban population		0.0018
(% of total population)		0.47
Youth population		−0.0082
(age 10–24, % of total population)		−0.42
Alcohol consumption		0.0459**
(liters of pure alcohol per capita)		2.06
Constant	0.4614	1.9053
	1.10	1.47
Number of observations	98	39
R-squared	0.00	0.28

Source: Authors' estimation.
Note: Method of estimation: ordinary least squares with robust standard errors; *t*-statistics are presented below the corresponding coefficients; ** denotes significance at the 5 percent level; variables are an average of 1997–2005 by country. See annex for their definitions and sources. PPP = purchasing power parity.

strong taste for drugs in the population). Finally, a larger share of youth population is linked to higher prevalence of cocaine consumption, even controlling for other development-related variables, such as per capita income and urbanization.

Unlike cocaine consumption, heroin consumption seems insensitive to price. Table 1.5 shows no significant own-price—or cross-price—effects and no significant link with per capita income or with other development-related variables. The only variable that seems to be related to the prevalence of heroin consumption is the consumption of alcohol, which is suggestive of a perhaps culturally or socially rooted taste for addictive or mood-altering drugs. In any case, it is not clear whether the inability of the econometric model to explain heroin consumption derives from problems of measurement in the data or from a very low responsiveness of heroin demand to any economic variable.

Estimates of the price elasticity matter because the efficacy of drug policies is often based on the estimated price effects of those policies rather than on direct measures of consumption. The previous section casts doubt on the ability of national enforcement efforts to affect the retail price of drugs in a given country. As also discussed there, however, this evidence does not mean that a radical shift in the drug prohibition regime would have no effect on drug prices: they would likely decrease significantly in consuming countries. By how much? The cross-country variation of prices can provide an indication of the possible range of change. Moreover, according to the consumption prevalence model we just estimated, cross-country comparisons can tell us the order of magnitude of the consumption increase that might occur if prices are drastically reduced.

The existing literature contains a number of within-country estimates of the effects of significant policy change on drug prices. Miron (2003) and Grossman (2004) estimate that the price of cocaine in the United States would drop by 50 to 80 percent in a legalized market. Assuming that liberalization has such an effect on prices, we can attempt to estimate the ultimate effect on consumption. For this calculation, the estimation of the price elasticity is crucial. If we adopt the significant assumption in much of the literature—that the price elasticities derived from small changes in prices also apply for large changes—in the case of heroin, given its low elasticities of –0.2 to –0.3 percent, the increase in consumption would be small even if prices were to decrease substantially. Cocaine is another matter, however. Given its range of price elasticities, –0.7 to –2.0 percent, demand would increase under legalization by 35 to 160 percent. This wide range denotes considerable uncertainty regarding the consumption response to significant price changes. Moreover, because of the estimation issues we have already underlined, this range of estimates seriously understates the range of potential effects of significant policy change on demand.

Our cross-country comparisons provide further information about the likely consumption response to a liberalization of current policies. They allow us to relax the assumption that elasticities estimated over small movements along the demand curve apply to large movements, given the large variation in drug prices and demand across countries. The cross-country data allow us to compare the experience of countries that span a large range of cocaine prices: from less than $5 per gram in Bolivia, Colombia, Ecuador, and Peru to more than $200 per gram in Australia, Norway, and Singapore.

If cocaine prices were to decrease from the 75th percentile of their distribution (around $95 per gram in, for instance, Austria and Great Britain) to the 25th percentile (around $12 per gram in Chile and Costa Rica), then the prevalence of cocaine consumption would increase by 0.4 percent of the population. (For comparison purposes, note that the world mean and standard deviation of cocaine consumption prevalence are 0.62 percent and 0.59 percent of the population, respectively.) Those calculations are based on the conservative estimates given by the empirical model where drug price and per capita income are the only explanatory variables (table 1.4, column 1). Using the extended empirical model (table 1.4, column 2) and considering a more drastic change in cocaine prices, from the 95th percentile of the distribution (corresponding to, for instance, Austria and Norway) to the 5th percentile (for example, Colombia and Peru), the increase in the prevalence of cocaine consumption would be 2.1 percent of the population. Given an initial consumption prevalence rate of 2.8 percent of the population, this change would represent a 75 percent increase.

In sum, as with the social and private costs of drug use, the effects on drug use of hardening or relaxing current drug policies are uncertain. It is undeniable that the relaxation of current policies would lead to an increase in drug consumption. The evidence we have reviewed indicates that, though substantial, this increase would not amount to widespread or epidemic drug use that would most clearly justify the high social costs of the current policy regime or the policy preference for prohibition-style policies over policies that emphasize harm reduction.

Policy Implications

The evidence presented in this chapter points to considerable uncertainty about the benefits and efficacy of current policies for combating drug consumption. Although this uncertainty makes it difficult to assess various policy choices properly, we can attempt an evaluation by first considering the social costs of current and alternative policies. We can start by asking what are the social costs of investing, say, $10 billion in the enforcement of prohibition and interdiction compared to the social costs of investing the same amount in education and treatment? In each case, the opportunity cost of using the funds is the same, so the question is how to rank the non-budgetary social costs of these expenditures. Because education and treatment entail none of the violent conflicts, institutional instability, incarceration, border delays, or other social costs of interdiction and prohibition enforcement, it seems reasonably certain that the social costs of current policy are much higher than those of alternatives. This fact would not constitute sufficient reason to abandon current policies if their social benefits (that is, the reduction of consumption-related harm) were sufficiently high. However, such benefits are entirely uncertain.

How should this uncertainty be taken into account? Our review of the relevant literature points to two main lessons: first, aggressive responses are justified only when the potential for error is small and, second, policy outcomes should be constantly verified and tested. Thus, drug policies that take into account the deep uncertainty regarding the efficacy of competing policies should embrace multiple sensible approaches, evaluate those approaches carefully, and invest more in "robust" policies—that is, those least likely to produce large social losses. This policy framework is precisely the opposite of current policies toward illicit drugs.

How, then, should the policy response to drug trafficking and consumption change?

- It should invest significant amounts in establishing the scope of the problem, including the social costs of drug consumption and the characteristics of its demand and market.
- It should give significantly greater emphasis to harm reduction, including education, treatment, and prevention of other diseases (such as HIV/AIDS, through needle exchange programs). As MacCoun and Reuter (2001, 10–11) point out, policy interventions can affect three dimensions of harm from drug use: the number of users, the average dose per user, and the harm per dose. Current strategies emphasize prevalence reduction (reducing total number of drug

users), while neglecting the other two.[16] A comprehensive policy intervention is particularly important in stable, mature drug markets, where a large body of analysis concludes that merely trying to reduce the number of users is least likely to succeed, even for less addictive drugs such as cocaine (Pacula 2008).

- It should treat different drugs differently. Tailoring policies to reduce specific drug abuse would consider these three questions. First, which drugs impose the largest social and private damage? Heroin (high cost) and marijuana (low), for example, are far apart in this regard. Second, which drugs are most responsive to market conditions, such as price and income? For instance, heroin consumption does not seem to respond to price changes, while cocaine consumption does. Policies toward more addictive heroin should emphasize treatment, while policies toward price-sensitive cocaine should include taxation. Third, how entrenched and large are current drug markets? For drugs that are not yet popular, addicted users are few and distribution networks unsettled. Repression may be the appropriate response to those drugs (for example, methamphetamines) even as treatment or taxation may be most appropriate for well-established drugs.

- Policy should draw back from aggressive eradication and interdiction strategies in producer and transit countries. Among all prohibition strategies, the empirical case demonstrating that these are efficacious is the weakest. Relatively small quantities of drugs are actually traded, so that it is easy to hide and smuggle them. The estimated imports of cocaine into the United States, for instance, amount to only around 400 tons, equivalent to the proverbial "needle in a haystack." In addition, interdiction and eradication efforts in producing and transit countries increase the price of production inputs and transportation, but because those increases are only a small fraction of the final price, even strong interdiction and eradication efforts will have little impact on retail drug prices in consuming countries. Moreover, stronger eradication and interdiction efforts are effectively counterattacked by drug traders, as they constantly innovate by changing the areas of cultivation, the inputs of production, and the method of transportation.

These may not be novel policy prescriptions.[17] We offer two additional rationales for them, however. First, the very uncertainty about the benefits of different strategies for reducing the use of drugs demands that public policy give greater weight to the social costs of those strategies. Second, we emphasize that many of the most serious social costs of current drug policies are borne by citizens of producer and transit countries, especially in the developing world.

Indeed, although the benefits and effectiveness of prohibition are uncertain, there is little uncertainty regarding its costs. Those costs are borne disproportionately by developing countries that grow crops for the production of drugs or that serve as trade routes to drug consumers in rich countries. They range from the direct expropriation of the wealth of poor farmers to the violence, corruption, and political instability brought about by organized crime. Policy makers in developing countries are increasingly aware of the negative consequences of prohibition, and their calls for change are becoming louder and louder. In a recent *Wall Street Journal* article,[18] three former Latin American presidents—Fernando Henrique Cardoso, César Gaviria, and Ernesto Zedillo—conclude:

> In this spirit, we propose a paradigm shift in drug policies based on three guiding principles: Reduce the harm caused by drugs, decrease drug consumption through education, and aggressively combat organized crime. To translate this new paradigm into action we must start by changing the status of addicts from drug buyers in the illegal market to patients cared for by the public-health system. . . . Each country's search for new policies must be consistent with its history and culture. But to be effective, the new paradigm must focus on health and education—not repression.

The uncertain success of prohibition efforts raises questions about the wisdom of the substantial resources they have demanded.[19] In the context of this debate, developing countries can play a role both by insisting that the costs and benefits of drug policies be shared more equitably and by helping design policies that improve on prohibition in every dimension: thus, by being less costly; by achieving greater reductions in drug abuse; and by shifting the burden of the policy away from drug consumers, poor farmers, and developing countries. But until now, organized crime has been the only clear winner from current policies.

Annex. Definitions and Sources of Variables

Variable	Definition and Construction	Source
Prevalence of cocaine consumption	Prevalence of abuse of cocaine as percentage of the population age 15–64	World Drug Report and Global Illicit Drug Trends (United Nations Office on Drugs and Crime [UNODC], various years)
Prevalence of heroin consumption	Prevalence of abuse of heroin (opiates) as percentage of the population age 15–64	World Drug Report and Global Illicit Drug Trends (UNODC, various years)
Cocaine retail prices	Typical retail (street) price of cocaine expressed in the constant 2000 US$ per gram (The consumer price index [CPI] is used to deflate. Prices of crack cocaine are not included. Also, prices of coca base are ignored unless no other price information is available.)	World Drug Report and Global Illicit Drug Trends (UNODC, various years), and World Development Indicators (World Bank, various years)
Heroin retail prices	Typical retail (street) price of heroin expressed in the constant 2000 US$ per gram (The CPI is used to deflate. Prices of black tar and homebake heroin are excluded. When multiple prices are available (for most cases, those of heroin no. 3 and no. 4), an average is used.)	World Drug Report and Global Illicit Drug Trends (UNODC, various years), and World Development Indicators (World Bank, various years)
Cocaine retail purity	Typical retail (street) purity level of cocaine in percentage (When only the range (minimum and maximum) of purity level is available, an average is computed. Purity levels of crack cocaine are excluded, and those of coca base are also ignored unless no other information is found.)	World Drug Report and Global Illicit Drug Trends (UNODC, various years)
Heroin retail purity	Typical retail (street) purity level of heroin in percentage (When only the range (minimum and maximum) of purity level is available, an average is computed. Purity levels of black tar and homebake heroin are not included. When multiple purity information is available, an average is used.)	World Drug Report and Global Illicit Drug Trends (UNODC, various years)
Cocaine producer countries	A dummy variable for countries where cultivation of cocaine is reported in any year during 1997 to 2005 (The following three countries are pertinent: Bolivia, Colombia, and Peru.)	World Drug Report (UNODC, 2007), Global Illicit Drug Trends (UNODC, 1999), and International Narcotics Control Strategy Report (U.S. Department of State, 1998)

(continued)

Annex. Definitions and Sources of Variables (*continued*)

Variable	Definition and Construction	Source
Opium producer countries	A dummy variable for countries where cultivation of opium is reported in any year during 1997 to 2005 (The following 10 countries are pertinent: Afghanistan, Colombia, Guatemala, India, Lao PDR, Mexico, Myanmar, Pakistan, Thailand, and Vietnam.)	International Narcotics Control Strategy Report (U.S. Department of State, 1998 and 2007)
Cocaine seizures	Seizures of cocaine (base and salts) expressed in kilogram equivalents per 1,000 population	Illicit Drug Seizure Reports (UNODC, data retrieved from www.unodc.org), and United Nations Common Database (UN, data retrieved from unstats.un.org)
Heroin seizures	Seizures of heroin expressed in kilogram equivalents per 1,000 population	Illicit Drug Seizure Reports (UNODC, data retrieved from www.unodc.org), and United Nations Common Database (UN, data retrieved from unstats.un.org)
Marijuana retail prices	Typical retail (street) price of marijuana (cannabis herb) expressed in the constant 2000 US$ per gram (The CPI is used to deflate.)	World Drug Report and Global Illicit Drug Trends (UNODC, various years), and World Development Indicators (World Bank, various years)
Ecstasy retail prices	Typical retail (street) price of ecstasy expressed in the constant 2000 US$ per gram (The CPI is used to deflate.)	World Drug Report and Global Illicit Drug Trends (UNODC, various years), and World Development Indicators (World Bank, various years)
GDP per capita	PPP-adjusted real GDP per capita (2000 international $), in logs	World Development Indicators (World Bank, various years), and Penn World Table 6.2 (Heston, Summers, and Aten, 2006, data retrieved from pwt.econ.upenn.edu)
People prosecuted for drug offenses	Number of people prosecuted for all drug offenses per 100,000 population, expressed in logs	United Nations Surveys of Crime Trends and Operations of Criminal Justice Systems (UNODC, various years, data retrieved from www.unodc.org), and United Nations Common Database (UN, data retrieved from unstats.un.org)
Police personnel	Number of police personnel per 100,000 population, expressed in logs	United Nations Surveys of Crime Trends and Operations of Criminal Justice Systems (UNODC, various years, data retrieved from www.unodc.org), and United Nations Common Database (UN, data retrieved from unstats.un.org)

(*continued*)

Annex. Definitions and Sources of Variables (continued)

Variable	Definition and Construction	Source
Outlays for public order and safety	PPP-adjusted central government expenditure on public order and safety (constant 2000 international $) per capita expressed in logs. Public order and safety includes (a) police services, (b) fire protection services, (c) law courts, (d) prisons, (e) research and development for public order and safety, and (f) not elsewhere classified	Government Finance Statistics Yearbook (IMF, various years), and World Development Indicators (World Bank, various years), United Nations Common Database (UN, data retrieved from unstats.un.org), and Penn World Table 6.2 (Heston, Summers, and Aten, 2006, data retrieved frompwt.econ.upenn.edu).
Urban population	Percentage of the total population living in urban agglomerations	World Development Indicators (World Bank, various years).
Youth population	Population age 10–24 as the percentage of the total population	World Population Prospects: The 2004 Revision (UN, 2005), LABORSTA-Internet (International Labour Organization, data retrieved from laborsta.ilo.org), United Nations Common Database (UN, data retrieved from unstats.un.org), and World Development Indicators (World Bank, various years).
Alcohol consumption	Per capita recorded alcohol consumption (liters of pure alcohol) among adults (age 15 years or older) (It is computed as the sum of alcohol production and imports, less alcohol exports, divided by the adult population.)	WHO Statistical Information System (World Health Organization, data retrieved from www.who.int).

Notes

1. As Van Ours and Pudney (2006) write, "Whereas in other, 'normal', markets there is plenty of research to back economic policy interventions, policy on illicit drugs is often driven more by emotions than by evidence-based evaluation of alternatives."

2. See, for example, "Route of Evil: How a Tiny West African Nation Became a Key Smuggling Hub for Colombian Cocaine, and the Price It Is Paying," *Washington Post*, May 25, 2008, p. A1.

3. See http://www.state.gov/p/inl/rls/nrcrpt/2006/vol1/html/62100.htm.

4. *Washington Post*, May 25, 2008, p. A1.

5. *Washington Post*, May 7, 2008, p. A13.

6. As Thoumi (this volume) argues, drug trafficking and cultivation tend to emerge in countries that already exhibit institutional weaknesses. Stephens (2009) argues

that Mexico's costly battle against traffickers is necessary *because* Mexican institutions are corrupt; most observers, though, argue that illegal drug trafficking
and the fight against it have significantly exacerbated institutional problems.

7. It may also be the case that prohibition is favored because the largest domestic
costs of prohibition are borne by groups that have less political influence (for
example, residents of inner cities).

8. According to biopsychological theories of addiction, exposure to drugs changes
the way the brain works, through enhancement of dopamine neurotransmis-
sion. In some cases, this change can be permanent, following repeated use of
addictive drugs (Robinson and Berridge 1993). This provides a biological basis
to time inconsistency in decisions related to drug consumption (as long as individuals are not fully aware of the change that they may be subject to).

9. Bhattacharya and Lakdawalla (2005) discuss time inconsistency under more
general settings and analyze the possibility of implementation of economically
efficient outcomes in these circumstances. Ample empirical evidence indicates
that time inconsistency is pervasive in economic decision, and not exclusive to
drug use. For example, time-inconsistent behavior is commonplace in individual saving and credit decisions (Shui and Ausubel 2005). It is also common in
individuals' decisions to use legal addictive substances, as evidence related to
smoking reveals (Gruber and Köszegi 2001).

10. See http://www.whitehousedrugpolicy.gov/publications/factsht/druguse/index
.html.

11. A large fraction of prisoners in the United States are incarcerated for violation
of laws against the possession of drugs, but Sevigny and Caulkins (2004) argue
that most of those prisoners are dealers who reached plea agreements with
prosecutors.

12. The appendix provides details on definitions and sources of all variables used in
the empirical analysis.

13. However, if this bias were large, then we would expect to see large changes in
consumption in law-abiding countries that relaxed prohibitions on consumption. This is not the case, however. In many relatively law-abiding countries, there
has been little evidence of a dramatic rise in drug use after decriminalization.

14. The latter can also indicate the strength of enforcement, but because this is controlled for by the other determinants, drug seizures' remaining explanatory
power is likely to be related to drug availability.

15. This exercise is not reported in the table, but its results are available upon
request.

16. Policies that focus on a reduction in the number of users, for example through
criminalization of drug use, may increase the harm per user/dose and may
increase the dose per user. Policies that reduce the harm per user/dose, such as
needle exchange programs, could increase the number of users (although in
their survey of many studies of needle exchange programs, MacCoun and
Reuter (2001) conclude that they do not increase drug consumption).

17. See Caulkins and Reuter (2006).
18. "The War on Drugs is a Failure," Feb. 23, 2009.
19. The sense of unfairness regarding who bears the costs of the "war on drugs" is perceived not only in developing countries. Increasingly, voices in developed countries are alerting to the limitations of this strategy, as the following concluding remarks in *The Economist* (2006) exemplify, "A 'clear-cut victory' over coca is impossible, Anne Paterson [the senior antidrug officer at the U.S. State Department and a former American ambassador in Colombia] concedes. 'It's just a question of containing it where it breaks out.' The problem is that containment carries heavy political costs for democratic governments in the Andes. The drug trade itself undermines democracy, but so do the heavy-handed American efforts to contain it. As long as rich-country governments insist on imposing an unenforceable prohibition on cocaine consumption, Andean governments will continue to be faced with the thankless task of trying to repress market forces."

References

Akram, Q. Farooq, Yakov Ben-Haim, and Øyvind Eitrheim. 2006. "Managing Uncertainty through Robust-Satisficing Monetary Policy." Working Paper ANO 2006/10, Research Department, Norges Bank, Oslo, Norway.

Becker, Gary S., and Kevin M. Murphy. 1988. "A Theory of Rational Addiction." *Journal of Political Economy* 96 (4): 675–700.

Becker, Gary S., Kevin M. Murphy, and Michael Grossman. 2006. "The Economic Theory of Illegal Goods: The Case of Drugs." *Journal of Political Economy* 114 (1): 38–60.

Ben-Haim, Yakov. 2006. *Info-Gap Decision Theory: Decisions under Severe Uncertainty.* 2nd ed. London: Academic Press.

Bernardo, Naissa P., Maria Elisa Pereira Bastos Siqueira, Maria José Nunes de Paiva, and Patrícia Penido Maia. 2003. "Caffeine and Other Adulterants in Seizures of Street Cocaine in Brazil." *International Journal of Drug Policy* 14 (4): 331–34.

Bewley, Truman F. 1987. "Knightian Decision Theory: Part II." Cowles Foundation Discussion Paper 835, Yale University, Cowles Foundation for Research in Economics, New Haven, CT.

Bhattacharya, Jay, and Darius Lakdawalla. 2005. "Time-Inconsistency and Welfare." NBER Working Paper 10345, National Bureau of Economic Research, Cambridge, MA.

Byrd, William. 2010. "Responding to Afghanistan's Opium Economy Challenge: Lessons and Policy Implications from a Development Perspective." In *Innocent Bystanders: Developing Countries and the War on Drugs,* ed. Philip Keefer and Norman Loayza. Washington, DC: World Bank.

Byrd, William, and Christopher Ward. 2004. "Drugs and Development in Afghanistan." Social Development Papers—Conflict Prevention and Reconstruction 18, World Bank, Washington, DC.

Cameron, Samuel, and Alan Collins. 2006. "Addict Death: A Lacuna in the Welfare Economics of Drug Policy." *American Journal of Economics and Sociology* 65 (4): 963–69.

Carpenter, Ted Galen. 2009. "Troubled Neighbor: Mexico's Drug Violence Poses a Threat to the United States." *Policy Analysis* 631, Cato Institute, Washington, DC.

Caulkins, Jonathan P., and Sara Chandler. 2006. "Long-Run Trends in Incarceration of Drug Offenders in the U.S." *Crime and Delinquency* 52 (4): 619–41.

Caulkins, Jonathan P., and Peter Reuter. 2006. "Reorienting U.S. Drug Policy." *Issues in Science and Technology Online* (Fall). http://www.issues.org/23.1/caulkins.html.

Colombian Government. 2003. "Defense and Security." Colombian Embassy, Washington D.C. http://www.colombiaemb.org/defense.

Dills, Angela K., and Jeffrey A. Miron. 2004. "Alcohol Prohibition, Alcohol Consumption, and Cirrhosis." *American Law and Economics Review* 6 (2): 285–318.

Dills, Angela K., Jeffrey A. Miron, and Garrett Summers. 2008. "What Do Economists Know about Crime?" NBER Working Paper 13759, National Bureau of Economic Research, Cambridge, MA.

Dills, Angela K., Mireille Jacobson, and Jeffrey A. Miron. 2005. "The Effect of Alcohol Prohibition on Alcohol Consumption: Evidence from Drunkenness Arrests." *Economics Letters* 86 (2): 279–84.

Drug War Chronicle (2007). "Latin America: Brazilian Governor Says Legalize Drugs to Fight Crime." March 9. http://stopthedrugwar.org/chronicle/476/brazilian_governor_says_legalize_drugs_to_reduce_crime.

Executive Office of the President. 2001. "What America's Users Spend on Illegal Drugs: 1988–2000." Washington: Office of National Drug Control Policy (December). http://www.whitehousedrugpolicy.gov/publications/drugfact/american_users_spend2002/index.html.

———. 2004. "The Economic Costs of Drug Abuse in the United States: 1992–2002." Washington: Office of National Drug Control Policy (December). http://www.whitehousedrugpolicy.gov/publications/economic_costs/economic_costs.pdf.

Fajnzylber, Pablo, Daniel Lederman, and Norman Loayza. 2002. "What Causes Violent Crime?" *European Economic Review* 46 (2002): 1323–57.

Godfrey, Christine, Gail Eaton, Cynthia McDougall, and Anthony Culyer. 2002. "The Economic and Social Costs of Class A Drug Use in England and Wales, 2000." Home Office Research Study 249 (July). Great Britain: Home Office Research, Development and Statistics Directorate. http://www.homeoffice.gov.uk/rds/pdfs2/hors249.pdf.

Godinho, Joana, and Jaap Veen. 2005. "Drug Policy and Its Impact on the HIV Epidemic in Europe." Draft policy note, World Bank, Washington, DC.

Gollier, Christian, Bruno Jullien, and Nicolas Treich. 2000. "Scientific Progress and Irreversibility: An Economic Interpretation of the 'Precautionary Principle.'" *Journal of Public Economics* 75 (February): 2, 229–53.

Gossop, Michael, John Marsden, and Duncan Stewart. 2001. "NTORS after Five Years: The National Treatment Outcome Research Study. Changes in Substance Use, Health, and Criminal Behaviour during the Five Years after Intake." London: National Addiction Centre. http://www.dh.gov.uk/en/Publicationsandstatistics/ Publications/PublicationsPolicyAndGuidance/DH_4084908.

Grossman, Michael. 2004. "Individual Behaviors and Substance Use: The Role of Prices." NBER Working Paper 10948, National Bureau of Economic Research, Cambridge, MA.

Gruber, Jonathan, and Botond Köszegi. 2001. "Is Addiction 'Rational'? Theory and Evidence." *Quarterly Journal of Economics* 116 (4): 1261–1303.

Heston, Alan, Robert Summers, and Bettina Aten. 2006. Penn World Table Version 6.2, Center for International Comparisons of Production, Income and Prices at the University of Pennsylvania, September.

ILO (International Labour Organization). Database on labor statistics, LABORSTA-Internet. http://laborsta.ilo.org.

IMF (International Monetary Fund). *Government Finance Statistics Yearbook.* Various years. Washington, DC: IMF.

International Crisis Group. 2008. "Latin American Drugs I: Losing the Fight." *Latin American Report* 25. Brussels, Belgium.

Kugler, Maurice, Thierry Verdier, and Yves Zenou. 2005. "Organized Crime, Corruption and Punishment." *Journal of Public Economics* 89 (9–10): 1639–63.

Lee, Li Way. 1993. "Would Harassing Drug Users Work?" *Journal of Political Economy* 101 (5): 939–59.

MacCoun, Robert J., and Peter Reuter. 2001. *Drug War Heresies: Learning from Other Vices, Times, and Places.* New York: Cambridge University Press.

Mejía, Daniel, and Carlos Esteban Posada. 2010. "Cocaine Production and Trafficking: What Do We Know?" In *Innocent Bystanders: Developing Countries and the War on Drugs*, ed. Philip Keefer and Norman Loayza. Washington, DC: World Bank.

Miron, Jeffrey. 2003. "Do Prohibitions Raise Prices: Evidence from the Market for Cocaine." *Review of Economics and Statistics* August 85 (3): 522–30.

Miron, Jeffrey, and Jeffrey Zwiebel. 1995. "The Economic Case against Drug Prohibition." *The Journal of Economic Perspectives* 9 (4): 175–92.

Monitoring the Future. 2008. "Long-Term Trends in Annual Prevalence of Use of Various Drugs in Grade 12." Institute for Social Research at the University of Michigan. Ann Arbor, MI. http://www.monitoringthefuture.org/data/08data/ pr08t16.pdf.

Pacula, Rosalie Liccardo. 2008. Testimony on "What Research Tells Us about the Reasonableness of the Current Priorities of National Drug Control before the U.S. House of Representatives" Oversight and Government Reform Committee, Subcommitttee on Domestic Policy, March 12. http://rand.org/pubs/testimonies/ CT302/.

Reuter, Peter. 2001. "The Limits to Supply Side Drug Control." *Milken Institute Review* (first quarter): 14–23.

Reuter, Peter, and Victoria Greenfield. 2010. "Measuring Global Drug Market: How Good Are the Numbers and Why Should We Care About Them?" *World Economics* 2 (4): 159–73.

Reuter, Peter. 2009. "Can Production and Trafficking of Illicit Drugs Be Reduced or Merely Shifted?" In *Innocent Bystanders: Developing Countries and the War on Drugs*, ed. Philip Keefer and Norman Loayza. Washington, DC: World Bank.

Reuter, Peter, K. Jack Riley, Justin L. Adams, Susan S. Everingham, Robert Klitgaard, and J. T. Quinlivan, with Kamil Akramov, Scott Hiromoto, and Sergej Mahnovski. 2004. "Mitigating the Effects of Illicit Drugs on Development." Project Memorandum PM-1645-PSJ-2, RAND, Santa Monica, CA.

Robinson and Berridge. 1993.

Sevigny, Eric, and Jonathan P. Caulkins. 2004. "Kingpins or Mules? An Analysis of Drug Offenders Incarcerated in Federal and State Prisons." *Criminology and Public Policy* 3 (3): 401–34.

Shui, Haiyan, and Lawrence M. Ausubel. 2005. "Time Inconsistency in the Credit Card Market." Unpublished manuscript, University of Maryland, College Park, Maryland.

Smith, Peter H. 2005. "The Political Economy of Drug Trafficking." Unpublished presentation, University of California at San Diego.

Soares, Rodrigo R. 2006. "The Welfare Cost of Violence across Countries." *Journal of Health Economics* 25 (5): 821–46.

Stephens, Bret. 2009. "In Praise of Mexico's War on Drugs: Complacency and corruption are the real enemies." *The Wall Street Journal,* March 3.

The Economist. 2009a. "On the Trail of the Traffickers." March 7.

The Economist. 2009b. "A Toker's Guide." March 7.

The Economist. 2007a. "Policing a Whirlwind." December 13.

The Economist. 2007b. "A Change of Mind on Coca." May 5.

The Economist. 2006. "One Step Forward in a Quagmire." March 18.

The Economist. 2004. "Always Coca." 2004. April 24.

The Economist. 2004. "Back on the Offensive." 2008. January 26.

The Economist. 2001. "Opinion: The Case for Legalization." July 26.

Thoumi, Francisco E. 2009. "Illegal Drugs, Politics, and Armed Groups in the Andean Region and Afghanistan." Chapter 6 in this volume.

United Nations Common Database.

UN, data.

United Nations Office on Drugs and Crime (UNODC). Various years. *World Drug Report.* United Nations Office on Drugs and Crime.

U.S. Department of State. 1998.

U.S. Department of State. 1998 and 2007.

Van Ours, Jan C., and Stephen Pudney. 2006. "On the Economics of Illicit Drugs." *De Economist* 154 (4): 483–90.

WHO (World Health Organization). Statistical Information System, Geneva. http://www.who.int.

Wilson, Suzanne, and Marta Zambrano. 1994. "Cocaine, Commodity Chains, and Drug Politics: A Transnational Approach." In *Commodity Chains and Global Capitalism,* ed. Gary Gereffi and Miguel Korzeniewicz, 297–315. Westport, CT: Greenwood Press.

World Bank (various years). *World Development Indicators.* Washington, DC: World Bank.

2

The Historical Foundations of the Narcotic Drug Control Regime

Julia Buxton

The international system of narcotic drug control is based on a complex series of accords and conventions administered by a dedicated drug bureaucracy within the United Nations and national partner agencies. These lock individual nation-states into the universal goal of eradicating the cultivation, production, distribution, and consumption of narcotic drugs. This obligation pertains to all states, irrespective of their position in the narcotic drug market, their financial capacity to dedicate resources to drug control measures, or the social, political, and structural consequences of eradicating the illicit trade within the national territory. The global drug conventions set out a comprehensive strategy for the achievement of a "drug-free world" (a goal that was restated at the 1998 United Nations General Assembly Special Session on the World Drug Problem), an end toward which all nation-states are obliged to work cooperatively. Underscoring the universal nature of the system, by 2005, 180 states were party to the 1961 Single Convention on Narcotic Drugs, 175 were party to the 1971 Convention on Psychotropic Substances, and 170 states had ratified the 1988 Convention against Illicit Traffic.

The drug control regime is a remarkable model of international collaboration and consensus. The core principle underpinning drug control—that states should step in and act coercively to prevent the use of dangerous substances—is accepted by all national governments regardless of regime type, religion, ideological orientation, or level of national development. This cohesion of action and principle owes much to the longevity and intensity of the campaign to prohibit narcotic drugs. The drug control system has evolved over a 100-year period, and during this time the prohibition model has become institutionalized, consolidated, and global.

The foundations of the international quest to eliminate the market for intoxicating substances were laid at a meeting of global powers held in Shanghai in 1909 convened by the United States. This meeting was the first significant foray by the United States onto the stage of global diplomacy. Through the antidrug initiative, the United States came to define and shape the drug "problem" and responses. The position maintained by the United States, a drug-consuming country, was that the trade in dangerous drugs had to be prohibited and that narcotic drug supply should be eliminated at its source. A century later, that remains the end goal of the control regime. This position, however, was not universally endorsed, with many cultivating countries—including Bolivia, Persia, Peru, and Turkey—positioning themselves on the outside of the control model from its foundation. A century later, these countries are party to the conventions, but their critique of the control model as one that inequitably distributes the cost of enforcing prohibition remains as pertinent and divisive today as it did 100 years ago.

The Shanghai conference was held against the backdrop of global, free, and mass markets for substances such as opium, cannabis, and cocaine and for derivative opiates such as morphine and heroin (Buxton 2006). U.S. steps to control and regulate the trade in intoxicating substances were revolutionary, given the pervasiveness of drug use and the powerful vested commercial interests in maintaining an unfettered trade. The U.S. initiative also went against a 2,000-year-long history of drug cultivation, production, trading, and use.

Intoxicating Substances in Historical Context

People have cultivated and ingested naturally occurring intoxicating and hallucinatory substances since the beginning of civilization. The most widely used naturally occurring drugs were opium from the opium poppy (*papaver somniferum*); the flowers, leaves, and resin of the cannabis plant (*cannabis sativa*); and the leaves of the coca plant (*erythroxylum*).

Drug Use

There were six main reasons for drug consumption in ancient and modern societies (Inglis 1975). The most significant was pain relief. Ancient Indian and Chinese manuscripts recommended the inhalation or eating of cannabis for a range of diseases such as gout, cholera, tetanus, and neuralgia and for pain relief in childbirth. Underscoring the medicinal value of cannabis, the U.S. pharmacopoeia recommended it for the primary treatment of more than 100 illnesses in its publications from 1850 to 1937. Owing to the presence of 46 alkaloids, including the analgesics codeine and morphine, opium was also highly valued for medical treatment, beginning with the Persians and Greeks. After Greek traders introduced opium to South Asia, the drug was used in medical practice in India and China, according to records dating from 400 A.D. (Booth 1999; Scott 1969).

The 17th century brought the commercialization of medical drug use, underscored by the launch of Sydenham's Laudanum, an opium-based medication in the United Kingdom in the 1680s. Competition among apothecaries and rising demand for self-medication among the new urban working classes in the 19th century spurred the opium-based patent medicine market, with products such as Gowan's Pneumonia Cure, Godfrey's Cordial, and Dr. Moffett's Teethina sold without prescription or regulation in grocery stores (Berridge 2001; Hodgson 2001).

After the isolation of morphine in 1803, the analgesic compound in opium, the German pharmaceutical firm E. Merck and Company began commercial manufacture, and morphine-based products such as Winslow's Soothing Sirup, Children's Comfort, Dr. Seth Arnold's Cough Killer, and One Day Cough Cure were launched as a superior form of pain relief. The popularity of morphine was in turn surpassed by diacetylmorphine, which was sold under the brand name Heroin by the German company Bayer. First synthesized from boiling morphine in 1874, it was 10 times stronger than morphine and marketed worldwide as a cure for bronchial problems. Indian-cultivated cannabis was also commercialized by the burgeoning pharmaceutical sector with Parke Davis, Squibb, Lilly, and Burroughs Welcome engaged in its manufacture and marketing.

After the active constituent of the coca leaf was identified in 1859 and named cocaine, this drug emerged as a popular remedy for a range of physiological and psychological illnesses such as allergies, nasal congestion, nymphomania, and morphine dependence, and it was recommended by *The British Medical Journal* for anesthesia in eye surgery. Produced and marketed by Merck and the American firm Parke, Davis, cocaine-based products such as Ryno's Hay Fever and Catarrh Remedy and Agnew's Powder, which contained 99 percent and 35 percent pure pharmaceutical cocaine respectively, gained mass markets in the United States and Western Europe (Streatfeild 2000).

A second driver of drug use was the need for physical stimulation. Coca, cannabis, and other natural plant–based stimulants such as betel, khat, and tobacco were traditionally ingested by indigenous and indentured laborers. In the Andean region of South America, Spanish colonists encouraged the chewing of coca by indigenous workers in the silver mines, because it boosted physical endurance and depressed the appetite. In the second half of the 19th century, the commercialization of coca leaves allowed for the development of a new mass market for stimulant tonics such as Vin Mariani, which was first marketed in Europe in 1863. Coca-based stimulants also found a receptive market in the United States, where French Wine Coca, a mixture of wine and cocaine manufactured in Atlanta, was marketed as a "brain-tonic." It was relaunched in 1886 as Coca-Cola after the alcohol prohibition movement objected to the wine content of the product.

A third factor accounting for the preponderance of drugs was their cultural and spiritual significance in religious, pagan, shamanic, and cultural ceremonies across the world. From the Dagga cults of West Africa and the indigenous Indian communities in North and South America to Hindu festivals in India, coca leaves, opium, cannabis, and hallucinogenic plants such as peyote and psilocybin were used as religious sacraments and venerated as gifts from nature or the gods (Schultes and Hoffman 1992).

Cannabis, coca, and the opium poppy were also cultivated as a food source. Hemp, a member of the *cannabis sativa* family, produces highly nutritious hemp seed and seed oil. It was a staple of rural diets in China, South and Central Asia, and the Balkan region for centuries. Hemp was also used for rope, rigging, paper making, and textiles. The utility of hemp was first recognized by the Chinese, and its cultivation spread to Central Asia and Europe in the 13th century and, following transplantation by the Spanish conquistadors and Pilgrims, into North and South America in the 17th century (Herer 1998). This history points to a fifth driver of drug cultivation—the use of these plants in early bartering and financial systems: the Spanish, for example, transformed coca leaves into one of the most highly commercialized products in the Andes by using coca as means of payment.

Relaxation, recreation, and experimentation were the final factor accounting for the popularity of drug use. In both ancient and modern societies, however, this purpose was the preserve of the elite. Although the synthetic drug revolution in the second half of the 19th century saw an increase in recreational drug experimentation, such use remained confined to Bohemian groups, literary and artistic figures, and secret societies that transformed nonmedical drug use into a "social signifier" of the rejection of the values of mainstream society (Keire 1998). The invention of the injecting syringe in 1843 created new recreational as well as medical markets for cocaine and opiates; the 1890s Sears Roebuck catalogue, for example, offered a syringe and vial of cocaine for $1.50.

A significant exception to the model of elite recreational use was the Chinese and the broader Southeast Asian market for opium. Opium consumption in China was common among all social classes, and, owing to the intensity of demand and addiction, domestic cultivation had to be reinforced by opium imports from India, Persia, and Turkey. Recreational opium smoking was also common among Chinese immigrants scattered across port cities such as London and San Francisco.

The Trade in Drugs

Drug cultivation and use have persisted across time, but there was a dramatic change in patterns of cultivation, production, and use during the 18th century when opium, and to a lesser extent coca, became commercialized. This change was catalyzed by Western efforts to expand their commercial and colonial presence in Asia. A brief assessment of the early opium trade puts into perspective the significance of the U.S. effort to regulate and ultimately eliminate what was one of the most important globally traded commodities in the international market.

Early Portuguese traders were responsible for initiating the mass market for opium. They first discovered opium poppy cultivation and opium production in India after their arrival in the country in 1501. As part of early efforts to enter the Chinese market, which was closed to foreign merchants, the Portuguese introduced the practice of smoking opium with tobacco shipped from Brazil. The Dutch deepened the Asian opium market through the commercial vehicle of the Vereenigde Oost-Indische Compagnie (VOC), which by the 1640s had pushed Portugal out of Indonesia and gained control of the profitable trade in spices and opium. Indicative of the rapid growth of the Dutch-controlled opium market after this date, imports of Bengal opium from India into Indonesia increased from 0.6 metric tons (mt) in the 1660s to 87 mt by 1699. The VOC realized profits in excess of 400 percent through the reexport of Bengal opium to China, and as a result of the lucrative nature of the opium enterprise, the spice trade declined in value and commercial significance (McCoy 1972; La Motte 2003).

The most dramatic change came in 1608, with the arrival in India of the British East India Company, which was originally created to boost Britain's commercial interest in the spice trade. Through military confrontation with the Indian opium merchants, the company gradually acquired control of the lucrative opium sector and absorbed peasant cultivators into a loose syndicate system. Opium for export was sold through its auction houses in Calcutta, while domestic demand was met through the sale of heavily taxed opium through a company monopoly of 10,000 retail outlets in India.

Opium as a commodity was of enormous fiscal and commercial significance for Britain, which expanded cultivation in the Bengal area from 90,000 acres in 1830 to 176,000 in 1840, reaching a high of 500,000 acres by 1900 (McCoy 1972; Richards 2003). Revenues from opium exports, which climbed from 127 mt in 1800 to 6,372 mt by 1857 (Ul Haq 2000), and domestic sales taxes contributed 11 percent of total revenues accruing to the British administration in India. Aside from financing the colonial enterprise in India and other British territorial possessions in Southeast Asia, opium was intensely valuable to Britain because it reversed a significant balance-of-trade deficit with China. While there was strong demand in the United Kingdom for Chinese goods like tea, silk, and ceramics, the Chinese market for British manufactured exports was limited, and no foreign traders were allowed to operate outside Canton. The export of Indian opium to China reversed this negative trade flow. The opium trade also enabled Britain to gain a strong commercial foothold in China. As in India, Britain gained that advantage through the use of military force. Successive Chinese emperors had sought to restrict the use of opium, which was seen as offensive to Confucian morality. However, prohibition decrees issued by Emperor Yung Cheng in 1729 and Kia King in 1799 met with resistance from British merchant smugglers. When the Chinese attempted to enforce the decrees, the British government launched naval attacks in defense of the smugglers. Under the resulting peace agreements following the two opium wars fought between Britain and China in 1839 and 1857, China was forced to open the treaty ports of Amoy, Tinghai, Chunhai, and Ningpo to the British; Britain gained Hong Kong; and the Chinese were forced to legalize the opium trade.

Summary

When the United States convened the first opium conference at the turn of the 20th century, opium cultivation and consumption were at an all-time high. Production levels were around 41,624 mt per year, the bulk of which was produced in China in Yunnan and Szechwan provinces. The Persian and Ottoman Empires had emerged as significant cultivator countries, having stepped up opium poppy cultivation and opium production in the second half of the 19th century to meet rising global demand. National governments, commercial trading houses, and the pharmaceutical sector all had significant interests in the opium trade. The colonial powers, the United Kingdom, Spain, and the Netherlands had operated opium retail monopolies across Southeast Asia for more than 150 years, and those monopolies contributed to meeting the administrative costs of the colonial enterprise. In Java, Indonesia, the Dutch administered 1,065 opium retail outlets, which covered 15 percent of administrative costs, while in the British colony of Malaya (Malaysia), opium sales contributed 53 percent (McCoy 1972).

Further developing the picture of a large global market and commercial interest in narcotic drugs, coca cultivation had expanded out of native areas in South America, such as the Yungas in Bolivia and Huanuco, Libertad, and Cuzco in Peru. British and Dutch pharmaceutical companies and commercial interests transplanted coca leaf cultivation to British

Guyana, India, Indonesia, Jamaica, Malaysia, and Sri Lanka, to reduce shipping times and to meet rising demand for cocaine. The Dutch had set up cocaine manufacturing facilities in Indonesia following the introduction of the coca leaf to Java in 1900, and by the turn of the century, the Dutch were the world's leading cocaine producer (Gootenberg 1999). As with opium production, national governments in coca cultivation areas also invested heavily in their new comparative advantage; the Peruvian government, for example, devised a strategy for national development based on the promotion of the coca paste export sector (Walker 1996).

Inaction and Detachment: The United States and the Early Opium Question

The United States was relatively marginal to the trade in opium, coca, and cannabis, and U.S. merchants were barred from the Calcutta opium auctions by the British. It was only at the beginning of the 20th century, when the use of narcotic substances was at a high point, that the United States became engaged in the nascent drug debate. When it did so, the country assumed a radical posture, pressing for the complete elimination of the trade, a position that "required little sacrifice from Americans while demanding fundamental social and institutional change from others" (McAllister 2000, 66).

The United States made a belated entry, particularly given that Christian-based anti-opium campaigns in countries such as the United Kingdom and India had been mobilizing around the "trade in misery" for more than 30 years. Three factors accounted for initial U.S. detachment from the opium question during the emerging debates of the mid-19th century. First, alcohol, rather than drugs, was seen as the most pressing social problem in the United States. The explosion of saloon bars associated with vice, gambling, and drunkenness catalyzed the emergence of a powerful Christian-based prohibition lobby that focused political attention on the need for a ban on alcohol rather than on regulation of the drug trade.

Second, even if the federal government were minded to intervene to regulate intoxicating substances, it was powerless to act. The constitutional separation of powers limited the responsibility of the federal government to foreign policy, interstate commerce, and revenue-raising measures such as taxation. As a result, it could not impose legislation on the states, which retained jurisdiction over policing, criminal and civil law, and the regulation of trade and transport (Whitebread 1995). This was despite evidence of a rising problem of morphine addiction among women and Civil War veterans in the second half of the 19th century. Middle-class women were the largest constituency of American opiate addicts, which totaled an estimated 300,000 people out of a population of 76 million. Intramuscular morphine injection was commonly prescribed for female "problems of mood" that included gynecological infection, depression, and nymphomania (Courtwright 1982; Keire 1998; Walker 1996, 39). An estimated 40,000 former combatants of the Northern army suffered from "soldier's sickness" or the "army disease," a morphine dependence that followed from its routine administration on the battle-field (Ul Haq 2000, 40; Whitebread 1995).

The absence of federal regulation contrasted with the situation in the United Kingdom, where the national government introduced the 1868 Pharmacy Act in response to a rise in overdose-related deaths. The U.K. legislation did not restrict the sale or use of drugs; it simply required that opiates and cocaine be clearly labeled as poisons. It was highly effective in reducing drug-related morbidity, particularly in small children. When anti-opium legislation was introduced in the United States in the 1870s and 1880s, it was on the initiative of individual states and was specifically targeted at Chinese nationals. The legislation was part of a wider anti-Chinese campaign led by organizations such as the American Federation of Labor and the Workingmen's Party, and it came as part of a package of measures that included restrictions on the rights of Chinese immigrants to marry, own property, and practice certain professions. As such, the first U.S. drug laws were premised on racial prejudice, not on a preoccupation with national health, and they were informed by the view that the drug threat was external and imported (Goode and Ben Yahuda 1994).

A final important factor accounting for the tardiness of U.S. engagement with the drug issue was the country's lack of overseas territorial possessions. Unlike Britain, the Netherlands, and Spain, the United States had no colonial enterprise, and the country maintained only a marginal trading presence in Southeast Asia. As a result, the United States was divorced from the broader debate on the morality of the opium trade and the operations of the market more generally. It was alcohol rather than drugs that preoccupied the moral conscience of white, Christian U.S. society (Behr 1996).

It was not until the end of the 19th century that a national debate on foreign policy and the need for "empire building" began to take hold in the United States. Preoccupation with the consolidation of national territory, unification of North and South, and prevention of foreign incursion into the Southern Hemisphere had inhibited aspirations of overseas expansion. It was not until 1898 that the United States acquired its first overseas possession, Hawaii, a move that followed intense pressure for expansion on Republican President McKinley from agricultural, media, and financial interests.

U.S. Narco-Diplomacy

The drastic change in the position of the U.S. federal government, from one of detachment from the opium question to leadership on the issue, was triggered by the acquisition of the Philippines from Spain, following the Spanish defeat in the Spanish-American War of 1898 and the subsequent ceding of Cuba, Guam, the Philippines, and Puerto Rico to the United States under the Treaty of Paris. Under ongoing pressure for U.S. territorial aggrandizement, the McKinley administration assumed direct responsibility for the Philippines on the basis that the territory had been entrusted to the United States "by the providence of God" (Bouvier 2001).

Having acquired direct responsibility over the Philippines, the U.S. federal government was forced to address the opium question. A decision had to be made on the retention of the opium retail outlets established by the Spanish, 190 of which operated in Manila alone. The immediate response of Governor General William Howard Taft was to allow opium sales to continue, with the sales revenues ring-fenced for education spending. This proposal provoked a vigorous response from Christian missionaries in the Philippines, including the Protestant Episcopal bishop of Manila, Charles H. Brent, and the Reverend Wilbur Crafts, the president of the International Reform Bureau, the main American missionary organization. Brent and Crafts intensively—and successfully— lobbied the federal government for a commission of inquiry into opium use in the Philippines.

The resulting Philippines Opium Commission of 1903 was the first federal government inquiry into the use and effects of intoxicating substances.

It was headed by Bishop Brent, and its findings contradicted those of the earlier British Royal Opium Commission, which had been convened in 1895. While the British commission had found opium-related problems in India "comparatively rare and novel," thereby legitimizing continued British participation in the trade, the Philippines commission found that the unregulated sale of opium had grave effects on the health and moral capacity of users. It recommended that the import, sale, and use of opium be based on medical need only, thereby ending a centuries-long tradition of unregulated and promiscuous use in Southeast Asia (McAllister 2000). The recommendations of the Philippines Opium Commission were accepted by the U.S. government, which put in place a three-year transition timetable phasing out the use of opium among the 12,000 registered consumers in the Philippines.

The influence of the Christian missionaries did not end with this measure. Brent and Crafts lobbied the Roosevelt administration to convene an international opium conference, an event that marked the beginnings of U.S. narco-diplomacy. Brent and Crafts argued that without an international agreement to curb the supply of opium, the domestic regulations put in place in the Philippines would fail. Two important principles had therefore been set out by the influential missionary groups: first, that the use of intoxicating substances was morally wrong and injurious and that national governments had the responsibility to step in to prevent people from doing harm to themselves and, second, that this result could be achieved only by eliminating the supply of narcotic substances from cultivator and producer countries. Once the supply had gone, demand and consumption would be terminated. This prohibitionist, supply-side–focused thrust shaped the structure and orientation of the international control regime that was to emerge (Buxton 2006).

The Shanghai Opium Conference, 1909

All the great powers—with the exception of the Ottoman Empire, a major opium cultivator—accepted the U.S. invitation to participate in an international opium conference on the understanding that national governments would not be bound by a final resolution.

The emphasis on prohibition that informed the views of the U.S. delegation to the meeting was a minority position. The British, Dutch, and other significant stakeholder countries were prepared to concede the need for regulation of the opium trade, but they emphasized regulation over prohibition on the basis that the latter was not feasible. In particular, the Europeans were cognizant of the extent to which cultivation was embedded in the agricultural systems and cultural traditions of their colonial outposts. The British had already moved toward a 10-year supply-reduction agreement with China. This 1907 accord proved highly successful in reducing opium cultivation and availability. There was also a strong view that banning opium would be futile—given the scale of the sector—and counterproductive. In previous experiences such as the prohibition of substances ranging from coffee to wine and tobacco, black markets had flourished as illicit supply and demand had persisted. Moreover, the U.S. delegation's emphasis on enforcement of prohibition through punishment of all individuals engaged in the drug trade as consumers, producers, or distributors (as proposed by the head of the U.S. delegation, Dr. Hamilton Wright) was viewed as punitive and extreme, specifically given long-standing social traditions of opium, cannabis, and coca use. The divisions between the United States and the other participant countries "remained central points of contention for decades" (McAllister 2000, 29).

Although no concrete agreement came out of Shanghai, the meeting was of enormous significance. It laid the foundations for international dialogue on opium and other drugs. This achievement was fully capitalized on by the U.S. missionary groups who successfully lobbied for a follow-up international conference that was held in The Hague in 1911. U.S. narco-diplomacy also forced the introduction of domestic antidrug legislation in the United States. It was recognized that the United States would have no credibility on the international stage if domestic restrictions were not in place. A circuitous route had to be devised so that the federal government could bypass constitutional obstacles to national regulation. In 1906, the Pure Food and Drug Act was introduced as an exercise of the right of the federal government to regulate interstate commerce. As with the earlier British Pharmacy Act, this law did not prohibit drug use; it simply required that alcohol, morphine, opium, cocaine, heroin, chloroform, and cannabis content be noted on the labels of medicines and tonics.

Although the new law was successful in reducing the use of patent medicines (Courtwright 1982), it did not meet the Christian lobby's position that all nonmedicinal drug use should be banned since consumption was immoral, degrading, and dangerous. This principle was finally realized in legislative form in 1909, when the federal government introduced the Smoking Opium Exclusion Act in line with its constitutional right to regulate overseas trade. This law prohibited the import of opium for non-medicinal purposes, making the 1909 law the first federal measure banning the nonmedical, "recreational" use of a substance.

The Exclusion Act was a triumph for the Christian missionary lobby, but the strategy for achieving support for the act's introduction was divisive. The lobby relied strongly on the use of racist language and imagery to galvanize popular and political support for strict antidrug measures, and this tactic was to become a core feature of antidrug measures in the United States. In his role as the first U.S. drug "czar," Hamilton Wright worked with William Randolph Hearst's newspaper empire to generate concern around substance use among minority groups. In an interview with *The New York Times* in March 1911, Wright focused public and media attention on the dangers posed to white American society by cocaine use among African Americans. This approach was further developed in *Literary Digest* and *Good Housekeeping*, where Wright elaborated on the danger posed to white women by "negro cocaine peddlers" and "cocainized nigger rapists." These "Negro fiends" with cocaine-induced superhuman strengths easily substituted for the opium-wielding Chinese "devils" of the earlier anti-opium propaganda. Public pressure for action was in turn channeled toward domestic legislation in the United States, while strengthening the hawkish, prohibition-oriented position of the U.S. delegation to The Hague conference of 1911 (Buxton 2006; Goode and Ben Yahuda 1994).

Building the Early Control Regime

Between The Hague meeting of 1911 and the outbreak of World War II, substantial progress was made in creating the founding structures of the international control regime (see table 2.1).

The 1912 International Opium Convention

In contrast to the Shanghai meeting of 1909, delegates to The Hague did have plenipotentiary powers, and as a result, participating countries were bound by the resulting International Opium Convention, which "raised

Table 2.1. Pre–World War II Drug Conventions

Date and Place Signed	Title	Date of Entry into Force
January 1912, The Hague, The Netherlands	International Opium Convention	February 1915 and June 1919
February 1925, Geneva, Switzerland	Agreement concerning the Manufacture of, Internal Trade in, and Use of Prepared Opium	July 1926
Februry 1925, Geneva, Switzerland	International Opium Convention	September 1928
July 1931, Geneva, Switzerland	Convention for Limiting the Manufacture and Regulating the Distribution of Narcotic Drugs	July 1933
November 1931, Bangkok, Thailand	Agreement for the Control of Opium Smoking in the Far East	April 1937
June 1936, Geneva, Switzerland	Convention for the Suppression of the Illicit Traffic in Dangerous Drugs	October 1939

Source: Author.

the obligation to co-operate in the international campaign against the drug evil from a purely moral one to the level of a duty under international law" (May 1950).

The convention institutionalized the principle that medical need was the sole criterion for the manufacture, trade, and use of opiates and cocaine. National governments were required to enact "effective laws or regulations" to control production and distribution and to restrict the ports through which cocaine and opiates were exported. Although the convention was a groundbreaking document, it did not create mechanisms to oversee implementation of the agreement, nor did it set targets for reducing the volume of drugs manufactured. It was loosely worded and, most problematic of all, could come into effect only if unanimously approved. Amid mounting suspicion and enmity between governments in the drift toward war in 1914, consensus was difficult to achieve, and only China, Honduras, the Netherlands, Norway, and the United States ratified the convention (Bewley Taylor 2001; McAllister 2000).

World War I removed the obstacles to ratification and administration of the Opium Convention. First, Austria-Hungary and the Ottoman

Empire—reluctant supporters of the measure—were defeated in the conflict, making it possible to craft a new consensus and for the United States and West European powers to impose the convention. This was achieved by conjoining ratification of the Opium Convention to the Versailles Peace Agreement of 1919 (McAllister 2000). Second, the League of Nations was created in the aftermath of the Great War and provided the international community with a centralized body for the administration of the convention.

On assuming responsibility for overseeing the Opium Convention, the league created specialized support bodies that included the Opium Section, which provided administrative and executive support to the League Council, and the Health Committee of the league, forerunner of the World Health Organization (WHO), which advised the league's secretariat on drug-related matters. The most important and specialized of these bodies within the new control regime was the Advisory Committee on the Traffic in Opium and Other Dangerous Drugs, known as the Opium Advisory Committee, which in turn created the Opium Control Board to assist it in its duties (Bewley Taylor 2001).

From this institutional foundation, the League of Nations went on to develop incrementally a comprehensive control regime. Knowledge and operational gaps in the system were identified and addressed through follow-up conferences and the introduction of new conventions. This process of building up the control system proceeded with two conferences in Geneva in 1924 that sought to address the problems encountered by the advisory committee in developing a comprehensive picture of the "legitimate" medical drug market.

The Geneva Convention

The Geneva Convention of 1928 expanded the manufacturing control system by establishing compulsory drug import certificates and export authorizations that were to be administered by national authorities and that were required for all drug transactions between countries. This system sought to prevent countries from importing or exporting drugs beyond medical and scientific requirement. To determine the level of legitimate medical drug requirements, parties to the convention were to provide annual statistics estimating production, manufacture, and consumption requirements for opiates, coca, cocaine, and, for the first time in drug control, cannabis. This information was to be supplemented by quarterly statistics detailing the volume of plant-based and manufactured drugs imported and exported and estimated figures for opium smoking. A new drug control organ, the eight-person Permanent Central Opium Board, which replaced the Opium Control Board, assumed responsibility for processing the statistical information. The new board had the authority to request explanations from national governments if they failed to submit statistical information or if stated drug import or export requirements were overshot. It could also recommend an embargo on drug exports or imports on any country that exported or imported in excess of stated production levels or medical need. These constraints extended to countries that were not party to the convention, universalizing the control system. Aside from refining the institutional structure and remit of drug control, the 1928 convention increased the number of drugs subject to the control regime and created an open-ended schedule that classified drugs according to their danger to health and relevance to science.

The 1924 Geneva conference also led to a second convention, the Agreement Concerning the Manufacture of, Internal Trade in, and Use of Prepared Opium, which came into force in 1926. This agreement established a 15-year timetable for the elimination of recreational opium use in Southeast Asia.

Convention for Limiting the Manufacture and Regulating the Distribution of Narcotic Drugs

The Geneva Convention failed to prevent legitimately manufactured drugs from seeping into the illegitimate market. The Opium Advisory Committee determined that between 1925 and 1929, legitimate demand for opium- and cocaine-based drugs was about 39 tons per year, while 100 tons of opiates had been exported to unknown destinations from licensed factories (Anslinger and Tompkins 1953). A follow-up conference addressing this weakness resulted in the 1931 Convention for Limiting the Manufacture and Regulating the Distribution of Narcotic Drugs. The convention set out that the quantity of manufactured drugs required globally was to be fixed in advance. This number was to be determined by a compulsory estimates system, under which all countries were required to detail the quantities of drugs needed for medical and scientific purposes for the coming year. The system of indirect limitations was administered by a new body, the four-person Drug Supervisory Board, which was authorized to draw up its own estimates of individual country needs as a means of checking the information submitted. It also devised estimates for those countries that did not submit drug requirements. No greater quantity of any of the drugs set out in the Drug Supervisory Board final report was to be manufactured.

In a further tightening of the control regime, the Permanent Central Opium Board was empowered under the 1931 convention to embargo directly any country that exported or imported beyond its stated manufacturing volumes or consumption needs. Signatory states were also required to establish a dedicated national drug enforcement agency to ensure compliance with domestic drug laws that had been introduced at the local level in line with international obligations.

Convention for the Suppression of the Illicit Traffic in Dangerous Drugs

The final element of the interwar control regime was the 1936 Convention for the Suppression of the Illicit Traffic in Dangerous Drugs, an initiative of the International Police Commission, the forerunner of Interpol. Unlike previous conventions, which sought to demarcate a legitimate trade in medical drugs, the 1936 convention addressed the illegal market. It imposed punitive and uniform criminal penalties for trafficking illicit substances, with Article 2 of the convention recommending that national antitrafficking laws be based on "imprisonment, or other penalties of deprivation of liberty." National governments were obliged to set up a dedicated agency responsible for monitoring drug traffickers and trafficking trends, in coordination with corresponding agencies in other countries.

Evaluating the Interwar Control Regime

The international community made remarkable progress in working collectively (an unprecedented development in itself) to control the supply of harmful substances. In 1933, the Opium Advisory Committee reported that "the sources of supply [of drugs] in Western Europe, as a result of the close control now exercised, appear to be rapidly drying up" (Renborg 1964). World opium production declined 82 percent between 1907 and 1934, from 41,624 tons to an estimated 16,653 tons. Legitimate heroin production fell from 20,000 pounds in 1926 to 2,200 pounds by 1931. Southeast Asia, the biggest "problem" market, saw a 65 percent fall in opium sales; in the Netherlands Indies (Indonesia), opium consumption fell 88 percent (McCoy 1972). This reduction was a major achievement, given the difficulties inherent in negotiating a universal agreement that had to reconcile diverse and competing interests and ensure an adequate global supply of medical drugs while altering patterns of individual behavior. The control model was all the more remarkable as it was the first instance in which states had surrendered overview of their sovereign affairs to an international body. Drug control was also groundbreaking, because it led to the introduction of uniform penal sanctions across countries and established principles of criminal law on an international basis.

The instauration of a comprehensive substance control regime was a major success for the U.S. Christian lobby groups that had first initiated the drug control discourse at the turn of the 20th century. The United States was able to pull dissenting national voices into the system and override competing regulatory proposals as a result of two key factors: evolving attitudes toward the drug trade in Europe and astute U.S. diplomacy.

As understanding of addiction and dependence evolved, West European states acknowledged the need for a stronger control framework, a paternalist orientation reinforced by the creation of rudimentary welfare state systems that placed responsibility for the health of citizens with the national government. The rollout of the European welfare state also eliminated the need for self-medication, further legitimizing medical and political arguments in favor of controlled drug use (Berridge 2001).

This is not to suggest that European and other governments were in full accord with the prohibition orientation of the United States, which was the driving force behind the introduction of increasingly punitive sanctions in the conventions. The Dutch, British, French, and Spanish all remained skeptical of the U.S. view that recreational drug use could be terminated through "shock" strategies, and they remained convinced of the importance of medical support for drug users over the penal approach advocated by the United States. Moreover, they did not accept that cultivation of opium or coca could be rapidly eradicated, and on this issue they did achieve a significant victory over the United States by introducing a protracted 15-year time frame for cultivation controls. As a result, by 1939, state opium monopolies continued to operate in British Malaya; Burma; Formosa; French Indo-China; Hong Kong China; Kwantung Leased Territory; Macao, China; the Netherlands Indies; and Siam. Overall, however, the U.S. delegation was effective in defining the shape and orientation of the control system—largely because of political posturing and by acting on the outside of the framework of the League of Nations.

European countries were determined to bring the United States into the league, and it was primarily through concern that the United States would not engage with the body that European powers acceded influence to the United States on drug-related matters. U.S. representatives at the drug conferences and within the control bodies—such as Harry J. Anslinger, director of the Federal Bureau of Narcotics, and Herbert May of the Permanent Central Opium Board—were forceful individuals, whose "beliefs, morals, ambitions and single-minded determination enabled them to exert exceptional influence over the shape of the international drug control regime" (Sinha 2001). When the American position was rejected, the United States withdrew from proceedings. The United States was not party to the most important founding conventions, including the 1928 Geneva convention and the 1936 trafficking convention, on the grounds that they were not rigorous enough (Bewley Taylor 2001; McAllister 2000; Sinha 2001). The United States also signed bilateral policing agreements with 22 countries during the interwar period. While such agreements went against the spirit of cooperation that the league was seeking to create, it allowed the United States to extradite and prosecute drug traffickers independently of the international control system (Anslinger and Tompkins 1953).

Consequently, the drug control framework that evolved reflected the core values of the United States and the internationalization of prohibition-oriented ideas and approaches that were culturally unique to that country. Owing to the influence of the United States, the control model that emerged was skewed toward supply as opposed to demand-focused activities; it emphasized punishment and suppression over consideration of why people cultivated, produced, and used drugs; and it institutionalized the influence of the police, the military, politicians, and diplomats while the opinion of stakeholders such as doctors, drug users, and peasant cultivators were marginalized (Sinha 2001).

Underscoring a further "internationalization" of North American approaches to drugs was a growing reliance on the demonization of drug users to justify repressive domestic legislative measures such as the 1919 Dutch Opium Act, the 1920 British Dangerous Drugs Act, and the 1929 German Opium Act. The emphasis on embattled nations under attack from subversive forces seeking to enslave, poison, and infiltrate the country; on dangerous substances; on threatening "out groups"; and on criminality—all of which were prevalent in early U.S. antidrug propaganda—became a stock element of international counternarcotics propaganda and "education." These stereotypes of drug users remain prevalent today (Reinarman and Levine 1997).

In the United States, themes of race, crime, and drugs were even more potent as the federal government labored around the constitutional separation of powers to introduce strict national prohibition measures. The Harrison Narcotics Tax Act of 1914 and the Marijuana Taxation Act of 1937 were introduced as taxation-based measures, in line with the jurisdiction of the federal government. They imposed punitively high taxes on the nonmedical exchange of cocaine and opiates, in the case of the 1914 act, and on cannabis transactions, including the sale of industrial hemp, in the case of the 1937 measure. Under the Harrison Act, doctors had to register with federal authorities, record all drug transactions, and pay a prescription tax. Any individual caught in possession of cocaine or opiates without a prescription was consequently charged with tax evasion rather than a criminal offense (Whitebread 1995). After 1922, doctors were not allowed to prescribe "narcotic drugs" to addicts to maintain their addiction (Berridge 2001; Courtwright 1982; Whitebread 1995). The Federal Bureau of Narcotics, which was created in 1930 and presided over by Harry J. Anslinger for 30 years, assumed a lead role in disseminating antidrug propaganda and acculturating Americans to the new drug laws. Among the reams of shockingly racist articles from the period was a New York Times piece by Edward Huntington Williams. The article claimed that cocaine made African-Americans resistant to bullets (New York Times, February 8, 1914). In the congressional hearings into the 1914 Harrison bill, cited by the article, the head of the State Pharmacy Board of Pennsylvania, Christopher Koch, testified that "most of the attacks upon the white women of the south are the direct result of the cocaine-crazed Negro brain." In the buildup to the 1937 Marijuana Tax

Act, Mexican migrants emerged as the new drug threat. It was claimed that "marijuana-crazed Mexicans" were committing violent acts after smoking the "loco weed." By emphasizing the threat faced by American society, the Federal Bureau of Narcotics was positioned to increase its share of federal revenues substantially.

After the alcohol prohibition movement was successful in amending the Constitution and achieving national prohibition in 1918, key activists such as Richmond Pearson Hobson of the Anti-Saloon League shifted their attention to the antidrug campaign. In the early 1920s, Pearson formed the International Narcotic Education Association, an organization responsible for distributing racist, eugenicist, hyperbolic, and medically incorrect "information" about the so-called narcotic peril. Support and pressure for drug prohibition persisted even after alcohol prohibition was lifted in 1933, despite the fact that alcohol prohibition had been a failure and that there were important lessons that remained to be learned from the experience. Even though alcohol prohibition had generated a flourishing, difficult-to-police, gangster-dominated illicit industry worth millions of dollars, pressure for domestic and international drug prohibition persisted and was institutionalized in the contemporary drug control framework that evolved after World War II.

The Contemporary Drug Control Regime

While World War I provided a strategic opportunity to advance the principle of drug control, World War II enabled the United States to shape the drug control regime and apparatus (see table 2.2). The framework that developed after 1945 addressed U.S. priorities: specifically, the prohibition of opium smoking, restrictions on drug-plant cultivation, extension of the control system to cannabis and other drugs, enhanced policing and enforcement, and the application of punitive criminal sentences for those engaged in illicit plant cultivation, drug production, trafficking, transportation, distribution, possession, and use (Bruun, Pan, and Rexed 1975). The U.S. ability to consolidate its influence can be attributed to a number of factors, including the geostrategic changes induced by the conflict and the exercise of U.S. political pressure and leverage.

The work of the Permanent Central Opium Board and the Drug Supervisory Board was transferred from Geneva to Washington in 1941.

Table 2.2. Post–World War II Drug Conventions

Date and Place Signed	Title	Date of Entry into Force
December 1946; Lake Success, New York, USA	Protocol amending the Agreements, Conventions and Protocols on Narcotic Drugs concluded at The Hague on January 23, 1912, at Geneva on February 11, 1925 and February 19, 1925 and July 13, 1931, at Bangkok on November 27, 1931, and at Geneva on June 26, 1936	December 1946
November 1948; Paris, France	Protocol Bringing under International Control Drugs outside the Scope of the Convention of July 13, 1931; for Limiting the Manufacture and Regulating the Distribution of Narcotic Drugs, as amended by the Protocol signed at Lake Success, New York, on December 11, 1946	December 1949
June 1953; New York, USA	Protocol for Limiting and Regulating the Cultivation of the Poppy Plant, the Production of, International and Wholesale Trade in, and Use of, Opium	March 1963
March 1961; New York, USA	Single Convention on Narcotic Drugs	December 1964
February 1971; Vienna, Austria	Convention on Psychotropic Substances	August 1976
March 1972; Geneva, Switzerland	Protocol amending the Single Convention on Narcotic Drugs	August 1975
December 1988; Vienna, Austria	Convention against Illicit Traffic in Narcotic Drugs and Psychotropic Substances	November 1990

Source: Author.

Reliant on federal funding, both bodies experienced a "considerable loss of freedom" (McAllister 2000, 146) as they were required to submit technical information to the U.S. government and assist in the development of new antidrug policies. The war also provided the United States with a strategic foothold in Southeast Asia. At a 1943 meeting with representatives from Britain, France, the Netherlands, and Portugal, the United States won the guarantee that opium monopolies would not be reestablished in colonial territories invaded by Japan that were liberated with the help of or by the United States. The subsequent U.S. military presence in the region enabled America to impose its model of prohibition. Opium dens and retail outlets were closed down by U.S. troops and, on conclusion of the war, strict antidrug legislation was introduced by the American administration in Japan and West Germany. The diplomatic environment also allowed for negotiations with opium-cultivating neutral governments such as Iran, Turkey, and the Yugoslavian governments in exile, allowing for preliminary agreements on cultivation controls.

In the aftermath of the war, the Lake Success protocol of 1946 transferred administration of the drug conventions from the defunct League of Nations to the newly established United Nations. The UN Economic and Social Council acquired primary responsibility for overseeing the conventions, and it was supported in this task by the Commission on Narcotic Drugs, which advised the council on drug-related matters and prepared draft international agreements. As such, the commission supplanted the Opium Advisory Committee. In a further innovation to existing control institutions, administrative support that had been provided by the Opium Section was transferred to a new body, the Division of Narcotic Drugs. The Permanent Central Opium Board and Drug Supervisory Board were transferred back to Geneva from Washington, where they continued in their role of compiling statistics from national estimates and administering the import-export certification system.

Another new institution, the World Health Organization, assumed the drug advisory responsibilities formerly exercised by the Health Committee of the League of Nations. The Drug Dependence Expert Committee of WHO was, in turn, given the task of determining the addictive potential of drugs and their position on the international schedule of controls (Fazey 2003).

The Paris Protocol

While there had been a collapse in illicit drug trafficking during the war, the international community had to address complex legacies of the conflict, such as stockpiles of medical opium and semisynthetic drugs and a burgeoning problem of the dependence on new synthetic drugs such as methadone and pethidine, which had been developed during the war but fell outside the control schedule established by the 1931 convention. The first postwar drugs conference resulted in the 1948 Paris Protocol. This agreement brought any drug liable to cause harm into the schedule of controlled drugs and required states to inform the UN secretary-general of any new drug developed that had the potential to produce harmful effects. The progress of the new convention was not without contention, with the Soviet Union reluctant to acknowledge the authority of the UN bodies on the issue or the existence of a drug problem within its territory. Similarly, the U.S. proposal to restrict opium cultivation ran into difficulties amid concerns from consumer states that there would be insufficient stocks of medical opium.

The resulting 1953 Opium Protocol was a compromise measure. It extended the import and export control system for manufactured drugs to opium poppy cultivation, and cultivating countries were required to detail the amount of opium poppy planted and harvested and the volumes of opium exported, used domestically, and stockpiled. The protocol built on an earlier negotiated agreement between the opium-producing countries of India, Iran, Turkey, and Yugoslavia to establish an opium monopoly, from which consumer countries were required to purchase opium stocks. This agreement was strongly resisted by those cultivators not incorporated into the accord and by consumer countries concerned that they would not have guaranteed access to opium stocks. The United States had been at the forefront of the campaign to establish an opium monopoly but was forced to accept stricter regulation and monitoring of opium cultivation. Imposing restrictions on coca cultivation, however, proved more contentious, and reporting requirements were not extended to this crop after Andean countries maintained that coca cultivation was integral to indigenous life and culture. By the time the Opium Protocol came into force in 1963, however, it was a redundant instrument as a result of the 1961 Single Convention on Narcotic Drugs.

Single Convention on Narcotic Drugs

The 1961 convention followed from a meeting of 73 countries to explore a single antidrug convention that would consolidate the nine drug conventions introduced since The Hague conference of 1911. The resulting Single Convention consolidated past convention provisions, introduced controls in new areas, and revised the existing control apparatus.

The Single Convention extended the system of licensing, reporting, and certifying drug transactions to all raw narcotic plant materials, including cannabis and coca leaves. Cultivator countries were required to

establish national monopolies to centralize and then phase out cultivation, production, and consumption, over 25 years in the case of coca and
15 years in the case of opium poppies, culminating in a full international
prohibition of the nonmedical cultivation and use of these substances by
1989. The convention further required immediate domestic legislation to
prohibit the nonmedicinal use of opium, cocaine, and cannabis (which
the United States saw as a so-called gateway drug); and, in a further tightening of restrictions on medicinal consumption, a new classification
schedule was introduced. Drugs considered addictive and scientifically
and medically obsolete, such as the opium poppy, coca, and cannabis and
their derivatives, were classified as schedule I or IV. Drugs that were considered less dangerous and of some medical value were classified as
schedule II or III (Bewley Taylor 2001; Fazey 2003; Sinha 2001). According to Article One of the convention, drugs presented "a serious evil for
the individual" and were "fraught with social and economic danger to
mankind." As such, signatory states were required to introduce more
punitive domestic criminal laws that punished individuals for engagement in all aspects of the illicit drug trade.

Intended as a final and definitive document, the 1961 convention also
restructured the international drug control apparatus. The Permanent
Central Opium Board and the Drug Supervisory Board were merged to
create a 13-person body of independent experts, the International Narcotics Control Board, which evaluated national statistical information,
monitored the import-export control system, and authorized narcotic
plant cultivation for medical and scientific need. These powers were subsequently extended under a 1972 amendment, which gave the board
responsibility for developing and implementing programs to prevent the
cultivation, production, manufacture, trafficking, and use of illicit drugs
and for advising countries that needed assistance in complying with the
conventions. The amendment also addressed extradition and required
that any bilateral agreement automatically include drug-related offenses.
While the thrust of the 1961 convention was toward a tightening of
criminal sanctions, the 1972 amendment introduced an important shift
toward addressing demand-side issues. Parties to the 1961 convention
were now requested to provide "treatment, education, after-care, rehabilitation, and social reintegration" for drug addicts and users. This
change was an attempt to respond to pressure from cultivating countries

to address demand-side issues. The thrust of counternarcotics strategy, however, remained heavily focused on supply-side strategies. Here, it is important to note that the fundamentals of drug control, as established in 1909, were not revisited. Instead, guiding principles were built upon in the 1961 Single Convention, despite major changes in the nature, scale, and dynamics of the illicit trade.

1971 Convention on Psychotropic Substances

Although the Single Convention was intended as "a convention to end all conventions" (May 1950), the international community met in 1971 to respond to the advances in chemistry and synthetic drug manufacture that had led to new mass markets for psychotropic substances such as amphetamines, barbiturates, and hallucinogens that were not incorporated into the existing regulatory framework. The resulting psychotropic convention introduced a regulatory regime for these drugs modeled on the manufacturing and cultivation control system set out in the 1961 convention. This regime included a schedule of four levels of control that were based, like the Single Convention, on a drug's therapeutic value and abuse potential.

The 1961 and 1971 conventions were followed through on the domestic level by repressive drug policies. There was a significant enhancement of police powers to stop, search, raid, hold without charge, and electronically tap suspected traffickers, dealers, and drug users, while the death sentence or mandatory life sentence for offences related to trafficking, production, and possession was routinely introduced. For critics of the approach, the uniformity of strategies owed much to the pressure on regimes stemming from youth rebellion, protest movements, revolutionary ideologies, social experimentation, and profound East-West tensions. In this interpretation, repressive, penal-oriented measures made it possible to suppress political dissent (Gamella and Jiménez Rodrigo 2004).

The domestic response in the United States was particularly noteworthy as it marked a deepening of unilateralism in drug strategy and a broader incorporation of counternarcotics policy into foreign policy. The Nixon administration launched a "war on drugs" in 1969 that was followed by the introduction of the 1970 Controlled Substances Act. That act, which is the basis for contemporary U.S. drug policy, brought together all previous federal drug legislation. It established a series of schedules, with cannabis among a number of drugs classified as the most dangerous drugs, or schedule I narcotics, and it was enforced by a new agency, the Drug Enforcement Administration, which was created in 1973 following the closure of the Federal Bureau of Narcotics. The reconceptualization of the drug issue as a matter of national security legitimized direct U.S. action in other countries to eliminate supply, starting with Mexico and U.S.-sponsored cannabis eradication in the early 1970s.

The war on drugs was relaunched by President Reagan, who in a 1982 speech outlined an aggressive new posture: "We're taking down the surrender flag . . . we're running up the battle flag" (*New York Times*, June 24, 1982). The Reagan administration introduced a plethora of punitive anti-drug measures that included the 1984 Comprehensive Crime Control Act, the 1986 Anti-Drug Abuse Act, the 1988 Anti-Drug Abuse Amendment Act, and the 1988 Drug Free Workplace Act. These measures raised federal penalties for all drug-related offenses and introduced mandatory minimum sentences and asset seizure without conviction; they also established the federal death penalty for drug "kingpins" (Chase Eldridge 1998). The Reagan period also saw the introduction of the Drug Abuse Resistance Education (DARE) program in schools and in 1986 drug testing of federal employees and contractors under Executive Order 12564. This effort was coordinated by a new agency, the Office of National Drug Control Policy, which was created by the 1988 National Narcotics Leadership Act.

This domestic legislative momentum continued into the 1990s and 2000s with the model 1999 Drug Dealer Liability Act that imposed civil liability on drug dealers for the direct or indirect harm caused by the use of the drugs that they distributed. In 2000, the Protecting Our Children from Drugs Act imposed mandatory minimum sentences on drug dealers who involved children under the age of 18 in the trade or who distributed near schools (Chase Eldridge 1998). The costs of this so-called hard security approach were significant. The federal prison budget, for example, increased 1,350 percent between 1982 and 2001 in line with the increase in the number of drug-related offenders in U.S. jails. The prison population increased from 1.27 million to 2.2 million, with an estimated one-quarter of prisoners incarcerated for drug offenses.

Of crucial significance, the U.S. drug war of the 1980s emphasized cultivation eradication, with a specific focus on South America. In the mid-1980s, the federal government introduced the drug certification system that terminated bilateral assistance to any country the State Department deemed uncooperative in the drug war. There was also an intense militarization of eradication and interdiction strategies, with the United States pressing for and financing the deployment of source-country military institutions in enforcement activities. This escalation of unilateral U.S. counternarcotics activities led to a sharp increase in the federal government's drug budget expenditures, from $1.8 billion in 1981 to $12.5 billion by 1993. The Drug Enforcement Administration's share of these revenues increased from $200 million to $400 million (Gray 2000), with additional finances available through the 1984 civil forfeiture law, which allowed enforcement agencies to confiscate drug-related assets. By the end of the 1980s, the 1984 law had contributed some $500 million to the agency, while the Justice Department received an estimated $1.5 billion in illegal assets between 1985 and 1991 (Blumenson and Nilsen 1998).

1988 Convention against Illicit Traffic in Narcotic Drugs and Psychotropic Substances

The final convention of the current drug control system was negotiated in 1988. As with the prewar drug control system, this agreement related to the traffic in illicit substances and addressed a mechanism for strengthening compliance with the control regime. The convention required states to cooperate and coordinate antitrafficking initiatives with international enforcement bodies and partner agencies in other countries; and, in response to the new challenges posed by the globalization of trade and services, it called on states to introduce domestic criminal legislation to prevent money laundering and to allow for asset seizure and extradition. The convention also introduced controls of the chemical precursors required for the production of synthetic and semisynthetic drugs, with states obliged to monitor the manufacture and trade in chemicals that could be used in illicit drug production. In addition, it set out procedures for the harmonization of national drug laws, identifying specific offenses that individual states were required to legislate against.

While no new conventions were introduced after 1988, the institutional apparatus of the drug control regime continued to evolve. In 1991, the separate, geographically dispersed UN agencies responsible for administering the conventions were unified under the United Nations Drug Control Program. This new body, which derived its authority from the Commission on Narcotic Drugs, absorbed the Division of Narcotic Drugs and the International Narcotics Control Board. As part of this restructuring process, the membership of the commission was expanded from 40 countries to 53, with seats allocated on the basis of the geographical groupings within the UN (Fazey 2003).

In response to the growing links between illicit trafficking activities, such as small arms, narcotics, and people, there was a further streamlining of agencies in 1997. The UN Drug Control Program was merged with the Centre for International Crime Prevention to form the United Nations Office for Drug Control and Crime Prevention, and in 2002 this agency became the UN Office on Drugs and Crime (see table 2.3).

Although there have been no new conventions after the Convention against Illicit Traffic in Narcotic Drugs and Psychotropic Substances, a U.N. General Assembly Special Session was convened in 1998. The meeting was of enormous significance—in part a response to a large expansion of the post–Cold War drug trade—allowing a period of reflection and thinking on drug strategy going forward. It was also an opportunity for a diverse coalition of countries and interests that were critical of

Table 2.3. The International Drug Control Apparatus

Body	Economic and Social Council	Commission on Narcotic Drugs
Function	Discusses and analyzes drug-related issues; initiates drug-related studies; drafts conventions; convenes drug conferences.	Analyzes drug traffic and trends; advises UN Economic and Social Council; prepares draft international drug agreements; provides forum for information exchange.
Body	International Narcotics Control Board	United Nations Office on Drugs and Crime
Function	Serves as control organ for the implementation of the drug control treaties; provides advice to WHO; determines worldwide medical and scientific drug requirements; processes technical and statistical information provided by states; allocates cultivation, production, manufacture, export, import, and trade quotas; advises status on antidrug measures.	Coordinates UN antidrug activities; provides secretariat services for the Commission on Narcotic Drugs and International Narcotics Control Board; advises countries on implementation of the drug conventions; executes antidrug initiatives in host countries.

Source: Author.

existing strategy to lobby for the reform of guiding principles. Here, four issues were given consideration in the resulting document:

- First, the need to advance alternative development strategies in cultivating countries, which followed from the lack of progress in reducing cultivation through eradication
- Second, the need to integrate harm-reduction approaches into demand-side strategies, with an emphasis on minimizing the harm done by drug use rather than simply on incarcerating offenders
- Third, acknowledgment of the role of coca, opium, and other narcotic drug crops in local cultures and indigenous traditions
- Fourth, a restatement of shared global responsibility for financing international drug control

In sum, the issues of contention in 1998 were the same as those that divided European countries, the United States, and developing countries in 1909.

Conclusion

Although the drug control regime has reached a high point in its universalism, comprehensiveness, and institutional integrity, it is also under unprecedented pressure. There are indications that the consensus underpinning the model is fracturing. The cultivation, production, and consumption of illicit substances are higher than they have ever been, and drug markets have become more complex, dynamic, and diversified. This situation has forced a questioning of first principles, along with a growing acknowledgment that the ideology of prohibition that underpins the control regime is counterproductive and unachievable. European and South American countries have taken the lead in experimenting with regulatory and liberalization-oriented strategies, a move informed by the limited progress made through the application of repressive approaches (Gatto 1999; Fazey 2003). Interest in liberalization and demand-side issues has run in parallel with a revision of strategy in supplying countries. The Europeans in particular now place emphasis on alternative development policy in cultivator states, a position that acknowledges the persistence of incentives to poor and marginalized people to cultivate narcotics for the global market.

There is a wider concern that the emphasis on repression, militarization, and enforcement is iatrogenic. The persistence of prohibition thinking and prohibition-oriented policies in an age of chemical advances, globalization, HIV/AIDS, and a growing interconnectivity among drugs, crime, and conflict may be doing more harm than good. The capacity of the current control regime to evolve from a source-focused, criminalization approach toward a more liberal, treatment-oriented, and developmentalist strategy, however, is constrained by the prohibition attitudes that continue among powerful country and regional players.

The conceptual frameworks used to understand and respond to drugs and drug consumption are more than a century old. They were framed in a period of colonial enterprise, social tension, racism, and a lack of medical and scientific understanding (Sinha 2001). That they continue to inform drug policy today is deeply problematic.

References

Anslinger, H., and Tompkins, W. 1953. *The Traffic in Narcotics.* New York: Funk and Wagnalls.

Behr, E. 1996. *Prohibition: Thirteen Years That Changed America.* New York: Arcade Publishing.

Berridge V., and G. Edwards. 1981. *Opium and the People: Opiate Use in Nineteenth Century England.* London: Allen Lane.

Berridge, V. 2001. "Altered States: Opium and Tobacco Compared." *Social Research* (Fall).

Bewley Taylor, D. 2001. *The United States and International Drug Control, 1909–1997.* London: Continuum.

Blumenson, E., and Nilsen, E. 1998. "The Drug War's Hidden Economic Agenda," *The Nation* (March 9) : 11–16.

Booth, M. 1999. *Opium: A History.* New York: Thomas Dunne Books.

Bouvier, M. 2001. *Whose America? The War of 1898 and the Battles to Define the Nation.* Santa Barbara, CA: Praeger.

Bruun, K., L. Pan, and I. Rexed, I. 1975. *The Gentlemen's Club: International Control of Drugs and Alcohol.* Chicago: University of Chicago Press.

Buxton, J. 2006. *The Political Economy of Narcotics: Production, Consumption and Global Markets.* London: Zed Books.

Chase Eldridge, D. 1998. *Ending the War on Drugs: A Solution for America.* New York: Bridge Works Publishing.

Courtwright, D. 1982. *Dark Paradise: Opiate Addiction in America before 1940.* Cambridge, MA: Harvard University Press.

Fazey, C. 2003. "The Commission on Narcotic Drugs and the United Nations International Drug Control Programme: Politics, Policies and Prospect for Change." *International Journal of Drug Policy* 14: 155–69.

Gamella, J., and M. Jiménez Rodrigo. 2004. "A Brief History of Cannabis Policies in Spain (1968–2003)." *Journal of Drug Issues* (Summer).

Gatto, C. 1999, "European Drug Policy: Analysis and Case Studies." National Organization to Reform the Marijuana Laws (N.O.R.M.L.) Foundation, http://www .norml.org/index.cfm?Group_ID=4415.

Goode, E., and N. Ben Yahuda. 1994. *Moral Panics: Social Construction of Deviance.* London: Blackwell.

Gootenberg, P., ed. 1999. *Cocaine: Global Histories.* London: Routledge.

Gray, M. 2000. *Drug Crazy: How We Got into This Mess and How We Can get Out of It.* New York: Random House.

Herer, J. 1998. *The Emperor Wears No Clothes: Hemp and the Marijuana Conspiracy.* http://www.jackherer.com/.

Hodgson, B. 2001. *In the Arms of Morpheus: The Tragic History of Laudanum, Morphine, and Patent Medicines.* New York: Firefly Books Ltd.

Inglis, B. 1975. *The Forbidden Game: A Social History of Drugs.* New York: Charles Scribner's Sons.

Keire, M. 1998. "Dope Fiends and Degenerates: The Gendering of Addiction in the Early Twentieth Century." *Journal of Social History* (Summer).

La Motte, E. 2003. *The Opium Monopoly.* Montana: Kessinger Publishing.

May, H. 1950. "The Evolution of the International Control of Narcotic Drugs." *Bulletin on Narcotics* 3.

McAllister, W. 2000. *Drug Diplomacy in the Twentieth Century: An International History.* London: Routledge.

McCoy A. 1972. *The Politics of Heroin in Southeast Asia.* New York: Harper and Row.

Reinarman, C., and Levine, H. 1997. *Crack in America: Demon Drugs and Social Justice.* Berkeley: University of California Press.

Renborg, B. 1964. "The Grand Old Men of the League of Nations. What They Achieved. Who They Were." *Bulletin on Narcotics* 4.

Richards, J. 2003. "The Opium Industry in British India." *The Indian Economic and Social History Review* 39 (2–3): 149–80.

Schultes, R., and Hoffman, A. 1992. *Plants of the Gods: Their Sacred, Healing and Hallucinogenic Powers.* Rochester, NY: Healing Arts Press.

Scott, J. 1969. *The White Poppy: A History of Opium.* New York: Funk and Wagnalls.

Sinha, J. 2001. "The History and Development of the Leading International Drug Control Conventions." Report prepared for the Senate Special Committee on Illegal Drugs. Law and Government Division, Library of Parliament.

Streatfeild, D. 2000. *Cocaine: A Definitive History.* London: Virgin.

The New York Times, February 8, 1914.

The New York Times, June 24, 1982.

Ul Haq, E. 2000. *Drugs in South Asia: From the Opium Trade to the Present Day.* London: Palgrave Macmillan.

Walker, W. 1996. *Drugs in the Western Hemisphere: An Odyssey of Cultures in Conflict.* Wilmington, DE: Scholarly Resources Inc.

Whitebread, C. 1995. "The Sociology of Prohibition or the History of the Non-Medical Use of Drugs in the United States." Speech to the California Judges' Association, 1995 annual conference.

3

Can Production and Trafficking of Illicit Drugs Be Reduced or Only Shifted?

Peter Reuter

Cocaine and heroin are produced in poor countries and exported to consumers in both poor and rich countries, where their consumption and sale cause considerable damage in the form of crime, disease, and addiction. The producing nations are then blamed by the rich countries for their failure to control production, accusations sharpened by the ubiquitous corruption around drug production and by the large rewards that accrue to some developing-country players in the trade. While there is increasing acceptance that the fundamental problem for rich countries is their inability to control domestic demand for drugs,[1] the search for ways of controlling production continues, with rich countries both aiding and coercing poor producer nations in their efforts.

Findings on the effects of interventions are discouraging. Little of a systematic nature is known about the effects of such programs as interdiction, crop eradication, "alternative development," or more general law

This chapter is based on earlier research conducted with RAND colleagues (Robert Klitgaard, K. Jack Riley, Justin Adams, Susan Everingham, and Jack Quinlivan) for the World Bank. A fuller statement of many of the ideas as they relate to heroin are contained in Paoli, Greenfield, and Reuter (2009). I thank Mara D'Angelo and Erica Schmeckpepper for research assistance and Norman Loayza for helpful comments. The author is solely responsible for opinions expressed here.

enforcement aimed at reducing drug production and trafficking. The general impression is that such programs have been ineffective. It is certainly the case that the world drug trade has continued to flourish even as the rhetoric of control has sharpened during the past quarter-century and as the flow of funds for suppression has increased. See European Commission (2009) for a review of how the world's drug problems and policies changed between 1998 and 2007.

This chapter focuses on cocaine and heroin for two reasons. First, cocaine and heroin are generally believed to account for the bulk of the income that flows to developing countries from illicit drugs, although the evidence is very soft; there are no systematic estimates of the flows from other drugs such as methamphetamines and marijuana.[2] Second, compared to drugs that are more widely used (in particular marijuana), cocaine and heroin produce particularly intense psychological and physical effects on users; cocaine use results in a form of psychological addiction by producing a high that encourages pursuit of more intense intoxication, whereas heroin use produces an actual physical dependence (Kleiman 1992). For example, opiates account for approximately 70 percent of all treatment demand in Asia, followed by 64 percent in Europe and 62 percent in Australia. They are the principal vector for the spread of HIV in a number of countries. Cocaine is the biggest problem drug in the Americas, accounting for 58 percent and 40 percent of total drug treatment in South America and North America, respectively.

The chapter begins by providing a description of how consumption, production, and trafficking are distributed among countries. The following section offers some hypotheses about why both production and trafficking are so concentrated in so few countries. The chapter then describes the ways in which governments have attempted to reduce both production and trafficking and summarizes what is known about the effectiveness of the different methods used. It concludes with comments on some major research questions.

Illicit Drug Trends and Developing Countries

This section provides background on the levels and trends in cocaine and heroin consumption; it shows which countries are most important and summarizes indicators of drug use in major developing countries.

Consuming Countries

There are no systematic estimates of worldwide consumption of illicit drugs. The United Nations Office on Drugs and Crime (UNODC) reports only the prevalence of illicit drug use (the percentage of the population using specific drugs) through surveys of countries' governments in its annual *Global Illicit Drug Trends*. But with the exception of the United States and (more recently) a few other industrialized nations, countries have not developed the necessary capability to collect such information (and some have little desire to do so).[3] Thus, the UNODC survey responses suffer from lack of data, varying estimation methodologies across different countries, and biases that governments bring to reporting the level of consumption.[4]

According to the UNODC (2008), cannabis is the most widely abused drug worldwide (around 160 million people), followed by amphetamine-type stimulants (35 million). Approximately 15 million people abuse cocaine, and a similar number abuse opiates. Tables 3.1 and 3.2 report

Table 3.1. Estimated Prevalence Estimates of Opiate Abuse Worldwide, 2007

Regions and Countries	Number of Persons (millions)	Percentage of Population (over 15)	Trends
Asia	9.56	0.3	
India	2.80	0.40	Slow growth
China	1.9	0.20	Increasing
Pakistan	.75	0.8	Stable to declining
Iran, Islamic Rep. of	1.3	2.8	Stable
Other	2.81	0.34	Mixed by region
Europe	4.17	0.70	
West and Central Europe	1.57	0.6	Stable to declining
Russian Federation	2.00	2.0	Stable
Other Eastern Europe	0.60	0.38	Mixed
Oceania	0.09	0.40	Declining
Americas	2.28	0.40	
United States	1.30	0.50	Declining
South America	0.98	0.30	Some increases
Africa	0.91	0.20	Increasing
Global	15.84	0.4	Increasing

Source: Paoli, Greenfield, and Reuter 2009, table 3.3, based on UNODC 2007.

Table 3.2. Estimated Prevalence of Cocaine Use Worldwide, 2007

Regions and Countries	Number of Persons (millions)	Percentage of Population (over 15)	Trends
Europe	4.01	.73	
West and Central Europe	3.89	1.22	Stable to increasing
Southeast Europe	.07	.08	
Eastern Europe	.05	.03	Mixed
Americas	10.20	1.74	
North America	7.10	2.42	Declining
South America	3.10	1.05	Increasing
Asia	.33	.01	
Oceania	.30	1.37	Stable to increasing
Africa	1.15	.22	
Global	15.99	.37	Stable

Source: UNODC 2008.

recent UNODC figures on opiates and cocaine for major nations and regions, along with my judgment of recent trends. Use of cocaine in Asia and Africa is minimal.

The use of opiates is very broadly distributed by both geography and relative wealth. The bulk of opiate users is in developing nations.[5] Even though China has a very low estimated prevalence rate, which may reflect the low investment in data collection, it has more opiate addicts than all but three or four other nations, simply because of its population.[6] India, with a moderate estimated prevalence, has by far the largest number of opiate addicts and for the same reason. In most of Western Europe and the United States, there has been little growth in opiate addicts; indeed, there has recently been a decline in many countries (European Commission 2009). Asia and Eastern Europe have seen sharp increases in recent years, with Central Asia being most affected (Ponce 2002; Roston 2002).

The bulk of cocaine users reside in a few rich countries. The United States dominates that market, but there has been substantial growth in Western Europe since about the mid-1990s, particularly in Spain and the United Kingdom.

Retail expenditures on heroin are dominated by rich-country consumers, simply because retail prices are so much higher in those nations.[7] The prices received by growers and traffickers, however, are not dependent on the final destination. A shift of consumption from Western Europe to China has no significance to the revenue of Afghanistan producers; the export price from Afghanistan is the same regardless of the final consumption destination. Hence, it is approximately true that consumers in the developing world account for most of the earnings of opium producers, as opposed to the revenues of traffickers and retailers in developed countries.

Although the data presented so far report only the numbers of users, estimates of the quantities consumed are needed to understand the market. Almost no data are available on the average quantities consumed annually by addicts in each country,[8] because users can report only how much they spend on cocaine and heroin, not how much of the active drug they purchased, since the purity is highly variable and cannot be observed. Some evidence suggests that U.S. heroin addicts consume less per year than their counterparts in Europe, but without more specific data, it is necessary to assume that for the rest of the world the distribution of quantities consumed does mirror the distribution of users.

Producing Countries

A small number of nations account for the bulk of the production of coca and opium. According to official estimates by the UNODC (2008), three countries—the Plurinational State of Bolivia, Colombia, and Peru—account for the entirety of commercial coca production. Small amounts of coca are reportedly being produced in Brazil and República Bolivariana de Venezuela, but nothing that reaches the market. Table 3.3 displays the global production of dry leaf coca for various years between 1990 and 2007.[9] As shown, most coca is currently produced in Colombia, although

Table 3.3. Production of Dry Leaf Coca in Bolivia, Colombia, and Peru, Selected Years 1990–2007
(in metric tons)

Country	1990	1995	2000	2002	2004	2006	2007
Bolivia	77,000	85,000	13,400	19,800	38,000	33,200	36,400
Colombia	45,300	80,900	266,200	222,100	164,280	154,130	154,000
Peru	196,900	183,600	46,200	52,500	101,000	105,100	107,800
Total	319,200	349,500	325,800	294,400	303,280	292,430	298,200

Source: UNODC 2008.

Peru was the primary producer a decade ago. Production in Bolivia increased between 2000 and 2002 but declined again after 2004. Production in Peru, however, declined sharply over the period of 2000 and 2002, although there has been a recent rebound in Peru.

Afghanistan and Myanmar accounted for more than 90 percent of global production of opium in 2004 (4,570 out of 4,850 metric tons). This two-country dominance in opium production has occurred in every year since 1988 (when systematic estimates began), except for 2001 when the Taliban successfully cut Afghanistan's production by more than 90 percent.[10] Table 3.4 reports estimated global production of opium for various years between 1990 and 2007. As shown by the table, second-tier opium producers include Colombia, Lao People's Democratic Republic, and Mexico. Pakistan, Thailand, and Vietnam comprise the third tier; once substantial producers in the 1980s and early 1990s, they now are almost insignificant.

It is useful to contrast those data with the data on cannabis, the other prominent psychoactive drug that has its source in a plant. In North America, the most recent data suggest that the Canadian market is now considered self-sufficient (Bouchard 2008; Royal Canadian Mounted Police 2004) and that in the United States more than 50 percent of the

Table 3.4. Global Production of Opium, Selected Years 1990–2006
(*metric tons*)

Country	1990	1995	2000	2001	2002	2004	2006	2007
Afghanistan	1,570	2,335	3,276	185[a]	3,400	4,200	6,100	8,200
Colombia	0	71	88	80	52	49	13	14
LAO, PDR	202	128	167	134	112	43	20	9
Mexico	62	53	21	91	58	73	108	107
Myanmar	1,621	1,664	1,087	1,097	828	370	315	460
Pakistan	150	112	8	5	5	40	39	43
Thailand	20	2	6	6	9	b	b	b
Vietnam	90	9	b	b	b	b	b	b
Other	45	78	38	32	56	75	16	38
Total	3,760	4,452	4,691	1,630	4,520	4,850	6,611	8,871

Source: UNODC 2008.
a. Reflects production crackdown by Taliban.
b. Included in other.

available cannabis is domestic (Gettman 2006). It is thought that the Netherlands accounts for a large share of the cannabis consumed in Europe.[11] Morocco and Mexico supply substantial quantities of cannabis resin and cannabis herb to Western Europe and the United States, respectively, but they are certainly not dominant. The exceptional status of cannabis probably rests on four factors:

- The bulkiness per unit value raises smuggling costs substantially.
- The high dollar yield per acre reduces risks of detection per dollar of production.
- A boutique market of users and growers is interested in developing better breeds of the plant. In addition, many users now "grow their own."
- Entry into the market is easy, because the seeds are widely available. There are probably few economies of scale in growing beyond quite a small number of plants, and there is no further processing.

Trafficking Countries

As with production, the trafficking of coca and opium involves a relatively small number of nations. One indicator of which countries are involved in trafficking is drug seizures, but it requires careful interpretation.[12] Seizures can be driven by production, local consumption, and transshipment; nations that experience large seizures but are neither producers nor major consumers are likely to be involved in trafficking to other countries. It is a one-sided indicator; some transshipment nations—as a result of either corruption or limited enforcement effort—may have few seizures. Illustrating the weakness of seizure as an indicator are the figures for Russia. It constitutes one of the three largest markets for heroin and serves as a transshipment country for Eastern Europe; yet Russia was seizing barely 1 ton of heroin annually in the early part of this decade.

Table 3.5 lists the highest-ranking countries for seizures of cocaine and opiates (that is, heroin, morphine, and opium) in 2006 by the percentage of the world total. The table shows that almost half the cocaine seized in 2006 was seized in two countries: the United States (21 percent), the largest consumer country, and in Colombia (26 percent), the largest producer country. Spain, which accounted for the next-largest amounts

Table 3.5. Highest-Ranking Countries for Seizures of Cocaine and Opiates, 2006
(*percentage of world total*)

Cocaine			Opiates in Heroin Equivalents[a]		
Country	%	Tons	Country	%	Tons
Colombia	26	181	Iran	37	52
United States	21	147	Pakistan	26	36
Spain	7	49	Turkey	8	11
Venezuela, República Bolivariana	6	39	Afghanistan	6	9
Panama	5	36	China	5	6
Portugal	5	34	Russian Federation	2	3
Ecuador	5	34	Myanmar	2	2
Costa Rica	3	23	Tajikistan	2	2
Mexico	3	21	United Kingdom	1	2
Peru	3	19	United States	1	2
Other countries	16	108	Other countries	10	12
Estimate of seizures in tons		413			139
Estimate of production in tons		984			606
Amount seized as percentage of estimated production	42			23	

Source: UNODC 2008.
Note: Individual countries' seizures as reported (street purity).
a. Heroin, morphine, and opium.

of seized cocaine, represents a gateway for cocaine traveling into Europe. Interestingly, Ecuador and Venezuela were also responsible for smaller, although significant, amounts of seized cocaine. Those countries border the important source countries of Colombia and Peru. As compared to heroin, total seizures of cocaine account for a much larger share of estimated production (42 percent as opposed to 23 percent).

Table 3.5 also shows that more than one-third of the opiates seized in 2006 came from Iran alone (37 percent). Pakistan accounted for 26 percent of the opiates seized, the second-largest amount. Other major countries with opiate seizures, Turkey and China, are located in Asia. Turkey, with a small domestic opiate market, is a principal transshipment route for European heroin, while China not only has a large domestic market but also serves as a transshipment route for heroin into some Western markets.[13] Afghanistan, where 6 percent of the world's seizures were made, is also a country noteworthy for its 2006 seizures.

Possible Explanations for The Pattern of National Involvement in the Drug Trade

The concentration of coca and opium production in those few developing countries is an important fact for policy makers. It creates the sense, probably illusory, that success is just around the corner because only two or three countries need to exit the industry. The concentration is a paradox for three reasons:

- First, many nations are capable of producing each drug. Historically, substantial opium production has been recorded in China, Iran, and Macedonia, for example, none of which now produces.[14] Australia, France, and Spain have entered the legal opiate market in recent times, obtaining production quotas from the International Narcotics Control Board under an international treaty agreement for that market (INCB 2002). Coca has been grown commercially in Java (while under Dutch rule) and Taiwan, China (while under Japanese rule), and could be grown in parts of the Andes that are not now involved (Spillane 2000).
- Second, technically it is possible to produce cocaine or heroin in industrialized nations. Hydroponic techniques, for example, can be used for both coca and opium poppies in regions with less than suitable climates. And with local production come associated savings in transportation costs and the elimination of interdiction risks. The enforcement risks faced by producers in the United States or Western Europe, however, are substantial, and the compensation costs for those risks are sufficiently high that local production has never developed.
- Third, many developing countries that neighbor coca and opium producers are not or have not been major producers, although they might be involved in trafficking. Consider Thailand, for example, which was a major producer of opium in the early 1970s. Thailand has had a substantial heroin addict population since the 1970s. It continues to suffer from high levels of corruption, both in the military and in the civilian government. Consequently, Thailand would seem to be a strong candidate for a large opium production sector. However, Thailand now produces very little opium and serves primarily as a consuming and transshipping country for Myanmar. Similarly, República Bolivariana de Venezuela and Ecuador have many of the preconditions for coca production and are regularly put on the list of

candidate producers but have, after two decades of being at high risk, not entered the industry. Very specific factors may account for the observed differences.

The concentration and precise pattern of trafficking, as opposed to production, is also not easy to explain. Transshipment across other countries is not a universal feature of the drug trade. Substantial quantities of cocaine are shipped directly from Colombia to Western Europe, although Argentina and Brazil, with close commercial connections to the Iberian Peninsula (as indicated by Spain's high seizures), also play a role. In the 1980s, some Pakistani-produced heroin was sent directly to the United Kingdom. Transshipment, then, is never simply geographic destiny, but geography is clearly a risk factor. Consequently, it is important to understand how the various economic, sociological, and political factors in different countries can drive the production and trafficking of coca and opium.

Structure of the International Drug Industry

One approach to exploring the question of which countries are more likely to produce and traffic in illicit drugs is to examine the structure of international drug industries. Table 3.6 provides approximate figures on the cost of cocaine and heroin at different points in the distribution system to the United States and Western Europe in 2007.[15] As shown, the principal costs of these drug industries are associated with distribution rather than production. One kilogram of pure cocaine exported from Colombia in 2007 cost traffickers $2,400; of this amount, $800 covered farmers' cultivation costs. Traffickers, however, priced this same kilogram of pure cocaine for U.S. importers at $19,000. And, moving down to the retail level (through perhaps four transactions), the kilogram can fetch about $122,000 from consumers. It is important to note that, along the distribution chain, purity and cost are often inversely related. That is, as the product drifts down to the retail level, buyers dilute the product to increase profits, meanwhile increasing prices for the next buyer. The story with heroin distribution was similar: a kilogram of pure heroin produced in Afghanistan for about $900 in 2007 was exported from Turkey for $10,000, and by the time it reached consumers in the United Kingdom, it was priced at $239,000 (at 100 percent purity).

Table 3.6. Price and Purity Estimates for 1 Kilogram of Cocaine and Heroin, 2007

	Cocaine				Heroin			
Stage	Raw Price ($)	Purity (%)	100% Pure ($)	Location	Raw Price ($)	Purity (%)	100% Pure ($)	Location
Farm price	800	100	800	Colombia	900	100	900	Afghanistan
Export	2,200	91	2,400	Colombia	3,400	73	4,700	Afghanistan's neighbors
Import at wholesale (kg.)	14,500	76	19,000	Los Angeles	10,000	58	17,000	Turkey
Mid-level wholesale (oz.)	19,500	73	27,000	Los Angeles	33,000	50	66,000	England/Wales
Typical retail price	78,000	64	122,000	United States	105,000	44	239,000	United Kingdom

Source: Kilmer and Reuter 2009.

The figures in table 3.6 suggest three general propositions:

- The cost of production, as opposed to distribution, is a trivial share of the final price. That statement holds true even if one adds the cost of refining to that of growing coca leaf or opium poppies.
- Smuggling, which is the principal transnational activity, accounts for a modest share but much more than production and refining.
- The vast majority of retail prices in Western markets are accounted for by domestic distribution in the consumer country. Most of the domestic distribution revenues go to the lowest levels of the distribution system. If the retailer and lowest-level wholesaler each raises their purchase price by 75 percent, which until recently was a low estimate of the margin, they account for two-thirds of the final price.

What explains these observations? A plausible, though still untested, explanation is that retail prices reflect the costs of the risks, both from the government and from others in the business,[16] that traffickers and dealers, rather than producers, must bear (Reuter and Kleiman 1986). First, coca and opium are grown in countries where prices for labor and land are low relative to those in North America and Europe (Kennedy, Reuter, and Riley 1993). The comparative advantage of these countries is reinforced by the reluctance or inability of governments in Bolivia and Peru (for coca) and Afghanistan and Myanmar (for opium and heroin) to act aggressively against growers or early-stage refiners. Low opportunity costs for factors of production in conjunction with low enforcement risks result in very modest prices for the refined product, and they also ensure that production does not move upstream geographically.

It should be noted, though, that cheap labor, plentiful land, conditions that support coca or opium production, corruption, and weak governments are found in many nations.[17] Francisco Thoumi (2003) contrasts the distribution of illicit drug production across nations with that for legitimate agricultural products. Thoumi notes that coffee can be grown in many countries and that, in fact, a large number of those countries do have producing and exporting industries. But very few potential producers are active in the coca and opium markets. With respect to government corruption, the totality of Myanmar's corruption and the need of the central government to allow indigenous groups to maintain independent export industries surely play a role in opium production, as does the extreme weakness of the central government in Afghanistan since 1989. In contrast, neither Bolivia nor Peru stands out as having a particularly weak government among those in the region. A history of illicit drug production is also a risk factor, but it is not essential. Mexico had no indigenous opium production until the U.S. government started limited production there during World War II because of interruptions to traditional sources.[18] Colombia also had no history of opium production before the development of poppy fields in the mid-1990s. Thus, we can suggest only the factors that lead specific countries to acquire important production roles.

One might ask whether the new republics of Central Asia are likely to become major players in the international heroin business, providing more than transshipment to the Russian and Eastern European market. They certainly have low-cost land and labor, as well as apparently favorable agricultural conditions for growing opium poppies and a traditional expertise. Some governments, such as those of Tajikistan and Turkmenistan, are desperate for foreign currency and have few alternative sources and little concern about their standing in international organizations; they are unlikely to aggressively enforce prohibitions against growing opium poppies or to have the capability to do so even if they desired to. They are certain to be low-cost producers.

But are they advantaged, compared to current low-cost producers, notably Afghanistan and Myanmar? Although they are closer to Europe and have significant populations resident in Russia and perhaps even in Western Europe, their commercial connections with Western Europe are likely to be weak compared to those of Myanmar, which has established Thai and Chinese trafficking networks. The Central Asian republics will probably become major players in the European opiate markets only if there are disruptions (including rapid economic development) in the current major supplier countries.

This discussion has identified factors that might make a nation attractive for drug production and trafficking but has not explained why the numbers of actively participating countries are so small. It may be that drug-related corruption shows sharply declining marginal costs per transaction or that there are high fixed costs to establishing international trading networks. The literature is silent on this matter, although Thoumi (2003) offers some suggestions on those noneconomic factors that are most likely to affect national participation in the drug trade.

The modest share of Western retail prices associated with cocaine smuggling and illustrated in table 3.6 is also easily explained.[19] Cocaine travels in large bundles at that stage; seizures suggest that shipments of 250–500 kilograms are quite common. Although large sums may be paid to American pilots for flying small planes carrying cocaine or to Honduran colonels for ignoring their landing, these costs are defrayed over a large quantity. A pilot who demands $500,000 for flying a plane with 250 kilograms generates costs of only $2,000 per kilogram, less than 2 percent of the retail price. Even if the plane has to be abandoned after one flight, the capital cost of replacing the plane adds only another $2,000 to the kilogram price. For shipments in container cargo, seizure constitutes little more than a random tax collection; replacement cost of the seized drugs is substantially less than the landed price, so that high seizure rates have modest effect even on wholesale prices.[20] Those costs contrast sharply with those of street-level dealing, where the risks of arrest and incarceration can be spread over only the few grams that the dealer sells (see Caulkins and Reuter 1998 for a discussion of such issues).

Heroin smuggling appears to be less efficient than cocaine smuggling, at least as measured in dollars per kilogram. Heroin that exits Afghanistan at $1,000 per kilogram (in bundles of 10 kilograms or more) sells on arrival in the United Kingdom for $50,000 per kilogram.[21] There have been a few multihundred kilogram shipments of heroin, but they are very rare compared to those for cocaine. The drug often travels in small bundles that are swallowed (typically wrapped in condoms) by individual couriers.[22] "Body-packing," where the couriers are low-wage earners, produces per kilogram smuggling costs of less than $10,000 in the United States. A body-packer can apparently carry about three-quarters of a kilogram. A payment of $5,000 for incurring a 1-in-10 risk of prison (perhaps acceptable for couriers whose legitimate wages are only about $2,000 per year), along with $3,000 in travel expenses, produces a per kilogram smuggling cost of just over $11,000 compared to a retail price of $500,000.[23] The remainder of the smugglers' margin is for assuming other kinds of risk.[24]

Smuggling costs depend significantly on the ability to conceal drugs in a flow of legitimate commerce and traffic. Colombia and Mexico serve as the principal smuggling platforms to the United States in part because they have large immigrant populations in the United States and extensive air traffic and trade.[25] Although Mexico is a high-cost producer—farm-gate prices for opium in Mexico being typically $2,000 to $5,000 per kilo, compared to less than $50 in Afghanistan before 2001—the low smuggling costs equalize total landed price. Colombia, a new source for heroin, also represents high farm-gate production with relatively low smuggling costs (Uribe 2005).[26] Although Colombia and Mexico are minor producers of opium worldwide, accounting for perhaps 3 percent of the total, they are now the source of nearly two-thirds of U.S. heroin.[27]

But geography also matters. Afghanistan's neighbors are at risk, for example. Iran's total dominance as a transshipment country until recently was probably a function of the existence of a substantial domestic Iranian market and the relatively good connections with Turkey, itself a traditional supplier of the United States and Western Europe until 1970.[28] As the Russian market grew after 1995, Tajikistan became an important transshipment country. The border between Afghanistan and Tajikistan was particularly porous, reflecting the flow of Tajik citizens to Afghanistan during the Tajikistan Civil War of the early 1990s, the weakness and corruption of the Tajikistan coalition government, and the ease of exit from Tajikistan through Kazakhstan to Russia. Uzbekistan, another Afghan neighbor with good links to Russia, has a much narrower, more defensible border and a stronger, richer central government; Uzbekistan, although suffering from a substantial drug-use problem, seems to have only a modest trafficking role.

Mexico is perhaps the nation for which geographic destiny is strongest; it has been called a "natural smuggling platform" for the United States. Mexico serves as the principal entry country for cocaine, heroin, marijuana, and methamphetamine imported by the United States. At various times, Caribbean nations and some nations in Central America have also served as transshipment countries; the latter are way stations to Mexico.

The drug trade readily uses indirect paths for smuggling. Seizures in Germany sometimes turn out to have traveled through Scandinavia into Russia and then exited through Poland to their final market. Ruggiero and South describe

> a joint Czech-Colombia venture to ship sugar rice and soya to Czechoslovakia.... This operation was used to smuggle cocaine, destined for Western Europe. In 1991, police say that 440 lbs. of cocaine were seized in Bohemia and at Gdansk in Poland, which would have been smuggled onward to the Netherlands and Britain. (1995, 75)

Nigeria is an interesting transshipment anomaly, a nation that seems to have little potential role in the international drug trade. It is isolated from any of the principal producer or consumer countries and lacks a significant base of traditional domestic production or consumption. Nonetheless, Nigerian traffickers have come to play a substantial role in the shipping of heroin between Southeast Asia and the United States and also to Europe; recently these traffickers have even entered the cocaine business, although the cocaine production centers are still more remote from their home country. Nigerians have been identified as pioneers in the heroin trade in Russia and Central Asia as well, implausible as that may seem.[29]

The explanation is perhaps to be found in a complex of factors. Nigerians are highly entrepreneurial, have been misruled by corrupt governments over a long period, and have large overseas populations, weak civil society, very low domestic wages, and moderately good commercial links to the rest of the world. Thus, it is relatively easy to buy protection for transactions in Nigerian airports (corruption and a weak governmental tradition), to establish connections in both the source and the rich consuming nations (large overseas populations), and to use existing commercial transportation (note that the drugs travel with passengers rather than cargo because Nigerian exports, apart from oil, are modest). Smuggling labor is cheap (low domestic wages). Moreover, Nigeria's entrepreneurial tradition produces many competent and enthusiastic smuggling organizers. Nigeria is not unique in most of these dimensions; however, its size and connections with the rest of the world distinguish it from other West African nations. Perhaps accident played a role in that country's initiation into the trade, but these other factors plausibly play a major role.

Immigrants in the destination country who are from the producing and trafficking countries have advantages in managing exporting, with better knowledge of potential sellers and corruption opportunities. Few potential U.S. importers speak any of the languages of the Golden Triangle (Lao People's Democratic Republic, Myanmar, and Thailand); English has more currency in Pakistan but not much in Afghanistan. Corrupt officials may be much more at ease in dealing with traffickers whose families they can hold hostage. Moreover, nonnative traffickers are likely to be conspicuous in the growing regions. Nor are the exporters merely agents for wealthy nations, in sharp contrast to the international trade in refined agricultural products. Khun Sa, a quasi-military leader associated with irredentist ethnic groups on the periphery of Myanmar, was the dominant figure in opium exports from the Golden Triangle for many years (Booth 1996). The Colombian cocaine trade has spawned some spectacular figures, such as Pablo Escobar and Carlos Lehder, all of them of Colombian descent. If there are major U.S. or European individuals in the exporting business in the source countries, they have managed to escape detection.

Supply-Side Controls Targeted at Producing and Trafficking Nations

Many different approaches are used to attempt to reduce illicit drug use and related problems. Few policies and programs have been subject to systematic evaluation. Particularly striking is the absence of any research on the effectiveness of the principal class of programs used in most Western nations (particularly the United States), namely, enforcement of prohibitions on selling drugs (Manski, Pepper, and Petrie 2001). Far more is known about the effectiveness of treatment of drug abuse and addiction.

Because almost all the research has been conducted in the industrialized world, predominantly the United States, evaluations reflect Western perspectives. In particular, there are almost no evaluations of interventions aimed at the demand side of poorer nations. This section reviews what is known about programs relevant to developing nations involved in production and trafficking; Boyum and Reuter (2005, chapters 3–4) provide a broader review.

Production and Refining Controls

Three types of programs have been used to reduce source-country drug production: eradication, alternative crop development, and in-country enforcement against refiners. Eradication, involving either aerial spraying or ground-based operations, has direct and indirect effects. It aims both to limit the quantity of the drug available for shipment to foreign consumers (in the short run) and to raise the cost of producing those drugs or otherwise discouraging farmers from growing them (in the long run).

Alternative development is the soft version of production controls; it encourages farmers growing coca or poppies to switch to legitimate crops by increasing earnings from these other products. Alternative development strategies include introducing new crops and more productive strains of traditional crops, improving transportation for getting the crops to market, and using various marketing and subsidy schemes. The concept can be broadened to alternative livelihoods, where the shift may be to nonagricultural activities (UNODC 2005a). Finally, source countries can pursue refiners more vigorously, perhaps using military equipment and training; much of the U.S. support for source-country control has taken this form. There is little discussion of aggressive use of criminal sanctions against the peasant farmers.

Eradication. Few producer countries use aerial eradication, which is believed by many observers to cause environmental damage.[30] It is also politically unattractive because the immediate targets, peasant farmers, are among the poorest citizens, even when growing coca or poppy. Colombia and Mexico, neither one a traditional producer of drugs, have been the source countries most willing to allow spraying. In a few other nations (for example, the Plurinational State of Bolivia), the government has allowed manual eradication, which is very labor intensive.

The term *eradication* has also been used for a program that mixes coercion and financial incentives: "voluntary eradication." In Bolivia in the 1990s, with U.S. funding, the national government offered farmers $2,000 per hectare for tearing out coca plants and agreeing not to cultivate any others (Riley 1996). Without a good registration of preexisting fields, this intervention also ran perilously close to being a price support program, because the unsuccessful coca farmer could sell his cultivated land to the government for the nominated price.

Little evidence suggests that eradication has been effective in recent years, but rigorous evaluations are not available and are difficult to carry out. The share of the crop eradicated has been quite high in some recent years; for example, in 2001 Mexico reported that it had eradicated 15,350 hectares out of the estimated 19,750 hectares in opium production (UNODC 2002). However, Mexico's estimated potential production has not consistently declined, perhaps because of the dubious nature of the estimates of eradication or the fact that poppy prices are high enough that eradication of 80 percent of crops still provides farmers with an incentive to plant poppies. Both explanations are plausible and both may apply.

In 2003, both the U.S. Department of State (2003) and UNODC reported substantial reductions in Colombian coca production, reasonably ascribed to increased spraying with U.S.-supplied planes and helicopters. The 2004 figure showed little change. In 2004, the U.S. government reported that voluntary eradication in Bolivia may have substantially reduced coca production there in the 1990s. Prices for cocaine in the United States dropped steadily through this period.

Eradication has one major success story in modern times: Mexican opium production in the mid-1970s. An industry that had operated fairly openly in five northern states, with large, unprotected fields, took approximately five years to adjust to the sudden introduction of spraying. Production subsequently became much more widely dispersed, and growing fields were smaller and more frequently hidden in remote locations; good data are lacking, but farm-gate prices may have been substantially higher as a result. By the early 1980s, Mexico was supplying as much heroin as before the spraying, but for about five years, there was a substantial reduction in availability in the United States, particularly in Western states where Mexican supply dominated heroin markets (Reuter 1992).

Alternative Development. In contrast to spraying, alternative development—a whole panoply of programs, almost always funded by Western donors—is politically attractive, since it provides resources for marginalized farmers.[31] However, there are numerous obstacles to successful implementation. For example, it requires persuading farmers that the government will maintain its commitment over a long period; otherwise, they will not be willing to incur the costs of shifting to new crops. In situations of political instability, there will understandably be skepticism about the ability of, say, the Peruvian government to ensure a dependable market and a reliable transportation infrastructure for tropical fruits from the Upper Huallaga Valley.[32] Moreover, in some regions, such as the Chapare in Bolivia, coca is grown in areas that have been cleared precisely for that purpose, and the land is not promising for other crops. In this case, finding ways of moving immigrant farmers back to their original communities has been an important part of the effort. In a few instances of well-executed local crop substitution programs, farmers in a small area have been persuaded to move from coca or poppy to legitimate crops. For example, in northern Thailand, replacing opium poppy with commercial flowers greatly increased annual revenues per acre. In Bolivia, rubber has turned out to be more profitable in some areas of the Chapare (Mansfield 1999). However, these programs do not appear to have reduced drug production in any region of the world, as opposed to the specific areas targeted by the interventions.

A recent report by the Independent Evaluation Unit of the UNODC reached very pessimistic conclusions:

> There is little empirical evidence that the rural development compo- nents of AD [alternative development] on their own reduce the amount of drug crops cultivated. Agriculture, economic and social interventions are not seen to overcome the incentive pressure exerted by the market conditions of the illicit drug trade. Where reduction in drug cropping occurs it seems other factors, including general economic growth, polic- ing, etc., can be identified as contributors to the change that takes place. (UNODC 2005a)

A recent study of the Chapare for the World Bank Institute (Reuter 2006) suggests that a combination of large-scale development funding and aggressive enforcement can move the locus of production. Whereas in the early 1990s, the Chapare was the principal producer of coca leaf for the illicit market in Bolivia, by 2005, before the election of Evo Morales as president, only 7,000 hectares were in coca cultivation (UNODC 2005b). As the result of heavy investment of aid by both the U.S. and European governments, the Chapare had become a relatively attractive rural area, with good-quality physical and social infrastruc- ture. Production had shifted both within Bolivia (to the Chapare) and to other countries.

There are two distinct frames for assessing production controls: those of the targeted nation and those of the global market. It is entirely plau- sible that a well-executed eradication or alternative development pro- gram could reduce production in a specific country or subnational region; less plausible is that successes even in a few nations could substan- tially reduce global production of either opium or coca. The reasoning is simple and rests largely on the fact that production costs (both cultivation and refining) constitute a trivial share of the retail price of drugs in the major Western markets. As noted earlier, the cost of the coca leaf that goes into a gram of cocaine is usually less than $0.50; the retail price of that same gram sold at retail in the West is more than $100.

Suppose that stepped-up eradication led to a doubling of the price of coca leaf, so that it cost $1 for refiners to buy the leaf that goes into one gram of cocaine. Assuming that the $0.50 per gram cost increase was passed along to traffickers and dealers, the resulting change in the retail price of cocaine would be negligible.[33] Indeed, leaf prices in the Andes have increased further since the mid-1990s, with no evident effect on the retail price of cocaine, which declined over the period.

The story for alternative development is analytically identical. If the introduction of new infrastructure in Afghanistan increases the returns from growing wheat, so that many farmers now switch from growing poppies, then refiners will raise their prices to keep sufficient land and labor in poppy production. That adjustment may lead to shifts in production across provincial or national boundaries or simply to increased payments to the current growers. The change in Western heroin prices from the higher farm-gate opium price is so slight that production will be unaffected. It should be noted, though, that the poppy farmers are now better off than they were before the alternative development programs; alas, they are still growing poppies.

This argument, however, views the issue exclusively from the side of the rich consumer countries. A very successful program in one country, whether it be eradication or alternative development, might raise poppy or coca costs sufficiently to make another nation more attractive as a production center. For the innovating country, this result is still desirable, even if global drug consumption is hardly changed. For the other nation or nations that see increases in production, or that enter the industry for the first time, the result is increased damage. We return to this issue later.

In-Country Enforcement. The United States has also invested in building institutional capacity to deal with the drug trade in major producer countries. Each year the State Department's *International Narcotics Control Strategy Report* (INCSR) argues that the central problem of drug control in other countries is political will and integrity. Training investigators, strengthening the judiciary, and improving extradition procedures are the stuff of efforts to deal with this issue. Unfortunately, in both Colombia and Mexico the corruption problems have seemed endless, embedded in a larger system of weak integrity controls. In Colombia, for example, where the army has taken on a major role in drug control, particularly with respect to coca growing, allegations of involvement in mass killings are well substantiated and have been a major source of controversy about U.S. funding (Youngers and Rosin 2004). Mexico has also had a succession of drug-related corruption scandals at the highest levels; for example, in 1998 the Mexican drug czar, an Army general, was convicted of involvement with major drug traffickers. Despite the election of a president (Felipe Calderon) in 2006 who had no ties to the old system of corruption, the problem continues, as illustrated by a flood of drug-related murders involving police both as victims and as assailants. The story for Pakistan and Thailand among Asian trafficking and producing nations differs only in that the violence is less conspicuous.

The United States has also promoted efforts to crack down on refining facilities in producer countries. This approach may have limited potential because refineries have little fixed capital and can be cheaply and rapidly replaced.

Trafficking and Smuggling Controls

Another set of control programs aims at the smuggling of drugs into the wealthy nations. Most large seizures are made through interdiction, that is, as cocaine or heroin is being moved across or toward borders. Indeed, interdiction seizures may account for as much as 42 percent of total cocaine production; large seizures are made by the exporting Andean countries, by some of the transshipment nations (particularly Mexico), and by the U.S. Coast Guard and U.S. Customs. Opiates seizures appear to be a much smaller share of total production, perhaps only 23 percent, as indicated in table 3.5.[34] Most of the opiates seizures are made in Asia, close both to the production centers (Afghanistan and Myanmar) and to the largest consumer populations (China, India, the Islamic Republic of Iran, Pakistan).

The effect of interdiction on the availability of cocaine has been examined in only a small number of studies (for example, Reuter, Crawford, and Cave 1988; Crane, Rivolo, and Comfort 1997). Interdiction is like a stochastic tax; shipments and agents (crew members, pilots, unloaders) are subject to a probability of interception, and the smuggler incurs the costs of replacing the shipment and providing compensation to agents for the risk of being incarcerated. This "tax" will be reflected in the margin that smugglers charge, that is, the difference between the price at which they purchase (export from source and transshipment country) and the price they charge in the destination country.

In table 3.7 (abbreviated from Reuter and Greenfield 2001), the difference between export and import values for world agricultural trade amounted to about 6 percent of the export value; in the absence of data for a particular product or market, the Food and Agricultural Organization typically applies a standard "add factor" of 12 percent. In glaring contrast, the cross-border markup on, for example, Tajikistan-Russia heroin shipments is thought to be vastly larger, perhaps a tenfold increase, even though what is crossed is just a pair of land borders.[35] Another indication of the effectiveness of interdiction is the high price per kilo of shipping drugs across international borders. It costs less than $100 to send a kilogram of coffee by express mail from Bogota to London; it costs $10,000 to send a kilo of cocaine between the same two cities.

Table 3.7. World Trade in Selected Agricultural and Industrial Commodities, 1999 (*billions of current U.S. dollars*)

Agricultural Products			Industrial Products		
	Exports	Imports		Exports	Imports
Cereals and preparations	54	57	Iron and steel	126	138
Fruits and vegetables	71	79	Chemicals	526	547
Sugar and honey	16	17	Automotive products	549	566
Coffee, tea, and spices	31	32	Office and telecom equipment	769	792
Beverages and tobacco	57	57	Textiles and clothing	334	352
Alcoholic beverages	30	30	Other manufactures	1,182	1,966
Tobacco	22	21			
Total agricultural products	417	441	Total industrial products	4,186	4,361

Source: Adapted from Reuter and Greenfield 2001.
Note: Exports valued free on board (FOB) and imports valued cost, insurance and freight (CIF); totals may not add due to rounding.

Unfortunately, tougher interdiction does not seem to raise prices much. Figures for the United States in recent years suggest that seizures of cocaine have increased as a share of total shipments, while import prices have fallen. Reuter, Crawford, and Cave (1988) built a simulation model in which smugglers used past interception data to make decisions about which routes to pursue. Given the low export price of cocaine and the low inputs of both equipment and personnel costs per gram, it turned out to be difficult to raise retail prices substantially with more aggressive interdiction. Crane, Rivolo, and Comfort (1997) examined the effects of temporary spikes in seizure rates in source zones and found that they did increase retail prices substantially; there has been considerable controversy about the researchers' development of a price series[36] and of their approach to modeling the short-run effects of interdiction events to reach this conclusion (see Manski, Pepper, and Thomas 1999).

That leaves open the question of why cross-border prices are so high, and yet more enforcement does not have the desired consequence. Consider again the border between Afghanistan and Tajikistan, whose passage increases the price of a kilogram of opium many fold. This border has been porous throughout the period in which the heroin trade between the two countries has developed. As a share of the estimated flow, seizures have been modest; Paoli, Greenfield, and Reuter (2009) present figures for seizures and flow that suggest the rate is less than 5 percent. Nor do smugglers face much threat of incarceration from law enforcement, requiring high payments to smuggling labor. Perhaps the border guards who seize a small share of the flow have the capacity to incarcerate the smugglers but are charging high prices for withholding their authority. Detailed descriptions of smuggling activities are inconsistent with this interpretation, however. Multiple border-control agencies (including, until recently, a Russian military division, staffed by Russian officers and Tajik soldiers) are thinly spread out along a border that has many difficult-to-guard mountain passes.

Perhaps the market for smuggling is characterized by cartel or monopoly control, which would account for both the high margin and the lack of sensitivity to the higher interdiction (that is, tax rate). Although a cartel or monopoly is possible in some markets, the best-known ones for shipment to the United States have been characterized by large numbers of small smuggling enterprises since the fall of the Cali and Medellín cartels in the early 1990s. Perhaps they continue to coordinate, but there is no obvious mechanism for them to impose the discipline that even legal cartels have rarely managed over sustained periods of time.

I can offer no good account for the high margins charged by drug smugglers in so many settings. The data on risks (seizure, incarceration) and prices (the difference between import and export prices) are not nearly precise enough to allow formal empirical modeling. The apparent lack of response to increased interdiction severity also remains a puzzle.

Nontraditional Drug Control Methods

In addition to the supply-and-demand interventions noted above, a variety of approaches—which I broadly label *nontraditional*—have not been widely discussed but probably bear closer examination: de facto legalization of production or trafficking, buying up the crop, and choosing a strategic location to allow production for the global market. Each has substantial operational or political risk, but explicating these risks helps clarify the considerations involved in policy toward drugs and development.

De Facto Legalization of Production or Trafficking

Can a nation simply ignore drug production and trafficking? In addition to treaties that require prohibition of such activities, legalization is so shocking to other nations that legalizing and openly taxing or regulating the production and distribution of these drugs for international markets are clearly not an option. It is very different, however, if a nation simply fails to enforce laws against producing or trafficking in these drugs as the result of explicit policy consideration. There are at least three reasons for considering this option:

- First, it might lead to minimal corruption around the trade; neither producers nor traffickers would have reason to pay police or other authorities if the latter are known to lack the political backing to eradicate crops or arrest producers and refiners.
- Second, it reduces political tension, since the government is not seen as opposed to the interests of small producers.
- Third, it increases earnings of peasant farmers, because it may induce a rise in their share of world production.

Pursuing such a policy, however, also poses substantial risks. Some important nations with major drug problems would object and might retaliate through official development assistance cuts, both bilateral and multilateral. Second, the state would not be able to tax the industry, which now takes a larger share of productive resources; to levy explicit taxes would be a move so close to legalization as to raise the question of treaty compliance. The Netherlands, which has de facto legalized the sale of small amounts of cannabis at coffee shops, has not been able to subject these sales to an explicit tax (MacCoun and Reuter 2001). Third, it creates ambivalence toward the role of the state in enforcing generally agreed-upon norms.

It is striking that no nation has actually adopted such a policy. In some regions of the world, such as the Shan State in Myanmar or the Upper Huallaga Valley in Peru in the 1980s, the national government took little action against producers or traffickers. Such examples, however, appear to be ones in which the state has generally weak authority; it simply could not take action.

Buying Up the Crop

The fact that global production and trafficking are quite concentrated presents an opportunity for effective interventions, particularly if it is possible to coordinate across sectors within countries and across nations. One policy option mentioned from time to time is preemptive purchase of the drugs in the dominant producing country by Western governments, perhaps acting through an international agency. The total cost of purchasing all of Afghanistan's opium production before 2001 might have been no more than $250 million,[37] a small fraction of what is spent by wealthy nations to deal with the problems of their heroin addicts. Such a preemptive purchase, if successful in making heroin much harder to obtain, might drive many addicts into treatment or otherwise lead them to desist from heroin use for a period of time.[38]

There are two standard objections to this approach, however: one practical and the other conceptual. The practical objection is that it would be impossible to make this preemptive purchase discreetly. Traffickers would soon become aware of the new entrants in the market and would bid against them. The price of opium in Afghanistan would soar, and the program would end up costing taxpayers a great deal more and still not prevent opium from continuing to flow into the illegal market, albeit at higher prices. The conceptual objection is that the intervention would exacerbate long-term problems. In face of the increase in demand at the farm-gate level, growers would now plant more, thus worsening the world heroin problem after the preemptive buying program ended.

Although both objections have some power, neither individually nor jointly are they decisive. The traffickers in the short run might not have access to funds to bid the prices very much higher than they are now; over time, they could increase their sales revenues enough to do so but perhaps not in the first year. Nor does failure to buy the whole crop mean that users would be unaffected by the program; if the governments succeed in purchasing half the product, for example, there could still be substantial hikes in export prices. These hikes might be large enough to raise retail prices in some countries, thus motivating a large number of addicts to desist, with or without formal treatment.

The fact that there will be an increase in production, and presumably lower prices, in the following years, has relatively little consequence for the global market. A decline in the price of opium has minimal effect on the price of heroin in the major consumer markets. The claim here is of an asymmetry. A sharp reduction in physical availability might generate a price spike that would in fact affect final demand. A glut, though, cannot have the opposite effect because declines in farm-gate prices of opium have minimal effect on retail prices. Thus, the short-term gain from the price spike may not be offset by any harm from the increased production that it generates, whether in Afghanistan or in some other nation that entered the market because of the perception that returns had increased.

I offer this example not as a complete analysis of the effects of a preemptive purchase but rather to indicate the kind of innovation that needs careful analysis. The sudden rise in prices might lead another nation to enter the market, thus spreading the problem and eliminating one of the attributes that make preemptive purchase possible. If crops can be expanded rapidly, then the program might be so short-lived as to be not worth the effort. One would have to consider not only whether it is possible to obtain the desired spike but also whether it is possible to coordinate treatment efforts in consumer countries to provide resources so that the system is able to take advantage of the short-term opportunity.

Strategic Location

It is plausible that even programs that succeed in raising the price of coca and opium will fail to reduce world consumption of cocaine and heroin substantially. The reason is simply that the elasticity of retail price with respect to the price of opium or of coca paste is too low; raising Afghan opium prices by 50 percent may generate, even in the Islamic Republic of Iran (a middle-income neighbor of Afghanistan), no more than a 5 percent increase in retail price[39] and thus a very modest decline in consumption. That has important policy implications, because it suggests that control efforts will result in shifts in location rather than in reductions in the volume of production. Afghanistan's decline in production will be compensated, perhaps with a lag, by increases in production elsewhere.

Drug production then becomes a global public "bad," like toxic waste disposal. Some nations will have to bear the consequences of the global demand for drugs so long as that demand cannot be suppressed.

The global policy decisions are, then, as follows: Is it desirable to have production dispersed across many countries or concentrated in a few? Should production be stably located in specific countries or moved around? Is it possible to determine which countries are likely to suffer the least bad consequences from becoming major producers and traffickers? And is it possible to develop compensation mechanisms for those nations that end up with the industry?

Many or Few? It may be argued that many countries with a small opium industry will result in less total harm than a few countries each with a large industry. A few hundred opium farmers scattered across a broad area will generate only opportunistic corruption, and the funds available from the farmers will not be sufficient to purchase central government protection. That may not be a stable equilibrium, however; subnational regional concentration may develop and pose a substantial threat to provincial, if not national, government integrity.

Allowing two or three nations to dominate production—in effect, the situation that has characterized the past 20 years—results in fundamental undermining of governmental authority in those countries. The term *narco-state* has been thrown around loosely,[40] but it is fair to say that the task of reestablishing the central government in Afghanistan has been made substantially more difficult by the flow of revenues from opium and heroin, a situation that has allowed regional warlords to maintain and equip substantial independent militias. Similarly, Colombia's long-running civil war has been deepened and prolonged by the ability of both FARC (the Revolutionary Armed Forces of Colombia) and the newer paramilitaries to finance their activities with funds from taxing coca production and refining. However, at the margin, shifting 25 percent of the industry to, say, Ecuador, might do less to reduce the damage in Colombia than it does to worsen Ecuadorian integrity and stability. It may be that globally it is preferable to manage the problem in Colombia, rather than pressure Colombia to act aggressively and motivate reemergence in Bolivia.

Move or Stabilize? The damage caused by the industry is also partly a function of whether it has been stably located. Systemic corruption is not irreversible, but once the norms and networks supporting it have developed, restoring good governance is difficult. Pushing Myanmar's production into Cambodia and then on into Vietnam may cause the other two countries great harm without much helping the fight to improve the welfare of the people of Myanmar.

Which Nations? If it is accepted that the global community can make a strategic choice about where the industry locates, then one can ask whether total harm can be reduced. For example, size is a consideration. A small nation such as Tajikistan may be substantially corrupted by accounting for trafficking even as little as 20 percent of Afghanistan's production, whereas Brazil is so large that a shift of trafficking networks for Colombia's cocaine output to that nation would have only modest effects. Brazil may also be more capable of moderating the adverse effects of the trafficking-related corruption. The population potentially affected by government failure, however, is very much greater in the larger nations. Should the world prefer that 5 million citizens of Tajikistan have their government totally captured by the drug trade, rather than have governance for 70 million Iranians somewhat worsened by trafficking?

Compensation Mechanisms. Whether it is possible to create a mechanism that is politically acceptable and that does not encourage weak nations to seek out the industry is another matter. Indeed, it could be argued that simply letting the producing nations keep the revenues from the drug trade without sanctioning them is compensation enough.

There is generally something disturbing about such policy realism, and it is not clear that it is a politically stable option. What if global public opinion does not accept the premise that drug production is demand driven? Can the government of Colombia responsibly accept that it will continue to be a major cocaine producer without acting aggressively to suppress the trade? The taint of the drug business may simply be too great for any nation that has prospects for attracting substantial legitimate foreign investment.

Concluding Observations

I have taken a speculative approach in this chapter because there is little empirical or conceptual literature. Gross facts about global drug problems are readily available: for example, Afghanistan produces most of the world's opium, and the United States consumes a large share of the world's cocaine production. However, magnitudes are imprecise; estimates of Colombian cocaine production, for example, have been revised by 50 percent around the year 2000 because of new information on yields of alkaloid and the frequency of crops, while the error bands around estimates of the number of heroin addicts in Europe are very broad indeed.

The body of research and evaluation on drug policy interventions, apart from drug treatment, is thin. No more than three empirical studies (using that term generously) of the effects of increased intensity of interdiction have been carried out. No evaluations of the consequences of crop eradication or lab seizure efforts for major drug markets in producer countries have been done.

Conceptual matters are no better. Barely a handful of articles by economists on the peculiar configuration of the global drug market have addressed the subject. Economists' curiosity has largely been confined to clever possible explanations for the paradoxical effects of enforcement (Poret 2003, for example). I will conclude this chapter by identifying three questions that seem worthy of economists' attention:

- What factors determine a nation's comparative advantage in the production or trafficking of illegal drugs?

- How stable is the configuration of producer and trafficker countries?
- Is long-term reduction in global supply possible?

Comparative Advantage

The factors of production for cocaine or heroin at first glance appear to be those of any agricultural commodity: labor and agronomically suitable land. Under conditions of prohibition, however, the scarce factor is some form of "domestic tranquility," with the ability to grow, process, and transport the commodity at low risk. In explaining Colombia's dominant role in the South American cocaine industry, Thoumi (2003) offers a conceptual model that emphasizes the lack of social capital and weak governance as the basis for low operating costs for the industry. He also notes the difficulty of disentangling the relationship between historically weak government institutions and the presence of the drug trade, which itself weakens those institutions.

The configuration is state dependent [pun intended]. A principal cost is presumably that of obtaining official cooperation. The cost of such cooperation is highest for the first transaction, because in subsequent transactions both sides know that the other can be trusted. An established producer country is one in which many such corrupt relationships have been created, providing lower costs for all phases of the industry within that country.

International transportation costs take on a new meaning in this setting as well; they are also determined less by the conventional factors than by the risk of seizure and the penalties faced by interdicted couriers; the relevant risks may those imposed by other countries. Thus, if it were possible to make transportation through all neighboring countries (China, Islamic Republic of Iran, Pakistan, Tajikistan, Turkmenistan, and Uzbekistan) very risky and expensive, Afghanistan might lose its attraction as a producing site. This observation is not intended as a policy option: closing trafficking is harder than eradicating production, which does require fixed sites.

Stability

Cocaine and heroin look like "footloose" industries. The specific knowledge, personnel, and capital required are minimal. Small changes in the profitability of specific nations should lead to rapid changes in location. Yet there has been surprising stability. The same three nations have dominated cocaine, and the same two have dominated heroin for the past 20 years. The only new entrant has been Colombia into heroin production.

At the subnational level, there has been much more change. For example, Afghanistan's opium production—long concentrated in a few southern and eastern provinces—is now spread throughout the country. Bolivian coca production was concentrated in the Jungas until about 1980, when unemployed tin miners moved to the Chapare; it is now moving back to the Jungas. What this movement suggests is that the nation is a relevant unit of analysis; there is a system of distribution and trafficking that can accommodate changes in the site of production.

Note that in the trafficking sector, nationalities rather than nations may be involved. Nigeria is not an important trafficking location. Rather, it is the diaspora of Nigerians throughout the world that serves as a supply of trafficking labor, linked loosely to the mother country. The decision may be which nations Nigerians find most advantageous to use for transshipment. However, the reverse relationship is also possible: some nations are advantaged for transshipment, and it is Nigerians as labor who are advantaged for certain roles in those countries.

Global Supply Reduction

This chapter reflects what is now nearly a traditional pessimism about the long-term prospects for reducing supply in source countries. The elasticity of demand for cocaine and heroin with respect to source-country prices appears to be almost zero. As noted earlier, the raw material costs of opium and coca are barely 1 percent of the retail price in rich countries and perhaps no more than 10 percent in the large markets in poorer nations.

This model of price formation, however, is static and crude. Is it possible to impose a series of short-run supply disruptions that might cumulatively make a difference? The market for these drugs appears to be less well integrated globally than markets for many legal commodities, perhaps reflecting the high fixed costs and risks of establishing new trafficking routes. Those drugs are the subjects of epidemics (see, for example, Caulkins and others 2004). A supply disruption for two or three years at the right moment in an epidemic can make a substantial difference for a particular country. Paoli, Greenfield, and Reuter (2009) expand considerably on this issue.

In addition, an implicit model of price formation underlies this assumption; small dollar but large percentage increases in raw material costs do not affect final prices because they are passed along additively. Caulkins (1990) has argued that the relationship might be multiplicative, at least for price increases somewhat further up the chain. The historical record is inconsistent with the multiplicative model for coca and opium prices. Those costs have been subject to large fluctuations that have not been seen in retail prices reported in the United States, although the quality of the price data is low. More serious testing might find that this model is not correct.

Cocaine and heroin appear likely to present global problems for the foreseeable future. A better understanding of the economics of production and trafficking would help policy makers both assess existing options and develop new ones.

Notes

1. President George W. Bush made such a statement in a meeting with President Vicente Fox of Mexico in 2001: "One of the reasons why drugs are shipped—the main reason why drugs are shipped through Mexico to the United States is because United States citizens use drugs. And our nation must do a better job of educating our citizenry about the dangers and evils of drug use" (Office of the Press Secretary 2001).

2. The most systematic effort to produce truly global estimates is contained in the 2005 *World Drug Report* (chapter 2), prepared by the United Nations Office on Drugs and Crime. Opium (mostly in the form of heroin) and cocaine are estimated to yield US$65 billion and US$70 billion in retail sales. Amphetamine-type stimulants (ATS) yield US$44 billion and cannabis resin US$25 billion. For cannabis herb (marijuana), the report cites a figure of US$113 billion but concedes this estimate has a weak base; the figure is far higher than can be reconciled with the systematic and well-documented estimates for the U.S. marijuana market (ONDCP 2001). The *World Drug Report* contains estimates of "wholesale revenues," but it is unclear what share should be assigned to developing nations. A recent study by Kilmer and Pacula (2009) has come up with lower estimates for the countries that are most important for those trades but could not estimate total global revenues. However, the results suggest that for cannabis the correct figure might be only half as large as the UNODC estimate. Kilmer and Pacula (2009) provide alternative estimates of market size for some major markets that suggest the UNODC estimates are overdated.

3. Among those that now regularly conduct general population surveys and attempt to estimate the number of *problematic drug users*, a term coined by the European Monitoring Center for Drugs and Drug Addiction, are Australia, the Netherlands, Switzerland, and the United Kingdom. There are good-quality data from school surveys of 15- to 16-year-olds in most European nations; the European School Project on Alcohol and Other Drugs can be found at www.espad.org.

4. On occasion, there are gross inconsistencies that undermine confidence; for example, a nation might report more opiate addicts than opiate consumers or wholesale purity that is lower than retail purity.

5. Opiates are products of the opium poppy; they include opium, which is usually smoked, morphine (rarely used), and heroin.

6. An unpublished estimate based on a 2004 survey by Chinese researchers (Chen Xiaobo, Xie Hua, and Zhou Tie) has generated an estimate of about 2 million heroin addicts.

7. For example, it was estimated that in Thailand, a relatively successful developing nation, the annual expenditure for a heroin addict in the mid-1990s was approximately $1,150, compared to $30,000 in Italy (UNDCP 1997).

8. The first fully documented quantity estimate outside the United States is provided in Singleton, Murray, and Tinsley (2006).

9. A kilogram of cocaine requires approximately 400 kilograms of leaf as input. The precise figure varies, depending on the alkaloid content. There is variation among regions within the Andes; however, there are no estimates of the quantities produced in each region and how they differ in terms of alkaloid content. See Drug Availability Working Group (2003).

10. Even in that year, Afghanistan still supplied large quantities of opium and heroin to the world market out of stockpiles.

11. No credible estimates of either marijuana consumption in Europe or of marijuana production in the Netherlands are available.

12. The annual series for most countries are quite noisy because a few large seizures can substantially affect the total. Over the long term, however, seizure data tend to suggest the actual level of trafficking. UNODC (2005) has shown that seizures track an independently generated estimate of total production well.

13. Although China does indeed share a border with Afghanistan, it appears that few of the seizures of heroin come out of that border; they occur either near the border with Myanmar or in the interior. See Townsend (2005) for a discussion of the risk that Afghanistan will become a major source of opiates for the China market.

14. On China's historic involvement in production, see Dikotter, Laamann, and Xun (2004). Iranian production before the 1979 Islamic Revolution is discussed in Hansen (2001).

15. I have chosen 2000 rather than 2002 because Afghanistan's opium price has been at a historic high following recovery from the cutback in production in 2001 and is now falling back closer to the levels of the late 1990s.

16. The government imposes costs through arrest, incarceration, and seizures. Other participants impose costs through violence and theft.

17. Norman Loayza (personal communication) has suggested that some countries may be advantaged in terms of how easily the drug production may be concealed. He suggests, for example, that Afghanistan's mountainous terrain makes it harder for the government to detect small fields.

18. Mexico has always had plentiful supplies of marijuana, but that drug appears not to have been commercially produced until the 1960s.

19. This analysis draws heavily on Reuter (1988).

20. This is not an argument for abandoning interdiction but for recognizing the limits of its effectiveness in making cocaine or heroin more expensive and less available in mature markets.

21. It is the absolute difference between export and import that measures smuggling efficiency. For purposes of final consumption, however, the absolute price difference is not the interesting figure here; heroin doses are much smaller than those for cocaine (25–50 pure milligrams versus 200 pure milligrams).

22. Nigerian traffickers seem to specialize in such smuggling. Mark Kleiman (personal communication) has estimated that Nigerian couriers body-packing heroin into New York in the early 1990s accounted for more than 500 kilograms per year, 3–5 percent of estimated U.S. consumption. That volume requires only three body-packers every two days.

23. The risk and payment figures here are moderately informed guesses; the purpose is simply to provide a sense of the magnitudes involved.

24. The body-packer costs are much lower for exports to Russia from Central Asia; body-packers in Tajikistan may receive only $500 for smuggling heroin. Russia seizes very little heroin, and the opportunity cost of the smugglers in legitimate wages is no more than a few hundred dollars per year. It is particularly difficult to explain the high markups for smuggling heroin into Russia.

25. The 2000 U.S. Census counted 9 million residents born in Mexico. The figure for Colombia was only 600,000, but this number was twice as many as for any other South American nation.

26. Uribe reports the price of a kilogram of opium latex, the raw production material in Colombia, as about $340 in 2000. A kilo of heroin requires roughly 10 kilos of opium latex; the same figure applies to opium.

27. There is substantial disagreement about the share from these two nations (Drug Availability Working Group 2003) but no disagreement that they are major suppliers to the United States and to no other major markets.

28. Turkey had a substantial traditional opium market until the 1970s; thus the poppy industry served both domestic and export markets. There is now little domestic consumption of opium.

29. On Nigerians in the Central Asia trade, see Reuter, Pain, and Greenfield (2004).

30. See, for example, Washington Office on Latin America (n.d.).

31. Thoumi (2003) offers the following list of programs under the general rubric of alternative development: (a) crop substitution, (b) development of markets for legal agricultural products, (c) industrialization of agricultural products to increase value added in rural areas, (d) providing social infrastructure, and, finally, (e) organization development in the communities involved and development activities in nonillicit crop-producing regions that expel migrants to coca and poppy areas (chapter 11).

32. Infrastructure development has potentially counterproductive effects. It is believed that the creation of better roads in the Chapare in Bolivia during the 1980s, which was intended to help the distribution of legitimate agricultural products, had the effect of providing easier access for small planes to pick up coca paste (Riley 1996).

33. There is a controversy over whether price increases are additive rather than multiplicative across successive distribution levels (Caulkins 1990). However, the arguments for a multiplicative relationship do not apply at the preimport level. Since the largest proportionate increases occur at the smuggling stage, even the Caulkins model would suggest very modest retail price increases from rising leaf prices. As a matter of historical observation, there appears to be substantial variation in coca leaf prices that is not reflected in retail cocaine prices in rich nations.

34. This is the percentage of estimated total world production reported as seizures in UNODC (2003). It may be an overestimate because seizures are not purity adjusted and are often very much less than 100 percent pure.

35. Tajikistan is separated from Russia by Kazakhstan. Citizens of both Kazakhstan and Tajikistan have the right to enter Russia without visas; the Russian border is, moreover, very long and lightly guarded.

36. That price series did not distinguish transactions by size but assumed a fractal distribution for transactions along the chain from import to wholesale.

37. The figure would be higher for 2002–05, given that opium prices have remained higher than before the Taliban opium ban (UNODC 2005).

38. A number of U.S. studies have found that higher prices for cocaine have increased treatment seeking.

39. The retail price of a kilo of pure heroin in Iran (sold in small and somewhat dilute units) in the year 2000 was about US$5,000–10,000 at a time when the 10 kilograms of opium required to produce that kilo of heroin cost less than US$500. The figures on Iranian prices come from the UNODC *Global Illicit Drug Trends*; they show broad ranges. For example, the 2002 report quoted the street price as US$0.70–2.30 for a gram that was 4–20% pure.

40. Shortly after Jacques Chirac became president of France in 1995, he canceled his first meeting with the Dutch prime minister, accusing the Netherlands, with its tolerant drug policies, of being a "narco-state." The Dutch were appropriately horrified at the mischaracterization of their country (Dejevsky 1996).

References

Booth, Martin. 1996. *Opium: A History.* New York: St. Martin's Press.

Bouchard, Martin. 2008. "Towards a Realistic Method to Estimate Cannabis Production in Industrialized Countries." *Contemporary Drug Problems* 35, (2/3): 291–320.

Boyum, David, and Peter Reuter. 2005. *An Analytic Assessment of U.S. Drug Policy.* Washington, DC: American Enterprise Institute.

Caulkins, Jonathan P. 1990. "The Distribution and Consumption of Illicit Drugs: Some Mathematical Models and Their Policy Implications." PhD diss., Massachusetts Institute of Technology.

Caulkins, Jonathan P., and Peter Reuter. 1998. "What Can We Learn from Drug Prices?" *Journal of Drug Issues* 28 (3): 593–612.

Caulkins, Jonathan, Doris Behrens, Claudia Knoll, Gernot Tragler, and Doris Zuba. 2004. "Markov Chain Modeling of Initiation and Demand: The Case of the U.S. Cocaine Epidemic." *Health Care Management Science* 7: 319–29.

Chen, Xiaobo, Xie Hua, and Zhou Tie. 2004. "An Empirical Study on Heroin Market in China." Unpublished paper.

Crane, Barry, Rex Rivolo, and Gary Comfort. 1997. *An Empirical Examination of Counterdrug Interdiction Program Effectiveness,* P-3219. Alexandria, VA: Institute for Defense Analyses.

Dejevsky, Mary. 1996. "Chirac Unveils New Jobs Deal for EU States for EU Summit." *The Independent.* March 26. http://www.independent.co.uk/news/world/chirac-unveils-new-jobs-deal-for-eu-states-foreu-summit-1344144.html.

Dikotter, Frank, Lars Laamann, and Zhou Xun. 2004. *Narcotic Culture: A History of Drugs in China.* Chicago: University of Chicago Press.

Drug Availability Working Group. 2003. *Drug Availability Estimates in the United States.* Washington, DC: Office of National Drug Control Policy.

Gettman, J. 2006. Marijuana Production in the United States [electronic version]. *The Bulletin of Cannabis Reform, December,* 1–29. Retrieved November 1, 2008, from http://www.drugscience.org/Archive/bcr2/MJCropReport_2006.pdf.

Hansen, Bradley. 2001. "Learning to Tax: The Political Economy of the Opium Trade in Iran, 1921–1941." *Journal of Economic History* 61 (1): 95–113.

International Narcotics Control Board (INCB). 2002. *Report of the International Narcotics Board Control.* http://www.incb.org/e/ar/2002.

Kennedy, Michael, Peter Reuter, and K. Jack Riley. 1993. "A Simple Economic Model of Cocaine Production." *Computer and Mathematical Modeling* 17 (2): 19–36.

Kilmer, Beau, and Rosalie Pacula. 2009. "Estimating the Size of the Illicit Drug Markets." *Report on Global Illicit Drugs Markets 1998–2007,* ed. Peter Reuter and Franz Trautmann. Brussels: European Commission.

Kilmer, Beau, and Peter Reuter. 2009. "Prime Numbers: The Drug Trade." *Foreign Policy.* November–December.

Kleiman, Mark. 1992. *Against Excess: Drug Policy for Results.* New York: Basic Books.

MacCoun, Robert J., and Peter Reuter. 2001. *Drug War Heresies: Learning from Other Vices, Times, and Places.* Cambridge: Cambridge University Press.

Mansfield, David. 1999. "Alternative Development: The Modern Thrust of Supply-Side Policy." *United Nations Bulletin on Narcotics* 51: 19–44.

Manski, Charles, John Pepper, and Carol Petrie, eds. 2001. *Informing America's Policy on Illegal Drugs.* Washington, DC: National Academy Press.

Manski, Charles, John Pepper, and Yvette Thomas, eds. 1999. *Assessment of Two Cost-Effectiveness Studies on Cocaine Control Policy.* Washington, DC: National Academy Press.

Office of the Press Secretary. 2001. "Remarks by President George W. Bush and President Vicente Fox of Mexico in Joint Press Conference." February 16, 2001. http://www.whitehouse.gov/news/releases/2001/02/print/20010216-3.html.

ONDCP (U.S. Office of National Drug Control Policy).

Paoli, Letizia, Victoria A. Greenfield, and Peter Reuter. 2009. *The World Heroin Market: Can Supply Be Cut?* New York: Oxford University Press.

Ponce, Robert. 2002. "Rising Heroin Abuse in Central Asia Raises Threat of Public Health Crisis." *Eurasia Insight.* http://www.eurasianet.org/departments/insight/articles/eav032902a.shtml.

Poret, S. 2003. "The Illicit Drug Market: Paradoxical Effects of Law Enforcement Policies." *International Review of Law and Economics* 22(4): 465–93.

Reuter, Peter. 1988. "Can the Borders Be Sealed?" *Public Interest* (Summer): 51–65.

Reuter, Peter, and Franz Trautmann, eds. 2009. "Assessing the Operations of the Global Illicit Drug Markets, 1998–2007." *Report on the Global Illicit Drugs Markets 1998–2007.* http://ec.europa.eu/justice_home/doc_centre/drugs/studies/doc_drugs_studies_en.htm.

Reuter, Peter, and Franz Trautmann, ed. 2009. *A Report on Global Illicit Drug Markets, 1998–2007.* ed. Brussels: European Commision. http://ec.europa.eu/justice_home/doc_centre/drugs/studies/doc/report_10_03_09_en.pdf.

———. 1992. "After the Borders Are Sealed: Can Domestic Sources Substitute for Imported Drugs?" In *Drug Policy in the Americas.* ed. Peter Smith, 163–77. Boulder, CO: Westview Press.

———. 2006. *Drug Control in Bolivia.* Unpublished paper. Washington, DC: World Bank Institute.

Reuter, Peter, Gordon Crawford, and Jonathan Cave. 1988. *Sealing the Borders: Effects of Increased Military Efforts in Drug Interdiction.* Santa Monica, CA: RAND, R-3594-USDP.

Reuter, Peter, and Victoria Greenfield. 2001. "Measuring Global Drug Markets: How Good Are the Numbers and Why Should We Care about Them?" *World Economics* 2 (4): 155–73.

Reuter, Peter, and Mark Kleiman. 1986. "Risks and Prices: An Economic Analysis of Drug Enforcement." *Crime and Justice: An Annual Review* 9: 128–79.

Reuter, Peter, and Emil Pain, with Victoria Greenfield. 2004. "The Effects of Drug Trafficking on Central Asia." Unpublished project report. Santa Monica, CA: RAND.

Riley, K. Jack. 1996. *Snow Job: The War against International Drug Trafficking.* New Brunswick, NJ: Transaction Publishers.

Roston, Aram. 2002. "Central Asia's Heroin Problem." *Nation.* March 25. http://www.thenation.com/doc/20020325/roston.

Royal Canadian Mounted Police. 2004. *Drug Situation in Canada—2003.* Criminal Intelligence Directorate. Royal Canadian Mounted Police, Ottawa.

Ruggiero, V., and N. South. 1995. *Eurodrugs: Drug Use, Markets, and Trafficking in Europe.* London: University College London Press.

Singleton, Nicola, Rosemary Murray, and Louise Tinsley. 2006. *Measuring Different Aspects of Problem Drug Use: Methodological Developments.* http://www.homeoffice.gov.uk/rds/pdfs06/rdsolr1606.pdf 16/06. London: Home Office.

Spillane, Joseph F. 2000. *Cocaine: From Medical Marvel to Modern Menace in the United States, 1884–1920.* Baltimore, MD: Johns Hopkins University Press.

Thoumi, Francisco. 2003. *Illegal Drugs, Economy, and Society in the Andes.* Baltimore, MD: Johns Hopkins University Press.

Townsend, Jacob. 2005. *China and Afghan Opiates: Assessing the Risk.* Silk Road Papers. School for Advanced International Studies, Johns Hopkins University. http://www.silkroadstudies.org/new/inside/publications/Townsend_Total.pdf.

United Nations Drug Control Program. 1997. *World Drug Report.* Oxford: Oxford University Press.

UNODC (United Nations Office on Drugs and Crime). 2002. *Global Illicit Drug Trends.* New York: United Nations.

———. 2004. *Global Illicit Drug Trends.* New York: United Nations.

———. 2005a. *Thematic Evaluation of UNODC's Alternative Development Programs.* Vienna: United Nations.

———. 2005b. *Bolivia Coca Cultivation Survey.* La Paz: United Nations.

———. 2005c. *Alternative Development: A Global Thematic Evaluation.* New York: United Nations.

———. 2007. *World Drug Report.* Vienna: United Nations.

———. 2008. *World Drug Report 2008.* New York: United Nations. http://www.unodc.org/unodc/en/data-and-analysis/WDR-2008.html

Uribe, Sergio. 2005. "Development of the Colombian Heroin Industry, 1990–2003." Unpublished project memorandum.

U.S. Office of National Drug Control Policy (ONDCP). 2001. *What America's Users Spend on Illicit Drugs, 1988–2000.* Washington, DC: White House.

U.S. Department of State. Annual. *International Narcotic Control Strategy Report.* Washington, DC: U.S. Department of State.

Washington Office on Latin America. N.d. *Aerial Fumigation: Stop U.S. Sponsored Chemical Spraying in Colombia.* http://www.wola.org/Colombia/citizen_action_guide_fumigation.pdf.

Youngers, Collete, and Eileen Rosin, eds. 2004. *Drugs and Democracy in Latin America: The Impact of U.S. Policy.* Boulder, CO: Lynne Rienner.

4

Evaluating Plan Colombia

Daniel Mejía

Many resources have been spent on the so-called war on drugs under Plan Colombia.[1] According to Colombia's National Planning Department (DNP) between 2000 and 2005, the U.S. government disbursed about $3.8 billion in assistance to the Colombian government for its war against illegal drug production and trafficking and the organized criminal organizations that claim the profits from those illegal activities.[2] Colombia, for its part, spent about $6.9 billion during the same period. About half of the Colombian expenses and three-quarters of the U.S. subsidies have gone directly to financing the military components of the war against illegal drugs. Together, the United States and Colombia spent on average about $1.2 billion per year between 2000 and 2005 on the military component of Plan Colombia, which corresponds to about 1.5 percent of Colombia's average gross domestic product (GDP) per year during that period.

I thank Pascual Restrepo and Maria José Uribe for excellent research assistance and close collaboration in the development of this research agenda. The author acknowledges financial support from Fedesarrollo's "German Botero de los Ríos" 2008 Prize for Economic Research and the Open Society Institute.

Apart from the military component of Plan Colombia, aimed at reducing the supply of illicit drugs and improving security, two nonmilitary components of the U.S. assistance are under the plan: one aimed at "promoting social and economic justice" and the other aimed at "promoting the rule of law." According to the U.S. Government Accountability Office (GAO), while the former accounts for about 15.3 percent of the total U.S. assistance to Colombia, the latter accounts for about 3.6 percent. The rest of the U.S. assistance under the plan, which accounts for more than 80 percent of the total program, applies to the military component (GAO 2008). Table 4.1 presents figures on U.S. assistance under Plan Colombia and the distribution among its three main components.

Motivation for the Research Agenda

Despite the resources spent during the current decade under Plan Colombia, however, most available measures show that trends in cocaine consumption in consumer countries have not decreased[3] (see figure 4.1), nor have the wholesale and retail prices increased significantly, as might have been expected given the intensification of the war on drugs during the current decade (see figures 4.2a and 4.2b).

Furthermore, according to the United Nations Office on Drugs and Crime (UNODC), while the number of hectares of land cultivated with coca crops decreased about 50 percent, from some 163,000 hectares in 2000 (just before Plan Colombia was initiated) to about 80,000 in 2006,

Table 4.1. U.S. Assistance for Plan Colombia by Program Objective
(fiscal year appropriations 2000 through 2008)

Dollars in Millions	Fiscal Year									
Program Objective	2000	2001	2002	2003	2004	2005	2006	2007	2008 (Est.)	Total
Reduce illicit narcotics and improve security	817.80	232.80	395.90	607.90	617.70	585.60	587.30	591.10	423.40	**4,859.50**
Promote social and economic justice	80.00	0.50	109.90	125.70	126.50	124.70	130.40	139.70	194.40	**1,031.80**
Promote rule of law	121.10	0.90	15.80	27.00	9.00	7.30	10.50	7.80	39.40	**238.70**
Total	**1,018.90**	**234.20**	**521.60**	**760.60**	**753.20**	**717.60**	**728.20**	**738.60**	**657.20**	**6,130.00**

Source: GAO (2008).

Figure 4.1. Trends in Cocaine Use in Consumer Countries, 1999–2006

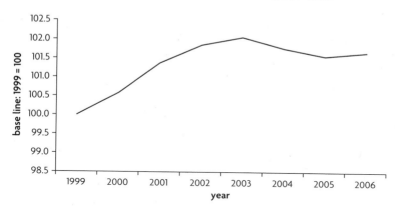

Source: UNODC, different years.

potential cocaine production in Colombia decreased only about 14 percent, from 687,500 kilograms per year in 2000 to about 610,000 in 2006. The White House Office of National Drug Control Policy (ONDCP), an alternative source of information for data on coca cultivation and potential cocaine production in Colombia (see Mejía and Posada, this volume), estimates that potential cocaine production in Colombia actually increased by about 4 percent between 2000 and 2006, from about 530,000 kilograms to about 550,000 kilograms (see ONDCP 2007; GAO 2008). In other words, the available evidence shows that almost the same amount of cocaine is being produced on half the land that was being used for the cultivation of coca crops before the start of Plan Colombia (see figure 4.3). Thus, while the plan's original intermediate target of reducing the cultivation of illicit crops by half by 2006 was met, the final target of reducing the processing and distribution of illicit narcotics was not.[4]

This apparently paradoxical outcome—the large decrease in the number of hectares of land cultivated with coca crops on the one hand and the relatively stable trend for potential cocaine production on the other— is mostly explained by large increases in productivity per hectare. Whereas in 2000, 1 hectare of land cultivated with coca crops produced about 4.7 kilograms of cocaine per year, by 2006 the yield per hectare was about 7.4 kilograms per year. Figure 4.4 presents the evolution of the

Figure 4.2. Trends in Cocaine Prices, 1999–2006

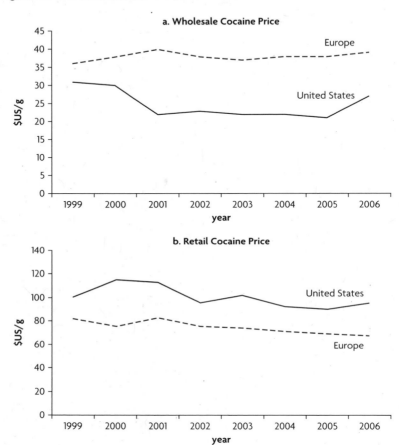

Source: UNODC, different years.

average yield per hectare per year between 2000 and 2006 implicit in UNODC figures.

The large increase in productivity between 2000 and 2006 has resulted from a number of factors, among others, the use of stronger and bigger coca plants, a higher density of coca plants per hectare, better planting techniques, and the spraying of coca plants with molasses to prevent the herbicides used in eradication campaigns from destroying the leaves. These productivity-related adaptations have constituted a strategic response by drug producers to the intensification of eradication campaigns under Plan

Figure 4.3. Number of Hectares Cultivated with Coca Crops and Potential
Cocaine Production in Colombia, 1999–2006

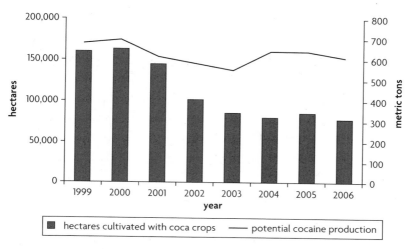

Source: UNODC, different years.

Figure 4.4. Productivity of Coca per Hectare per Year in Colombia, 1999–2006

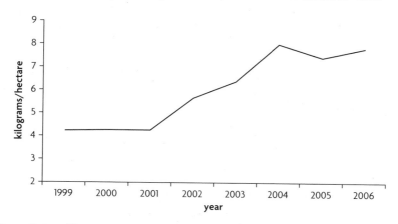

Source: UNODC, different years.

Colombia and have rendered the plan ineffective in reducing the amount
of cocaine produced.

To make things even worse, according to the figures produced by
UNODC and ONDCP, the small reduction in potential cocaine production
in Colombia between 2000 and 2006 was more than offset by increases in

production in the Plurinational State of Bolivia and Peru, the other two cocaine-producer countries in Latin America. As a result, potential cocaine production in the Andean region as a whole increased between 2000 and 2006. According to UNODC, potential cocaine production in the region increased from about 880,000 kilograms in 2000 to about 984,000 kilograms in 2006, an increase of about 12 percent (see figure 4.5).

The interdiction of cocaine in producer and transit countries has shown a steady increase since 2000. According to UNODC, about 90,000 kilograms of cocaine were intercepted in Colombia in 2000, whereas by 2006 the amount of cocaine seized from the country's illegal drug producers and traffickers reached more than 127,000 kilograms. Figure 4.6a presents the evolution of cocaine seizures in Colombia between 2000 and 2006. The same pattern holds with the interdiction of drug shipments in transit countries (see figure 4.6b). According to GAO (2008), the amount of cocaine interdicted or disrupted on its way toward U.S. markets increased from about 140 tons in 2000 to roughly 220 tons in 2006. Figure 4.7 compares UNODC figures on the interdiction of cocaine with those from GAO.

In Peru and Bolivia, the amount of cocaine interdicted has also increased, although not as much as production has. In fact, despite the increase in the amount of cocaine interdicted in Colombia and in the

Figure 4.5. Potential Cocaine Production in Bolivia, Colombia, and Peru, 1999–2006

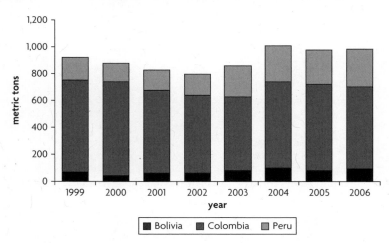

Source: UNODC, different years.

Figure 4.6. Interdiction in Producer and Transit Countries, Since 2000

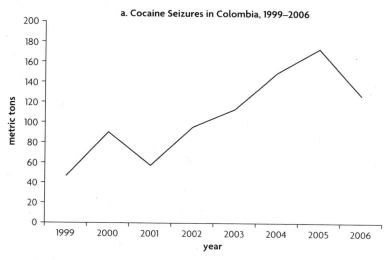

a. Cocaine Seizures in Colombia, 1999–2006

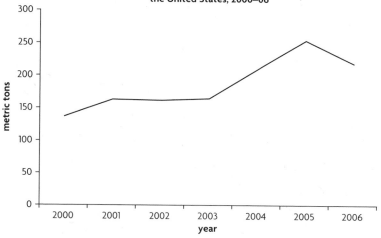

b. Total Seizures and Disruptions of Cocaine Flowing toward the United States, 2000–06

Sources: UNODC, different years; GAO (2008).

other two producer countries, the amount of cocaine flowing toward the United States has not decreased because the increase in production was larger than the increase in the quantities interdicted.

According to GAO (2008), the amount of cocaine flowing toward U.S. markets increased between 2000 and 2006 from about 460 metric tons to

Figure 4.7. Amount of Cocaine Interdicted and Disrupted from Flows toward the United States, 2000–06

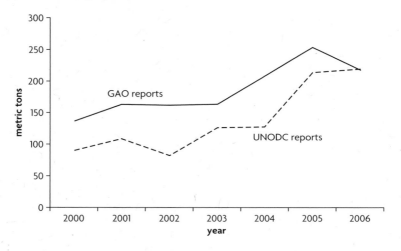

Source: GAO (2008); UNODC, different years.
Note: The UNODC data correspond to cocaine seizure reports specified by country; the figures are not corrected for purity levels.

about 620 metric tons. Once the amount of cocaine interdicted and disrupted is subtracted from the amount of cocaine estimated to be flowing toward the United States (that is, the amount of cocaine leaving producer countries), we can obtain an estimate of the amount of cocaine reaching the U.S. borders. Our estimates, based on GAO's figures, suggest that the amount of cocaine reaching the U.S. borders increased from about 322,000 kilograms in 2000 to about 402,000 in 2006 (see figure 4.8). Those figures are consistent with the pattern of wholesale prices observed in the United States between 2000 and 2006 presented in figure 4.2.

A Research Agenda to Evaluate Plan Colombia's Antidrug Policies

Given the facts reviewed above, the general impression is that programs aimed at reducing the production and trafficking of illegal drugs have proved ineffective in reducing the amount of drugs reaching consumer countries. Some observers have even argued that the war on drugs is "self-defeating," because the potential decrease in the supply of drugs

Figure 4.8. Estimated Quantity of Export-Quality Cocaine Flowing toward the United States, 2000–06

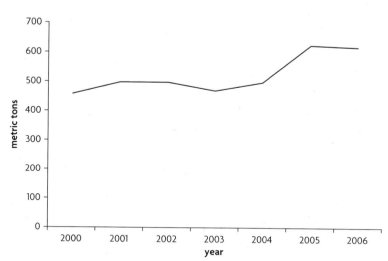

Source: GAO (2008).

induced by the war on drugs in producer countries tends to increase drug prices in consumer countries, thus creating larger profits and an incentive for more production and trafficking of illegal drugs. Instead, we argue that the relevant policy question is, What is the cost of making "important" advances in the war against illegal drug production and trafficking?

A recent report by GAO recognizes that although security in Colombia has improved significantly during the current decade, the drug reduction goals of Plan Colombia were, after almost six years of implementation (and more than $10 billion spent), not fully met.[5] Despite the large expenditures on the program by Colombia and the United States during the current decade, however, little of a systematic nature is known about the effects, costs, and efficiency of the antidrug policies implemented under Plan Colombia.[6] In short, the main objective of the research agenda summarized in this chapter is to fill that gap.

Mejía and Restrepo (2008) provide a thorough and independent economic evaluation of the antidrug policies implemented in Colombia between 2000 and 2006. In this chapter, we identify the key fundamentals behind the low effectiveness (and high costs) of policies aimed at reducing the supply of illegal drugs that reach consumer countries. We use the model and the calibration results to evaluate the future prospects of the war against illegal drug production and trafficking. In particular, we estimate the impact of changes in the U.S. budget for Plan Colombia on different outcomes of the war on drugs and drug markets.

Mejía (2008) extends the framework developed in Mejía and Restrepo (2008) to study the key role played by the type of antidrug policies in consumer countries on the effectiveness of antidrug policies in producer countries. In this chapter, we study how treatment and prevention policies (aimed at reducing the demand for illegal drugs) and enforcement policies (aimed at reducing the supply of illicit drugs) affect the efficiency of the antidrug policies in producer countries. We show how the consumer countries' optimal allocation of resources in the war on drugs crucially depends on the price elasticity of demand for drugs and on the effectiveness of *demand prevention* policies vis-à-vis the effectiveness of *supply reduction* policies.

A Game Theory Model of the War on Drugs

To evaluate the effectiveness, costs, and efficiency of the antidrug policies implemented in Colombia between 2000 and 2006 under Plan Colombia, we develop a game theory model of the war against illegal drugs in producer countries.[7] Using a game theory setup allows us to model the strategic interactions among the actors involved in the war on drugs and capture the strategic responses of different actors to changes in policies.

A Sequential Game

We model the war on illegal drug production and trafficking as a sequential game. The actors are the governments of the drug-producer and -consumer countries, the drug producers, the drug traffickers, and a wholesale drug dealer in the consumer country. On the one hand, we assume that while the objective of the government of the drug-producer country is to minimize the total costs arising from illegal drug production, trafficking, and the war against these two activities, the objective of the drug-consumer country's government is to minimize the illegal drugs reaching its borders. On the other hand, we assume that the objective of both the drug producers and the drug traffickers is to maximize the profits derived from their respective activities.

One of our modeling assumptions is that the government of the drug-producer country faces a net cost, c_1, for each dollar received by the drug producers and a net cost, c_2, for each dollar received by the drug traffickers. The rationale for this assumption is that organized criminal organizations use part of the proceeds from illegal drug production and trafficking to finance their attacks against the state and civilians, to corrupt politicians, and to weaken the institutional arrangement. Yet another fraction of the proceeds from illegal drug production and trafficking activities is reinvested in legal companies in the form of money laundering. Thus, c_1 and c_2 capture the net cost from illegal drug production and trafficking activities.

We assume (as seems to have been the case in Colombia) that the war on drugs in producer countries occurs on two main fronts:

- a conflict between the government and the illegal drug producers over the control of the arable land suitable for cultivating the illegal crops
- a conflict between the government and the drug traffickers over the control of the drug routes necessary to transport illegal drug shipments to consumer countries.

Drug producers combine the land they control after the conflict with the government with other complementary factors such as chemical precursors, workshops, and power plants to produce illegal drugs. Drug traffickers, for their part, combine the drug routes with the cocaine bought in the producer country to "produce" illegal drug shipments.

The Six Stages of the Game

The sequential game evolves as follows. First, the government of the drug-consumer country, hoping to minimize the quantity of drugs entering its territory, subsidizes a fraction $1-\omega$ of the expenses of the government of the drug-producer country in the conflict over the arable land and a fraction $1-\Omega$ of the expenses of the government of the drug-producer country in the conflict over the drug routes. The fractions ω and Ω need not be equal. Second, the government (whose objective at this stage is to minimize the costs arising from illegal drug production and the war against this activity) and the drug producers (whose objective is to maximize profits) engage in a conflict over the control of the land suitable for cultivating illegal crops. The outcome of this conflict is the fraction of arable land controlled by the drug producers, q (the remainder fraction, $1-q$, is controlled by the government). The fraction q depends positively on the amount of resources invested by the drug producers in this conflict, x, and negatively on the amount of resources invested by the government, z, in this conflict. Formally, $q = q(\phi x, z)$ with $q_x > 0$, and $q_z < 0$. The parameter ϕ captures the relative effectiveness of the resources invested by the drug producers in the conflict over the arable land with the government. In the third stage of the game, the drug producers fight against each other over the control of the land that the government does not control. The outcome of this conflict is symmetric because we assume that all drug producers are of the same size and are equally effective at fighting against each other over the control of that land.

Once the drug producers know how much land they control (after confronting the government and the other drug producers), in the fourth stage of the game they have to decide how much to invest in the factors that are complementary to land in the production of illegal drugs (chemical precursors and workshops, for example), r. At this stage of the game, we obtain the supply of drugs in the producer country. We assume that drugs are produced by combining the land that drug producers control with the complementary factors, according to the following production technology:

$$Q_d^s = \lambda r^\alpha (qL)^{1-\alpha},$$

where $\lambda > 0$ is a scale parameter, L is the total land suitable for cultivating illegal crops in the producer country, and α and $1-\alpha$ are the relative importance of the complementary factors and land in the production of illegal drugs.

Fifth, the drug trafficker and the government engage in a dispute over the routes that are used for transporting illegal drugs to consumer countries. The outcome of this conflict is given by the probability, h, that a drug route will not be intercepted by the government. The probability h depends positively on the amount of resources invested by the drug trafficker to try to avoid the interdiction of its drug shipments, t, and negatively on the amount of resources invested by the government in interdiction efforts, s. Formally, $h = h(\gamma t, s)$ with $h_t > 0$ and $h_s < 0$.

Once the drug trafficker knows the expected probability, h, of having a drug route intercepted by the government, in the sixth stage he has to decide the quantity of illegal drugs he buys in the producer country, Q_d^d. At this stage, we obtain the demand for drugs by the drug trafficker in the producer country and the supply of drugs by the drug trafficker in the consumer country. We assume that the drug trafficker combines drug routes, κ, with illegal drugs bought in the producer country, Q_d^d, to "produce" illegal drug shipments, Q_f^s, according to the following drug-trafficking technology:

$$Q_f^s = (\kappa h)^{1-\eta} (Q_d^d)^\eta,$$

where $1 - \eta$ and η are, respectively, the relative importance of drug routes and cocaine in the trafficking technology. Not all the illegal drugs that the drug trafficker buys in the producer countries reach the border of the consumer country because a fraction h of the drug routes are intercepted by the government and, thus, a fraction of illegal drug shipments is disrupted.

Finally, in the last stage of the game the drug trafficker sells the illegal drugs that survive the government's interdiction efforts to a wholesale drug dealer located at the border of the consumer country. We assume that the wholesale illegal drug dealer demands drugs according to the following (generic) demand function:

$$Q_c^d = a/P_f^b,$$

where $a > 0$ is a scale parameter of the demand function, P_f is the wholesale price of illegal drugs in the consumer country, and b captures the price elasticity of demand for illegal drugs at the wholesale level in the consumer country.

Drug Markets

In our model, market prices are determined endogenously by market-clearing conditions in both producer and consumer countries. Such modeling allows us to account for potentially important feedback effects between policies and market outcomes likely to arise as a result of such large-scale policy interventions as Plan Colombia. The main building blocks of the model are described in figure 4.9.

The solution of the model as a whole is characterized by the equilibrium conditions for the conflict over the control of arable land between the drug producers and the government in the drug production subgame, equilibrium conditions for the conflict between the drug trafficker and the government in the interdiction subgame, and market-clearing conditions in both producer and consumer countries.[8]

One of the natural extensions of the framework developed in Mejía and Restrepo (2008) is to include the optimal choice of antidrug policies

Figure 4.9. The Model in a Nutshell

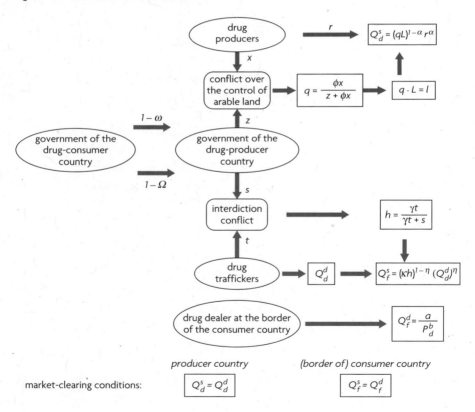

market-clearing conditions:

producer country
$$Q_d^s = Q_d^d$$

(border of) consumer country
$$Q_f^s = Q_f^d$$

Source: Author.

in consumer countries and study how this choice, made by the government of the drug-consumer country, affects the effectiveness of antidrug policies in producer countries. Mejía (2008) extends the original model of Mejía and Restrepo (2008) to include the trade-off faced by the governments of the drug-consumer countries: they can choose to emphasize enforcement policies, which are aimed at curtailing the supply of illegal drugs from producer countries and involve subsidizing the producer-countries' governments in efforts to reduce production and trafficking of illegal drugs; or they can emphasize treatment and prevention policies, aimed at reducing the demand for drugs inside their own countries through education, prevention, and treatment. The basic assumption in Mejía (2008) is that increases in treatment and prevention policies decrease the demand for drugs in consumer countries, whereas enforcement policies, in the form of subsidies to the governments of drug-producer countries, decrease the supply of drugs inside consumer countries. We assume that treatment and prevention policies, l, affect the scale parameter, a, of the demand for illegal drugs as follows:

$$Q_c^d = a(l)/P_f^b,$$

where $a_1 < 0$. When extending the model, we assume that the term $a(l)$ takes the functional form $a(l) = A/l^\theta$. With this particular functional form, the parameter θ captures the elasticity of demand for drugs at the wholesale level to changes in treatment and prevention in consumer countries. More precisely, θ measures the reduction of cocaine demand (in percentage terms) that would follow after a 1 percent increase in the amounts spent on treatment and prevention policies.

The Carrots and Sticks of Antidrug Policies in Producer Countries

Yet another natural extension of the original framework developed in Mejía and Restrepo (2008) is to take into account the "carrot" component of antidrug policies in producer countries. This component consists of alternative development programs (ADPs) aimed at convincing farmers who cultivate illegal crops (mainly coca in the case of Andean countries) to switch to legal crops in exchange for support in the form of ADPs. Those programs take many different forms: temporary cash transfers, training and technical support for farmers who shift to legal crops, subsidized credit, and preferential access to markets in developed economies, among others. Mejía, Restrepo, and Uribe (2009) extend the basic framework developed in Mejía and Restrepo (2008) to include the optimal decision of farmers between the cultivation of legal and illegal crops.

Under this extension, we assume that farmers who are making such decisions trade off the expected benefits of cultivating illegal crops with the expected benefits of cultivating legal ones. On the one hand, although the benefits of cultivating illegal crops are significant because of the high relative price of illegal crops, they are also negatively affected by the government's threat of destruction through eradication campaigns (the "stick" component of antidrug policies). On the other hand, although the relative price of legal crops is low, the benefits from the cultivation of legal crops are positively affected by ADPs aimed at increasing the productivity of legal crop cultivation. In this extension of the basic framework, our target is to assess the effectiveness, costs, and sustainability of alternative development projects aimed at reducing the supply of illicit drugs in consumer countries by convincing farmers to change from illegal to legal crops.

The Calibration of the Model

Using the solution of the model (and its extensions), we then take the next step of using available data for the outcomes of the war on cocaine production and trafficking as well as observed outcomes from the cocaine markets in producer and consumer countries to calibrate the parameters of the model.[9] We use available information from different sources on coca cultivation, eradication, cocaine production, productivity per hectare, interdiction of cocaine, and cocaine prices in Colombia and in the United States and Europe, among others. We also use the information about the expenditures of the United States and Colombia in the war on drugs under Plan Colombia.[10]

Among other parameters of the model, we calibrate the following:

- the price elasticity of demand for cocaine at the wholesale level in consumer countries, b;

- the importance of land in the production of cocaine (relative to the importance of complementary factors such as chemicals, electricity, workshops, and the like), $1-\alpha$;
- the relative importance of the drug routes in the drug-trafficking technology, $1-\eta$;
- the relative effectiveness of the resources invested by the drug producers in the conflict with the government over the control of arable land, ϕ;
- the relative effectiveness of the resources invested by the drug traffickers in the conflict with the government over the fraction of drug routes that are not intercepted, γ;
- the costs the Colombian government perceives from illegal drug production activities, c_1, and from illegal drug-trafficking activities, c_2.[11]

Using the results from the calibration exercise, we then proceed to estimate important measures of the costs, effectiveness, and efficiency of the war on drugs in Colombia. For instance, we estimate the marginal cost to the United States and Colombia of decreasing the amount of cocaine reaching consumer countries by 1 kilogram. We also estimate the elasticity of cocaine reaching consumer countries to changes in the U.S. budget allocated to eradication efforts and to interdiction efforts. Those elasticities capture the reduction (in percentage terms) in the amount of cocaine reaching consumer countries due to a 1 percent increase in the U.S. assistance to Plan Colombia targeted to subsidize Colombia's eradication or interdiction efforts. Both the two marginal costs and the two elasticities are direct estimates of the costs and effectiveness of the war on illegal drug production and trafficking under Plan Colombia. A higher marginal cost or a lower elasticity indicates that the war on drugs is more costly and less effective in reducing the amount of cocaine reaching consumer countries.

We also construct a measure of the intensity of conflict under the war on drugs: that is, the sum of the resources by all the actors involved in it. From the model and the calibration results, we are also able to obtain different measures of the profits and rates of return from illegal drug production and trafficking.

Finally, we carry out simulation exercises to assess the impact of an increase (or a reduction) in the U.S. budget allocated under Plan

Colombia. In particular, we estimate the effect of changes in the total U.S. budget allocated to the war on drugs in Colombia on many of the endogenous variables of the model, such as the quantity of drugs reaching consumer countries, the number of hectares of land under the control of the drug producers, the fraction of drug shipments surviving the government's interdiction efforts, market prices in consumer and producer countries, and our measure of the intensity of the conflict. The simulations shed light on the costs and benefits of making "important" advances in the war on drugs. For instance, we estimate the reduction of coca cultivation, domestic cocaine production, and the amount of cocaine reaching consumer countries in response to an increase (or decrease) in the total U.S. assistance for antidrug policies in Colombia. The simulations take into account not only the strategic responses of all the actors involved in the war on drugs to changes in the U.S. budget for Plan Colombia but also the potentially important feedback effects through endogenous drug-market outcomes.

Main Findings

From the calibration of the model in a baseline scenario, where we use data from primary sources such as UNODC and the U.S. and Colombian governments, among others, we find that the price elasticity of demand for cocaine at the wholesale level, b, is about -0.64. Thus, consistent with evidence from empirical studies, we find that the demand for cocaine at the wholesale level is inelastic to changes in the wholesale price of cocaine. A low price elasticity of demand for drugs in consumer countries implies that a contraction in the supply of drugs, induced by the war on illegal drug production and trafficking in Colombia, has relatively minor effects on the quantity of drugs transacted in equilibrium. As explained next, the price elasticity of demand turns out to be one of the key parameters in explaining the low effectiveness and high costs of antidrug policies in producer countries.

On the one hand, according to our estimations in the baseline exercise, the relative effectiveness of the resources invested by the Colombian government in the conflict over the control of arable land with the drug producers, $1/\phi$, is about 0.29. In other words, each dollar invested by the drug producers in this conflict is 3.4 times more effective $(1/0.29)$ than each dollar spent by the Colombian military forces in the conflict over the control of that land. On the other hand, we find that the Colombian expenses in the interdiction front of the war on drugs, $1/\gamma$, are about four times more effective in detecting and disrupting illegal drug shipments than each dollar spent by the drug traffickers in trying to avoid the interdiction of their drug shipments.

We estimate that the relative importance of land in the production of cocaine, $1-\alpha$, is about 22 percent. That is, although essential, land is a relatively unimportant factor when it comes to producing cocaine. The remainder 78 percent corresponds to the relative importance of the other factors that are complementary to land in the production of cocaine such as chemical precursors, workshops, and power plants. In the case of the trafficking technology, we find that the drug routes are the most important factor, with a relative importance, $1-\eta$, of about 92 percent, with the relative importance of cocaine in the "production" of illegal drug shipments accounting for the remaining 8 percent.

We also find that the U.S. government has paid for about 42 percent $(1-\omega)$ of the expenses related to the Colombian government's conflict with drug producers over the control of arable land, in the form of eradication equipment, chemicals, and other materials, as well as military equipment and training for the Colombian armed forces. With respect to interdiction, we find that the U.S. assistance has funded about 67 percent $(1-\Omega)$ of the related expenses. We estimate that the cost to the Colombian government arising from illegal drug production activities, c_1, is about $0.55 per dollar received by the cocaine producers (a cost of about $990 per kilogram of cocaine successfully produced). The cost from drug-trafficking activities, c_2, is estimated to be about $0.02 per dollar received by drug traffickers (a cost of about $590 per kilogram of cocaine successfully exported). As it turns out, the estimated total yearly cost to Colombia arising from drug production is about $620 million, whereas that arising from illegal drug trafficking is about $250 million. Once we add to those figures, the costs of the resources invested in fighting on the two fronts of the war on drugs—that is, fighting against the drug producers over the control of arable land and against the drug traffickers over illicit drug shipments—we estimate that the total cost of the war on drugs to Colombia is about $1.45 billion (approximately 1.5 percent of Colombian GDP between 2005 and 2006).

We estimate that the marginal cost to the United States of reducing the successful production and trafficking of cocaine by 1 kilogram, which results from subsidizing the Colombian government in its war against drug production, is about $163,000. By contrast, the marginal cost of subsidizing the Colombian government in its war against drug trafficking is estimated to be about $3,700. The large difference between these two marginal costs and the fact that both activities have been subsidized under Plan Colombia tell us that the allocation of subsidies has not been efficient. In other words, the current allocation of subsidies is not consistent with the one that would minimize the amount of cocaine reaching consumer countries. Had the allocation been efficient, our estimates would show that the marginal cost to the U.S. government of decreasing the amount of cocaine reaching consumer countries by subsidizing the war against production and the war against trafficking should be equal, but this is clearly not the case, according to our estimations.

We go on to estimate the efficiency cost of the misallocation of subsidies. We estimate that under an efficient allocation, the United States should be funding the Colombian government only on the interdiction front. Under such a scenario—that is, one in which all the funding to Plan Colombia (about $465 million per year) is used to subsidize interdiction efforts—the marginal cost of reducing the successful production and trafficking of cocaine by 1 kilogram would be about $8,800. This figure represents the marginal cost of decreasing the amount of cocaine reaching consumer countries by 1 kilogram through subsidizing the Colombian military's interdiction efforts. Had the subsidies been allocated efficiently during the period in question, we find that cocaine supply in consumer countries would have been 14.4 percent lower than it actually was, that is, instead of having been about 428,000 kilograms between 2005 and 2006, it would have been about 366,400 kilograms (about 62,000 kilograms lower).

The Effectiveness of Antidrug Policies under Plan Colombia
Another way of looking at the effectiveness of fighting the two-front war on drugs is by estimating how a 1 percent increase in the U.S. budget for Plan Colombia would affect the amount of cocaine reaching consumer countries. We estimate that such an increase would reduce the amount of cocaine reaching the U.S. borders by about 0.007 percent if

it were allocated to the conflict over the control of arable land. However, if the increase in the budget were assigned to fund interdiction efforts, the reduction in cocaine reaching the U.S. borders would be about 0.29 percent. Thus, we find that both elasticities are relatively low. Consistent with the results using the marginal-cost approach described above, however, the amount of cocaine reaching consumer countries is much larger if the U.S. resources are allocated to funding interdiction efforts.

Colombia's Preferred Allocation of Subsidies

Ironically, another interesting result from our estimations is that, if allowed to choose the allocation of U.S. subsidies, the Colombian government would allocate all U.S. assistance under Plan Colombia to funding its war over the control of arable land and none of it to funding interdiction efforts. We find that one extra dollar of U.S. assistance used in the conflict over the control of land reduces the total cost to Colombia by about $1.37. If an extra dollar of U.S. assistance is used to fund interdiction efforts, however, the total cost to Colombia is reduced by only $0.09. The reason for this difference, according to our estimates, is that Colombia faces a much higher net cost for each dollar received by drug producers (about $0.55 per dollar) than the cost it faces for each dollar received by drug traffickers (about $0.02 per dollar).

Thus, even though we estimate that the Colombian government is much more efficient at interdicting illegal drug shipments than it is at fighting over the control of arable land, it still prefers to attack the drug producers' sources of income rather than those of drug traffickers. This finding is consistent with the view that the cocaine producers (mainly FARC and the paramilitaries) generate a much larger cost to Colombia than do illegal drug traffickers, who are less visible nowadays than in the times of the Medellín and Cali cartels during the 1990s. The large difference in the costs generated by the drug producers and the drug traffickers more than counteracts the difference in the relative effectiveness of the Colombian government in the conflict over the control of arable land vis-à-vis its relative effectiveness in the interdiction of illegal drugs.

Despite the fact that both Colombia and the United States have an interest in fighting against illegal drug production and trafficking, they are not necessarily in agreement on the optimal strategy. Colombia's goal is to reduce the sources of income that criminal organizations derive from illegal drug production and trafficking activities to finance attacks against infrastructure, civilians, and the armed forces; to corrupt politicians; and to create institutional instability. The goal of the U.S. government, however, is to curtail the supply of drugs reaching the U.S. markets. This disparity creates an asymmetry between the two countries in the preferred means, but not the ends, of the war on drugs. In fact, when we allow the available data to determine what the optimal allocation of resources has been between the two fronts, we find that resources were allocated to both fronts and not to only one of them, as each country separately would have preferred if deciding on its own. According to our interpretation, both countries need the other and are thus willing to move away from their preferred allocations to collaborate. Another interpretation is that the United States has moved away from its preferred allocation because the results from the war against illegal drug production (proxied by the amount of land used for coca crops cultivation) are much easier to monitor than the results from interdiction efforts. Yet another explanation is that the United States also cares about the security conditions in Colombia and not only about reducing the amount of cocaine reaching consumer countries. This explanation is potentially important, given the fact that Colombia has been a long-time ally of the United States in the war on terror and that many of the organized criminal organizations that are now profiting from illegal drug production and trafficking in Colombia are internationally recognized as terrorist groups.

Results of the Simulation

Turning now to the results of our simulation exercises, we find that a threefold increase in the U.S. budget allocated to Plan Colombia would reduce the amount of cocaine reaching consumer countries by about 19.3 percent. Assuming that the subsidies to the two fronts of the war on drugs are allocated efficiently, an increase in the U.S. budget for the plan from about $465 million to about $1.5 billion would reduce the quantity of cocaine reaching consumer countries from about 366,000 to roughly 296,000 kilograms.

Furthermore, such an increase in the U.S. budget would also increase the fraction of drugs interdicted from about 28 percent to about 41 percent.

Inasmuch as under an efficient allocation of subsidies the United States would not be funding the Colombian government in its war against drug producers, the fraction of land under control of the producers would remain constant at about 25 percent, implying about 100,000 hectares cultivated with coca crops. The marginal cost to the United States of reducing the production and successful exportation of cocaine by 1 kilogram would increase from about $8,900 per kilogram to slightly more than $22,500. Also, following a threefold increase in the U.S. budget allocated to the war on drugs in Colombia, the intensity of the war would increase by about 70 percent, from about $6 billion to more than $10 billion per year.[12] Thus, the increase in the U.S. assistance to Colombia would also induce an intensification of conflict in Colombia, as measured by the sum of the resources invested by all the actors involved in the war on drugs. Finally, a threefold increase in the U.S. budget allocated to the plan would decrease drug traffickers' profits by about 11.5 percent (from about $10 billion per year to roughly $8.8 billion), while increasing the drug producers' profits by about 12 percent (from about $42 million per year to about $47 million).

Robustness Checks

To check the robustness of our results, we use different variations in data sources and reference years for before and after Plan Colombia. For instance, instead of using the UNODC estimates for the number of hectares of land cultivated with coca crops, we can use the estimates provided by ONDCP (see ONDCP 2007). The same holds for potential cocaine production and for cocaine seizures and interceptions. As for the price data, we conduct robustness checks using weighted averages for Europe and the United States, rather than only the U.S. prices, and alternative sources for the U.S. wholesale price of cocaine from the System to Retrieve Information from Drug Evidence (STRIDE) price data. Furthermore, recall that in our baseline calibrations, we were using an average of the outcomes observed between 1999 and 2000 as a reference point for before Plan Colombia and averages for 2005 and 2006 as the reference years for after the plan. In some of the robustness checks, we change the reference years for before and after the plan (including the outcomes for 1998 and 2004 for before and after) and find that the results summarized above are all robust to these changes in data sources and reference years. For some key parameters such as the price elasticity of demand for illegal drugs and productivity measures, we also conduct robustness checks. Although the price elasticity of demand for drugs is a key parameter in most of our estimations of the costs and effectiveness of the war on drugs, we show that relatively large variations in this parameter do not change the results significantly. The same holds true for changes in productivity measures before and after Plan Colombia.

When we calibrate the extended model, which includes the choice of antidrug policies in consumer countries, we find that the price elasticity of demand for drugs at the wholesale level is about -0.66, very close to the one estimated in Mejía and Restrepo (2008). We also estimate, using the extended model, that a 1 percent increase in prevention and treatment policies would decrease the demand for illegal drugs at the wholesale level by about 0.17 percent (see Mejía 2008).

Why Is the War on Drugs in Producer Countries So Costly and Ineffective?

According to our estimates, the elasticity of the quantity of cocaine reaching consumer countries with respect to changes in the U.S. budget allocated to Plan Colombia is about 0.007, if resources are allocated to the war against illegal drug production, and about 0.296, if resources are allocated to interdiction efforts. In other words, if the U.S. budget for Plan Colombia increases by 1 percent (an increase of about $4.6 million) and this increase is assigned entirely to the war on production, the quantity of illegal drugs reaching consumer countries would be reduced by about 0.007 percent (about 50 kilograms). If the same funding were allocated to interdiction efforts, the amount of cocaine reaching consumer countries would be reduced by about 0.296 percent (about 1,075 kilograms). Both elasticities are relatively low, but the one associated with illegal drug trafficking is many times greater than the one associated with illegal drug production. One of the key factors underlying these low elasticities is the low price elasticity of demand for drugs (that is, a low level of the parameter b described before). The intuition behind the key role played by the price elasticity of demand on the effectiveness of policies aimed at reducing the supply of drugs is very simple: if the demand for drugs is inelastic, a contraction of the supply of illegal drugs induced by the war against illegal drug production and trafficking would have only a minor effect on the quantity of drugs transacted and, depending on the shape of the supply curve, potentially a large effect on drug prices.

Arable Land versus Drug Routes

We identify four more factors that play a key role in the effectiveness of the war on illegal drug production and trafficking. The first is the relative importance of the factor being contested in each of the two fronts of the war on drugs. The second is the relative effectiveness of the resources invested by the government in each of the two fronts (vis-à-vis the resources invested by drug producers and drug traffickers in each of the two fronts).Regarding the first factor, we find that the relative importance of land in the production of cocaine, $1-\alpha$, is about 22 percent, whereas factors complementary to land in illegal drug production have a relative importance, α, of about 78 percent. In other words, the war on illegal drug production (that is, the conflict over control of land) targets a relatively unimportant factor of production. We find that the war on illegal drug trafficking, however, which targets the routes used to transport illegal drugs, focuses on a relatively important factor: the drug routes: which have a relative importance, $1-\eta$, of about 92 percent in the "production" of illegal drug shipments (the remaining 8 percent represents the relative importance of cocaine bought in the producer country, η). On the one hand, we estimate that the resources invested by drug producers in the conflict with the government over the control of arable land are about 3.4 times more efficient than the resources invested by the Colombian government in this conflict. On the other hand, we estimate that the resources invested by drug traffickers to try to avoid the interdiction of drug shipments are only about one-fourth as efficient as the resources invested by the government in interdiction efforts. We thus find that the Colombian government is much more efficient, relatively speaking, in fighting against illegal drug trafficking than in fighting against illegal drug production.

Both the relative importance of the factors being contested and the relative effectiveness of the resources invested by the government determine the size of the contraction of the supply of drugs induced by an increase in the resources invested in the war on drugs in producer countries. In other words, if the factor being contested is relatively unimportant in the production or the trafficking of drugs or the government's resources invested in the war on drugs are relatively ineffective, then the contraction of the supply of drugs generated by an increase in the expenditures will be relatively small. To make things even worse, if, as seems to be the case according to our results, the demand for drugs is inelastic, then the small shift in the supply function will have only minor effects on the quantity of drugs transacted in equilibrium.

A third element that reduces the effectiveness of the war on drugs in producer countries is the type of antidrug policies implemented in consumer countries. When the focus of antidrug policies in consumer countries is on the reduction of supply (by means of enforcement policies, stiffer penalties, and the prosecution of drug dealers), the price of drugs in consumer countries will tend to increase, thus leading to an increase in the profit margins associated with illegal drug production and trafficking and a larger incentive to engage in these activities in producer countries. If the focus is on policies aimed at reducing the demand for drugs, however, drug prices in consumer countries would be lower, making antidrug policies in producer countries more effective. In other words, the type of antidrug policies implemented in consumer countries has an indirect (through drug prices) but potentially important effect on the effectiveness of antidrug policies in producer countries.

Finally, a fourth factor that makes the war on drugs costly and ineffective has to do with the strategic responses of drug producers and traffickers to the specific types of antidrug policies implemented under Plan Colombia. More precisely, drug producers and traffickers respond to antidrug policies by using the uncontested factor more intensively (the complementary factors to land in the case of the war against drug production and cocaine bought in the producer country in the case of the war against drug trafficking). This response, in turn, increases the productivity of drug production and trafficking activities, thus partially rendering inefficient the war on drugs. In particular, we estimate that a 1 percent decrease in the amount of land under the drug producers' control resulting from a more intense war against drug production leads to an increase of about 0.79 percent in the productivity of land (that is, in the amount of cocaine produced from one hectare of land in one year). Conversely, a 1 percent decrease in the fraction of drug routes not detected by government authorities leads to an increase of about 0.11 percent in the productivity of drug routes. Thus, while the war against drug production activities leads to relatively large incr-eases in productivity, the increases in productivity in drug-trafficking activities resulting from the war against illegal drug trafficking are rela-tively small.

Conclusion

Many resources have been spent on the war on drugs in Colombia under Plan Colombia. By most available measures, however, the results have not been the expected ones. The amount of cocaine reaching consumer countries remains relatively stable seven years after the initiation of Plan Colombia, and the price of cocaine at different stages has not risen. Thus, the general impression is that policies aimed at reducing the amount of drugs reaching consumers by curtailing their production and trafficking have been relatively ineffective. Despite the substantial resources invested in this war, no independent evaluation of the antidrug policies imple-mented under Plan Colombia had been done until now. Our principal aim in the research agenda summarized in this chapter is to fill this gap. In particular, the research agenda provides an economic evaluation of the antidrug policies implemented in Colombia during this decade with a strong focus on the costs, efficiency, effectiveness, and future prospects of the war against illegal drug production and trafficking under the plan.

We go a step further and identify the key factors that have made the war against drugs relatively inefficient and costly: among others, the strategic (and probably not anticipated) response of the drug producers and traffickers to the specific policies implemented under Plan Colom-bia, the low response of the demand for illegal drugs to changes in drug prices, the low relative importance of the factor being targeted in the war against illegal drug production (that is, land), and the low relative effec-tiveness of the resources invested by the United States and Colombia in the war against illegal drug production.

The results from this chapter should help policy makers shape more effective (and less costly) antidrug policies and should encourage future research to evaluate the costs and benefits of alternative policies, such as demand-side controls (treatment, prevention policies, and harm-reduction policies) or legalization (with the appropriate controls) of currently illegal drugs.

Notes

1. This section summarizes the main stylized facts that motivate a research agenda aimed at evaluation of antidrug policies implemented in Colombia between 2000 and 2006. For a thorough description of other stylized facts on cocaine production, cocaine markets, and cocaine in general, the reader is referred to Mejía and Posada (2008).

    Plan Colombia is the official name of the program that, among other things, provides the institutional framework for the military alliance between the United States and Colombia in the war against illegal drug production and trafficking and the organized criminal groups associated with these activities.

2. Recent estimates of the U.S. Government Accountability Office (GAO) indicate that the total U.S. assistance under Plan Colombia between 2000 and 2007 reached $5.5 billion (see ONDCP 2007; GAO 2008).

3. The global trend of cocaine consumption has remained relatively stable during the past few years. However, this stability is a result of recent contractions in cocaine use in North America, where the highest prevalence rates of cocaine use (2.4 percent) still prevail, and where increases in cocaine use in most of the other regions of the world: Western and Central Europe, with a prevalence rate of about 1.2 percent; Oceania, with the second-highest prevalence rate in 2006–7 of about 1.4; South and Central America, with a prevalence rate of about 1.1 percent; Africa, with a prevalence rate of 0.2 percent; and Southeast Europe, with a prevalence rate of 0.1 percent (see UNODC 2008).

4. Plan Colombia also had the goal of improving security conditions in Colombia. In this dimension, the plan has been viewed by different analysts as very successful, especially in reducing the number of kidnappings, extortion events, terrorist attacks against municipalities, and ambushes against the military forces, among others.

5. The first goal of Plan Colombia was to reduce the cultivation, processing, and distribution of illicit narcotics in Colombia by 50 percent over a six-year period (starting in 2000).

6. Other government programs of about the same size in terms of the resources invested such as the Subsidized Health Care Regime (Regimen Subsidiado de Salud) and Familias en Acción (the largest conditional cash transfer program in Colombia), which accounted for about 1.25 percent and 0.08 percent of Colombian GDP in 2006, respectively, have been subject to constant program evaluations (see, among others, Attanasio, Gomez, and Murgueitio 2004; Attanasio and others 2005; Gaviria, Mejía, and Medina 2006; Camacho and Conover 2008; and Santa María and others 2008).

7. Game theory is a branch of applied mathematics that is widely used in the social sciences (most notably economics). Game theory attempts to mathematically capture behavior in strategic situations, in which an individual's success in making choices depends on the choices of others.

8. The reader is referred to Mejía and Restrepo (2008) for the complete characterization of the solution of the model as well as the derivation of all the results.

9. We use different sources of information to check the robustness of the calibration results, finding that the results are very robust to changes in the sources of information, to the data used as the reference point for before and after Plan Colombia, and to variations in some of the crucial figures that we use in the calibration exercises.

10. The reader is referred to Mejía and Restrepo (2008) for a detailed description of the data sources used in the calibration of the model. Mejía and Posada (2008) provide a thorough description of the data sources and of how the data are collected as well as the possible sources of bias.

11. The complete calibration strategy is described in detail in Mejía and Restrepo (2008).

12. This measure of the intensity of conflict generated by the war on drugs is defined as the sum of the resources spent by all the involved actors.

References

Attanasio, O., E. Battistin, E. Fitzsimons, A. Mesnard, and M. Vera-Hernández. 2005. "How Effective Are Conditional Cash Transfers? Evidence from Colombia." Briefing Note 54, Institute for Fiscal Studies, London.

Attanasio, O., M. E. Gómez, and C. Murgueitio. 2004. "Baseline Report on the Evaluation of *Familias en Acción.*" Centre for the Evaluation of Development Policies, Institute for Fiscal Studies, London.

Camacho, A., and E. Conover. 2008. "Effects of Subsidized Health Insurance on Newborn Health in Colombia." Documento CEDE 16, Universidad de los Andes, Bogotá, Colombia.

GAO (U.S. Government Accountability Office). 2008. *PLAN COLOMBIA Drug Reduction Goals Were Not Fully Met, but Security Has Improved; U.S. Agencies Need More Detailed Plans for Reducing Assistance.* GAO 00-71. Washington, DC: GAO.

Gaviria, A., C. y Mejía, and P. Medina. 2006. "Evaluation of the Impact of Health Care Reform in Colombia: From Theory to Practice." Documento CEDE 6, Universidad de los Andes, Bogotá, Colombia.

Mejía, D. 2008. "The War on Illegal Drugs: The Interaction of Anti-Drug Policies in Producer and Consumer Countries." CESifo Working Paper 2459, Munich.

Mejía, D., and C. E. Posada. 2008. "Cocaine Production and Trafficking: What Do We Know?" Policy Research Working Paper 4618, Washington, DC: World Bank.

Mejía D., and P. Restrepo. 2008. "The War on Illegal Drug Production and Trafficking: An Economic Evaluation of *Plan Colombia.*" Documento CEDE 19. Universidad de los Andes, Bogotá, Colombia.

Mejía, D., P. Restrepo, and M. Uribe. 2009. "The 'Sticks' vs. the 'Carrots' of Anti-Drug Policies in Producer Countries: What Works and at What Cost?", Unpublished paper. Universidad de los Andes, Bogotá, Colombia.

ONDCP (U.S. Office of National Drug Control Policy). 2007. *National Drug Control Strategy, 2007Annual Report.* Washington, DC: ONDCP.

Santa María, M., F. García, S. Rozo, and M. J. Uribe. 2008. "Un Diagnóstico General del Sector Salud en Colombia: Evolución, Contexto y Principales Retos de un Sistema en Transformación." Fedesarrollo, Bogotá, Colombia.

UNODC (United Nations Office on Drug Control). 1999–2008. *World Drug Report.* Vienna: United Nations.

5

Evo, Pablo, Tony, Diego, and Sonny: General Equilibrium Analysis of the Market for Illegal Drugs

Rómulo A. Chumacero

> Cronauer: Speaking of things controversial, is it true that
> there's a marijuana problem here in Vietnam?
> Funny voice: NO, it's not a problem, everybody HAS it.
> —*Good Morning, Vietnam*, 1987

Drug use is widely blamed for a broad range of personal and social ills. Drug users are said to suffer diminished health and decreased earnings. Similarly, the market in illegal drugs is said to promote crime and to corrupt law enforcement officials and politicians (Miron and Zwiebel 1995).

The most common response to these perceptions is the belief that governments should prohibit the production, sale, and use of illegal drugs. Policy measures often adopted to decrease the demand for illegal drugs include stiff penalties to consumers, treatment of heavy users, and educational campaigns. Policies intended to reduce the supply include crop eradication, interdiction, and heavy penalties on producers and

I would like to thank Philip Keefer, Norman Loayza, Felipe Morandé, Klaus Schmidt-Hebbel, and the participants in the Global Development Network conference for useful comments and suggestions. Cintia Külzer Sacilotto provided able research assistance. The usual disclaimer applies.

traffickers. Although significant resources have been allocated to these activities, the results appear discouraging. A small but vocal minority suggests that prohibition may be the cause of many of the problems associated with illegal drugs and that policies other than prohibition (including legalization) might be preferable.

According to the Office of National Drug Control Policy, between 1986 and 2008 the U.S. government spent an average of almost $14 billion a year (in 2008 dollars) on policies intended to control the production and consumption of illegal drugs (marijuana, cocaine, crack, stimulants, LSD, PCP, and heroin). These expenditures increased rapidly from 1986 to 1992, growing at an annual rate of 22 percent. From 1992 to 2001, they grew at an average annual rate of 2 percent. Beginning in 2002, these expenditures have declined significantly (by almost $7 billion between 2001 and 2003), reaching levels comparable to those of 1989–1990 (table A5.1). From 2001 to 2008, the expenditures increased at a 1.9 percent annual growth rate.

On average, 34 percent of the expenditures supported efforts to decrease the demand for illegal drugs (prevention and treatment), and the remaining 66 percent went toward reducing the supply of illegal drugs (domestic law, interdiction, and international expenditures).[1] These shares have not been constant, and, beginning in 2002, the proportion of expenditures on treatment and antinarcotics activities outside the United States has increased.

According to the Federal Bureau of Investigation and the Department of Justice, the number of drug users in the United States has remained stable since 1989 (approximately 31 million persons).[2] Furthermore, in 2004, 12.5 percent of the arrests made in the United States (1.7 million out of 14 million) involved drug abuse violations. This figure does not consider crimes that may have been drug related. Despite the prevalence and magnitude of the problem, the methodological framework commonly used to analyze it relies on partial equilibrium models.[3] In a market with complex interactions, key aspects that can help explain how different policies shape prices and modify incentives are certain to be missed with this approach. By its own nature, a partial equilibrium approach will ignore the feedback effects among prices, policies, and the consequent reactions of the agents. In general, equilibrium, prices, and actions are endogenous to policies.

This chapter presents a general equilibrium model that can be used to assess the effects of alternative policies. The model is dynamic, stochastic, and internally consistent. Optimal actions and prices are determined as a result of how agents perceive the laws of motion of the state variables and the policies undertaken by the authorities. Furthermore, the model assumes that markets are competitive but that risks are involved in devoting resources to illegal activities.

The chapter is organized as follows. After a presentation of the dynamic general equilibrium model, the following section calibrates the model and tailors it to the cocaine market.[4] The next section reports the long-term effects of alternative policies, and the final section summarizes the findings and offers some concluding observations.

A General Equilibrium Model

The dynamic stochastic general equilibrium model presented below considers the existence of five representative agents:

- Crop producer (agent E)
- Drug producer (agent P)
- Drug trafficker (agent T)
- Drug consumer (agent D)
- Government or law enforcement agency (agent S)

Next, we describe the optimization problem faced by each agent, the optimality conditions, and the equilibrium conditions that jointly determine actions and prices.

The Crop Producer

This model generalizes the acreage supply response model of Chavas and Holt (1990). At any point, the representative agent can devote his time to producing a good (crop) that is used as an input in a drug or to producing a good that is directly consumed.

The first activity is illegal, and the second is not. His consumption of the legal good is $c_{0,t}^E$ if he is not caught producing the illegal crop and $c_{1,t}^E$ if he is. With π_t^E denoting the probability of getting caught producing the illegal crop, we have

$$c_t^E = \begin{cases} c_{0,t}^E & \text{with probability } 1-\pi_t^E \\ c_{1,t}^E & \text{with probability } \pi_t^E \end{cases},$$

$$c_{0,t}^E = p_t y_t^E + h_t^E$$
$$c_{1,t}^E = \left(1-\tau_t^E\right) p_t y_t^E + h_t^E, \tag{5.1}$$

where p is the price (relative to the legal good) at which the illegal crop is sold to the drug producer, y_t^E is the amount of the illegal crop produced, h_t^E is the amount of the legal good produced, and $0 < \tau_t^E \le 1$ is the penalty that is paid if the producer is caught producing the illegal crop.

The agent is endowed with one unit of time and derives no utility from leisure. This unit of time can be devoted to producing the illegal crop $\left(l_{1,t}^E\right)$, to producing the legal good $\left(l_{2,t}^E\right)$, or to reducing the probability of getting caught in the production of the illegal crop $\left(l_{3,t}^E\right)$.[5] The production functions y^E and h^E are increasing and strictly concave in $l_{1,t}^E$ and $l_{2,t}^E$ respectively. Finally, $\pi_t^E = \pi^E\left(g_t^E, l_{1,t}^E, l_{3,t}^E\right)$ is increasing in the first two arguments and decreasing in the third, where g^E is the level of government expenditures aimed at detecting the illegal activity.[6]

The problem of the representative agent can be summarized by the value function that satisfies

$$V\left(x^E\right) = \max_{l_1,l_2,l_3}\left\{\pi^E u\left(c_1^E\right) + \left(1-\pi^E\right) u\left(c_0^E\right) + \beta \mathcal{E}\left[V\left(x_{+1}^E\right)\right]\right\},$$

subject to (1) and the perceived laws of motion of the states x^E, where $u(\cdot)$ is the utility function that is increasing and concave in consumption, and $\mathcal{E}$ is the conditional expectation operator.[7]

The first-order optimality conditions are

$$\frac{\partial \pi}{\partial l_1^E}\left[u\left(c_1^E\right) - u\left(c_0^E\right)\right] + p\frac{\partial y^E}{\partial l_1^E}\left[\pi^E\left(1-\tau^E\right)\frac{\partial u}{\partial c_1^E} + \left(1-\pi^E\right)\frac{\partial u}{\partial c_0^E}\right] = Z^E$$

$$\frac{\partial \pi^E}{\partial l_3^E}\left[u\left(c_1^E\right) - u\left(c_0^E\right)\right] = Z^E, \tag{5.2}$$

where

$$Z^E = \frac{\partial h^E}{\partial l_2^E}\left[\pi^E\frac{\partial u}{\partial c_1^E} + \left(1-\pi^E\right)\frac{\partial u}{\partial c_0^E}\right].$$

The intratemporal optimality conditions state that the marginal benefits of devoting time to producing the illegal crop, to reducing the probability of getting caught producing it, and to producing the legal good must equate.

The Drug Producer

The representative drug producer (agent P) demands the illegal crop from the crop producer (y^P). He can devote his time to combining with y^P to produce the illegal drug or to produce the legal good. His consumption of the legal good can be $c_{0,t}^P$ or $c_{1,t}^P$ depending on whether or not he is caught producing the illegal drug (which happens with probability π_t^P). Then,

$$c_t^P = \begin{cases} c_{0,t}^P & \text{with probability } 1-\pi_t^P \\ c_{1,t}^P & \text{with probability } \pi_t^P \end{cases},$$

$$c_{0,t}^P = q_t w_t^P + h_t^P - p_t y_t^P$$
$$c_{1,t}^P = \left(1-\tau_t^P\right)q_t w_t^P + h_t^P - p_t y_t^P, \tag{5.3}$$

where q is the price at which the illegal drug is sold to the trafficker (relative to the legal good), w_t^P is the amount of drug produced, h_t^P is the amount of the consumption good produced, and $0 < \tau_t^P \le 1$ is the penalty that is paid if the producer is caught producing the illegal drug. The agent is endowed with one unit of time and derives no utility from leisure. This unit of time can be devoted to producing the illegal drug $\left(l_{1,t}^P\right)$, to producing the legal good $\left(l_{2,t}^P\right)$, or to reducing the probability of getting caught $\left(l_{3,t}^P\right)$. The production function h^P is increasing and strictly concave in $l_{2,t}^P$. The production function $w^P = w\left(l_1^P, y^P\right)$ is increasing and strictly concave in both arguments. Finally, $\pi_t^P = \pi^P\left(g_t^P, l_{1,t}^P, l_{3,t}^P\right)$ is increasing in the first two arguments and decreasing in the third, where g^P is the level of government expenditures aimed at detecting the illegal activity.

The problem of the representative agent can be summarized by the value function that satisfies

$$V\left(x^P\right) = \max_{l_1,l_2,l_3,y} \left\{\pi^P u\left(c_1^P\right) + \left(1-\pi^P\right)u\left(c_0^P\right) + \beta E\left[V\left(x_{+1}^P\right)\right]\right\},$$

subject to (5.3) and the perceived laws of motion of the states x^P.

The first-order optimality conditions are

$$\frac{\partial \pi}{\partial l_1^P}\left[u(c_1^P)-u(c_0^P)\right]+q\frac{\partial w^P}{\partial l_1^P}\left[\pi^P(1-\tau^P)\frac{\partial u}{\partial c_1^P}+(1-\pi^P)\frac{\partial u}{\partial c_0^P}\right]=Z^P$$

$$\frac{\partial \pi}{\partial l_3^P}\left[u(c_1^P)-u(c_0^P)\right]=Z^P \quad (5.4)$$

$$\pi^P\frac{\partial u}{\partial c_1^P}\left[(1-\tau^P)q\frac{\partial w^P}{\partial y^P}-p\right]+(1-\pi^P)\frac{\partial u}{\partial c_0^P}\left[q\frac{\partial w^P}{\partial y^P}-p\right]=0,$$

where

$$Z^P=\frac{\partial h^P}{\partial l_2^P}\left[\pi^P\frac{\partial u}{\partial c_1^P}+(1-\pi^P)\frac{\partial u}{\partial c_0^P}\right]$$

The first two optimality conditions state that the marginal benefits of devoting time to producing the illegal drug, to reducing the probability of getting caught, and to producing the legal good must equate. The third equation states that the marginal benefit from demanding an extra unit of the illegal crop must equate with the marginal cost of acquiring it.

The Drug Trafficker
The representative drug trafficker (agent T) demands the illegal drug from the drug producer (w^T). He can devote his time to selling the illegal drug or to producing the legal good. His consumption of the legal good can be $c_{0,t}^T$ or $c_{1,t}^T$ depending on whether he is caught trafficking the illegal drug (which happens with probability π_t^T).
Then,

$$c_t^T=\begin{cases}c_{0,t}^T & \text{with probability } 1-\pi_t^T\\ c_{1,t}^T & \text{with probability } \pi_t^T\end{cases},$$

$$c_{0,t}^T=r_t n_t^T+h_t^T-q_t w_t^T$$
$$c_{1,t}^T=(1-\tau_t^T)r_t n_t^T+h_t^T-q_t w_t^T, \quad (5.5)$$

where r is the price at which the illegal drug is sold to the drug consumer (relative to the legal good), n_t^T is the amount of the product sold by the trafficker,[8] h_t^T is the amount of the legal good produced, and $0<\tau_t^T\leq 1$ is the penalty that the trafficker pays if caught trafficking the illegal drug.

The agent is endowed with one unit of time and derives no utility from leisure. This unit of time can be devoted to trafficking the illegal drug $\left(l_{1,t}^T\right)$, to producing the legal good $\left(l_{2,t}^T\right)$, or to reducing the probability of getting caught $\left(l_{3,t}^T\right)$. The production function h^T is increasing and strictly concave in $l_{2,t}^T$. The production function $n^T = n\left(l_1^T, w^T\right)$ is increasing and strictly concave in both arguments. Finally, $\pi_t^T = \pi^T\left(g_t^T, l_{1,t}^T, l_{3,t}^T\right)$ is increasing in the first two arguments and decreasing in the third, where g^T is the level of government expenditures aimed at detecting the illegal activity.

The problem of the representative agent can be summarized by the value function that satisfies

$$V\left(x^T\right) = \max_{l_1, l_2, l_3, w} \left\{\pi^T u\left(c_1^T\right) + \left(1 - \pi^T\right)u\left(c_0^T\right) + \beta E\left[V\left(x_{+1}^T\right)\right]\right\},$$

subject to (5.5) and the perceived laws of motion of the states x^T.

The first-order optimality conditions are

$$\frac{\partial \pi}{\partial l_1^T}\left[u\left(c_1^T\right) - u\left(c_0^T\right)\right] + r\frac{\partial n^T}{\partial l_1^T}\left[\pi^T\left(1 - \tau^T\right)\frac{\partial u}{\partial c_1^T} + \left(1 - \pi^T\right)\frac{\partial u}{\partial c_0^T}\right] = Z^T$$

$$\frac{\partial \pi}{\partial l_3^T}\left[u\left(c_1^T\right) - u\left(c_0^T\right)\right] = Z^T \quad (5.6)$$

$$\pi^T \frac{\partial u}{\partial c_1^T}\left[\left(1 - \tau^T\right)r\frac{\partial n^T}{\partial w^T} - q\right] + \left(1 - \pi^T\right)\frac{\partial u}{\partial c_0^T}\left[r\frac{\partial n^T}{\partial w^T} - q\right] = 0,$$

where

$$Z^T = \frac{\partial h^T}{\partial l_2^T}\left[\pi^T \frac{\partial u}{\partial c_1^T} + \left(1 - \pi^T\right)\frac{\partial u}{\partial c_0^T}\right].$$

These optimality conditions have interpretations similar to the ones for the drug producer.

The Drug Consumer

The problem of the drug consumer is more complex. It relies on the "rational addiction" literature pioneered by Becker and Murphy (1988). The model generalizes the framework of Orphanides and Zervos (1995). The representative drug consumer (agent D) demands the illegal drug from the drug trafficker (n^D). His consumption of the legal good can be

$c_{0,t}^D$ or $c_{1,t}^D$ depending on whether or not he is caught consuming the illegal drug (which happens with probability π_t^D).

Then,

$$c_t^D = \begin{cases} c_{0,t}^D & \text{with probability } 1 - \pi_t^D \\ c_{1,t}^D & \text{with probability } \pi_t^D \end{cases},$$

$$(1 + \phi_t)c_{0,t}^D = h_t^D - r_t n_t^D$$

$$(1 + \phi_t)c_{1,t}^D = h_t^D - (1 + \tau_t^D)r_t n_t^D, \tag{5.7}$$

where h_t^D is the amount of the legal good produced, ϕ_t is a consumption tax levied by the government, and $0 < \tau_t^D \leq 1$ is the penalty that is paid if the consumer is caught consuming the illegal drug.

At each period, the agent is endowed with one unit of time and derives utility from leisure.[9] This unit of time can be devoted to demanding leisure $(l_{1,t}^D)$, to producing the legal good $(l_{2,t}^D)$, or to reducing the probability of getting caught $(l_{3,t}^D)$. The production function h^D is increasing and strictly concave in $l_{2,t}^D$. The probability $\pi_t^D = \pi^D(g_{1,t}^D, n_t^D, l_{3,t}^D)$ is increasing in the first two arguments and decreasing in the third, where g_1^D is the level of government expenditures aimed at detecting the illegal activity.

As the illegal drug is potentially addictive, the long-lasting effects of past consumption of n^D are summarized by the stock variable d^D that has the following law of motion:

$$d_{t+1}^D = (1 - \delta)d_t^D + n_t^D, \tag{5.8}$$

where $0 < \delta < 1$ acts as a depreciation rate.

The momentary instantaneous utility of the individual is

$$\pi^D u(c_1^D, n^D, l_1^D) + (1 - \pi^D)u(c_0^D, n^D, l_1^D) + \theta^D k^D,$$

where $u(\cdot)$ is increasing and concave in leisure and in the consumption of the legal and illegal goods. The third term is itself composed of two terms. The first is $\theta_t^D = \theta(g_{2,t}^D, d_t^D)$ and denotes the probability that the agent will experience the detrimental effects of the consumption of the illegal good; it is decreasing in g_2^D and increasing in the stock of illegal drugs.[10] The second is $k_t^D = k(n_t^D, d_t^D)$ and represents the detrimental side effects of past consumption. It is increasing in the first argument and decreasing in the second. Thus, the second reflects the fact that the agent is rationally addicted in the sense that he knows that there are negative side effects to increased consumption.

The problem of the representative agent can be summarized by the value function that satisfies

$$V(x^D) = \max_{l_1, l_2, l_3, n} \left\{ \begin{array}{l} \pi^D u\left(c_1^D, n^D, l_1^D\right) + \left(1 - \pi^D\right) u\left(c_0^D, n^D, l_1^D\right) \\ + \theta^D k^D + \beta E\left[V\left(x_{+1}^D\right)\right] \end{array} \right\},$$

subject to (5.7), (5.8), and the perceived laws of motion of the states x^D.

The first-order optimality conditions are

$$\frac{\partial u}{\partial l_1^D} = Z^D$$

$$\frac{\partial \pi}{\partial l_3^D}\left[u\left(c_1^D\right) - u\left(c_0^D\right)\right] = Z^D$$

$$\frac{\partial \pi}{\partial n^D}\left[u\left(c_1^D\right) - u\left(c_0^D\right)\right] + \frac{\partial u}{\partial n^D} + \theta \frac{\partial k}{\partial n^D} = \lambda + M^D \qquad (5.9)$$

$$\beta E\left[(1-\delta)\lambda_{+1} + \frac{\partial \theta_{+1}^D}{\partial d_{+1}^D} k_{+1}^D + \theta_{+1}^D \frac{\partial k_{+1}^D}{\partial d_{+1}^D}\right] = \lambda,$$

where

$$Z^D = \frac{1}{1+\phi} \frac{\partial h^D}{\partial l_2^D}\left[\pi^D \frac{\partial u}{\partial c_1^D} + \left(1 - \pi^D\right) \frac{\partial u}{\partial c_0^D}\right]$$

$$M^D = \frac{r}{1+\phi}\left[\pi^D \left(1 + \tau^D\right) \frac{\partial u}{\partial c_1^D} + \left(1 - \pi^D\right) \frac{\partial u}{\partial c_0^D}\right].$$

The first two optimality conditions state that the marginal benefits of devoting time to leisure, of reducing the probability of getting caught, and of producing the legal good must equate. The third and fourth equations determine the optimal demand for the addictive good, where the agent considers all benefits and costs (including the detrimental effects of becoming addicted).

The Government

The government (agent S) has no explicit objective function to maximize. It chooses the tax rate (ϕ) on the consumption of the legal good by agent $D(C^D)$ that is necessary to finance its total expenditures:

$$G_t^S \equiv g_t^E + g_t^P + g_t^T + g_{1,t}^D + g_{2,t}^D + g_t^S = \phi_t C_t^D, \qquad (5.10)$$

where g^S denotes other expenditures made by the government that do not affect the probabilities of detecting illegal activities.

As the production and consumption of the illegal goods that are confiscated by agent S are assumed to be destroyed (not taxed), they do not constitute a source of revenue for the government.

Market-Clearing Conditions

The market-clearing conditions are

$$
\begin{aligned}
\left(1 - \tau_t^E \, \pi_t^E\right) y_t^E &= y_t^P, \\
\left(1 - \tau_t^P \, \pi_t^P\right) w_t^P &= w_t^T, \\
\left(1 - \tau_t^T \, \pi_t^T\right) n_t^T &= n_t^D,
\end{aligned}
\qquad (5.11)
$$

which state that the supply and demand of the illegal crop, illegal drug produced, and illegal drug trafficked must equate.

Competitive Equilibrium

A competitive equilibrium is a set of allocation rules $l_i^j = L_i^j(x)$, for $i = 1,2,3$ and $j = E,P,T,D$, a set of pricing functions $p = P(x), q = Q(x)$ and $r = R(x)$ and the laws of motion of the exogenous state variables $x_{+1} = X(x)$ such that

- Agents E, P, T, and D solve their respective optimization problems taking x and the form of the functions $P(x)$, $Q(x)$, $R(x)$, and $X(x)$ as given, with the equilibrium solution to this problem satisfying $l_i^j = L_i^j(x)$, for $i = 1, 2, 3$ and $j = E, P, T, D$.
- The market-clearing conditions (5.11) hold each period, and the legal good market clears:

$$h_t^E + h_t^P + h_t^T + h_t^D = C_t^E + C_t^P + C_t^T + C_t^D + G_t^S + \tau_t^D \pi_t^D r_t n_t^D. \qquad (5.12)$$

The final equation states that the amount produced by all agents must equate with the sum of private consumption, government expenditures, and the resources lost when agent D is detected consuming the illegal good. Thus, the equilibrium consumption of the legal good for each agent is given by

$$C_t^j = \left(1 - \pi_t^j\right)c_{0,t}^j + \pi_t^j c_{1,t}^j, \text{ for } j = E, P, T, D.$$

Functional Forms and Calibration

The model just described can be used to analyze any illegal market. Next, we focus on the analysis of the cocaine market for several reasons: (a) the cocaine market has agents in different locations (coca leaves are produced mainly in the Plurinational State of Bolivia, Colombia, and Peru); (b) cocaine is produced mainly in Colombia and is transported to consumption centers in the United States and Europe; (c) a relatively comprehensive database includes prices and quantities is available for this market (see the annex); and (d) because of the heterogeneity of agents involved, several supply and demand policies have been implemented or proposed.

Tables 5.1 and 5.2 present the functional forms and parameters used in the exercise. The utility functions of all agents display constant relative risk aversion with respect to the consumption of the legal good (with the risk aversion coefficient set equal to 2 in all cases). Agent D's utility also depends on leisure and on the stock and flow of consumption of the illegal drug.[11] Consistent with the empirical literature on rational addictions, the depreciation rate is high and set equal to 80 percent.

The production functions of the legal good are identical for all agents, and the share of labor is set equal to 0.3 (a number consistent with the macro literature). The production functions of the illegal goods for agents E, P, and T differ. Illegal crop production is assumed to be more labor intensive than the production of the illegal drug or the legal good. The production of w and n are less labor intensive. The parameters Aj (for $j = E, P, T$) are calibrated to match the average relative prices q/p and r/q observed on the data (7.19 and 17.45 respectively, see the annex).[12]

Government expenditures (G^s) are set such that, in steady state, ϕ is equal to 0.0025 (0.25 percent), which corresponds to the ratio between

Table 5.1. Functional Forms

Agents	Forms
E (crop producer)	$$u\left(c_i^E\right)=\frac{\left(c_i^E\right)^{1-\gamma_E}}{1-\gamma_E}, \text{ for } i=0,1$$ $$y^E = A_E\left(l_1^E\right)^{\upsilon_E}$$ $$h^E = B_E\left(l_2^E\right)^{\varphi_E}$$ $$\ln\left(\frac{\pi^E}{1-\pi^E}\right)=\alpha_1^E+\alpha_2^E\ln g^E+\alpha_3^E l_1^E+\alpha_4^E l_3^E$$
P (drug producer)	$$u\left(c_i^P\right)=\frac{\left(c_i^P\right)^{1-\gamma_P}}{1-\gamma_P}, \text{ for } i=0,1$$ $$w^P = A_P\left(l_1^P\right)^{\upsilon_P}\left(y^P\right)^{1-\upsilon_P}$$ $$h^P = B_P\left(l_2^P\right)^{\varphi_P}$$ $$\ln\left(\frac{\pi^P}{1-\pi^P}\right)=\alpha_1^P+\alpha_2^P\ln g^P+\alpha_3^P l_1^P+\alpha_4^P l_3^P$$
T (drug trafficker)	$$u\left(c_i^T\right)=\frac{\left(c_i^T\right)^{1-\gamma_T}}{1-\gamma_T}, \text{ for } i=0,1$$ $$n^T = A_T\left(l_1^T\right)^{\upsilon_T}\left(w^T\right)^{1-\upsilon_T}$$ $$h^T = B_T\left(l_2^T\right)^{\varphi_T}$$ $$\ln\left(\frac{\pi^T}{1-\pi^T}\right)=\alpha_1^T+\alpha_2^T\ln g^T+\alpha_3^T l_1^T+\alpha_4^T l_3^T$$
D (drug consumer)	$$u\left(c_i^D,n^D,l_1^D\right)=\frac{\left(c_i^D\right)^{1-\gamma_D}}{1-\gamma_D}+\psi_1\ln n^D+\psi_2\ln l_1^D, \text{ for } i=0,1$$ $$k^D\left(n^D,d^D\right)^D\zeta\ln d^D+(1-\zeta)\ln n^D$$ $$\ln\left(\frac{\theta^D}{1-\theta^D}\right)=\vartheta_1+\vartheta_2\ln g_2^D+\vartheta_3\ln d^D$$ $$h^D = B_D\left(l_2^D\right)^{\varphi_D}$$ $$\ln\left(\frac{\pi^D}{1-\pi^D}\right)=\alpha_1^D+\alpha_2^D\ln g_2^D+\alpha_3^D n^D+\alpha_4^D l_3^D$$

Source: Author.

total expenditures on drug control and private consumption for the year 2000.

Finally, the parameters that describe the laws of motion of the probabilities $\pi^j\left(j=E,P,T,D\right)$ and θ^D, were obtained by estimating econometric models with proportions data. To do so, time series realizations of proxies for the probabilities must be constructed. We proxied for π_t^E by

Table 5.2. Parameter Values

Parameter	Values
Preferences	$\beta = 0.95,\ \gamma_E = \gamma_P = \gamma_T = \gamma_D = 2$
	$\psi_1 = \psi_2 = 0.1,\ \delta = 0.8,\ \zeta = -0.3$
Illegal goods production functions	$A_E = 1, A_P = 0.24, A_T = 0.12$
	$\upsilon_E = 0.4, \upsilon_P = 0.2, \upsilon_T = 0.1$
Legal good production functions	$B_E = B_P = B_T = B_D = 70$
	$\varphi_E = \varphi_P = \varphi_T = \varphi_D = 0.3$
Government	$\tau^E = 0.6,\ \tau^P = 0.8,\ \tau^T = 0.9, \tau^D = 0.2$

Source: Author.

using the ratio of the surface of coca eradicated to the surface cultivated in Bolivia and Colombia; for π_t^P by using the ratio of the cocaine seized to that estimated to have been produced in Colombia; for π_t^T by using the ratio between the cocaine seized and that estimated to have been produced outside Colombia; for π_t^D by using the ratio of the number of people arrested for drug possession to the number of drug users; and for θ^D by using the percentage of chronic and occasional cocaine users.[13]

Econometric models using variables proxying for g^j were estimated, based on time series of probabilities. Table 5.3 reports the results of the models in which π^j $(j = E, P, T, D)$ were made to depend only on variables exogenous to the agent. In particular, π^E and π^P were found to depend on the component of international expenditures, π^T on expenditures on interdiction and domestic law, and π^D only on expenditures on domestic law.[14] For the estimation of the parameters that determine the probability of addiction, we need to construct time series for the stock of addictive good (d). We do it as follows:

$$d_t \simeq \sum_{i=0}^{2} (1-\delta)^i\, n_{t-i},$$

where (as noted earlier) δ was set equal to 0.8 and n_t is the consumption of cocaine. Finally, the constants on the specifications of the probabilities were set so that in equilibrium they matched the average probabilities of table A5.3 in the annex.[15]

Figure 5.1 presents the fitted probabilities π^j for each agent given different values of ln g. As can be inferred from the coefficients reported in

Table 5.3. Probabilities

Agents	Probabilities
E (crop producer)	$\alpha_2^E = 1.771, \; \alpha_3^E = \alpha_4^E = 0$ ${\scriptstyle(0.83)}$
P (drug producer)	$\alpha_2^P = 1.139, \; \alpha_3^P = \alpha_4^P = 0$ ${\scriptstyle(0.56)}$
T (drug trafficker)	$\alpha_2^T = 0.621, \; \alpha_3^T = \alpha_4^T = 0$ ${\scriptstyle(0.15)}$
D (drug consumer)	$\vartheta_2 = -0.890, \; \vartheta_3 = 1.288$ ${\scriptstyle(0.35)} {\scriptstyle(0.28)}$ $\alpha_2^D = 0.760, \; \alpha_3^D = \alpha_4^D = 0$ ${\scriptstyle(0.22)}$

Source: Author.
Note: Standard errors in parenthesis.

Figure 5.1. Fitted Probabilities and Expenditures
(logs of billions of US$)

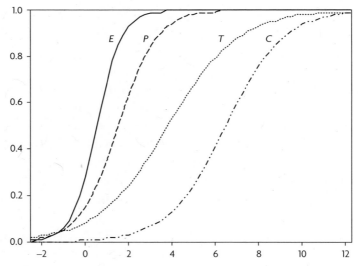

Source: Author.

table 5.3, expenditures are almost uniformly more effective in detecting crop production than drug production, drug trafficking, and drug consumption. The estimated probabilities imply that to obtain $\pi^E = 0.5$, the value of international expenditures should be three times higher ($1.7 billion) than it has been on average; to obtain $\pi^P = 0.5$, the value of international expenditures should be 8.1 times higher ($4.6 billion) than it has been on average; to obtain $\pi^T = 0.5$, the value of expenditures on interdiction and domestic law should be 5.8 times higher ($46.3 billion) than it has been on average; and to obtain $\pi^D = 0.5$, the value of domestic law expenditures should be 107 times higher ($653.9 billion) than it has been on average. Of course, those figures convey only an idea of the resources that would be needed to make these activities riskier without assessing the means by which they would be financed and their impact on welfare. That question is addressed in the next section.

Assessment of the Effects of Alternative Policies

Several policies have been proposed and enacted in the war on drugs. In this section, we use the general equilibrium model presented earlier along with the functional forms and parameter values of the previous section to evaluate the long-run effects of alternative policies.[16] Given the structure of the model, we consider three types of policies and evaluate their effects on the actions taken by each agent and the prices that are determined as a result:

- *Increased risk*: The first set of policies evaluates the effects of increases in different components of G^S. This exercise evaluates the effect of policies that affect the risks involved in each activity but maintains the penalties (τ^j) constant. Because the increased expenditure must be financed, we also compute the increases required in the consumption tax on the legal good.
- *Stiffer penalties*: Next, we consider the case in which the level of expenditure is maintained constant (thus, not changing the risks involved in each activity), but the penalties of the agents when they are caught are increased.
- *Legalization*: There are two equivalent ways by which legalization can be modeled. One is to force π^j to be equal to 0, in which case the level of τ^j would be irrelevant. The other is to set τ^j to 0, in which case the level of π^j would be irrelevant.

Making Illegal Activities Riskier

Because our specifications of π^j depend on different components of government expenditures, we make an activity riskier by increasing the appropriate expenditure. We also compute the new level of the consumption tax required to finance this increase.

The effect of increasing risks in a partial equilibrium model can be compared to an adverse supply shock that reduces the quantity produced. In general equilibrium, an increased risk for one agent may actually foster illegal activities by the other (as the latter's relative risk has decreased).

Five experiments are conducted by increasing different components of G^S. They share the characteristic that overall expenditures are increased by 10 percent (table 5.4). The first experiment increases all the components of G^S proportionally to their average share. In this case, the risks of producing the illegal crop and producing, trafficking, and consuming the illegal drug are all higher. As expenditures on prevention are also increased, the probability of addiction decreases. As the share of international expenditures (the most effective in increasing risk) is relatively small, a 10 percent increase in overall expenditures produces relatively modest increases in risks. Production of the illegal goods (and the consumption of the illegal good) decreases, and the relative prices of the illegal goods increase with respect to the legal good. The net result for agent D is that it decreases its expenditures on the illegal good, providing an income effect that makes him demand more of the legal good. Even though agents E, P, and T reallocate labor from the illegal to the legal activity and produce more of the legal good, it is not automatic that their consumption of the legal good will increase.[17] As the increased consumption of the legal good by agent D is relatively modest, financing this policy would imply that the consumption tax must be almost doubled (from its original level). In terms of welfare, agents E and T would be worse off as they experience the highest increased risks, and agents D and P would be better off.[18] The bottom line of this exercise is that if government expenditures continue to be distributed as they are—and the structure of our model provides a reasonable approximation of the long-run characteristics of this market—drug producers and consumers would favor continuing this policy.

We arrive at similar conclusions with the second experiment in which the increased expenditures are channeled solely to international antinarcotics expenditures. In this case, the risks for agents, and particularly for E, increase substantially, leaving the risks for other agents unchanged.

Table 5.4. The Effects of Increased Risks

	Proportional	International	Interdiction	Domestic Law	Prevention
			Illegal good		
y^E	−1.22	−5.34	−0.73	−0.77	−0.82
w^P	−4.10	−29.17	−0.99	−1.04	−1.10
n^T	−5.04	−35.73	−1.12	−1.18	−1.25
n^D	−6.20	−35.73	−3.13	−3.18	−1.25
			Prices		
P	1.52	33.00	−1.60	−1.67	−1.78
Q	3.29	58.50	−1.50	−1.58	−1.67
R	4.87	48.01	2.81	2.63	−3.71
			Probabilities		
π^E	4.92	44.23	0.00	0.00	0.00
π^P	1.54	15.70	0.00	0.00	0.00
π^T	1.06	0.00	1.77	1.77	0.00
π^D	0.21	0.00	0.00	0.50	0.00
θ^D	−0.28	−0.87	−0.08	−0.08	−0.81
			Legal good		
C^E	−0.39	−1.34	−0.34	−0.36	−0.38
C^P	0.17	2.44	−0.10	−0.11	−0.11
C^T	−0.05	−1.36	0.57	0.50	−1.37
C^D	1.43	4.24	0.33	0.61	4.28
			Welfare		
E	−	−	−	−	−
P	+	+	−	−	−
T	−	−	+	+	−
D	+	−	+	+	+
Expenditure[a]	−1.33	−4.56	−0.07	−0.30	−4.93
Tax[b]	0.02	0.01	0.02	0.02	0.01

Source: Author.
Note: E, P, D, and T are actors, and + and − refer to improvement or deterioration in their welfare.
a. Change of expenditures of agent D on the illegal good (in terms of the legal good).
b. Change on the consumption tax needed to finance government expenditures.

In equilibrium, production and consumption of illegal goods fall drastically, while their relative prices increase. The income effect of reduced expenditure on the illegal good makes agent D consume more of the legal good than in the first experiment, thus making the increased tax on the consumption of the legal good smaller. However, in this experiment, the only agent that is better off now (due to favorable changes in relative prices) is agent P. Agent D is worse off because the decreased probability of addiction does not compensate for the reduction of consumption of the illegal good. Summing up, the drug producer (not the crop producer) might actually desire a policy that makes it riskier to produce the drug.

The next two experiments focus on increasing the expenditures on interdiction (increasing the risk of the illegal activity of agent T) and on domestic law (increasing the risk of the illegal activities for agents T and D). Those experiments can be seen as negative demand shocks for agents P and E, decreasing the relative prices of the illegal goods they produce. Agent T, however, reallocates labor from illegal to legal activities, but because r rises and the reduction of expenditures on the illegal good by agent D is relatively modest, agents T and D are better off in both cases.

The last experiment increases expenditures solely on prevention, which decreases the probability of addiction. This experiment produces a reduction in the demand for and relative prices of the illegal goods. It makes agents E, P, and T reallocate labor from illegal to legal activities and makes them worse off. Only agent D is better off, because the decreased expenditure on the illegal good produces an income effect that increases his demand for leisure and consumption of the legal good more than any other of the experiments considered. This last fact makes the increase in the consumption tax more modest than in the other cases.

Imposing Stiffer Penalties

The second set of policies considered does not make the illegal activities riskier, but it makes them costlier if the agents are caught. We consider three experiments in which the penalties for performing illegal activities by agents E, P, and T are increased (table 5.5).[19]

Stiffer penalties on the crop producer can be seen as a negative supply shock for him. Production of the illegal crop decreases, and its relative price (p) increases. The increased cost for agent P makes him produce less of the illegal good (another negative supply-side shock) and increases the price of the illegal good sold (q) but not to the same extent of the increase in p. The same argument can be made for agent T. The increased price also reduces the demand for the illegal good by agent D, making

Table 5.5. The Effects of Stiffer Penalties

	$\tau^E = 1$	$\tau^P = 1$	$\tau^T = 1$
	Illegal good		
y^E	−2.92	−1.28	−4.65
w^P	−8.35	−1.74	−6.23
n^T	−7.59	−3.00	−7.01
n^D	−7.59	−3.00	−9.88
	Prices		
P	10.83	−2.79	−9.72
Q	8.52	3.20	−9.05
R	7.15	2.70	9.55
	Probabilities		
θ^D	−0.19	−0.08	−0.25
	Legal good		
C^E	0.47	−0.59	−2.03
C^P	−0.02	1.11	−0.56
C^T	−0.28	−0.11	3.87
C^D	0.85	0.33	1.11
	Welfare		
E	−	−	−
P	−	+	−
T	−	−	+
D	+	+	+
Expenditure[a]	−0.98	−0.38	−1.28
Tax[b]	−0.002	−0.001	−0.003

Source: Author.
Note: E, P, D, and T are actors, and + and − refer to improvement or deterioration in their welfare.
a. Change of expenditures of agent D on the illegal good (in terms of the legal good).
b. Change on the consumption tax needed to finance government expenditures.

him consume the legal good as a substitute. As government expenditures are not changed and the consumption of the legal good by agent D increases, the consumption tax decreases. Agent D is the only one better off in this experiment.

The other two experiments are very interesting because they provide results that can be obtained only when considering general equilibrium models. The second experiment imposes stiffer penalties on the drug producer (agent P). As it makes his activity costlier, its production falls and its relative price increases (q). This precise experiment, however, can be seen as a negative demand shock for agent E. The result is that the production of the illegal crop falls as does its relative price (p). As a result, the relative price q/p increases, and the consumption of the legal good by agent P increases, making him better off, not worse off, with this policy.[20] Agent T is worse off given that this experiment can be seen as a negative supply shock and that the relevant relative price for him (r/q) increases. Finally, agent D is better off, given that the increased price of the illegal good makes him consume less of it and more of leisure and the legal good.

The last experiment considers increasing penalties for the drug trafficker. Following the reasoning provided above, this increased cost reduces the demand and price of the drug produced by agent P, which in turn reduces the demand and price of the illegal crop produced by agent E (making them worse off). However, as the activities of agent T are costlier, the relative price r increases, and even though the volume of drug trafficked by agent T decreases, he is better off as his terms of trade have improved (r/q), and he can consume more of the legal good. As in other experiments, the consumption tax and expenditures on the illegal drug by agent D decrease, making him consume more of the legal good and demand more leisure (making him better off).

Increasing Legalization

The last set of exercises considers the progressive legalization of each of the activities (table 5.6). It starts by legalizing crop production[21]; then it legalizes drug production as well and follows with legalizing drug trafficking and finally drug consumption. The last exercise takes into account that legalization makes expenditures on everything but prevention and treatment unproductive. Given that condition, we also consider the case of legalizing all activities and allocating all the expenditures to prevention (to reduce the probability of addiction).

Legalizing crop production increases the production and consumption of illegal drugs and decreases their relative prices. Notably, as p decreases significantly, consumption of the legal good by agent E decreases. Even so, as this is no longer a risky activity, the welfare of the crop producer increases. Production and trafficking of the illegal good also increase, and their relative prices fall (though not as sharply as p does).

Table 5.6. The Effects of Legalization

	E	E + P	E + P + T	E + P + T + D	E + P + T + D + Prevention
			Illegal good		
y^E	1.18	2.92	18.13	18.89	12.57
w^P	10.07	12.62	35.78	36.98	27.13
n^T	9.08	17.79	45.32	46.77	34.92
n^D	9.08	17.79	85.78	87.64	72.48
			Prices		
P	−10.68	−7.36	28.34	30.51	13.69
Q	−8.59	−15.55	11.37	12.99	0.41
R	−7.28	−13.24	−41.21	−40.42	−46.54
			Probabilities		
θ^D	0.23	0.46	2.36	2.41	−1.34
			Legal good		
C^E	−0.12	0.67	9.96	10.57	6.00
C^P	0.03	−1.41	−0.76	−0.71	−1.06
C^T	0.32	0.63	−14.19	−14.18	−14.28
C^D	−0.98	−1.87	−7.71	−11.44	6.54
			Welfare		
E	+	+	+	+	+
P	+	−	−	−	−
T	+	+	−	−	−
D	−	−	−	−	+
Expenditure[a]	1.14	2.19	9.23	11.79	−7.80
Tax[b]	0.002	0.005	0.020	0.030	−0.015

Source: Author.
Note: E, P, D, and T are actors, and + and − refer to improvement or deterioration in their welfare.
a. Change of expenditures of agent D on the illegal good (in terms of the legal good).
b. Change on the consumption tax needed to finance government expenditures.

Agents P and T increase their consumption of the legal good and are better off in this experiment. The only loser here is the drug consumer, because the increased expenditure on the illegal good forces him to demand less leisure and consume less of the legal good. Furthermore, and as a consequence of the latter, the consumption tax must also increase.

When crop production and drug production are legal, production and consumption of illegal drugs increase, and their prices with respect to the legal good decrease, especially q. This in turn makes the drug producer worse off in this experiment. The winners are the crop producer and the drug trafficker, who obtain more income because of the increased demand for their products. As in the first case, agent D is worse off because he expends more for the illegal good, consumes less of the legal good, demands less leisure, and is more likely to become addicted.

In the third and fourth experiments, drug trafficking and consumption are also legalized. In these cases, the only winner is agent E. What happens is that as the relative price of the illegal good decreases significantly for agent D and his demand for it increases, the trafficker and the drug producer demand more of the production of agent E, increasing the price p. Agent E then has more resources that he can allocate to consume the legal good. Agent P also produces more of the illegal good, increasing q, but its costs (p) increase more. As a result, agent P consumes less of the legal good and is worse off. Agent T is in an even more uncomfortable situation, as the price at which he sells his product decreases (r), while the cost of the input he uses increases (q). As in the first exercise, agent D is also worse off as he expends more on the illegal good, sees the consumption tax increased, reduces the consumption of the legal good, and is more likely to become addicted.

The previous exercises considered that even though the formerly illegal activities were legalized, the government was still expending the same amounts on interdiction, domestic law, and international expenditures. As these resources would cease to be necessary, they could be used in the only productive activity left (prevention) that could reduce the probability of the addiction of agent D. When that happens, even though the production of the previously illegal goods and their prices follow the same pattern of the previous exercise, the increased expenditure on prevention now reduces the probability of addiction. This simple difference accounts for the fact that now agent D expends less on the illegal good (even though he consumes more of the drug). This income effect makes him consume more of the consumption good, demand more leisure, and witness a reduction in the consumption tax. As a result, agents D and E benefit from this experiment, while the trafficker and drug producer are still worse off. Thus, without resorting to arguments such as imperfect competition and without (at least explicitly) considering benefits that could follow from reduced crimes, legalization is bad for traffickers and drug producers but is good for the crop producer and may be good for the drug consumer.

Conclusion

As drug use is blamed for a broad range of personal and social ills, governments have prohibited their production, sale, and use. Among the policy measures adopted to decrease the demand for illegal drugs are stiffer penalties on consumers, treatment of heavy users, and educational campaigns. Policies intended to reduce the supply include crop eradication, interdiction, and stiffer penalties on producers and traffickers.

Although significant resources have been allocated to these activities, the results appear not to be encouraging. More important, a coherent general equilibrium approach that can help assess the effects of alternative policies has not been developed, and the analysis has focused on partial equilibrium models. This failure is dangerous because policies not only determine responses by the actors but also modify prices and change incentives. In general equilibrium, prices and actions are endogenous to policies.

This chapter develops a general equilibrium model that considers the production, trafficking, and consumption of illegal goods. The model uses characteristics of popular partial equilibrium models (such as production under uncertainty and rational addictions) and integrates them in a coherent framework.

The model is calibrated to characterize the market for cocaine and is used to analyze the effects of three types of policies: making the illegal activities riskier, increasing the penalties for conducting illegal activities, and legalizing previously illegal activities. Assessing the effects of these policies using the powerful tool of a general equilibrium model provides illuminating (and in some cases surprising) results.

For example, increased expenditures intended to deter illegal activities may actually make drug producers better off. What appears to be consistent in all scenarios is that increasing the risk of any illegal activity makes crop producers worse off. Imposing stiffer penalties on illegal activities, however, makes crop producers worse off and drug consumers better off, while stiffer penalties on drug producers and traffickers may make them better off. Finally, legalization of previously illegal activities is good for crop producers and is generally disliked by drug producers and traffickers. As the consumption of illegal drugs can increase substantially, the drug consumer is usually worse off. Nevertheless, if resources were invested in diminishing the probability of addiction, legalization might be good for the consumer.[22]

Even though the model is quite general, it is used in a narrow context. In particular, we do not consider strategic interactions by which agents may invest resources that allow them to reduce the probability of getting caught. We also consider that all the markets are competitive. The chapter also addresses steady-state (long-run) effects and does not analyze transitional dynamics. Furthermore, even though this structure lends itself to incorporating more dynamic and stochastic features (technology shocks and time-to-grow constraints, among others), these and other features are promising avenues for further research.

Annex: The Data

The annex presents the series used to calibrate the model and estimate the probabilities.

- Government expenditures, table A5.1
  - *Total*: U.S. government expenditures on controlling marijuana, cocaine, crack, stimulants, LSD, PCP, and heroin
  - *Prevention*: Development and implementation of programs that prevent illicit drug use, keep drugs out of neighborhoods and schools, and provide a safe and secure environment for all people
  - *Treatment*: Inclusion of behavioral therapy (such as counseling, cognitive therapy, or psychotherapy), medications, or a combination
  - *Domestic law*: Cocaine seizures, asset seizures, and arrests of drug dealers and their agents by federal, state, and local law enforcement agencies; imprisonment of convicted drug dealers and their agents
  - *International*: Coca leaf eradication; seizures of coca base, cocaine paste, and the final cocaine product in the source countries (Bolivia, Colombia, and Peru)

Table A5.1. Distribution of the Expenditures of the U.S. Government on Control of Marijuana, Cocaine, Crack, Stimulants, LSD, PCP, and Heroin, 1986–2003 (*billions of 2000 dollars*)

Year	Prevention	Treatment	Domestic Law	International	Interdiction	Total
1986	0.3	1.1	1.8	0.2	1.2	4.5
1987	0.8	1.4	2.7	0.3	2.0	7.2
1988	0.8	1.4	3.0	0.3	1.4	6.9
1989	1.1	1.8	3.9	0.4	2.0	9.3
1990	1.8	2.4	5.7	0.7	2.3	12.9
1991	2.1	2.6	5.8	0.8	2.6	13.9
1992	2.1	2.9	6.4	0.8	2.4	14.6
1993	2.1	3.0	7.1	0.6	1.8	14.5
1994	2.1	3.1	7.1	0.4	1.5	14.2
1995	2.0	3.3	7.9	0.3	1.4	15.0
1996	1.8	3.1	8.1	0.3	1.5	14.8
1997	2.0	3.3	8.5	0.4	1.8	16.2
1998	2.3	3.5	9.0	0.5	1.7	17.0
1999	2.0	3.0	9.1	0.6	1.9	16.6
2000	2.1	3.1	8.6	0.8	2.4	17.0
2001	2.5	3.2	9.2	0.6	2.0	17.6
2002	2.0	3.0	3.1	1.0	1.8	11.0
2003	1.8	3.1	2.8	1.0	1.8	10.5
Average	13.2	21.0	45.4	4.6	15.8	100.0

Source: Author.

Note: Average is expressed in percentage points of total expenditures.

- o *Interdiction*: Cocaine seizures and asset seizures by the U.S. Customs, Service, the U.S. Coast Guard, the U.S. Army, and the U.S. Immigration and Naturalization Service
- Prices, table A5.2
  - o q/p: Ratio of the price of cocaine exported from Colombia to the price of coca base
  - o r/p: Ratio of the consumer price of cocaine to the price of cocaine exported from Colombia

Table A5.2. Relative Prices, 1981–98

Year	q/p	r/q
1981	2.57	8.13
1982	2.58	8.33
1983	1.57	14.78
1984	1.86	14.54
1985	4.65	14.91
1986	3.61	21.00
1987	4.55	19.47
1988	4.49	19.83
1989	5.26	20.55
1990	6.92	24.27
1991	7.01	20.64
1992	8.33	20.36
1993	13.20	18.09
1994	10.43	17.81
1995	10.05	18.67
1996	16.15	16.67
1997	13.46	18.57
1998	12.65	17.43
Average	7.19	17.45

Source: Author.

- Risks, table A5.3
  - π^E: Ratio of surface of coca leaves eradicated to the surface cultivated in Bolivia and Colombia (see Bureau for International Narcotics and Law Enforcement Affairs)
  - π^P: Ratio of cocaine seized to that estimated to be produced in Colombia
  - π^T: Ratio of cocaine seized to that estimated to be produced (excluding Colombia)
  - π^D: Ratio of the number of arrests resulting from drug possession to the number of drug users (see Uniform Crime Reports)
  - θ^D: Percentage of chronic and occasional cocaine users (see ONDCP 2009)

Table A5.3. Risks
(*percentage points*)

Year	π^E	π^P	π^T	π^D	θ^D
1986	n.a.	1.2	16.6	n.a.	n.a.
1987	2.3	2.6	17.3	n.a.	n.a.
1988	2.0	5.2	20.1	n.a.	n.a.
1989	3.2	8.0	22.1	2.5	n.a.
1990	9.1	10.1	23.3	2.4	2.7
1991	7.0	13.7	17.5	2.0	2.9
1992	4.7	6.3	22.5	2.5	2.2
1993	3.5	5.6	23.2	2.8	2.0
1994	6.0	6.7	35.6	3.5	1.9
1995	12.5	7.6	27.5	3.8	1.9
1996	10.2	7.1	31.4	3.7	2.0
1997	17.2	8.0	33.6	4.0	1.9
1998	24.1	15.5	n.a.	3.7	1.9
1999	29.2	n.a.	n.a.	3.7	1.6
2000	26.7	n.a.	n.a.	3.7	1.3
2001	33.1	n.a.	n.a.	n.a.	1.6
2002	44.8	n.a.	n.a.	n.a.	2.2
2003	51.0	n.a.	n.a.	n.a.	n.a.
Average	16.9	7.5	24.2	3.2	2.0

Source: Author.
Note: n.a. = data not available.

Notes

1. The main difference among these components is that expenditures on domestic law are incurred inside the United States, expenditures on interdiction are incurred along the U.S. border, and expenditures on international antinarcotics efforts are incurred outside the United States (see annex 5.1).
2. The preferences of drug users in the United States have changed in the past years. On the one hand, cocaine use has decreased and has been substituted by consumption of synthetic drugs that are more potent, addictive, cheaper, and easier to produce. On the other hand, consumption of cocaine in Europe and Latin America has continued to increase.
3. Examples of theoretical and empirical papers dealing with drug consumption are Becker and Murphy (1988); Becker, Grossman, and Murphy (1991); Orphanides and Zervos (1995); Grossman, Chaloupka, and Brown (1998); and Beherens and others (1999). Examples of models for drug trafficking (distribution) are Caulkins

(1993, 1997). Models that discuss optimal allocations of resources for prevention, treatment, and enforcement are Rydell, Caulkins, and Everingham (1996); Behrens and others (2000); and Tragler, Caulkins, and Freichtinger (2001).

4. The choice of this drug is due to the availability of information. The model is general enough so that it can be used to study other illegal markets.

5. This variable can be seen as proxying for activities such as violence and corruption of law enforcement officials and politicians, among others.

6. The timing of uncertainty is such that once the agent commits resources to each activity, a fraction π^E is caught and $1 - \pi^E$ is not. Note that π^E is, in equilibrium, a function of the decisions of the agent. The same is true for the problems faced by the other agents.

7. For brevity, time t subscripts are eliminated.

8. We assume that n is different from w as the trafficker may modify the properties of w (such as "quality").

9. Because this agent does not have to devote resources to produce illegal goods, we force him to derive utility from leisure to avoid trivial solutions for the labor supply.

10. The difference between g_1^D and g_2^D is that the first considers expenditures that make the demand of the illegal good riskier for the consumer, while the second deals with expenditures that diminish the effects of its use (for example through educational campaigns or treatment for heavy users).

11. It is assumed that agent D is the only demander of the illegal good. Furthermore, it is assumed that the illegal crop is used exclusively to produce the illegal drug. GTZ (a German technical cooperation agency) estimates that no more than 6 percent of the total production of coca leaves is used for traditional consumption in Bolivia, Colombia, and Peru.

12. The model assumes perfect competition in every market. Thus, markups in each stage are due solely to technological and risk factors.

13. The annex presents the time series constructed and sources used.

14. As the coefficients α_3^j, α_4^j are restricted to be equal to 0 (avoiding strategic interactions), the optimization problem of the agents with respect to the choice of l_3^j is trivial $\left(l_3^j = 0\right)$, because there are no benefits to devoting resources to reduce the probability of getting caught. Models with endogenous probabilities are not considered here.

15. In particular, the constants were set so that in steady state $\pi^E = 0.169$, $\pi^P = 0.075$, $\pi^T = 0.242$, $\pi^D = 0.032$, and $\theta^D = 0.020$.

16. Transitional dynamics are not considered in this chapter.

17. Agent D actually reduces his production of the legal good given that the positive income effect of the reduced expenditure on the illegal good makes him demand more leisure.

18. The case of agent P is interesting. The modest increase in the probability of getting caught, compounded by an increase in the relative price of the price at which it sells the good he produces (q) with respect to the price at which he buys the input (p), makes him actually better off with this policy.

19. Stiffer penalties such as "three strikes and you are out" come to mind. We do not report the case of stiffer penalties on consumption as in our model it can be seen as a consumption tax.
20. This is the case given that π^p does not change.
21. The president of Bolivia (and acting president of the union of coca leaf producers), Evo Morales, has been flirting with the idea of legalizing coca leaf production, although he is said to vehemently oppose cocaine production and trafficking. Because most of the coca crop production is destined for cocaine production, this attitude can be considered similar to that of a missile producer that favors their production but vehemently opposes their firing.
22. One crucial positive effect of legalization, namely the reduction of crime and violence, is overlooked here.

References

Becker, G., M. Grossman, and K. Murphy. 1991. "Rational Addiction and the Effect of Price on Consumption." *American Economic Review Papers and Proceedings* 81(2): 237–41.

Becker, G., and K. Murphy. 1988. "A Theory of Rational Addiction." *Journal of Political Economy* 96 (4): 675–700.

Behrens, D., J. Caulkins, G. Tragler, and G. Feichtinger. 2000. "Optimal Control of Drug Epidemics: Prevent and Treat—But Not at the Same Time?" *Management Science* 46 (3): 333–47.

Behrens, D., J. Caulkins, G. Tragler, J. Haunschmied, and G. Feichtinger. 1999. "A Dynamic Model of Drug Initiation: Implications for Treatment and Drug Control." *Mathematical Biosciences* 159: 1–20.

Bureau for International Narcotics and Law Enforcement Affairs. "International Narcotics Control Strategic Report." Annual reports for various years.

Caulkins, J. 1993. "Local Drug Markets: Response to Focused Police Enforcement." *Operations Research* 41 (5): 848–63.

———. 1997. "Modeling the Domestic Distribution Network for Illicit Drugs." *Management Science* 43 (10): 1364–71.

Chavas, J., and M. Holt. 1990. "Acreage Decisions under Risk: The Case of Corn and Soybeans." *American Journal of Agricultural Economics* 72: 529–38.

Federal Bureau of Investigation. "Uniform Crime Reports." Annual reports for various years.

Grossman, M., F. Chaloupka, and C. Brown. 1998. "The Demand for Cocaine by Young Adults: A Rational Addiction Approach." *Journal of Health Economics* 17 (4): 427–74.

Miron, J., and S. Zwiebel. 1995. "The Economic Case against Drug Prohibition." *Journal of Economic Perspectives* 9 (4): 175–92.

ONDCP (Office of National Drug Control Policy). "National Drug Strategy: Budget Summary." *Annual Reports, 1988–2005*. Washington, DC: ONDCP.

————. 2009. "National Drug Control Strategy, Data Supplement 2009." Washington, DC: ONDCP.

Orphanides, A., and D. Zervos. 1995. "Rational Addictions with Learning and Regret." *Journal of Political Economy* 103 (4): 739–58.

Rydell, P., J. Caulkins, and S. Everingham. 1996. "Enforcement or Treatment: Modeling the Relative Efficacy of Alternatives for Controlling Cocaine." *Operations Research* 44 (5): 687–95.

Tragler, G., J. Caulkins, and G. Feichtinger. 2001. "Optimal Dynamic Allocation of Treatment and Enforcement in Illicit Drug Control." *Operations Research* 49 (3): 352–62.

6

Competitive Advantages in the Production and Trafficking of Coca-Cocaine and Opium-Heroin in Afghanistan and the Andean Countries

Francisco E. Thoumi

Coca can grow in at least 30 countries and poppy in at least 90, but most countries do not grow those crops despite the profitability. Furthermore, cocaine refining from coca paste and heroin refining from opium can take place anywhere in the world. Profitability, natural resources, and the availability of labor skills do not explain the high concentration of coca-cocaine and opium-heroin in producing countries. If those three were determining factors, illegal drugs industries would be spread around the world, and all countries that could be involved in it would be. Instead, with the exception of marijuana, plant-based drug production does not take place in many countries; indeed, it is remarkably concentrated, and most countries that can produce drugs do not. Today, Colombia produces about 70 percent of the world's coca and cocaine, and Afghanistan produces more than 80 percent of the opium poppy and heroin.

For comments on earlier drafts, the author thanks Marcela Anzola, Phil Keefer, and an anonymous referee who are exonerated of all responsibilities for the ideas herein expressed.

Brief Overview of Drug Production

In 1970, Colombia was not known for its production of illegal drugs, and Afghanistan had been a minor producer of opium for a long time.[1] According to the United Nations Office on Drugs and Crime (UNODC), opium was not really a "traditional" crop in Afghanistan and was not cultivated in most parts of the country until the 1990s. Unlike most countries in the region, Afghanistan did not have much of an "opium culture," and its consumption remained relatively low (UNODC 2003, 87–88). Only in the past 35 years have those two countries became large producers of opium poppy or coca and significant players in international drug markets.

Some 100 years ago, when cocaine had extensive medical applications, the largest exporters of coca to the drug labs in Europe and the United States were the islands of Java and Sumatra. Coca also grew on Formosa and in other Southeast Asian nations. Bolivia and Peru had been the original coca exporters, but in the 1870s the Dutch took coca plants from Surinam to their Southeast Asian colonies and developed plantations there (Gagliano 1994). The War of the Pacific (1879–83) blocked exports from Bolivia and Peru, but coca continued to be produced for domestic demand, mainly traditional uses within native communities. When illegal cocaine demand surged in the 1970s, coca production expanded in Bolivia and Peru, and Colombia became the center of cocaine refining and trafficking. Although Bolivia and Peru had cocaine traffickers, they did not match the large Colombian cartels, and many of them were subordinate to the Colombian organizations. In the 1990s, the Colombian coca crop also expanded; by the late 1990s, that country became the largest coca producer in the world. Today, cocaine is illegal, and none of the Southeast Asian countries that supplied the legal cocaine industry grows coca. In contrast, Colombia did not export a single coca leaf or a gram of cocaine while such exportation was legal.

The main objective of this chapter is to explore the reasons coca and poppy cultivation and cocaine and heroin refining are concentrated in only a few countries, as we look at case studies for four countries. The explanation is rooted in institutional economics that emphasize the importance of formal and informal norms of behavior. Those norms are, in turn, rooted in historical and sociological factors that weaken the enforcement capacity of the central government, strengthen informal norms at the expense of formal ones, and favor the emergence of violent networks that have a competitive advantage in trafficking. The case studies herein illustrate how those factors—more than the technical conditions required to cultivate and manufacture plant-based illegal drugs—drive cultivation and trafficking location. The case studies about Afghanistan, Colombia, Bolivia, and Peru also demonstrate a vicious circle: the emergence of the illegal drug industry has a corrosive effect on political and social organizations precisely because it changes informal norms to make lawbreaking and violence more socially acceptable.

The Causality of Plant-Based Drug Production

In countries that produce coca-cocaine and opium-heroin, the formal rules emanating from the state conflict significantly with the norms by which individuals are socialized through tribe, family, religious groups, political parties, and other entities.[2] Those conflicts vary among countries. Afghan tribal regions have implicit norms that oppose many of those of the central state. The same occurs within the native and peasant communities of Bolivia and Peru. In Colombia, the situation is more complex. As shown in the case study, Colombia never had strong tribal loyalties, and its geography produced many autonomous urban settlements that influenced surrounding regions but were highly independent from the central state. In Colombia, the violence and upheaval that accompanied modernization weakened informal norms. In many regions of Colombia, the state has not been able to resolve that upheaval and to impose the rule of law. Contraband and other illegal activities have been socially legitimate, and many formal laws and rules have been de facto illegitimate. Informal norms vary among regions, generating further clashes among norms.

Conditions Conducive to Developing an Illegal Drug Industry

In the four countries, one can find some strong institutions such as the central bank, some courts, or producer associations that might project an image of strength. The problem, however, is not just the lack of strong organizations but the conflicts among norms. Conflicts between formal and informal norms are sometimes "settled" when pressure groups succeed in changing formal norms, often resulting in unclear laws and regulations that allow multiple interpretations or that respond to the interests of one pressure group at the expense of another. Such laws further weaken the citizenry's support for the rule of law. It is easy to see how the clash of norms could encourage the cultivation of plant-based illegal drugs by farmers. The enforcement of antidrug laws becomes more costly and draconian as the illegitimacy of those laws, or simple indifference to them, increases in a society.

Conflicts among norms and their erosion facilitate the emergence of an illegal drug industry. The cultivation of plant-based illegal drugs, like that of any agricultural product, requires markets for the processing, transport, and sale of the products. The organization of these activities is not trivial. Producing illicit opium-heroin and coca-cocaine requires the performance of a series of illegal activities:

- purchasing illegal inputs, which are frequently controlled substances and have to be smuggled or obtained from an underground market
- cultivating illicit crops
- creating clandestine manufacturing facilities
- developing domestic and international criminal distribution networks to sell at home and to smuggle and distribute drugs abroad
- transporting illegally obtained currency across international borders and exchanging these funds from one currency to another without revealing their origin
- laundering and investing illegally obtained funds
- managing portfolios of illegally obtained capital

This chapter contends that the need to minimize risks in performing such illicit activities determines the location of the illegal industry.

Factors in Determining the Location of Illegal Drug Activity

The successful performance of these tasks requires special "illegal skills" to develop illegal business organizations and the social support networks to protect the industry from law enforcement efforts, to provide contract enforcement and conflict resolution systems within the criminal organizations, and to have the will to break economic laws and regulations and to use violence if necessary (Thoumi 2003a, 56). Individuals are more likely to have these skills—and to be organized—in countries with a history of violence. In the country cases, Colombia and Afghanistan exhibit the most extreme and long-standing history of violence, internal conflicts, and wars and the most pervasive presence of traffickers. Violence has one additional and important effect that is evident in Afghanistan: it drives down the rates of return on legitimate forms of economic activity, further weakening norms of compliance with laws that forbid illegitimate forms of activity. The emergence of drug markets also requires central governments that are too weak to break up trafficking organizations.

In brief, the argument developed in the context of four case studies is that illegality is a key factor in determining the location of the coca and poppy fields and of the refining and trafficking activities. A combination of factors such as geography, history, institutions, and culture has resulted in strong competitive advantages for the illegal production and trafficking of poppy and heroin in Afghanistan; of coca and cocaine in Colombia; and of coca, coca paste, and cocaine base in Bolivia and Peru.

The four case studies also illustrate that many factors that influence the emergence of an illegal drug industry are themselves affected by that industry once it is in place. For example, the weakness of central governments encourages the emergence of illegal drugs, but traffickers can and do infiltrate governments and do purchase or extort government leniency in the enforcement of antitrafficking laws. Similarly, norms of non-compliance with central government laws may deepen and spread as the share of the economy devoted to illegal activity grows. The illegal drugs have a number of direct effects, among them:

- influencing and corrupting politics
- changing social attitudes toward compliance with the law, thus weakening the rule of law
- increasing expectations for quick profits that can easily lead to speculative investments
- increasing criminality and violence
- requiring shifts in the government budget from investment and social expenditures to law enforcement
- increasing the risk of expanding local drug consumption
- strengthening some social groups (overtly criminal and otherwise) and weakening others

Such negative changes are cumulative through time and produce changes in institutions and culture. This vicious circle exacerbates the concentration of the illegal drug industry in a few countries: countries that have moderately favorable conditions for the emergence of a drug industry become ever more favorable as the drug industry expands. This chapter attempts to sort through the multiple causal chains at work in the emergence of a drug industry.

Two Caveats

Two caveats are in order. First, an important characteristic of the structure of illegal activities is that they do not have a sufficiency factor. In other words, there is no factor that once in place will always result in an illegal activity. There are two necessary factors: an illegal demand and an illegal supply. Both require a wide gap between formal and informal norms, at least within a part of the society. In addition, the illegal supply requires informal norms that disregard negative effects on others or that tolerate the will to commit crime to achieve a so-called higher goal, the ability to develop illegal networks and links, and the physical resources to produce illegal drugs. To develop coca and poppy plantings and cocaine and heroin production and exports, countries must have the full set of necessary conditions. A wide spectrum of other factors—poverty, economic crises, and the like—are also possible contributors. Those factors might trigger the development of the illegal industry only if all the necessary conditions are present.

Because no single factor is sufficient, a society with all the conditions for the development of the illegal industry may not have, in fact, developed it. Such a society, however, is very vulnerable and could develop one. The appearance of a new contributing factor, for example, may be the trigger. Criminal activities develop as a result of evolutionary processes, not Newtonian ones with well-defined causality of the type "$Y = f(X)$"— that is, "if X, then Y happens." For that reason, some societies with all the necessary conditions for the development of an illegal drug industry do not currently have it.[3]

The second caveat is that some important consequences of the illegal drugs industry may not be classified as either positive or negative. Because the illegal industry is instrumental in changes in institutions and culture, the evaluation of these changes requires strong value judgments. For example, the growth of illegal coca plantings and the government responses to it in Bolivia resulted in the rise of a strong *cocalero* movement with deep Indian roots and the election of Evo Morales, the head of the Coca Growers Confederation, to the country's presidency. This development may be seen as positive from the point of view of the long-suppressed Indian population but as highly negative by the country's traditional elite and some foreign investors.

The Drug Industry Development and Its Links with Politics and Armed Groups

The operation of any illegal industry requires the support of a social network that protects the industry against law enforcement efforts and attacks and challenges by possible competitors. In the four cases studied, the illegal drugs industry has obtained such support. Furthermore, it has offered armed subversive and countersubversive groups the opportunity to participate in highly profitable activities that can support their own agendas.

Case Study: Afghanistan

Opium has been produced in Afghanistan for centuries, but only relatively recently did it present significant domestic or international problems. The United Nations asserts that only in Badakshan was there "something of an opium tradition" whose roots could be traced only to the 18th century, a recent date by standards of that part of the world (UNODC 2003, 88). The emergence of widespread poppy cultivation in Afghanistan followed external factors in combination with the three factors identified earlier: informal norms that conflict with and did not include compliance with state laws, a structurally weak central government, and violence.

Conditions Favoring Opium Production. The first external condition was that from 1972 onward, Iran, Pakistan, and Turkey enforced bans on opium cultivation that encouraged the displacement of those crops to Afghanistan. By 1980, the country accounted for 19 percent of the world's output. The second was the invasion by the Soviets in 1980, following which its market share of opium rose rapidly. Informal norms, a weak central government, and violence explain why those external events triggered the rapid expansion of poppy cultivation.

Afghanistan comprises many tribes with differing cultures and loyalties, a condition that undermines the development of a strong central government and promotes informal norms that diverge from those of the central government and among themselves. The Hazaras who occupy the western region have affinities with Iran, speak mostly Persian, and are Shiites. The Pashtuns and Beluchis on the east and southeast have loyalties with the Indian subcontinent and are Sunni. The tribes in the northeast have roots in Tajikistan, Turkmenistan, and Uzbekistan and are also Sunni. The different ethnic and cultural groups are themselves not unified, because each one is made up of several tribes. They all have strong tribal and ethnic identities even among their most modern members. It is not surprising that the "creation of the Afghan State was thus not sufficient, in itself, to create a pan-Afghan national identity" (UNODC 2003, 84).

Afghanistan as a country dates from the mid-18th century, but it was never consolidated as a state. The Durrani dynasty of the Pashtun Abdali tribe ruled Afghanistan from 1747 to 1973.[4] The more than two centuries of Durrani rule witnessed the development of warlordism, as the Durranis had to negotiate continually with tribesmen and mercenaries who had great autonomy. During the 1950s and 1970s, the government in Kabul was isolated from the rest of the country: "the troika of Khan (feudal lord), malik (tribal chieftain), and mullah (Muslim priest) controlled the country side quite effectively; had no need for a central government; and objected strongly and violently whenever the central government made any attempt at reform and change" (UNODC 2003, 86).

There is ample evidence of clashes between informal norms and state laws, because tribal leaders have appealed to holy wars or jihads to move the populations in defense of the status quo and ancestral traditions. Social uprisings have not sought to achieve revolutions but to protect their institutions from modernizing efforts.

For example, in April 1978, a Communist group led by Nur Mohammed Taraki, a Pashtun from the Ghilzai tribe, which is a traditional enemy of the Abdalis, took power. Taraki had strong links with the Soviet Union and tried to implement a drastic modernization program with a Socialist bent that, as in the past, generated strong widespread opposition from tribal leaders and communities. According to one observer,

The main reason for the upheavals was the state's encroachment on the traditional way of life and its social, economic, and cultural patterns. The agrarian reform program introduced by the People's Democratic Party of Afghanistan (PDPA), without providing a viable alternative to it, threatened the social structure, which was based on a landowner/tenant relationship that politically and socially functioned as a patron/client relationship. Other reforms—the abolition of the dowry; the enforcement of compulsory literacy courses; the appointment of young, inexperienced and dogmatic urbanites as local administrators, followed by mass arrests of popular labor leaders labeled 'feudalists'—antagonized rural communities and rekindled defiance toward state and government encroachment. (Roy 1993, 496)

The Soviet Invasion. The assassination of Taraki in 1979 and the invasion of the Soviet Union ushered in a long period of violence, which both increased farmer incentives to cultivate poppies and favored the emergence of the illegal networks crucial to drug trafficking. During 11 years of a war of liberation from the Soviet invaders, poppy plantings expanded.[5] Several factors contributed to this rapid expansion. The very dramatic negative impact of the war on rural sector production and employment directly affected the great majority of the population (at the beginning of the war, 85 percent of the population was rural). Bombings of legal plantings by the Soviet air force, for example, induced peasants to migrate to mountainous zones where less productive lands made it difficult to survive with small plantings of legal crops. The war also destroyed the country's financial and monetary system and completely disrupted education. Government funding for education virtually disappeared, and the generation that grew up during the 1980s, including many young Pashtun boys, was educated in religious schools (madrassas) controlled by Muslim priests (ulemas) who followed the Deobandi Islamic tradition that sprang up in 19th-century India to oppose modernization efforts within Islam (UNODC 2003, 91). Those schools were the cradle of the Taliban.

Rise of the Taliban. Conflict also strengthened the autonomy of local warlords, who received substantial funding directly from American, Chinese, and Saudi sources, channeled mainly though the Pakistani Inter Services Intelligence (ISI) (Labrousse 1991). The Soviet-backed government's lack of control over the territory allowed the development of a large contraband network of many goods, including weapons for the Mujahideen, who received substantial foreign funding. These networks, which specialized in violence and "illegal" activity (the expulsion of Soviet occupiers), adapted themselves easily to the marketing of opium. The Pakistani secret service purchased large quantities of opium, the profits from which were used to support Muslim rebels in Kashmir (Labrousse 2004).

By 1990, at the time of the Soviet Union's collapse and the end of the liberation war, Afghanistan accounted for 41.7 percent of the world's illegal opium. Opium remained a main source of funding for the subsequent civil war. In 1995 when the Taliban took control of the government, Afghanistan's share of the world's opium crop output reached 52.4 percent, a figure that ballooned to 79 percent in 1999 (UNODC 2004).

War and the deep ethnic ties among Afghan tribes and those of neighboring countries also uniquely promoted the emergence of opium trafficking networks. During the past 25 years, Afghan opium has been exported mainly through Iran, Pakistan, and Tajikistan. The opium and heroin networks involve organizations of traders from those countries who specialize in contraband of various types, including weapons. Afghanistan is also a trade corridor between Iran, Pakistan, Tajikistan, Turkmenistan, and Uzbekistan. This trade frequently includes contraband, and during the war, local warlords imposed "taxes" on it. Those routes are also used to export illegal drugs. While Afghans participate in those illicit trade networks, most opium exports are done by others, mainly Pakistanis and Tajiks (UNODC 2003).

After 1995, the Taliban government controlled most of the territory and, following established tribal behaviors, opposed modernization efforts and imposed an extreme version of Islam (Goodson 2001). Members of the government initially considered banning poppy, which according to their interpretation of the Koran was prohibited, but realized that they could not have succeeded given the weak rural economy and the role of opium in society. Their efforts were limited to banning cannabis. Eventually, though, on July 27, 2000, Mullah Omar imposed a total ban on poppy cultivation in the areas under Taliban control. Farrell and Thorne (2005), without praising or defending the Taliban, argue that "this may have been the most effective drug control action of modern times." To achieve that outcome, however, the Taliban had to resort to fairly extraordinary measures: the threat of punishment, the close local monitoring and eradication of continued poppy farming, and the actual and public punishment of transgressors. The Taliban intimidated the peasantry by arguing that the three-year drought that had devastated the rural sector had been God's punishment for the cultivation of an evil plant, and they then used their power to implement the ban. The Taliban's success was remarkable. UNODC (2004) estimates that in 2000 Afghanistan had 82,171 hectares under cultivation and produced 3,276 tons of opium. In 2001, these figures had dropped to 7,606 hectares and 185 tons, virtually all in Badakshan, the area outside the Taliban's control. Because of bumper crops in 1999 and 2000, despite the drought, traffickers had accumulated significant stocks of heroin. Thus, the effects of the ban on wholesale and retail prices in Europe and the United States were felt only marginally (UNODC 2007).

U.S. Invasion. After the Taliban were driven out of power by the U. S. invasion of Afghanistan, the poppy crop rebounded in 2002 to 71,100 hectares and 3,400 tons and continued increasing to 80,000 hectares and 3,600 tons in 2003. The importance of the illegal drugs industry in the Afghan economy has reached extraordinary levels. Bird and Ward (2004) estimate that it generates a little over one-third of the country's gross national product (GNP), making Afghanistan a true narco-economy in which drugs are the largest income-generating sector.

The foregoing illustrates that cultivation of illegal opium in Afghanistan responded not only to the particular technical conditions needed to raise poppies for opium production but also to a variety of additional circumstances. Some conditions were external: the prohibition of cultivation by neighbors, the Soviet invasion, and war. Others were internal: the deep difficulties of forming a central state out of diverse groups and the weak or nonexistent norms of obedience to laws emanating from the central state.

Case Study: Colombia

An extensive and growing literature (Herrán 1987; Thoumi 1987, 1999, 2003a; Kalmanovitz 1989; Lemoine 2000; Yunis 2003; Puyana-García 2005) argues that Colombian society lacks solidarity, reciprocity, and trust and that social capital has characteristically been of the bonding type within small social circles. The "bridging" social capital that links groups to one another has been scarce.

A Vulnerable Social Structure. Gómez-Buendía (1999) goes so far as to conclude that Colombians have a remarkable individual logic but a disastrous social one, because informal norms lead individuals to take little account of the social effects of their actions. The vulnerability of the Colombian social structure made it a favorable location for the illegal drug-trafficking industry to get a start. Once established, this industry has acted as a catalyst accelerating a process of social change that has continued to devastate traditional social controls (Thoumi 1995).

Colombia, for example, is apparently (a) a principal producer of counterfeit U.S. dollars and a producer of first-quality counterfeit euros and passports (BBC 2006), (b) the first or second exporter of Latin American prostitutes to Europe, (c) the second country in the world in the number of displaced citizens and warring children (United Nations High Commissioner for Refugees 2007), and (d) the country with the largest number of land mine victims (UNIDIR 2006).[6] It has also been known in the recent past for exceptional rates of extortive kidnappings and assassins for hire (*sicarios*).

Destructive informal norms contrast with some strong organizations such as the central bank and constitutional court, armed forces respectful of civilian government, and some robust producer associations (Cepeda 2004). The roots of conflict between well-functioning formal institutions and dysfunctional informal norms can be traced to the country's geography, history, and the organizations it developed.

Colombia's History and Geography. Colombia emerged from colonial periods as an ensemble of distinct regions with scant communication and trade exchanges among them. Physical obstacles were (and remain) great, and regions tended to develop as almost completely self-sufficient units. In many of them, urban centers grew, and today Colombia is a country of many cities that are regional centers. Today, large areas of the country are still isolated from national markets. Regional heterogeneity has resulted in cultural diversity. Area loyalties are strong, and the conformation of a national identity has been slow and incomplete.[7]

Because of its geography, Colombia was, at least until the coffee boom of the 1920s, a Latin American country with atypically low per capita international trade and, therefore, a central state with few resources.[8] Although export production drove the infrastructure development that linked a few Colombian regions with the coast and foreign markets, it contributed little to national integration. Geography also increased the cost of tax collection enormously and led to its privatization through auctions that permitted entrepreneurs to profit from it.[9] The need to respond to growing urban constituencies and the scarcity of resources made the central state's presence precarious in large portions of the country. Indeed, the Colombian state has never controlled its territory.[10]

During colonial times, peasants and runaway slaves fled to isolated regions where they could subsist independent of the state and out of reach of landowning Spanish colonists. During the 18th and 19th centuries, settlements of these runaway slaves and others were established beyond the control of the state, church, and other dominant social institutions. By the late 19th century, population in the *minifundia* areas in the central plateau had increased beyond what those smallholdings could support, and peasants migrated again, mostly to the emerging coffee-growing regions. The migrations led "to the spontaneous formation of societies marginalized from the social, family, religious, and political controls that characterized their original locations" (González 1998, 151).

At the time of the Spanish conquest, Colombia's native communities were not unified under a central government as in Bolivia, Ecuador, Guatemala, Mexico, Paraguay, and Peru but formed an array of fairly autonomous chiefdoms that frequently fought each other. Natives did not have a concept of a strong central state, and neither did the Spanish, who arrived just as Spain was becoming unified. Indian communities experienced a fast process of *mestizaje* (race mixing), blended into the mainstream, and lost their identities (Jaramillo-Uribe 1991). In contrast with other Andean countries, the tribes that survive represent a small share of the Colombian population and are located in inhospitable locations in the jungle or arid areas without much economic activity. In these communities, social norms are strong, and deviant behaviors are punished. Most Colombian peasants, however, are the result of *mestizaje* and have weak communal ties.[11]

Colombia was settled by Spaniards, who came with medieval values and norms. The informal norms that they brought with them were less diluted by non-Spanish immigration than were those in any other Latin American country: Colombia has had the fewest number of non-Spanish, non-Catholic immigrants relative to the size of its population. Colombia was not an attractive destination for European immigration because it did not offer significant investment and business opportunities. At the same time, government policies set significant obstacles to non-European and non-Catholic immigration. The 1886 Constitution, which remained in force with some amendments until 1991, aimed at strengthening the Spanish identity of the country. The Concordat with the Holy See in place from 1887 to 1986 granted the Catholic Church substantial power over family law and education. Citizenship was cumbersome to acquire, and few foreigners achieved it.

Colombia's Economy. A history of economic booms and busts further stunted the development of the "bridging" social capital that would build stable organizations and communities. During the 19th and early 20th centuries, Colombia had a series of primary-product export booms and busts: indigo, quinine, cocoa, rubber, and bananas in different locations, which generated short-lived settlements that did not produce social capital or cohesion. Until the 1920s, when Colombia received compensation from the United States for the loss of Panamá and experienced a coffee boom, Colombia endured a chronic external debt crisis caused by the large foreign debt that Bolivar had incurred to finance his campaign to liberate Bolivia and Peru. For most of the 19th century, the country's foreign debt crisis prevented it from obtaining the needed resources to integrate the country (Junguito 1995).

Politics in Colombia. These social and historical phenomena are reflected in the structure of Colombian political parties. Many parties in Latin America are organized centrally and attempt to present a distinct political agenda. Others respond to a leader with a strong personality. In both cases, the structure is organized from the top down. In contrast, the two traditional parties in Colombia, Liberal and Conservative, have tended to be organizations of local leaders who joined to influence the central government. In many regions, they have substituted for the state and mediated between the central state and the citizenry. Until recently, many Colombians were Liberal or Conservative by birth rather than by choice. In the words of one commentator, "That sense of belonging represented a transcendental element of civil life that marked and defined personal identities" (Acevedo-Carmona 1995, 41). Strong party loyalty has been an obstacle for the development of other parties. Diverging political views are most frequently expressed as dissident factions of the traditional parties or as independent, nonparty movements.

Colombia is the only Latin American country that never had a populist government. Instead, it developed a strong clientelistic system (Robinson 2007). While populist governments generated many economic pitfalls in Latin America that were avoided by Colombia (Urrutia 1991), clientelism allowed for a strong influence of technocrats in macroeconomic policy formulation that resulted in macroeconomic stability. Because in this system the state becomes a bounty for the politicians, however, the rule of law and the ability of the state to enforce its norms are greatly undermined. Not surprisingly, despite significant improvement in living standards, the political system in Colombia has not been responsive to the grievances of many Colombians, whose claims for social reforms have been frustrated. Some of the reform advocates have resorted to violent, nonpolitical means.[12]

History of Violence. In addition to a weak central state and informal norms that are individualistic rather than supportive of "bridging" social capital, Colombia has suffered wrenching violence. During the 1940s and 1950s, Colombia experienced La Violencia, an ambiguous rural civil war between the two parties that killed between 200,000 and 300,000 people out of a population of 11–12 million. The war ended in an agreement among the leaders of the Liberal and Conservative parties (the National Front) that alternated the presidency and distributed all public jobs evenly between the parties. This peculiar arrangement succeeded in ending La Violencia but, in so doing, depoliticized the parties and replaced them with electoral machines whose main goal was to distribute government bounty.[13]

La Violencia generated large rural-urban migrations to urban slums. One salient effect of that violence-induced migration was the loss of links between the migrants and their original communities, which were often destroyed, again disrupting the informal norms that reinforced the social obligations of individuals and thus making them extremely resentful. Furthermore, there was a significant rural-rural migration that went into the "empty lands" (*terrenos baldíos*) that, once again, established many settlements outside state control. Among the Latin American countries with large peasant populations, Colombia is the only one that has never had meaningful land reform.

During the 20th century, Colombia experienced a dramatic expansion of the agricultural and ranching frontier, a process highly influenced by a population explosion and rural violence. Individual settlers spontaneously undertook most of this expansion with little if any state support. Many settlers were armed, and many were displaced by rural violence. Settlements were often violent and unstable, and settlers frequently welcomed guerrilla organizations because they imposed order in the existing power vacuum.[14]

Colombia's Military

The military generates a strong sense of national identity in most countries. Consistent with the historical pattern of social fractionalization and with the fact that the military is not representative of Colombian society (military service by elite children has been exceptional), such is not the case in Colombia. While the armed forces have shunned military coups and respected civilian government, Colombian military personnel have generally not been active in politics, even after retirement.[15] Finally, the military has not contributed to national cohesion because it has never controlled the national territory and has in particular lacked a significant presence in the large border areas.

Beginnings of the Illegal Drug Industry. The historical and social circumstances, capped by widespread violence, provide an explanation of Colombia's vulnerability to illegal drug trafficking when the international demand for marijuana grew in the early 1970s, followed by cocaine demand later that decade. Until the early 1970s, illegal drugs were an unimportant policy issue. Coca was grown in a few areas where mostly Indian peasants would chew it. Marijuana grew around the country, but there were few users, although it had been considered an important social problem in a few places, such as the conservative Caldas Department

(Saénz-Rovner 2007). Cocaine and heroin had been trafficked in small quantities (a few kilograms). In 1954, for instance, two brothers from Medellín's upper class were caught in Cuba with a few kilos of heroin that had been smuggled in from Colombia (Saénz-Rovner 2005).

Colombia's participation in the illegal drug business began in earnest in the late 1960s in response to the growth in U.S. demand. Ruiz-Hernández (1979) argues that American traffickers went looking for new supply sources and found the Colombian environment to be suitable. They distributed seeds and booklets with instructions on how to grow the plant and returned to purchase and export the product. Colombians caught on quickly and replaced the foreign traffickers. Colombia's marijuana business grew rapidly but did not last long as the Colombian varieties found it difficult to compete against the stronger *sin semilla* variety that was hydroponically produced and became common in the United States.

Early Cartels. The experience with marijuana led Colombians to seek other products, leading them to cocaine, a product with a high value relative to weight and volume and, therefore, more attractive for trafficking. Colombians started with small trafficking organizations that obtained coca paste or cocaine base in Bolivia and Peru, that refined cocaine, and that smuggled it to the United States. In the United States, Colombians wrested the business from the Cuban criminal organizations that had controlled cocaine trafficking since before the Cuban Revolution and used the large number of new Colombian migrants to develop their distribution networks.[16] The illegal business produced high profits and grew quickly. By the late 1970s, the large Medellín and Cali cartels were well established, controlled most of the international cocaine market and the drug-trafficking industry, and had become entrenched in Colombian society. The illegal drug business funded political campaigns, made large purchases of rural land and urban real estate, and became a factor to reckon with in many aspects of Colombian society (Thoumi 2003a).

By 1980, Colombia had ratified an extradition treaty with the United States that became the main source of conflict between the illegal industry and the government. Indeed, the threatened traffickers called themselves "the extraditables" and waged a terrorist war against the state (Gugliotta and Leen 1990; Lee 1990; Thoumi 1995). With large amounts of capital at their disposal, the trafficking organizations enjoyed an extensive social support network and began to seek political power. Carlos Lehder established a national-socialist party, and Pablo Escobar "bought" himself a senator with a large constituency who placed Escobar as his substitute in Congress. The need to protect their large illicit capital assets and to evade extradition led to the organization of armed groups. Those groups confronted left-wing guerrillas who had controlled large areas of the country for decades and had expelled peasants from lands that drug traffickers wanted to control. They fought each other in intradrug trade wars. The extradition threat led traffickers to a narco-terrorist campaign that claimed the lives of many government officials, politicians, and law enforcement agents. This conflict reached its climax in 1989, when three presidential candidates were assassinated.

The two large cartels developed strong links with regional law enforcement agencies. The Medellín drug lords invested heavily in rural lands. To protect the lands, they organized self-defense groups that fought the guerrillas and became one of the roots of a paramilitary movement. The cartel then built an alliance with traditional landlords and army personnel that supported the paramilitary (Medina-Gallego 1990; Betancourt-Echeverry 1998).

The Cali cartel developed an extensive social support network in that city and led a social cleansing campaign "that targeted marginal urban dwellers such as vagrants, unfortunate 'expendables,' thieves, beggars, prostitutes, and drug addicts" (Clawson and Lee 1996, 58). The social network also provided intelligence and support to cartel members. In addition, the drug industry developed strong links with sectors of the political establishment, which made it difficult to coordinate police and army antidrug efforts.

During the 1990s, the role of Colombia in the illegal drug industry and in drug trafficking evolved and became more complex. Cocaine demand in the United States stagnated, while cocaine production increased. The resulting lower prices encouraged traffickers to search for new markets and products. Trafficking organizations became more international and established links with European criminal organizations (Clawson and Lee 1996; Krauthausen 1998).

After the United States increased interdiction efforts in the Caribbean, traffickers shifted their routes to Mexico. The development of links between Colombian and Mexican traffickers, however, allowed the latter to increase their market share at the expense of the former. This change has led to the generation of strong Mexican cartels that today control an increasing share of the American market.

The Barco government (1986–90) declared a "war against narco-terrorism." Acknowledging the state's weaknesses, President César Gaviria (1990–94) applied a *"sometimiento"* policy that allowed traffickers to turn themselves in, plead guilty to one crime, and receive a reduced sentence that averaged about five years. Many took advantage of this offer. Pablo Escobar built his own jail on top of a hill overlooking Medellín and negotiated its control with the government. When the government tried to move him to a real jail in July 1992, he escaped and declared an all-out war against the establishment. This conflict led to another period of terrorism during which frequent bomb attacks targeted civilians and politicians. This wave of violence ended on December 2, 1993, when Escobar was killed in a gunfight with the police. By then, however, the Medellín cartel had been destroyed.

The fight against the Medellín cartel allowed the Cali cartel to gain power and market share. The cartel leaders' low-profile strategy and their emphasis on "purchasing" politicians instead of confronting the establishment proved successful (Thoumi 2003a). The 1994 election of Ernesto Samper to the presidency led to a major national and international scandal when it became evident that the Cali cartel had provided significant funding to his campaign. The open conflict that followed led the U.S. government to "decertify"[17] Colombia in 1996 and 1997. President Samper, who then had to devote almost all his energy to responding to the drug-funding accusations, failed to confront the growing social and political problems of the country. Under pressure, he pursued the Cali cartel until almost all its leaders were in jail or killed. By the end of his administration, the large cartels had lost their importance, and most of their leaders were dead or jailed.

Fragmentation of the Cocaine Syndicates. As the two large cartels weakened, a large number of smaller trafficking organizations sprouted up. Those groups have followed low-profile strategies, have had more educated leaders, and have been more difficult to track down. The largest of the organizations, the North Valle cartel, did not achieve the dominance enjoyed by earlier drug syndicates. The new cartels developed strong ties with paramilitary groups, and some became symbiotic with them. Their number is uncertain, but several documents from the U.S. Drug Enforcement Administration suggest that there have been some 200–300 smaller trafficking organizations.

The fragmentation of the cocaine syndicates encouraged local coca production (Thoumi 2007, 2008). In addition, left-wing guerrillas that lost Soviet and Cuban economic support found illegal plantings and drug traffickers an excellent source of "taxes." The growth of the paramilitary movement that confronts the guerrillas also required funding, and illegal crops and cocaine and heroin processing provided a good share of it. The confrontation between guerrillas and paramilitaries over territorial control displaced a large number of peasants, many of whom settled in illicit crop–producing areas.

The opening of the economy after 1990 and the growth of coffee in Vietnam substantially increased competition in the markets for agricultural products, and a rural crisis ensued that provided a willing labor force for coca and poppy. Many peasants migrated from coffee, rice, and other farms to unsettled areas where they started coca and poppy fields. Royalty transfers to coal- and oil-producing municipalities increased substantially, as those industries expanded in the 1990s. The 1991 Constitution granted greater autonomy to local governments, which became more prone to corruption (Hernández-Leal 2004). The econometric study of Sánchez and Chacón (2006) shows that decentralization policies implemented from the mid-1980s in areas the state could not control by force or administer justice created strong incentives for irregular armed groups to use violence and control local governments. It can be argued that coca plantings developed as a "backward link" to the cocaine industry. In 1990, Colombia was the third-largest coca grower in the world. By the late 1990s, Colombia had become by far the largest world producer of coca.

Guerrillas and Paramilitary Groups. The large Cali and Medellín cartels had security organizations to protect their business. Small *cartelitos* do not have the size or resources to do so. Guerrillas and paramilitary groups have supplied their protection needs. The paramilitary movement started in part to protect landowners from guerrilla extortions and kidnappings. In the past, they fought guerrillas for control of coca-producing areas and trafficking corridors. In the past few years, however, common interests in drug trafficking have led some guerrilla and paramilitary fronts to collude to profit from the illegal drugs industry (Reyes-Posada, Thoumi, and Duica-Amaya 2006). In some places, those fronts agree to divide control of coca- and poppy-growing regions, manufacture cocaine and heroin, and sell to the same trafficking networks. In other locations, the Revolutionary Armed Forces of Colombia (FARC) oversees coca production and sells coca to the paramilitaries that refine it and sell cocaine to traffickers. The packages of some cocaine shipments that have been seized have carried both guerrilla and paramilitary markings, indicating joint shipping.

Drugs have altered the nature of paramilitary and guerrilla groups and their relationships (Lee and Thoumi 1999; Gutiérrez and Barón 2006). The military power of these groups has allowed them to control the illegal industry. Guerrillas provided protection and gained control mostly over coca- and poppy-planting regions. The paramilitaries have prevailed in the more advanced stages of the production chain. It has been more difficult for guerrillas to develop international marketing networks than for paramilitary groups with strong links to the mainstream capitalist society. "Pure" traffickers have become dependent on such groups (Duncan 2006). In effect, the illegal industry evolved from being controlled by common criminal organizations (cartels) to being controlled by warlords (Thoumi 2008).

Drugs and Politics. Drug money has allowed traffickers to gain political influence. Drug money has funded elections for at least three decades, and drug traffickers have gained influence in Congress and local governments. Paramilitary leaders in Ralito openly claimed that they "owned" 35 percent of Congress.

The Pastrana administration (1998–2002), in an attempt to start a peace process, granted a "distension" zone to FARC. In this 42,000-square-kilometer zone, which included large coca-growing areas and was out of bounds to the Colombian police and armed forces, FARC became a de facto government that imposed its own laws and a primitive justice system. FARC used this area to deepen its participation in the illegal drug industry.

President Andrés Pastrana Arango realized that it was imperative for the Colombian state to control the country's territory and to eliminate the armed groups and illicit crops. In late 1998, with the collaboration of the U.S. government, Plan Colombia was created to achieve those goals. The U.S. government provided a significant amount of resources but limited them to fighting drugs, thereby preventing the Colombian government from using them against guerrilla and paramilitary organizations.

During the Pastrana administration, the "peace process" with FARC floundered. Perhaps FARC realized that it was gaining military strength against a weak state, or perhaps its goal was to delay negotiations indefinitely or at least until it had a stronger bargaining position. After more than three years of frustrations, the Pastrana administration canceled the so-called distension zone in early 2002 and regained control of that area, forcing FARC to move.

The failure of the peace process with FARC disillusioned many Colombians over attempts to achieve peace through negotiations and facilitated the election of Álvaro Uribe in 2002 on a hard-line platform against FARC. Uribe's agenda emphasized control over Colombian territory and a "democratic security" program to allow citizens to reclaim their right to move freely around the country without fear of kidnapping or extortion. The success of this strategy forced FARC into retrenchment and a more passive position. It has also been applied to drug traffickers. Indeed, Uribe has extradited more than 1,000 traffickers, more than 10 times the number extradited from 1984 to 2002.

Demobilizing the Paramilitaries. After September 11, 2001, the United States declared terrorists the main violent Colombian actors and allowed the use of Plan Colombia funds to fight guerrillas and paramilitary groups, not just to fight illegal drugs, thus adding a most important external actor to the Colombian conflict. In 2004, President Uribe started negotiations with paramilitary groups and introduced a "peace, justice, and reparation" bill. After a bitter debate, the bill became the 2005 "justice and peace" law. This provided a framework for the government to negotiate with paramilitary leaders at a haven in Ralito, a small borough in Tierralta, a municipality of Córdoba Department. The negotiations resulted in a massive paramilitary demobilization. In 2004, the government estimated that there were 17,000 fighters. More than 30,000, however, demobilized. Implementation of the 2005 "justice and peace" law nevertheless allowed paramilitary leaders to retain substantial assets, although the law officially required confiscation of assets and victims' reparation (Duncan 2006).

Drug traffickers have taken advantage of this opportunity to pass as paramilitary members and attempted to cleanse their assets. Some drug traffickers have purchased paramilitary groups to protect their business (Vargas-Meza 2005). This tactic allowed them to take part in the negotiations and induced other traffickers to do the same (Reyes-Posada, Thoumi, and Duica-Amaya 2006). During the past three decades, drug traffickers have accumulated very large land holdings (Medina-Gallego 1990; Reyes-Posada 1997). Some were purchased from their owners, but a significant number have been obtained after threatening peasants who own small plots. In many cases, paramilitary groups have accused peasants of being guerrilla supporters and have forced them to flee their lands. This process has resulted in significant land concentration. Some fear that negotiations with the paramilitaries, which have not been defeated in battle, may lead to the legalization of titles to large tracts of illegally obtained land and other assets, not only of the paramilitaries but also of drug traffickers (Thoumi 2008).

The demobilization of the paramilitaries has created a power vacuum in some regions. Guerrilla organizations have tried to fill it, but former paramilitaries and their supporters have acted to prevent that. In addition, the illegal drugs industry has undermined the ideologies of left- and right-wing guerrillas and has shifted its focus to illegal moneymaking. Through drugs, many guerrilla and paramilitary fronts have gained autonomy from their central organizations, which are having increasing difficulties controlling them. The breakaway guerrilla and paramilitary groups have tended to become bands of common criminals.[18]

As a result, some former paramilitaries have recycled themselves into criminal organizations that now cannot claim a political motive. Many of these groups were formed to control drug trafficking. The demobilization of the large paramilitary warlords that controlled the drug industry has led to significant uncertainty about the future evolution of the industry.

In summary, the structure of Colombia, both physical and institutional, prevented the development of a cohesive society and over time led to a very individualistic culture. The failure of the central government to control the country's territory and to impose the rule of law in many regions has made Colombia an attractive place for growing illicit crops and for trafficking cocaine and other drugs. Once established, the illicit industry strengthened local groups whose norms differed from the laws of the central state, generated stronger individualism even within formerly revolutionary groups, and weakened some state institutions. In the meantime, the government's efforts to eliminate the illicit industry might at best make short-term gains but will not ultimately succeed at getting rid of the industry. As argued earlier, the illegality of the coca-cocaine industry determines which locations have a competitive advance in its production and trafficking. Colombia concentrates the coca-cocaine industry because it is illegal, that is, because in that country it is easier to grow coca, refine it, and traffic cocaine than in other locations. The only long-term solution to the Colombian drug problem requires lowering the gap between formal and informal norms of behavior. In other words, it requires the construction of a law-abiding society. This is no doubt a mighty challenge.

Case Study: The Plurinational State of Bolivia

Bolivia is a country deeply divided between white and native societies. Whites have dominated politics and the economy. Indians have resided mostly in rural areas, have had very low levels of formal education, and have remained poor. Until about a generation ago, Bolivia had been the most politically unstable country in the Western Hemisphere. García-Meza's July 1980 takeover, for example, was the "189th coup in Bolivia's 154 years of independence" (Hargreaves 1992, 102). Throughout the country's history, the military has unarguably played a key political role. Of the 20 presidents and dictators that Bolivia has had from the 1952 revolution until the establishment of a new electoral regime in 1982, 16 were military and 6 civilian (Lavaud 1998). From November 1964 to October 1982, constitutional governments were in power for 476 days and de facto military regimes for 3,488. The reinstatement of democracy in 1982 opened the door to political participation to the excluded Indian communities.

Bolivia's Cultural Divide. Conflicts induced by the emergence of illegal drug cultivation reinforced deep social cleavages in Bolivia, a multicultural country with serious problems of social integration. Indians have their own languages (Quechua and Aymara) and, more important, their own non-Western conceptions of life and their relationship with Pachamama, the mother earth.[19] Since the conquest in the 16th century, the more "European" society has attempted to impose its own values and to "civilize" the Indians. What from the European perspective is an issue of civilization, from the Indian viewpoint is domination. The cultural divide is a big obstacle to effective communication between the two main groups and leads to frequent misunderstandings, distrust, and resentment.

Bolivia's History. For centuries, Bolivia's economy was based on traditional haciendas and mining exploitations controlled by a small white and *mestizo* minority. The situation changed in the second half of the 20th century. Some modern agricultural sectors developed, and new regions were settled, thus sharing neither the economic nor the cultural attributes of the traditional sectors. During this time, La Paz lost importance relative to Santa Cruz, where the more modern groups (*Cambas*) established their bases. New cultural and regional differences developed, becoming a significant obstacle to national unity and producing strong movements that seek political and economic autonomy in Santa Cruz and Tarija.

Political instability generated one additional social cleavage. Following the revolution in 1952, a large land reform program was implemented, and many haciendas were split up and distributed among peasants. Peasants who worked in the haciendas subjected to the land reform formed *sindicatos*, that is, workers' unions that evolved into strong community and political organizations. The three main social groups—the decaying traditional elites associated with haciendas and mines, the Indian and peasant communities, and the new *Cambas*—have differing norms. The state has its own norms, many of which conflict with those of the three social groups.

Despite persistent social conflicts, Bolivia is a pacific society. The Indian culture avoids direct confrontations and shuns violence as a conflict-resolution instrument. Other groups also have significant cohesion and are not prone to violence.[20] The illegal drug industry is always linked to increased levels of violence, but in Bolivia those levels are much lower than in Colombia.[21]

Coca in Bolivia. In Bolivia, there is traditional coca, produced and consumed for millennia, and new coca. Traditional coca comes from the Yungas region where it was produced in haciendas until the mid-20th century. The Yungas' landlords developed a tight-knit association (SPY) that became a strong coca lobby against international pressures in the League of Nations to restrict coca cultivation and consumption and against domestic opposition to coca chewing (Lema 1997).

During the first half of the 20th century, coca chewing was so common that it was considered a staple in the Bolivian diet. Seeking new coca uses, SPY funded studies showing "that coca's vitamin content was indeed high" (Lema 1997, 109), but traditional uses dominated consumption. The 1952 revolution and the 1953 land reform brought about changes that resulted in a fall in coca demand. Some argue that the overall increase in rural standards of living resulting from the land reform increased the food intake of the rural population and lowered the need to placate hunger by chewing coca. Others claim that breaking up the hacienda system resulted in a lower coca supply because marketing systems were destroyed (Quiroga 1990; Bascopé 1993). Another element was the slow but continuous Westernization of the peasantry and rural-urban migration. In the 1980s, traditional coca uses were also discouraged by higher prices resulting from the high cocaine demand (Blanes and Mansilla 1994).

New coca plantings were developed in the 1970s in response to increased world demand for cocaine. Most of the new plantings were in Chapare, but there were also smaller plantings in other regions. The colonization of Chapare had been encouraged by many governments, particularly from 1940 on, as an attempt to solve the land tenancy problem. Accompanying the settlement of this region were increases in coca production, and by 1967, more than 50 percent of Bolivian coca acreage was in Chapare (Painter 1994). While the government sponsored many Chapare settlements and others developed spontaneously, the state was always involved. Large infrastructure projects were partially financed by the World Bank, the Inter-American Development Bank, and the U.S. Agency for International Development (USAID) (Painter 1994). Government investment in Chapare has been so significant that it has by far the best infrastructure of any rural Bolivian region.

Sindicatos. Peasant *sindicatos* have played a key role in this process. *Sindicato* membership is determined by residence: each one covers an area, and each family that settles on a parcel of land within it becomes a member. *Sindicatos* require their members to attend periodic meetings where many of the community's problems are discussed. The groups have developed systems for resolving conflicts, the decisions of which are enforced by the community (Healy 1991). The *sindicatos* are grouped in federations that form confederations, which provide coca growers with political representation and act as mediators among peasants, the state, and foreign donors like the United Nations Office on Drugs and Crime (UNODC) and USAID. Bolivia has had extensive alternative development (AD) programs, and peasant *sindicatos* have played a key role in mediating between foreign donors and the government on one side and coca growers on the other. In addition to his position as president of the country, Evo Morales is also president of the Sindicato Confederation.

Sindicatos were organized after the 1952 revolution in the sierra communities. Their cohesion reflects the strong social fabric among Bolivian peasants. Sierra peasants from a particular village migrated to the same Chapare area, and sierra *sindicato* members are also members of the same *sindicato* in Chapare. Most sierra Chapare immigrants kept their links with their original sierra communities, and many migrants maintained their small plots in the sierra and established new ones in Chapare, where they worked only part of the year (Sanabria 1993). Migrants were a blend of former highland peasants and former miners.

After the large migration to Chapare in the 1970s, the collapse of the Bolivian economy and the closings of the tin mines in the mid-1980s accelerated the mass movement of population and resulted in another significant increase in coca acreage. In July 1988, the Bolivian government, bowing to pressures emanating primarily from the United States, enacted the Ley del Regimen de la Coca y Substancias Controladas, known as Law 1008 (Léons and Sanabria 1997, 22). This law defined legal and illegal coca and decreed stiff penalties for drug-trafficking activities. It established three coca-planting categories: legal coca, grown in Yungas; "surplus" coca, grown in Chapare to be eradicated gradually after compensating peasants; and illegal coca plantings in other regions subject to rapid eradication without any compensation. This law passed despite strong nationalist and anti-imperialist arguments in defense of cultural values. Nevertheless, there was substantial accommodation: aerial spraying was banned as well as the use of defoliants and herbicides in coca eradication efforts (Malamud-Goti 1994). In addition, international funding was required for AD and peasant compensation programs in Chapare.

Law 1008 has remained a subject of political debate. Some argued that it is unconstitutional and erodes civil liberties. Others claim that its implementation has been biased against the poor, who are the great majority of those detained and jailed (Farthing 1997). From the point of view of many peasants, "lack of compliance with the requirement for provision of viable alternatives invalidates the other requirements of the law" (Léons and Sanabria 1997, 27), including eradication, dismissing the relevance of coca as part of the illegal cocaine trade.

Two Branches of the Drug Industry. The illegal drug industry in Bolivia developed two distinct branches. One, composed of peasants and their hired laborers (*Collas*) in Chapare, is closely tied to traditional Indian values and used the "seignorial" production system that prevailed in Bolivia before the 1952 revolution (Rodas 1996). The other branch is made up mostly of *mestizos* and whites from Santa Cruz (*Cambas*) and other low-prairie departments that have adopted Western attitudes. They devoted themselves to the more profitable aspects of the industry: providing a cocaine base and cocaine refining, marketing illegal coca derivatives, smuggling precursor chemicals, and exporting cocaine base and cocaine. The differences in culture, ethnicity, and social class between the two groups have traditionally fostered confrontation and mistrust.

During the 1970s, Bolivian trafficking organizations emerged but did not evolve into complex export syndicates, as in Colombia. They coordinated the purchase of coca paste, the refining of cocaine base and cocaine, and the in-country sales of most of the products to foreigners—mainly Colombians linked with the Medellín and Cali cartels. Rodas (1996) asserts that trafficking organizations primarily incorporated members from within single families, that they did not try to interfere with organizations of other families (that were their friends), and that they shunned violence. Levine (1991) argues that in the mid-1980s, drug traffickers in Bolivia organized themselves under the leadership of William

"Pato" Pizarro into one very large group. La Corporación, as it was known, controlled most Bolivian manufacturing and exports, but its members did not take high risks, shunned violence, and sold their cocaine only in Bolivia. In other words, they were satisfied to make enough money to live comfortably but did not attempt to compete significantly in international exports, where they would have needed more complex armed organizations.

The largest Beni trafficker was Roberto Suárez ("the king"), who became the main Bolivian supplier to the Colombian cartels. Suárez was a friend of General Hugo Banzer Suárez and was protected by the authorities. He also hired Klaus Barber, once head of the Gestapo in Lyon, France, who organized a group of thugs to terrorize his critics (journalists, analysts, law enforcers) and competitors and to protect him from Colombian traffickers (Hargreaves 1992). The illegal drug industry boomed during the Banzer dictatorship (1971–78), which protected it or at least condoned it (Hargreaves 1992; Gamarra 1994). In the late 1970s, a cocaine lab was found on Banzer's ranch, El Potrero.

Links with the Military. The authoritarian tradition emanating from the seignorial society, the grip that the military had on power, and the small size of the country made it infeasible for the illicit drug industry to operate in the country without strong links to the military. Compounding this problem, land reform allowed the government to distribute unsettled lands, and during the 1960s and 1970s many military officers received land grants in the departments of Beni and Santa Cruz. Some of them became prominent traffickers whose labs and airstrips were located on those distant ranches and farms.

Links between military personnel and the drug industry were tolerated by the governments of the 1970s and by the U.S. bureaucracies, whose main goal at the time was to prevent a possible expansion of communism in Latin America (Gamarra 1999). By the late 1970s, a number of Bolivian military personnel were profiting from the illegal business. Roberto Suárez's organization developed strong links with a group of military personnel, particularly General Luis García-Meza Tejada. However, several groups, especially those related to organized labor, were willing to denounce their involvement. On July 18, 1980, García-Meza orchestrated a military coup "to prevent the rise to power of the left-leaning coalition of the Popular Democratic Unity (UDP) that won the June 1980 election" (Gamarra 1994, 25). García-Meza's regime used the group of thugs previously employed by Suárez to concentrate the illegal industry's sales to foreign buyers under his authority and that of his inner group, including Roberto Suárez. The narco-government led by García-Meza was short-lived. General García-Meza was overthrown in August 1981 by a military junta primarily interested in preserving some semblance of institutional honor (Gamarra 1994, 26). The García-Meza episode has been the only case of a true "narco-government" in the Andean countries.

Bolivian Drug Production, 1990s. Most Bolivian production was marketed internationally by foreigners, but there were smaller, independent cocaine-exporting operations run by Bolivians. The best known was run by Roberto Suárez's nephew, Jorge Roca-Suárez. Although he developed an international cocaine production and trafficking network that achieved a medium-size smuggling network in the United States, he was arrested in December 1990 in Los Angeles (Painter 1994).

In the 1990s, the stagnation of cocaine demand in the United States and the demise of the Medellín cartel encouraged Bolivians and other traffickers to export to Europe (Irusta 1992; Malamud-Goti 1994). In Bolivia, many export organizations from Beni and Santa Cruz were disrupted. The capture of Roberto Suárez destroyed the largest trafficking organization (Bedregal and Viscarra 1989). In 1991, the Paz-Zamora administration, following César Gaviria's example in Colombia, offered not to extradite and to give relatively short sentences to traffickers who turned themselves in and confessed to one crime. A group of "repentants," ranchers and pilots from Santa Ana de Yacuma in the Beni Department, took the offer (Irusta 1992).

The vertical integration of production evidenced in Colombia also occurred in Bolivia. Since at least the mid-1980s, most peasants had been producing coca paste, a good number had been producing cocaine base, and some had been producing cocaine (Mansilla 1994). The best-known traffickers of the 1980s were apprehended, but their arrest did not have a significant impact on coca acreage, which remained relatively stable until 1998. Trafficking organizations also evolved, although available information is weak and sketchy. Production of cocaine base and cocaine increased, and a few export networks to the main markets developed.

It is likely that these organizations were multinational and included traffickers from Bolivia, Brazil, Colombia, and other nations as well (Clawson and Lee 1996). Bypassing Colombian intermediaries, some of the networks established direct links with Mexican traffickers and searched for markets outside the United States.[22]

The second Banzer administration, inaugurated in August 1997, implemented Plan Dignidad to get rid of the drug "scourge" (República de Bolivia 1998). This plan emphasized eradication without compensation,[23] some actions against money laundering, and drug treatment and prevention. Attacking trafficking organizations was not one of its main concerns. The plan's implementation was very aggressive and focused on a vigorous eradication campaign with strong support from the U.S. government.

The success of Plan Dignidad was remarkable. Coca plantings from 1990 to 1997 were estimated between 45,000 and 50,000 hectares. They declined to 38,000 in 1998, 21,800 in 1999, and 14,600 in 2000, leaving a "surplus" of only 2,600 coca hectares over the 12,000 legal ones. Coca hectares rebounded to 27,500 in 2005 (UNODC 2007).

Forced eradication, however, contributed to a large decline in the real standard of living of Chapare peasants and led to serious social unrest and protests, some violent.[24] The income decline in Chapare was also caused by important changes in external conditions. The economic crisis in Brazil in 1998, followed by a deeper one in Argentina (the two main markets for many Bolivian agricultural products), as well as the collapse of the international coffee market caused by the large increase in Vietnamese production, all resulted in lower prices for Chapare products. Alternative development projects, therefore, became more difficult to implement, and peasants increasingly mobilized. Beginning in April 2000, the government faced frequent confrontations with the federations of coca growers that demanded an end to forced eradication and other counternarcotic measures. The conflicts led to repeated agreements between peasant organizations and the government, in which the government promised policy changes that it could not possibly implement. The government did institute "a new criminal procedures code, fully enacted in June 2001, [that] eliminated some of Law 1008's most egregious problems while providing key due process and guarantees" (Ledebur 2005 167). Despite such changes, though, the culture of the government bureaucracy and military still allowed impunity (Ledebur 2005).

The main coca representatives in Congress led an active political opposition to the forced eradication program. In early 2002, Evo Morales, the principal coca leader, was expelled from Congress and in reaction ran for president. The 2002 presidential election was remarkable: Gonzalo Sánchez de Losada was elected with only a 22 percent plurality. Evo Morales was a surprising runner up with just over 20 percent of the vote; other Indian candidates also did well.

Political Upheavals. Coca was not the only peasant issue. In some regions, the lack of access to land was the main grievance. Education, health care, access to utilities, and use of natural resources were also important. Yet coca was at the forefront of the political debate. Peasant pressures forced President Sánchez de Losada to stop forced eradication and, in early 2003, to consider allowing every peasant family in coca-growing regions to cultivate a "cato," a 1,600-square-meter coca plot. The U.S. embassy forcefully opposed this measure and prevented its implementation. Peasant protests continued. In September, a government proposal to export gas to the United States through Chile triggered "widespread protests . . . [and] ultimately encompassed a large range of concerns. These included demands for better wages, reform of antidrug legislation, rejection of a law imposing prison terms for people participating in road blockades, and repudiation of the proposed Free Trade Area of the Americas" (Ledebur 2005, 161). The government tried to repress the protests with force, but on October 17, after more than 60 people had been killed, Sánchez de Losada resigned. In accord with the Constitution, Vice President Carlos Mesa took over.

Mesa's government was marked by constant conflict. The 1996 hydrocarbon law that had facilitated foreign investment in the energy sector became the main focus of contention. Peasant marches, road blocks, and urban protests were organized to demand 50 percent royalty payments to the state, a much higher percentage than what is common in the industry. Ethnic and regional conflicts over that issue grew intense, as the oil- and gas-rich *Camba* regions of the west demanded more autonomy in managing their resources. Mesa attempted to hold a binding referendum on the gas export plan, to rally the population behind his demands that Chile return a stretch of land lost during the War of the Pacific in the 1880s, and to convene a Constitutional Assembly to "found again" the country. After 20 frustrating months, he resigned on June 7, 2005, in favor of the caretaker government of Eduardo Rodriguez, the chief justice of the Supreme Court.

On January 22, 2006, Evo Morales became the first Bolivian president of Indian ancestry. He is the founder and leader of the Movement toward Socialism (MAS), a political party with an antiglobalization agenda. He has increased the area allowed for legal coca to 20,000 hectares and is requesting that the UN reconsider the classification of coca to remove it from schedule I of the conventions that limit its uses to medical and scientific research. Recent reports indicate that coca plantings have come back and that Bolivia is supplying a large share of Brazil's cocaine market, the second largest in the world by volume. Morales convened a Constitutional Assembly to make drastic social reforms. He is opposed by *Camba* groups from Santa Cruz, Beni, Tarija, and other areas that are demanding autonomy from the central government. This secession movement has grown and so has the power of the *Collas*.

The Bolivian case, then, illustrates how existing illicit drug cultivation and strenuous efforts to eradicate it have interacted with preexisting cleavages to generate significant social and political instability. One effect of this instability has been the unprecedented emergence of a Bolivian president of Indian ancestry. Another, however, has been growing rifts between social and regional groups, renewed threats to democratic institutions, and increasing challenges to the authority of the central government.

Case Study: Peru

Peru offers another example of how the illicit drug industry takes root in a socially divided country and undermines political and social stability. Peru has three distinct geographical regions: the coast, the sierra, and the jungle (*selva*) (Palmer 1980). With strong links to the outside world, the coast is the center of the modern economy and has a large share of the population. Peru also has a substantial peasant population of Indian ancestry, a powerful white minority, and a large urban *mestizo* population, many of Indian origin. Black, Chinese, and Japanese communities make up the rest of the urban population. Assimilation of the Indians into mainstream society has been slow.

The coast is made up of an arid desert with patches of productive irrigation-based agriculture, including large sugarcane plantations and other agricultural crops (Palmer 1980). The bulk of the Indian population has lived in the sierra, where there are also large traditional haciendas. Very sparsely populated, the jungle east of the sierra is a region where mythical riches await exploitation and where the cultivation of illegal coca crops is concentrated.

Peruvian Society. Peasants have maintained many of their ancestral traditions, but they are less well organized than their Bolivian counterparts. Peruvian society has seignorial roots, like those of Bolivia. Until the mid-20th century, hacienda landlords were the most politically powerful group. There was a tight nexus between the armed forces and the landlords, and military leaders were frequent presidents and dictators.[25] Peru's Indian communities are weaker than those in Bolivia, although they are still well structured.[26] Peru's modern sector is larger, and parts of the society are more cosmopolitan. In contrast to Colombia, Peru appears to exhibit greater family and religious controls on individual behavior. However, it is a more stratified society than that in Colombia; social mobility is more restricted. Finally, in contrast to Colombia, the military generates national loyalties and identity.

Peruvian Coca Society. As in Bolivia, coca has been used in Peru from time immemorial, and coca chewing has been widespread among the peasantry and mine workers who have used it to endure long shifts inside silver and other mines and in rural activities. Coca is also used as a social mediator and in native religious rites; it also has a few industrial uses like coca tea.

Traditional coca chewing was looked down on by white urban society. In the first half of the 20th century, there were substantial debates about coca use. Coca is an anorexic that allows workers to undertake long shifts without food. Progressive forces argued against coca chewing because that practice was seen as an instrument of exploitation of the peasantry and mine workers. The well-known novels of the Indian author Ciro Alegria, for example, express opposition to coca chewing. Others argued that the practice prevented the assimilation of Indians into the Peruvian social mainstream and contributed to the Peruvian defeat by Chile in the War of the Pacific in the 1880s. Hacienda and mine owners, however, paid part of their workers' salaries in coca and supported the practice (Gagliano 1994; Gootemberg 1999). A significant group of Andean public health workers and politicians believed that coca was a key factor in the "degeneration of the Indian race."

Coca and Politics. The military government that came to power in 1968 advocated broad state intervention in the economy, including extensive land reform and nationalism. Coca plantings expanded during the 1970s. Observing this expansion, the government also tried to control the coca market. In 1978, the military government of General Francisco Morales-Bermúdez Cerruti enacted Decreto Ley 22,095 to repress the "traffic of dependency producing drugs, prevent their inappropriate use, psycho-socially rehabilitate addicts, and reduce coca cultivation." The law also established the Multisectoral Drug Control Committee made up of the ministers of interior, presidency, foreign relations, agriculture, health, education, industry, and justice and the attorney general (Cotler 1996, 61).

A few months later, the government established ENACO, the National Coca Enterprise that replaced Coca Estanco (the government agency in charge of purchasing all coca from peasants and selling it to coca wholesalers). ENACO was charged with conducting a census of coca growers; establishing itself as the only coca grower, distributor, and processor; and controlling the markets of inputs required to process coca. From that moment on, coca growers not included in the census were illegal. The census was conceived as a temporary measure while ENACO consolidated its monopoly.

Law 22,095 did not establish a permanent right to grow coca. It allowed growers to continue growing coca only until ENACO assumed its duties, something that never occurred. Individuals and not land were registered in the census. The law is confusing because it did not establish what happens when the registered peasant dies or plants in a different field. ENACO never had the funds or organization required to become a coca monopolist, and registered peasants and their heirs have continued growing the legal coca sold to ENACO. The current interpretation of the 1978 census is even more confusing. Law 27,436 of January 15, 2002, asserts that through ENACO, the state "would industrialize and market coca leaves from registered farms." This language implies that the census applies to the land and not to individuals. The National Strategy against Drugs 2002–7 supports Law 27,436, which recognizes the right of the heirs of the original registered peasants to continue planting coca for traditional uses.

Originally, ENACO was a "rural sector public enterprise" supported by the state, but in 1982 it was changed to a "private law public enterprise," whose bureaucracy had to be self-supporting. Because legal coca is spread around the country, ENACO has offices even in regions where legal coca production is quite limited. ENACO's mandate requires maintaining detailed records and keeping stocks of coca. All this activity translates into an expensive bureaucracy funded out of a large differential between coca prices paid to peasants and those charged to customers; this arrangement encouraged the development of a black market for licit coca uses.

The registry of coca growers has become shorter through time. Some peasants have died, and others just stopped growing coca. ENACO (2002) shows a great variation in the ratio of coca sold to ENACO and the surface allotted to planting, indicating that many registered peasants are selling their product in the black market. A former ENACO manager estimated that ENACO buys only about 20 percent of all coca devoted to licit uses (Thoumi 2003b).

ENACO does not know the size of licit coca demand. A rule of thumb used by official documents is that 12,000 coca hectares are needed to satisfy licit demand. It is likely, however, that the area needed to satisfy such demand has fallen over time:

- First, improved agricultural technologies have increased coca plants' productivity.
- Second, food availability and nutrition levels have increased in rural Peru, and the demand for coca to suppress hunger has probably declined.
- Third, the large peasant migration to urban areas has changed consumption patterns, and "modern" peasants and urban dwellers use less coca.

Illegal coca has been grown primarily in the "jungle's eyebrow" (*Ceja de Selva*), the mountainous jungle on the east side of the Andes that remained almost totally unpopulated for centuries. Settling and colonizing this region was an old goal of Peruvian governments and elites, who believed that the Amazon region was to become not only Peru's but also the world's food basket (Cotler 1996; Tarazona-Sevillano 1990). In the 1960s and 1980s, President Fernando Belaúnde's governments made the development of that region a high priority.

Belaúnde promoted the settlement of the jungle to integrate that region into Peru's coastal markets, and in 1966 the Inter-American Development Bank financed a settlement project in the Upper Huallaga Valley (Tarazona-Sevillano 1990). After the 1968 military coup, the government implemented a land reform along the coast and high sierra, promoted cooperatives in the Huallaga, and increased the pro-urban bias of government policies. According to Cotler (1996), the persistence of those policies led to a gradual decline in rural incomes and an increase in rural poverty that made illegal coca–related activities increasingly attractive. During this period, coca plantings notably expanded and substituted for traditional legal crops in the Upper Huallaga Valley. The military government's obligatory cooperative organization in the valley also resulted in lower outputs of legal crops, and the low fertility of the jungle soil resulted in quickly declining crop yields (Tarazona-Sevillano 1990). Coca is one of the most suitable crops for conditions of declining soil fertility.

Gonzales-Manrique (1989) traces coca cultivation in the Upper Huallaga back to the 1940s, but it disappeared a decade later when cocaine was declared illegal. His work documents that Peruvians had the know-how and ability to produce cocaine before the coca boom of the 1970s. During the 1970s and 1980s, Peru produced mainly coca paste that was exported almost exclusively by Colombians. Cuánto S.A. (1993) argues that over time Peruvians increased their production of cocaine and that by 1992 they were producing 165 tons. Macroconsult S.A. (1990) claims that by 1989 Peru was not exporting any coca paste, only cocaine base and cocaine. Those studies argue that poverty was the main cause of the growth in the supply of coca paste.

Two Parallel Branches of the Drug Industry. In the 1970s, two parallel illegal industrial branches developed. The artisan, Peruvian branch produced and exported small quantities. The other branch—commercial, Colombian—dominated large-scale exports. The commercial networks included coca-growing peasants; *traqueteros* or coca collectors; *storers* who processed coca and stored coca paste or cocaine base; and the "boss's chargé," who organized shipments and worked directly under the "boss" (generally a Colombian who resided outside Peru). The network also included, among others, suppliers of chemical inputs; chemists and lab assistants; guards, bodyguards, and other security personnel; and pilots who transported the product out of the country. Morales (1989) asserts that in Peru there is an ethnic division of labor similar to the one in Bolivia. Indian peasants cultivate coca and process it into paste, and *mestizos* do the more profitable downstream processes. In the early 1990s, there were 40–50 "firms" (Alvarez and Associates 1996). Cabieses (1998) argues that these groups were so loosely organized that they should be referred to as "bands" rather than "firms."

Morales (1989) found that natives in traditional coca-growing regions, many of them authorized to produce legal coca, had learned to process coca paste and base; some produced cocaine marketed in Lima. Coca paste produced in small quantities in other regions was also sent to Lima, where it was processed into cocaine. This trade was independent of the large "firms" that produced the cocaine smuggled in small quantities by "mules," frequently caught at Lima's airport.

Illegal drug crops were recognized as a problem in the late 1970s. When the electoral regime was reinstated and Belaúnde elected for the second time, the Peruvian government under pressure from and supported by the United States started the Special Coca Control and Eradication Project in the Upper Huallaga (CORAH). This initiative was complemented a year later by a crop substitution initiative, the Special Upper Huallaga Project (PEAH).

CORAH eradicated coca manually, a very labor-intensive and slow process: it takes 30 workers one full day to eradicate 1 hectare (Obando 1993). Slow progress led to proposals for aerial spraying of coca plantings using tebuthiuron (aka Spike), which generated a strong public reaction because of fears of environmental damage; Ely Lilly, producer of tebuthiuron, refused to supply it to coca eradication programs in Latin America. After 10 years, CORAH had eradicated only 18,000 hectares (Obando 1993).

Shining Path. Despite PEAH's efforts to develop alternative crops for the Upper Huallaga and although CORAH was considered unsuccessful by advocates of eradication, the eradication program triggered significant peasant unrest; peasants considered the police and government officials involved in eradication as their enemies. This situation provided an opportunity for Shining Path guerrillas that had entered the Upper Huallaga Valley in 1984 (Obando 1993), an incursion facilitated by the relative weakness of peasant organizations compared to the Bolivian *sindicatos* (Lee 1990). At the end of 1984, after the military offensive in the Ayacucho and Huancavelica Departments, Shining Path moved to the Huallaga supported by Puka Llacta (Red City), another Maoist group (Labrousse 1995). They systematically attacked government officials working in eradication and crop-substitution programs, as well as the leaders of peasant organizations (Dreyfus 1999). Shining Path set minimum coca prices and became "the only intermediary between the traffickers and the peasants ... [and] the only source of protection for both groups against the police" (Dreyfus 1999, 382). Shining Path also required peasants to maintain their food crops.

The army was called to action in the Huallaga Valley to confront the guerrillas. It realized the necessity of avoiding confrontation with the peasantry and opted not to fight drug trafficking and to focus strictly on the guerrillas (Obando 1993; Labrousse 1995). Furthermore, the army refused to provide protection to CORAH's eradication teams, some of whom were massacred by Shining Path guerrillas and drug traffickers (Dreyfus 1999). "This move quickly turned the support of the peasants (and, paradoxically, of the traffickers) in favor of the army" (Dreyfus 1999), a turn of events that became key to the army's success and to the eventual expulsion of Shining Path from the valley:

> The succeeding administration of President García took the position that the guerrilla movement stemmed from socioeconomic problems; therefore, programs of social assistance and economic development in poor rural areas should take precedence over repression. Moreover, it sought to reduce the high degree of autonomy that the armed forces had in managing the repression of Shining Path in areas that were declared under a state of emergency. (Dreyfus 1999, 283)

Garcia then ordered the army out of the Upper Huallaga Valley. His policies were more aggressive against illegal crops and traffickers, which weakened the peasants' support for the government.

The deep economic crisis during Garcia's presidency offered new opportunities for Shining Path and the Tupac Amaru Revolutionary Movement (MRTA) to get established in Huallaga. In the subsequent confrontation between the two groups, Shining Path was the victor (McClintock 1988; Obando 1993). Garcia then changed tactics and had the police focus on capturing *traqueteros, storers,* and traffickers, while leaving peasants alone. This approach worked in the short run and produced a substantial decline in coca leaf prices (McClintock 1988). When peasants realized that the police were responsible for their income losses and that the government did not provide any reasonable income alternative, they once again turned against the police and the government (Obando 1993).

Shining Path took the opportunity to establish, once again, strict control of the Huallaga. It "reorganized all narco-trafficking relations: fixed coca leaf prices, got rid of all intermediaries, determined how leaves were to be weighted, fixed the dollar exchange rate and established a system of Delegations"[27] (Obando 1993, 85):

> To be allowed to buy, traffickers had to register with the delegation [a group of guerrillas charged with negotiating with traffickers][28] at a cost of $15,000 of which 50 percent went to the central Shining Path accounts, 40 percent was used to purchase communication equipment, and 10 percent was left with the Delegation. (Obando 1993, 85)

Shining Path also benefited from drugs in other ways. For example, it violently replaced the traffickers' security guards with Shining Path members, establishing a tax of $15,000 on each trafficking airplane that landed to pick up coca paste (Obando 1993).

Shining Path's control of the Huallaga rang Washington's alarm bells. Several U.S. government reports charged the Peruvian military with incompetence and accused the army of corruption and human rights abuses. In some cases, the threat of decertification was clear.[29] Alan García reacted by decreeing an emergency zone to allow the army to regain control. According to Clawson and Lee (1996), Shining Path responded by capturing the Uchiza police post in the center of the Upper Huallaga after a bloody nightlong battle. The interior minister resigned in disgrace, and a new commander was appointed for the Huallaga emergency zone.[30] Afterward, the focus of government policy shifted from fighting drugs to fighting guerrillas:

The new commander, Brigadier General Arciniega-Huby, realized that he could not destroy the peasants' livelihood and win the war against Shining Path. He threatened to destroy Uchiza if the citizenry did not support the government, restricted eradication activities [and] carried out aggressive military actions against Shining Path without particular regard for human rights. (Dreyfus 1999, 385)

General Arciniega mediated between peasants and police and managed to restore peasants' support for the government. Backed by the air force, the army once again defeated the guerrillas in the Huallaga (Clawson and Lee 1996).

The Fujimori Presidency. By the time Alberto Fujimori was elected in 1990, the Peruvian economy was in shambles, and the government's ability to implement a strong antidrug campaign was limited. The new president sought improved bilateral relations with the United States, but its first priority was to eliminate Shining Path, not illicit drugs. The United States was eager to cooperate with Fujimori, whose policy was based on his close adviser Hernando De Soto's analysis of Peru's informal economy (De Soto 2002). De Soto considered the coca problem to be one of poverty, not of criminal behavior, and emphasized alternative development programs that would secure land titles for the peasants and markets for their products. The so-called Fujimori Doctrine defined coca growers as individuals outside the criminal drug organizations. His policies required large infrastructure development in transportation, storage, and other facilities and aid from the international community, including private sector companies that would guarantee markets and purchase prices for alternative development products (Obando 1993; Rojas 2005). Fujimori's policy postponed attacking drug trafficking directly until the subversion was eliminated.

Most migrants to the "jungle's eyebrow" came from the sierra and belonged to structured communities. Even though their communal organizations were not reproduced in the settled areas, the colonization of the Huallaga Valley was relatively pacific. Huallaga coca growers organized themselves first against eradication and later on against Shining Path. The guerrilla group at first protected the peasants against traffickers and government policies, but its strong Maoist ideology, which required indoctrination of the peasants and changes to their ancient mores, forced them to undertake many actions that the communities rejected (Obando 1993).[31] Furthermore, in 1991 Fujimori depenalized coca growers, making it unnecessary for them to get protection from guerrillas or organized crime. This measure left coca plantings in limbo: they could be eradicated, but peasants could not be prosecuted.

Coca growers, who had been victims of Maoist guerrillas, became organized, with the help of the state, to protect themselves. Peasants organized 175 Committees in a Defense Front against Coca Eradication in the Upper Huallaga and a smaller Agrarian Federation of the Selva Maestra. These organizations had the support of the National Agrarian Confederation. Many were armed and organized peasant self-defense groups (Rondas Campesinas) to fight Shining Path (Obando 1993). This broad-based development transcended the Huallaga Valley. The most important *Rondas* developed in areas where Shining Path had been strong and had massacred peasants on several occasions, particularly in Ayacucho Department. Taking advantage of these conditions, the government encouraged the creation of the *Rondas*, which had played an important role in weakening Shining Path (Degregori and others 1996).

The assertion of military control over Huallaga had an undesirable by-product, as the army and some politicians developed significant links with traffickers who also fiercely opposed Shining Path (Rojas 2005). The growing military involvement and the shift from a social approach to solving the coca issue to a strong punitive one led to the resignation of De Soto in January 1992.

The growing power of the military became consolidated after April 1992, when Fujimori closed down Congress and started a process for changing the political system dominated by old, fossilized, and corrupt parties and for putting the executive in total control of the state. This authoritarian "autogolpe" succeeded because of the support of the armed forces. A main goal of the autogolpe was to eliminate opposition. That intent, however, distanced Fujimori from the country's political establishment and made him more dependent on the military. Such events produced a de facto civil dictatorship supported by the armed forces (Rospigliosi 2001; Dammert-Ego-Aguirre 2001).

Changes in the Peruvian Illegal Drug Industry. During the 1990s, the structure of the Peruvian illegal drug industry experienced substantial changes. The most obvious was a steep decline in coca acreage in response to a sharp fall in prices for coca (Cabieses 1998; Ronken, Ledebur, and Kruse 1999). Coca plantings declined dramatically and generated a deep crisis in coca-growing areas. UNODC (2005) estimates 1995 acreage at 115,300 hectares. Beginning in 1996, estimates of hectares under cultivation dropped sharply, reaching 51,000 in 1998 and 38,700 in 1999.

The decline in coca acreage was due to a combination of factors. One was the infestation of about 5,500 hectares by a Fusarium oxysporum fungus (Rojas 2005). Although forced manual eradication also played a role, the most important determinant was the fall in coca prices below production costs that led to a massive abandonment of coca fields. U.S. government officials report off the record that about one-third of the decline was attributable to eradication and two-thirds to the abandonment of many fields in response to very low prices.

Interestingly, the United Nations Office of Drug Control and Crime Prevention, UNODCCP (2000) attributes that decline to the success of alternative development. Government officials believe that coca prices declined because of the "air bridge denial" policy and argue that in 1995 it "neutralized" 20 airplanes, causing coca prices to fall (see table 6.1). In 1996, the United States removed some radars, and the air bridge denial program was abandoned. Official data from the Peruvian Air Force draw a very different picture. They show that the program to shut down airplanes began in 1990. The 1991–95 period shows the number of neutralized planes reached a maximum in 1993. UN data, however, show that between 1991 and 1995 coca prices remained stable in the main coca-growing regions (UNODC 2003).

The figures indicate that the air bridge denial program did not have a significant effect for several years on illicit acreage and that other factors were relevant. Indeed, the illegal industry appears to have adapted quite well to the Air Force program (Thoumi 2003b).

The main factor behind the coca price collapse appears to have been exogenous to Peru: Colombian traffickers quit buying from Peruvian

Table 6.1. Number of Neutralized Drug-Running Planes in Peru, 1991–2001

Year	1991	1992	1993	1994	1995	1996	1997	1998	1999	2000	2001
Number	11	11	25	15	20	3	10	0	0	2	2

Source: Thoumi 2003b, based on author's interview with Colonel Pedro Gracey, Peruvian Air Force, Lima, November 2002.

growers because the dismemberment of the Cali cartel in Colombia eliminated export networks and spawned many smaller "*cartelitos*" that had a strong preference for purchasing coca-derived products in Colombia. In addition, the Colombian guerrillas and paramilitaries encouraged Colombian peasants to grow coca as a means for developing a financial and political base. Those factors resulted in a large expansion of coca plantings in Colombia (Thoumi 2003b; Rojas 2005).

In the early 1990s, the coca industry also changed its geographical distribution in response to the fungus:

> Farmers moved into areas where land was readily available, primarily to the east. Some went directly east into the Aguaytía Valley; others went northeast into the Central Huallaga; still others went southeast into the Apurimac Valley. Those regions generally lack economical access to the legal market, making coca the most attractive crop. (Clawson and Lee 1996, 136)

Alvarez and Associates (1996) concluded that by 1995 all Peruvian peasants had learned to produce coca paste. In many locations, there was no coca price because there was no coca market. "Firms" exported almost exclusively high-quality cocaine base and had developed their own facilities for reprocessing lower-quality cocaine base and making it exportable. Transportation costs had increased substantially, because the air bridge denial program made it necessary to transport coca paste, cocaine base, or cocaine by surface to distant landing strips, many of which were near the Colombian and Brazilian borders. Even though Peruvians' participation in the export market had increased, they had not been able to satisfactorily substitute for the Colombian "bosses." Only two Peruvian "families" were found that could export their products on their own.

The 1995 coca price collapse encouraged Peruvians to refine cocaine and to develop their own trafficking networks. These networks established links with Mexican traffickers and bypassed Colombian trafficking organizations. The increased cocaine production also offered opportunities for small trafficking groups to develop. A substantial increase in "mules" captured at Lima's international airport attests to this development.

Peruvians have not been successful in developing large international drug distribution networks. Increased cocaine seizures in Peru, however, indicate increases in cocaine-processing capacity and point in the direction of efforts to develop new export channels. Coca prices bottomed out in 1997 and increased steadily afterward, so that by 2002 they were four times higher (Rojas 2005). Peruvians clearly succeeded in developing new drug export networks. This rebound in coca prices was also influenced by the strong eradication campaign of the Banzer government in Bolivia. Most likely, Bolivian cocaine producers and traffickers substituted Peruvian coca and cocaine for domestic. The rebound of the Peruvian coca-cocaine industry appears to have followed. UNODC estimates 2006 coca acreage at 51,400 hectares (2007, 64). Journalistic reports give higher figures, in the 60,000–70,000 range.

Extensive Corruption. During the 1980s and early 1990s, Shining Path provided significant protection to the illegal industry. The policies of the Fujimori government in the early 1990s weakened the guerrilla group, but the government agencies that controlled coca-growing regions were vulnerable to the corruption generated by the illegal industry and became involved in drug trafficking themselves (Rospigliosi 2001; Dammert-Ego-Aguirre 2001). The role of Vladimiro Montesinos, de facto head of the National Intelligence Service (SIN) and the closest official to Fujimori, was particularly important. The relationship between the illegal industry and the power centers in the state became symbiotic.

Data on coca prices and acreage support the interpretations of Rospigliosi (2001) and Dammert-Ego-Aguirre (2001) that coca prices remained relatively stable and that total coca acreage increased somewhat during the years in which more airplanes were neutralized. These facts support the contention that Montesinos had strong oversight over the market. Airplanes of traffickers that competed with his organization and a few others were neutralized to show results. Indeed, the air bridge denial program had significant problems and generated substantial conflicts within government agencies and with foreign ones (Rojas 2005).

Worrisome Developments. Soon after Alejandro Celestino Toledo Manrique took office as president in July 2001, he "demonstrated the political will to confront drug trafficking" (Rojas 2005) and reorganized the government agencies dealing with illegal drugs. He created a high-ranking "drug czar" to coordinate antidrug policies and activities. In October 2001, he started a round of negotiations with representatives of coca growers that did not advance. A failed attempt to restart the talks the following March produced "an explosion of conflict in the coca-growing valleys" (Rojas 2005). Toledo acceded to some peasant demands: a temporary halt to forced eradication, the creation of a commission to investigate rumors of fumigation, a reevaluation of alternative development programs, and changes in the policy of legal coca purchases (Rojas 2005).

Toledo formulated a gradual eradication plan that satisfied neither the peasants, who wanted strong alternative development programs before eradicating, nor the U.S. Embassy, which wanted a stronger eradication effort. Since then, peasants have strengthened their organizations and are demanding a right to grow coca. Several projects for a new coca law have been debated in Congress, where lawmakers are considering the permanent legalization of coca crops. The worsening armed conflict in Colombia and the labeling of FARC, ELN, and paramilitary groups in Colombia as terrorists by the United States have created new incentives for Colombian traffickers to return to Peru to purchase coca paste, cocaine base, and cocaine. Furthermore, subversive Peruvian organizations appear to have learned from the Colombian experience. Recent reports indicate that a resurgent Shining Path has been purchasing coca paste from peasants and that FARC representatives are doing the same and are also providing "technical assistance" to the guerrilla group.

All these changes indicate that the illegal drug industry in Peru is experiencing a deep restructuring process. The possible growing involvement of Peruvian guerrilla organizations in drug trafficking is particularly worrisome, because it can have gravely destabilizing political effects at a time when a sharp drop in law enforcement resources places all government agencies involved at a very high risk of corruption.

As in Bolivia, eradication has strengthened coca-growing peasant organizations. In January 2003, they organized a national meeting and formed the National Confederation of Farmers in the Coca-Growing Valleys of Peru. Nelson Palomino—its secretary general and head of the Federation of Farmers in the Apurimac and Ene River Valley, one of the largest coca-producing regions—was arrested in February 2004 and sentenced to 10 years of jail time after being accused of abetting terrorism (Rojas 2005). A few months later, in an automotive accident during a jail transfer, he was injured and became a paraplegic. His followers have continued opposing government polices and have become radicalized, following the example of Bolivian peasants. Peruvian peasants have not achieved the political power and organization of the Bolivians, but they could become an important force. When Alan García returned to office as president in mid-2006, he inherited a bleak situation. The illegal drug industry will unquestionably continue to generate great uncertainty in Peru's future.

A Few Conclusions

All four countries surveyed in this chapter have conflicting formal and informal norms. In these countries, their significant unresolved social issues have become intertwined with the illegal drug industry. The societies had all the elements necessary for development of the industry, although no single factor was determining. Not all societies with the individual elements that make them susceptible fall prey, but those that are vulnerable may become involved when a contributing event like an economic crisis occurs. Once the illegal industry becomes established, the numbers of actors and interests involved in drugs proliferate over time. Illegal drugs then become a major influence on the country's politics and can change its power structure. In the countries discussed here, the illegal industry was able to establish itself because the social structures, institutions, and cultures made them fertile grounds for such activities.

The structure of the illegal industry reflects each country's institutional weaknesses. In tribal Afghanistan, for example, the illegal drugs industry has remained concentrated in opium and heroin manufacture, while foreigners have dominated trafficking. Illegal poppy growing began to expand after the Soviet invasion, increased during the war between the Mujahideen and Taliban, and accelerated dramatically after the U.S. invasion. In Colombia—a country where people never developed strong loyalties to the nation and where La Violencia, large migrations, and modernization changed social norms, weakened social controls, and led to extreme individualism—sophisticated trafficking organizations developed. In their wake, illegal plantings flourished. Bolivia and Peru have a long history of coca use among Indians, who have historically wielded little social power. These societies have remained more traditional and have not developed large trafficking organizations. There, coca has become a symbol of the Indian and peasant identity and an instrument of rebellion for those that have been politically disenfranchised and socially marginalized.

The illegal drug industry is a symptom of deeper problems that result in social tolerance for illegal economic activities. Once the illegal industry develops, it becomes a catalyst for accelerated social change and intensifies the latent unresolved social conflicts of each society. Antidrug policies try to lower the profitability and raise the risk of some parts of the industry, but they cannot make them legal, and the countries' competitive advantage requires illegality. Therefore, although repressive policies may have partial successes, they cannot eliminate the illegal industry and have only heightened the social conflicts in each country.

The solution to the "drug problem" in the countries studied requires social changes that close the gap between formal and informal behavioral rules. These are slow processes that require social reforms. Illegal coca-cocaine and poppy-heroin concentrate in countries where the central state lacks legitimacy across the population, the formal justice system is weak or inoperative, significant social groups feel excluded, and bridging social capital is lacking (Thoumi 2003a). In these countries, the long-term solution to the drug problem requires strengthening governability and regime legitimacy. Without question, this prescription is not attractive, because it requires a long time and a strong social commitment to building more equitable societies. In its defense, one can point out that the "war on drugs" proclaimed by Richard Nixon in 1970 and reaffirmed by Ronald Reagan in 1980 has yet to be won—and today would be the very "long run" of 1970.

Not surprisingly, the consequences of the illegal industry have varied substantially among the four countries. They have been more important and negative in Afghanistan and Colombia, where drugs fund internal conflicts. In Peru, they have been less severe. Guerrillas have been and are involved, but the lack of large Peruvian trafficking organizations and the large number of peasants involved resulted in a relatively wide distribution of the illegal income among many low-income citizens. And the peaceful culture of the country (relative to Colombia or Afghanistan, for example) makes for fewer negative consequences. In Bolivia, the effects have been more benign in terms of violence, although coca has played a key role in changing the political spectrum.

A paradigm change, indicating a shift in public opinion in the Andean countries, should also be highlighted. When the Single Convention was signed in 1961,[32] there was widespread agreement that coca chewing had to be eliminated if Bolivia and Peru were to develop. In the meantime, coca has become a symbol of Indian identity, and today there is broad support for traditional uses of coca, still prohibited by the UN conventions. This paradigm change has added fuel to the conflicts over drug policies. At this time, it is important to evaluate convention changes to allow licit coca uses besides those in medicine and research.

In the four countries studied, the growth of the illegal drug industry has brought foreign actors into policy formulation, implementation, and funding. The illegal industry changed what were domestic policy issues into "intermestic" ones and curtailed the policy leeway of national governments. In this sense, the drug industry has resulted in a loss of sovereignty and has forced the governments to confront the external world.

Traditional societies are sometimes strongly segmented into different groups, each with its own social norms and socially accepted discrimination against the other groups; often the social norms conflict with certain legal norms. Yet, such societies may be stable for a long time. Technological change and globalization, however, have made these societies increasingly vulnerable to the development of international organized crime and the illegal drugs industry. Many countries have become increasingly prone to hosting illegal economic activities as the gap between formal and informal norms and rules widens and as some of the social differences of the past become increasingly less accepted by groups that find illegal economic activities and illegal drugs in particular as a good option for improving their economic and social standing. The four cases studied show how traditional social structures have placed Afghanistan, Bolivia, Colombia, and Peru in a vulnerable position regarding an increased world demand for illegal drugs. In all these countries, the large gap between the legal and the socially accepted norms of at least some groups has permitted the development of important illegal drug activities. Many other countries are in similar conditions today and could become involved in illegal economic activities as their societies increase their exposure to illegal global markets.

Antidrug policies may decrease the illegal drug activities in one location, but they will only shift the activity to other vulnerable societies. Colombia, for example, could lose its prominence in the cocaine industry if illegal plantings and drug trafficking gain a foothold in Venezuela, Ecuador, or parts of Brazil and tropical Africa. In Southeast Asia, Papua New Guinea also appears susceptible to such developments. Poppy shifts are harder to forecast as Afghanistan's conflict is likely to continue. Some Central Asian regions, however, are good candidates for future poppy growth.

A big question raised by this study is this: Can the development of illegal economic industries be prevented? The only answer is simple: there is no substitute for a rule of law that arises from a social consensus. Of course, this is a broad and perhaps fuzzy answer, but it highlights the importance of having strong social capital, solidarity, trust, reciprocity, and what one may vaguely call a reasonable society. Chances are, of course, that most vulnerable countries will not undertake the reforms required and will develop various forms of illegal economic activities.

Notes

1. Thoumi (2007) presents a detailed comparison of the development of the illegal drug industry in these two countries.
2. As North (1990, 3) emphasized, compliance with laws depends on both the state's ability to enforce them and the internal controls that individuals develop during their socialization processes that lead them to adhere to laws independent of active state enforcement.
3. This situation is similar to a case in which a patient is diagnosed with a terminal illness such that every person with it has a deficiency of vitamin xyz that, if corrected, cures the patient. The patient, however, finds that many people who have such a deficiency do not develop the illness. In this case, the patient will not take the vitamin xyz pills until a physician explains to him why others did not develop the illness.
4. The Durrani come from the Abdali tribe; the first king changed the name from Abdali to Durrani.
5. Data on illegal crops are very weak and vary substantially among sources. The differences are frequently very large. The U.S. Department of State (1992, 223) estimated the 1991 poppy-cultivated area in Afghanistan as 17,790 hectares while UNODC (2004, 217) places that figure at about 51,000 hectares.
6. In the first five months of 2006, Colombia had 526 victims, 1,110 in 2005, and 882 in 2004.
7. This is what Yunis (2003) calls "regional cultural endogamy."
8. Palmer (1980, 45) provides data on Latin American government revenues per capita for 1860, 1870, 1880, and 1890. For the first three dates, Colombia had the lowest revenues, and its levels are significantly less than the rest of the countries. In 1890, it exceeded only those of Bolivia and the Dominican Republic. Bulmer-Thomas (1994, chapter 3) estimates exports per capita in Latin America

for 1850, 1870, 1890, and 1912. Colombia is consistently at the bottom. Those data, however, overestimate exports per capita of current day Colombia because the dates include Panama. Ocampo (1984, 53) presents estimates of exports per capita in Latin America for 1913, separating Colombia and Panama. The Colombian figure is 34 percent of the region's average and exceeds only those of Haiti (31 percent) and Honduras (27 percent).

9. Deas (1982) gives several examples. Those that auctioned alcohol and tobacco taxes appeared to have prospered, but there were instances in which private collectors actually lost money.

10. It may be argued that this has also been the case in other Latin American countries. Colombia, however, is different because of the dispersion of its population among small urban centers. In countries like Bolivia, Brazil, or Peru, the central government did not have a presence in large parts of the territory, but most of the population lived in areas where the central government did have a presence, which was not the case in Colombia.

11. For example, the classic work on peasants in the highlands near Bogotá (Fals-Borda 1961) showed that nuclear families were isolated and that only the Catholic Church and local alcohol drinking places provided social links.

12. Colombia has had reform-oriented movements. For example, liberation theology originated in the country. However, their effects on government policies have been marginal at best.

13. The National Front and the growth of clientelism have been studied extensively (Berry, Hellman, and Solaún 1980; Hartlyn 1988; Leal-Buitrago 1989; Leal-Buitrago and Dávila 1990).

14. This process is in stark contrast to the Chapare settlements in Bolivia, where many peasants migrated communally and where the state promoted migrations and had some presence. Indeed, today Chapare has the best rural infrastructure of any Bolivian region, while the Colombian coca- and poppy-growing zones have almost none (Thoumi 2003a).

15. Elected members of the Colombian Congress, for example, include several former guerrillas and only one former military person.

16. This emigration wave was particularly significant among *Antioqueños*. Not surprisingly, Medellín and the coffee-growing region became very important in drug trafficking.

17. After DEA officer Enrique Camarena was killed in Mexico in 1986, the U.S. Congress enacted a law that requires the government to annually "certify" the cooperation of foreign governments with U.S. antidrug policies. Since then, on the first of every March, the U.S. president has to take to Congress a list of countries involved in activities related to illicit drug traffic and either certify, decertify, or certify for reasons of national interests. Decertified countries are subject to sanctions: elimination of U.S. foreign aid to those countries except for that related to fighting drugs, elimination of any loans from the multilateral agencies, elimination of insurance from the Overseas Private Investment Corporation for

U.S. private investments in the country, and the executive may take measures against trade with it.

18. There have been several recent reports of guerrilla and paramilitary members defecting with large amounts of cash.

19. The Centro de Cultura, Arquitectura y Arte Taipinquiri (1996) presents an elaborate defense and analysis of diverse aspects of the Indian culture and world vision.

20. An example is provided by the confessions of the main traffickers from Santa Ana de Yacuba in Beni that accepted the government's offer of leniency in exchange for their surrender in the early 1990s. In their confessions, they explained that they had repented and had turned themselves in to cleanse their family names (Irusta 1992).

21. In 2003, I had the opportunity to interview coca leader and current president Juan Evo Morales Ayma, who argued that the situation in Chapare had become intolerable because in the previous year's confrontations with the state's forces there had been four casualties among the peasantry—exceedingly low by Colombian standards. Coca traffickers introduced arms to Chapare, but social organizations prevented generalized increases in violence (Irusta 1992, 34–35). The avoidance of violence, peaceful conflict resolution, and respect for human life are crucial Indian values (Spedding 1997).

22. The seizure of a cocaine-loaded Boeing 727 in Lima's airport in 1993 in a fueling stopover on a La Paz to Mexico route attests to this level of violence.

23. Law 1008 granted compensation only for the eradication of plants in existence in Chapare in 1988.

24. Ledebur (2005, 164) presents a table based on data from the Chapare human rights ombudsman that shows 23 peasant and 19 police and military fatalities during 1998 through 2002. The number of coca growers injured reached 454 and the police and military 103.

25. Cotler (1994, 1999) presents a good summary of Peru's institutional characteristics. See also Gagliano (1994) and Morales (1989).

26. Peruvian peasants are mainly Indian and have strong social ties and rituals (Bolin 1998), but they have not developed anything comparable to the Bolivian *sindicatos* and have not achieved the political organization of the Bolivian Indians.

27. Peasants had frequent complaints that traffickers used altered weights.

28. Dreyfus (1999, 383) places the first Delegations in 1984 during the first Shining Path incursion of the valley. They were composed of peasants led by a guerrilla.

29. Many in Washington's intelligence community were concerned. The Center for Strategic and International Studies published Tarazona-Sevillano's (1990) book warning about the establishment of an imminent narco-terrorist threat by Shining Path.

30. The authors believe that Shining Path's action was triggered by a field test in preparation of CORAH's eradication with tebuthiuron (aka Spike).

31. Labrousse (1995) argues that the MRTA had greater appeal to the peasantry because it promoted traditional populism rather than the ascetic Shining Path.

32. The Single Convention incorporates and supersedes the international norms that had been developed in earlier conventions. It followed the principle of limiting the uses of controlled drugs to those in medicine and scientific research. It bans all experimental, recreational, religious, and other ritualistic uses. This convention was complemented by the 1971 Convention on Psychotropic Substances and the 1988 Convention against the Illicit Traffic in Narcotic Drugs and Psychotropic Substances. The three conventions are the core of the International Drug Control Regime.

References

Acevedo-Carmona, Darío. 1995. *La Mentalidad de las Elites sobre la Violencia en Colombia (1936–1949)*. Bogotá: IEPRI-El Ancora Editores.

Alvarez, Elena, and Associates. 1996. "Economic Structure, Size, and Economic Implications of Illicit Drugs in Peru." New York: United Nations Development Programme.

Bascopé, René. 1993. *La Veta Blanca: Coca y Cocaína en Bolivia*. 3rd ed. La Paz: Ediciones Gráficas E.G.

Bedregal, Guillermo, and Ruddy Viscarra. 1989. *La Lucha Boliviana Contra la Agresión del Narcotráfico*. La Paz: Los Amigos del Libro.

Berry, R. Albert, Ronald G. Hellman, and Mauricio Solaún, eds. 1980. *Politics of Compromise: Coalition Government in Colombia*. New Brunswick, NJ: Transaction, Inc.

Betancourt-Echeverry, Darío. 1998. *Mediadores, Rebuscadores, Traquetos y Narcos*. Bogotá: Edición Antropos.

Bird, William, and Christopher Ward. 2004. "Drugs and Development in Afghanistan." In *Conflict Prevention and Reconstruction*. Social Development Papers Series 18. World Bank, Washington, DC.

Blanes, José, and H. C. F. Mansilla. 1994. *La Percepción Social y los Hechos Reales del Complejo Coca/Cocaína: Implicaciones para la Formulación de una Política Nacional*. Investigación para el Debate No. 9. La Paz: SEAMOS.

Bolin, Inge. 1998. *Rituals of Respect: The Secret of Survival in the High Peruvian Andes*. Austin: University of Texas Press.

British Broadcasting System. 2006. "Colombia: Pasaportes falsos para al-Qaeda." January 27. http://news.bbc.co.uk/hi/spanish/latin_america/newsid_4653000/4653604.stm

Bulmer-Thomas, Victor. 1994. *The Economic History of Latin America since Independence*. Cambridge: Cambridge University Press.

Cabieses, Hugo. 1998. "Nuevas Tendencias sobre la Coca y el Narcotráfico en el Perú." *Debate Agrario* (March) (27): 200–217.

Centro de Cultura, Arquitectura y Arte Taipinquiri. 1996. *Cosmovisón Andina*. La Paz: Taipinquiri.

Cepeda, Fernando, ed. 2004. *Fortalezas de Colombia*. Bogotá: Editorial Planeta Colombiana, S.A.

Clawson, Patrick L., and Rensselaer Lee III. 1996. *The Andean Cocaine Industry*. New York: St. Martin's Press.

Cotler, Julio. 1994. *Política y Sociedad en el Perú. Cambios y Continuidades*. Lima: Instituto de Estudios Peruanos.

———. 1996. "Coca Sociedad y Estado en el Perú." Lima: UNDP.

———. 1999. *Drogas y Política en el Perú. La Conexión Norteamericana*. Lima: Instituto de Estudios Peruanos.

Cuánto, S.A. 1993. "Impacto de la Coca en la Economía Peruana: Perú, 1980–1992." Lima: USAID.

Dammert-Ego-Aguirre, Manuel. 2001. *Fujimori-Montesinos: el Estado Mafioso*. Lima: Ediciones El Virrey.

Deas, Malcolm. 1982. "Colombian Fiscal Problems during the XIX Century." Pt. 2. *Journal of Latin American Studies* 14 (2).

Degregori, Carlos Iván, J. Coronel, P. Del Pino, and O. Stam, eds. 1996. *Las Rondas Campesinas y la Derrota de Sendero Luminoso*. Lima: Instituto de Estudios Peruanos.

De Soto, Hernando. 2002. *The Other Path: The Economic Answer to Terrorism*. New York: Basic Books.

Dreyfus, Pablo G. 1999. "When All the Evils Come Together: Cocaine, Corruption, and Shining Path in Peru's Upper Huallaga Valley, 1980 to 1995." *Journal of Contemporary Criminal Justice* 15 (4): 370–96.

Duncan, Gustavo. 2006. *Los Señores de la Guerra: De paramilitares, mafiosos y autodefensas en Colombia*. Bogotá: Editorial Planeta.

Empresa Nacional de la Coca (ENACO). 2002. Oficio No. 028-2002-ENACO S.A. Lima: ENACO.

Fals-Borda, Orlando. 1961. *Campesinos de los Andes*. Estudio Sociológico de Saucío. Bogotá: Editorial Iqueima.

Farrell, G., and J. Thorne. 2005. "Where Have All the Flowers Gone? Evaluation of the Taliban Crackdown against Opium Poppy Cultivation in Afghanistan." *International Journal of Drug Policy* 16 (2): 81–91.

Farthing, Linda. 1997. "Social Impacts Associated with Antidrug Law 1008." In *Coca, Cocaine, and the Bolivian Reality*, ed. M. B. Léons and H. Sanabria. Albany: State University of New York Press.

Gagliano, Joseph. 1994. *Coca Prohibition in Peru*. Tucson: University of Arizona Press.

Gamarra, Eduardo A. 1994. *Entre la Droga y la Democracia: La cooperación entre Estados Unidos-Bolivia y la lucha contra el narcotráfico*. La Paz: ILDIS.

———. 1999. "La Guerra Contra las Drogas en Bolivia: Donde los Instrumentos de la Guerra Fría Siguen Vigentes." In *Drogas Ilícitas en Bolivia*, ed. E. Gamarra and F. E. Thoumi. La Paz: UNDP.

Gómez-Buendía, Hernando. 1999. "La Hipótesis del Almendrón." In *¿Para Dónde Va Colombia?* ed. H. Gómez-Buendía. Bogotá: TM Editores-Colciencias.

González, Fernán, S. J. 1998. "La Guerra de los Mil Días." In *Las Guerras Civiles Desde 1830 y su Proyección en el Siglo XX*. Memorias de la II Cátedra Anual de Historia "Ernesto Restrepo Tirado." Bogotá: Museo Nacional.

Gonzales-Manrique, José E. 1989. "Perú: Sendero Luminoso en el Valle de la Coca." In *Comisión Andina de Juristas, Coca, Cocaína y Narcotráfico: Laberinto en los Andes*. Lima: Comisión Andina de Juristas.

Goodson, Larry P. 2001. *Afghanistan's Endless War: State Failure, Regional Politics, and the Rise of the Taliban*. Seattle: University of Washington Press.

Gootemberg, Paul 1999. "Reluctance or Resistance? Constructing Cocaine (Prohibitions) in Peru, 1910–1950." In *Cocaine Global Histories*, ed. P. Gootemberg. New York: Reutledge.

Gugliotta, Guy, and Jeff Leen. 1990. *Kings of Cocaine*. New York: Harper and Row Publishers.

Gutiérrez, Francisco, and Mauricio Barón. 2006. "Estado, Control Territorial Paramilitar y Orden Político en Colombia. Notas para una Economía Política del Paramilitarismo, 1978–2004." In *Nuestra Guerra Sin Nombre. Transformaciones del Conflicto en Colombia*, ed. F. Gutiérrez, M. E. Wills, and F. Sánchez. Bogotá: IEPRI and Grupo Editorial Norma.

Hargreaves, Clare. 1992. *Snow Fields: The War on Cocaine in the Andes*. New York: Holmes & Meier Publishers, Inc.

Hartlyn, Jonathan. 1988. *The Politics of Coalition Rule in Colombia*. Cambridge: Cambridge University Press.

Healy, Kevin. 1991. "Political Ascent of Bolivia's Peasant Coca Leaf Producers." *Journal of Interamerican Studies and World Affairs* 33 (1): 87–121.

Hernández-Leal, Germán H. 2004. "Impacto de las Regalías Petroleras en el Departamento del Meta." Serie Ensayos Sobre Economía Regional, Centro Regional de Estudios Económicos. Villavicencio: Banco de la República.

Herrán, María Teresa. 1987. *La Sociedad de la Mentira*. 2nd ed. Bogotá: Fondo Editorial CEREC-Editorial la Oveja Negra.

Irusta, Gerardo. 1992. *Narcotráfico: Hablan los Arrepentidos. Personajes y hechos reales*. La Paz: Gerardo Irusta M.

Jaramillo-Uribe, Jaime. 1991. *Ensayos de Historia Social*. Vol. 1. Bogotá: TM Editores-Ediciones Uniandes.

Junguito, Roberto. 1995. *La Deuda Externa en el Siglo XIX. Cien Años de Incumplimiento*. Bogotá: TM Editores—Banco de la República.

Kalmanovitz, Salomón. 1989. *La Encrucijada de la Sinrazón y otros Ensayos*. Bogotá: Tercer Mundo Editores.

Krauthausen, Ciro. 1998. *Padrinos y Mercaderes. Crimen organizado en Italia y Colombia*. Bogotá: Planeta Colombiana Editorial.

Labrousse, Alain. 1991. *L'Argent, la drogue et les Armes*. Paris: Fayard.

———. 1995. "Pérou: Enjeux politico-militaires de la production et du trafic des drogues," *Problèmes d'Amérique Latine*, New Series 18 (July–September): 101–11.

———. 2004. "La drogue: Principal obstacle a la reconstruction de l'Afghanistan?" Report for the Transnational Institute, Amsterdam.

Lavaud, Jean-Pierre. 1998. *El Embrollo Boliviano. Turbulencias Sociales y Desplazamientos Políticos: 1952–1982*. La Paz: IFEA-CESU-Hisbol.

Leal-Buitrago, Francisco. 1989. *Estado y Política en Colombia*. 2nd ed., exp. Bogotá: Siglo Veintiuno Editores and CEREC.

Leal-Buitrago, Francisco, and Andrés Dávila, 1990. *Clientelismo. El Sistema Político y su Expresión Regional*. Bogotá: Tercer Mundo Editores and IEPRI.

Ledebur, Kathryn. 2005. "Bolivia: Clear Consequences." In *Drugs and Democracy in Latin America: The Impact of U.S. Policy*, ed. C. A. Youngers and E. Rosin. Boulder, CO: Lynne Rienner Publishers.

Lee III, Rensselaer W. 1990. *The White Labyrinth*. New Brunswick, NJ: Transaction Publishers.

Lee III, Rensselaer W., and Francisco E. Thoumi. 1999. "The Criminal-Political Nexus in Colombia." *Trends in Organized Crime* 5 (2): 59–84.

Lema, Ana María. 1997. "The Coca Debate and Yungas Landowners during the First Half of the 20th Century." In *Coca, Cocaine, and the Bolivian Reality*, ed. M. B. Léons and H. Sanabria. Albany: State University of New York Press.

Lemoine, Carlos. 2000. *Nosotros los Colombianos del Milenio*. Bogota: TM Editores-Cambio.

Léons, Madelaine Barbara, and Harry Sanabria. 1997. "Coca and Cocaine in Bolivia: Reality and Policy Illusion." In *Coca, Cocaine, and the Bolivian Reality*, ed. M. B. Léons and H. Sanabria. Albany: State University of New York Press.

Levine, Michael. 1991. *Deep Cover. The Inside Story of How DEA Infighting, Incompetence, and Subterfuge Lost Us the Biggest Battle of the Drug War*. New York: Dell Publishing.

Macroconsult S.A. 1990. "Impacto Económico del Narcotráfico en el Perú." Lima: Macroconsult.

Malamud-Goti, Jaime. 1994. *Humo y Espejos. La Paradoja de la Guerra Contra las Drogas*. Buenos Aires: Editores del Puerto.

Mansilla, H. C. Felipe. 1994. *Repercusiones Ecológicas y Éticas del Complejo Coca/Cocaína*. La Paz: SEAMOS, Investigación para el Debate No 7.

McClintock, Cynthia. 1988. "The War on Drugs: The Peruvian Case." *Journal of Interamerican Studies and World Affairs* 30 (1–2): 127–42.

Medina-Gallego, Carlos. 1990. *Autodefensas, Paramilitares y Narcotráfico en Colombia*. Bogotá: Editorial Documentos Periodísticos.

Morales, Edmundo. 1989. *Cocaine: White Gold Rush in Peru*. Tucson: University of Arizona Press.

North, Douglass C. 1990. *Institutions, Institutional Change, and Economic Performance*. Cambridge: Cambridge University Press.

Obando, Enrique. 1993. "El Narcotráfico en el Perú: Una Aproximación Histórica." *Análisis Internacional* (2) (April–June).

Ocampo, José Antonio. 1984. *Colombia y la Economía Mundial, 1830–1910*. Bogotá: Siglo Veintiuno Editores.

Painter, James. 1994. *Bolivia and Coca: A Study in Dependency*. Boulder, CO: Lynne Rienner Publishers.

Palmer, David Scout. 1980. *Peru. The Authoritarian Tradition*. New York: Praeger Publishers.

Puyana-García, Germán. 2005. *Cómo somos? Los Colombianos. Reflexiones Sobre Nuestra Idiosincrasia y Cultura.* Bogotá: Panamericana Editorial.

Quiroga, José Antonio. 1990. *Coca/Cocaína: Una Visión Boliviana.* La Paz: AIPE-PROCOM/CEDLA/CID.

República de Bolivia. 1998. *¡Por la Dignidad! Estrategia Boliviana de la Lucha Contra el Narcotráfico, 1998–2002.* La Paz: Ministerio de Gobierno.

Reyes-Posada, Alejandro. 1997. "Compra de Tierras por Narcotraficantes." In *Drogas Ilícitas en Colombia. Su Impacto Económico, Político y Social,* ed. F. Thoumi. Bogotá: PNUD, DNE, Editorial Ariel.

Reyes-Posada, Alejandro, Francisco E. Thoumi, and Liliana Duica-Amaya. 2006. "Drug Trafficking and the Colombian Border Regions." Research and Monitoring Center on Drugs and Crime, Universidad del Rosario, Bogotá. June.

Robinson, James. 2007. "¿Un típico país Latinoamericano? Una perspectiva sobre el desarrollo." In *Economía Colombiana del Siglo XXI. UN Análisis Cuantitativo,* ed. J. Robinson and M. Urrutia. Bogotá: Fondo de Cultura Económica and Banco de la República.

Rodas, Hugo. 1996. *Huanchaca: Modelo Político Empresarial de la Cocaína en Bolivia.* La Paz: Plural Editores.

Rojas, Isaías. 2005. "Peru: Drug Control Policy, Human Rights, and Democracy." In *Drugs and Democracy in Latin America: The Impact of U.S. Policy,* eds. C. A. Youngers and E. Rosin. Boulder, CO: Lynne Rienner Publishers.

Ronken, Theo, Kathryn Ledebur, and Tom Kruse. 1999. *The Drug War in the Skies: The U.S. "Air Bridge Denial" Strategy; The Success of a Failure.* Amsterdam: Transnational Institute and Acción Andina.

Rospigliosi, Fernando. 2001. *Montesinos y las Fuerzas Armadas. Cómo Controló Durante una Década las Instituciones Militares.* Lima: Instituto de Estudios Peruanos.

Roy, Olivier. 1993. "Afghanistan: An Islamic War of Resistance. In *Fundamentalisms and the State: Remaking Politics, Economics, and Militance.* ed. Martin E. Marty and Scott Appleby. Chicago: University of Chicago Press.

Ruiz-Hernández, Hernando. 1979. "Implicaciones Sociales y Económicas de la Producción de la Marihuana." In *Marihuana: Legalización o Represión.* Bogotá: Biblioteca Asociación Nacional de Instituciones Financieras .

Sánchez and Chacón. 2006.

Saénz-Rovner, Eduardo. 2005. *La Conexión Cubana. Narcotráfico, contrabando y juego en Cuba entre los años 20 y comienzos de la revolución.* Bogotá: Universidad Nacional de Colombia.

———. 2007. "La Prehistoria de la Marihuana en Colombia: Consumo y Cultivos entre los Años 30 y 60." Cuadernos de Economía XXVI (47): 205–22.

Sanabria, Harry. 1993. *The Coca Boom and Rural Social Change in Bolivia.* Ann Arbor: University of Michigan Press.

Spedding, Alison L. 1997. "The Coca Field as a Total Social Fact." In *Coca, Cocaine, and the Bolivian Reality,* ed. M. B. Léons and H. Sanabria. Albany: State University of New York Press.

Tarazona-Sevillano, Gabriela, with John B. Reuter. 1990. *Sendero Luminoso and the Threat of Narcoterrorism*. New York: Praeger Publishers.

Thoumi, Francisco E. 1987. "Some Implications of the Growth of the Underground Economy in Colombia." *Journal of Interamerican Studies and World Affairs* 29 (2): 35–53.

———. 1995. *Political Economy and Illegal Drugs in Colombia*. Boulder, CO: Lynne Rienner Publishers.

———. 1999. "The Role of the State, Social Institutions, and Social Capital in Determining Competitive Advantage in Illegal Drugs in the Andes." *Transnational Organized* Crime 5 (1): 76–96.

———. 2003a. *Illegal Drugs, Economy and Society in the Andes*. Baltimore: Johns Hopkins University Press for the Woodrow Wilson International Center for Scholars.

———. 2003b. "Las Drogas Ilegales en el Peru." Unpublished internal report. Washington, DC: Inter-American Development Bank.

———. 2007. "The Rise of Two Drug Tigers: The Development of the Illegal Drugs Industry and Drug Policy Failure in Afghanistan and Colombia." In *The Organized Crime Community: Essays in Honor of Alan A. Block*, ed. F. Bovenkerk and M. Levi. New York: Springer.

———. 2008. "From Drug Lords to Warlords: Illegal drugs and the 'Unintended' Consequences of Drug Policies in Colombia." In *Governments of the Shadows*, ed. T. Lindsey and E. Wilson. London: Pluto Press.

United Nations High Commissioner for Refugees (UNHCR/ACNUR). 2007. *Balance de la política pública de atención integral a la población desplazada por la violencia, 2004–2006*. Bogotá: UNHCR/ACNUR.

United Nations Institute for Disarmament Research (UNIDIR). 2006. "Monitor de Minas Terrestres 2006: Hacia un mundo libre de minas." Geneva: UNIDIR.

United Nations Office of Drug Control and Crime Prevention (UNODCCP). 2000. "UNDCP Alternative Development Work in Peru: A Success Story in Progress." February Vienna.

United Nations Office on Drugs and Crime (UNODC). 2003. *The Opium Economy in Afghanistan: An International Problem*. New York: United Nations.

———. 2004. *World Drug Report 2004*. New York: United Nations.

———. 2005. *World Drug Report 2005*. New York: United Nations.

———. 2007. *World Drug Report 2007*. New York: United Nations.

Urrutia, Miguel.1991. "On the Absence of Economic Populism in Colombia." In *The Macroeconomics of Populism in Latin America*, ed. Rudiger Dornbush and Sebastián Edwards. Chicago: University of Chicago Press.

U. S. Department of State. Bureau of International Narcotics Matters. 1992. *International Narcotics Strategy Report*. Washington, DC: U.S. Department of State.

Vargas-Meza, Ricardo. 2005. *Narcotráfico, Guerra y Política Antidrogas. Una perspectiva sobre las drogas en el conflicto armado colombiano*. Bogotá: Acción Andina.

Yunis, Emilio. 2003. *¿Por Qué Somos Así? ¿Qué Pasó en Colombia? Análisis del Mestizaje*. Bogotá: Editorial Temis.

7

Cocaine Production and Trafficking: What Do We Know?

Daniel Mejía and Carlos Esteban Posada

The nature of illegal and so-called black markets makes it very difficult to collect data such as quantities of goods traded, intermediate and final prices, and other relevant market characteristics, including the quality of the product and the distribution of profits within the industry. Illegal drug markets are not the exception.[1] For instance, in measuring consumption "buyers cannot report a price in dollars per standardized unit, but only how much they spent on some quantity of white powder, the contents of which is unknown" (Reuter and Greenfield 2001, 169). Notwithstanding the difficulties of collecting accurate data, estimates of the size, quantities, and prices of the market always attract a good deal of attention—not only from policy makers who want to request appropriations, governments that want to measure the success of antidrug policies, and analysts who want to identify those who profit from the illegal drugs business but also from journalists who want to inform the public. Many times the numbers are, voluntarily or not, misused "to buttress

The authors wish to thank Norman Loayza, Phil Keefer, and workshop participants at the World Bank for helpful comments and suggestions. Diana Jaramillo provided excellent research assistance. As usual, the views expressed in this article are solely those of the authors and not those of the Banco de la República, Colombia, or its board of governors.

preconceived and personal agendas." And, as one researcher has put it, "[T]he emotional and ideological charge carried by most data users leads to widespread data misuse" (Thoumi 2005a, 186).

This chapter describes the available data for measuring the incidence and prevalence of cocaine production and trafficking. It also describes the main data sources and the collection methodologies, if available, and examines the accuracy and biases of those sources. The chapter poses some key empirical questions and hypotheses that should drive future research into the determinants of cocaine production and trafficking and of the outcomes and side effects of the war against illegal drugs. If the price elasticity of demand is a crucial aspect of the effectiveness of the war on drugs, for example, what are the short- and long-term price elasticities of demand for cocaine? What factors underlie the estimation of potential cocaine production? Have illegal drug producers made technological advances that counteract the measures taken in the war on drugs? What are the results of that war? Is the war sustainable in the long run? What are its side effects?

The chapter also studies the outcomes of the war against the production of cocaine in the producer countries, the role of consumer countries in the implementation of specific antidrug policies, and the effectiveness of these policies and some of their possible side effects. Finally, the chapter briefly discusses the sustainability of policies aimed at reducing the production of cocaine in source countries. Before describing the data and collection methodologies, we provide some basic information on our main topic: cocaine.

A Brief Introduction to Cocaine

Cocaine is a powerful addictive drug produced in large quantities in only a few Latin American countries: the Plurinational State of Bolivia, Colombia, and Peru.[2] The main ingredient used to produce cocaine is cocaine alkaloid, a chemical compound extracted from the leaves of coca plants.[3] Coca was grown in the Andes long before the arrival of European settlers. The local indigenous population in the Americas chewed its leaves (and, in some cases, still does) to help relieve fatigue caused by altitude sickness and to achieve a mild stimulant effect. Today, prevailing indigenous populations in Bolivia and Peru still use coca leaves in religious and social ceremonies.[4]

The coca plant is a very hardy, medium-sized bush that grows in a tropical rainforest climate anywhere between 100 and 1,700 meters above sea level. The time between planting and harvesting ranges from six to nine months, depending on the coca variety, climate, and geographical conditions. Coca bushes can be grown and harvested year-round, but most growth occurs from December to April. Coca is harvested, on average, four times a year (a minimum of three and a maximum of eight, depending on the variety and location of the coca) and requires up to 300 man-days to harvest 1 hectare—about 2.5 acres—for one year (CIA 2004).

Although more than 250 different varieties of the coca plant exist, only a few are widely used today to produce cocaine for the illegal drug markets.[5] Cocaine production is a relatively simple process that can take place in small local workshops. The process of producing cocaine consists of three main steps:

- The coca leaves are harvested, dried, and converted into coca paste.
- The coca paste is then converted into cocaine base.
- The cocaine base is made into the final product: cocaine (cocaine hydrochloride). The manufacturing process requires a few chemicals (precursors), such as sulfuric acid, potassium permanganate, ether, hydrochloric acid, acetone, and ethyl ether; water, filters, and microwave ovens are also needed.

Depending on coca variety, geography, bushes per hectare, and the like, 1 hectare planted with coca bushes produces, on average, between 1,000 and 1,200 kilograms of fresh coca leaf per harvest. Between 1.1 and 1.4 grams of cocaine can be produced from 1 kilogram of coca leaf. Using an average of four harvests per year and the yields described above, we arrive at a general production estimate of between 5 and 6 kilograms of cocaine per hectare per year.[6]

Cocaine hydrochloride, a white crystalline powder,[7] is a highly potent and addictive stimulant.[8] It is either snorted or dissolved in water and injected. Because of the high price of cocaine, by the late 1970s and beginning of the 1980s, drug dealers discovered a new and cheaper alternative for low-income users: crack—a rocky crystal obtained by mixing cocaine, baking soda, and water in a saucepan—whose name derives from the crackling sound produced when the ingredients are being burned to create the vapors that are then inhaled (see Levitt and Dubner 2005).

Cocaine is the second most consumed illegal drug in the United States (after marijuana) and the third in most European countries (after marijuana and heroin). Cocaine consumption triggers different physical effects. In moderate doses, it causes disturbances in heart rates, elevated blood pressure, dilated pupils, decreased appetite, irritability, and argumentative behavior, among other effects. In large doses, it can lead to loss of coordination, collapse, blurred vision, dizziness, anxiety, heart attacks, chest pain, respiratory failure, strokes, seizures, headaches, abdominal pain, nausea, and paranoia. The duration of the euphoric effect of cocaine (the "high") depends on the route of administration. With faster absorption, the high is more intense but shorter. When the cocaine is snorted, the high can last from 15 to 30 minutes; when the cocaine is smoked, the high can last from 5 to 10 minutes.

Data Sources

The two main sources of data for illegal drug production, prices, extent of cultivation of illegal crops, and seizures of drug shipments are the United Nations Office on Drugs and Crime (UNODC) and the U.S. Office of National Drug Control Policy (ONDCP). In addition to these two sources, other institutions—many times government departments in producer countries—either gather their own statistics or collaborate in the gathering of data with UNODC or ONDCP.

UNODC

Established in 1997, UNODC has become the main source for data on illegal drug markets. It employs about 500 staff members worldwide and has 21 field offices located in the main producer countries, as well as in those countries used as traffic corridors. According to its mandate, UNODC is to assist member countries in their struggle against illegal drugs, crime, and terrorism.[9] UNODC relies on voluntary contributions—mainly from just a few countries—for almost 90 percent of its budget.[10] UNODC works jointly with the appropriate government institutions in the producer countries to undertake the Coca

Cultivation Survey each year. Through the Illicit Crop Monitoring Programme, UNODC uses the interpretation and processing of satellite images to monitor illegal crops in producer countries: coca in the three Andean producer countries and opium poppy in South and East Asian countries.[11] Using surveys and studies on yields, this institution also produces an estimate of potential cocaine production, gathers prices of intermediate goods such as dry coca leaf and coca base, and collects other crucial statistics such as eradication measures, seizures of drug shipments, and the number of cocaine-processing laboratories destroyed as reported by different governmental institutions in producer countries.[12]

ONDCP

ONDCP's data on coca cultivation are prepared by the U.S. Director of Central Intelligence, Crime and Narcotics Center (CNC), and are published each March in the *International Narcotics Control Strategy Report* as part of the U.S. president's determination of whether to provide assistance to drug producer and transit countries. In preparing its estimates of coca cultivation, CNC analyzes black-and-white, high-resolution satellite imagery and aerial photographs. These photographs are taken only between November and January of each year, weather permitting. The satellite images and aerial photographs cover a representative area of the known or suspected drug-growing locations in the producer countries. The technique for analyzing the satellite images and aerial photographs is similar to the one used to estimate agricultural crops throughout the United States (see ONDCP 2005). However, according to a study conducted by ONDCP in 2002, the CNC's methodology has not adopted a "statistically rigorous accuracy assessment, commonly known as an error rate" in its methodology for measuring coca cultivation. Moreover, the technology used by CNC is inappropriate because it did not account for image distortions or variations in the terrain and the atmosphere, such as cloud cover.

UNODC's methodology for collecting data on coca cultivation covers almost the entire territories in the producer countries, whereas ONDCP's covers only a representative sample. UNODC also makes more corrections than ONDCP for possible biases and mistakes in the interpretation of aerial imagery. Finally, UNODC has been actively involved in conducting the Coca Cultivation Surveys in each of the producer countries, which are complemented by continuous efforts to undertake field studies to update yields per hectare and other information relevant for estimating potential cocaine production. Although UNODC stands as a more reliable source of data on coca cultivation, cocaine production, and related issues, we will also be referring to the other two data sources in the following section of the chapter for comparison purposes.

Cocaine Production: Stylized Facts

This section describes in detail the available evidence regarding the evolution over time in coca cultivation; coca leaf, coca base, and cocaine prices; potential cocaine production; and purity levels. When available, we compare estimates from different sources.

Coca Cultivation

According to ONDCP, coca cultivation in the three Andean countries remained relatively stable throughout the 1990s. On average, while coca cultivation covered about 200,000 hectares, each country's share of total cultivation changed dramatically during the decade. In 1990, Peru had the largest number of hectares under coca cultivation (about 62 percent of the total), and Colombia the lowest (14 percent). By 1999, these shares had completely reversed, with Peru having 21 percent of the total, Bolivia, 12 percent, and Colombia 67 percent (figure 7.1). On the one hand, this change was, in part, a result of the increasing eradication efforts of the Bolivian and Peruvian governments and of the aerial interdiction efforts of the Peruvian government to close the air bridge between coca-producing centers in Peru and cocaine-processing laboratories in Colombia. On the other hand, in Colombia, after the demise of the Medellín and Cali cartels in the mid-1990s, the Fuerzas Armadas Revolucionarias de Colombia (FARC), and the Autodefensas Unidas de Colombia—their historical origins as leftist guerrillas and right-wing paramilitaries notwithstanding—became increasingly involved in the production and commercialization of cocaine to finance their insurgent activities against each other and against the Colombian state.[13]

Figure 7.1. Estimates of Coca Bush Cultivation in Bolivia, Colombia, and Peru, 1987–2005

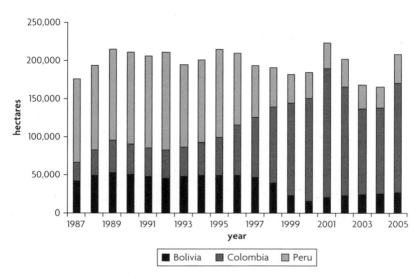

Source: ONDCP 2009.

As a result, coca cultivation reached its highest levels ever recorded in Colombia (about 163,000 hectares) by 2000. The Colombian government responded to the large increase in coca cultivation with Plan Colombia, the official name of a multiyear, comprehensive strategy designed and implemented in 2001 to bring about lasting peace by reducing the production of illegal drugs. As a result, from 2000 to 2003 coca cultivation in Colombia decreased by more than 47 percent, whereas in Bolivia and Peru it remained relatively stable.

According to the latest UNODC report, total coca cultivation in the three producer countries has remained relatively stable during the past eight years (figure 7.2a). ONDCP's figures (presented in figure 7.2b) are available only until 2005. Those figures should be treated with care as they expanded by 81 percent the size of the landmass that was imaged and sampled for coca cultivation, and, when the new areas covered are taken into account, there is an increase of 39,000 hectares cultivated with coca.[14] As ONDCP noted in a press release,

Figure 7.2. Estimates of Coca Bush Cultivation in Bolivia, Colombia, and Peru by UNODC and ONDCP, 2000–08

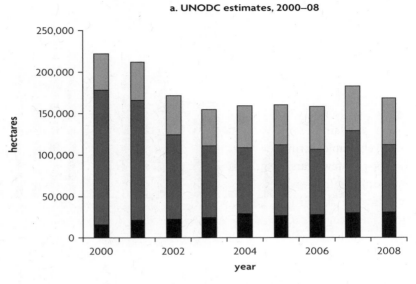

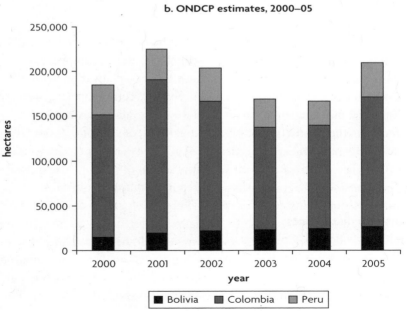

Because these areas were not previously surveyed, it is impossible to determine for how long they have been under coca cultivation. . . . The higher cultivation figure in this year's estimate does not necessarily mean that coca cultivation increased in the last year, but rather reflects an improved understanding of where coca is now growing in Colombia. (ONDCP 2005)

Summarizing, according to the two sources, total cultivation in the three Andean countries shows a large decrease between 2001 and 2003, due largely to the substantial decrease in Colombia after the implementation of Plan Colombia. If anything, coca cultivation has remained relatively stable during the past five years reported. Although the figures for the past few years are not enough evidence to conclusively support a ballooning effect—where a decrease in cultivation in one area because of "effective" antidrug policies leads to the reallocation of crops to new areas, resulting in unchanged or even increased total cultivation—it does send a warning signal of the potential for large increases in Bolivia and Peru if antidrug policies and monitoring are not maintained in all areas where coca can and has been grown in the past (see U.S. Department of State 2005).

Because UNODC started the Illicit Crop Monitoring System in Colombia only in 1999, in Peru in 2000, and in Bolivia in 2003, data between the two main sources of information can be compared only for those years. Figure 7.3 shows the evolution of coca bush cultivation in Colombia according to the two main sources between 1999 and 2005. Although the levels are different, with an almost constant average difference between the two sources of about 32,000 hectares, the tendencies in the two sources are very similar. The same pattern is observed for Bolivia, Colombia, and Peru—that is, an almost constant level of coca cultivation with a small increasing tendency in the last year.

Intermediate Prices

Although Bolivia, Colombia, and Peru have an active market for coca leaf, in Colombia that market is very limited because most farmers process the coca leaves into coca base themselves in small "kitchens" located on their farms. Thus, UNODC collects monthly data on prices of sun-dried coca leaf in Bolivia and Peru and of coca base in Colombia, based on semistructured interviews of farmers, storekeepers, and others who

Figure 7.3. UNODC and ONDCP Estimates of Coca Bush Cultivation in Colombia, 1999–2005

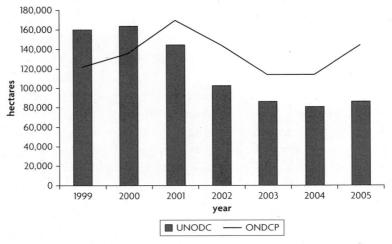

Sources: UNODC 2009; ONDCP 2009.

participate in the cultivation of coca and the production of coca base. In many instances, the prices are collected in only a few regions where coca is grown, and, as a result, the selected sample may be far from representative and should be treated with care. For instance, during 2004 the prices of coca leaf in Bolivia were collected only in the Yungas of La Paz by UNODC and in the Chapare region by the Dirección de Reconversión de la Coca (DIRECO), in 13 different locations in Peru, and in five departments in Colombia.

The price of dried coca leaf in Bolivia, Colombia, and Peru increased dramatically from 1996 to 2001 as a direct result of the eradication measures of the Bolivian, Colombian, and Peruvian governments and the efforts of the Peruvian government to close the air bridge connecting the coca- and coca paste–producing centers in Peru and the coca-processing laboratories in Colombia. Figures 7.4a and 7.4b show the evolution of coca leaf prices in Bolivia and Peru along with potential coca leaf production as calculated by UNODC according to yields per hectare.

In Colombia, despite the large decrease in coca cultivation between 2001 and 2006, neither the price of coca base nor coca base production showed any increasing tendency between 2000 and 2007 (see figure 7.5).

Figure 7.4. Potential Dried Coca Leaf Production and Prices in Bolivia and Peru, 1990–2007

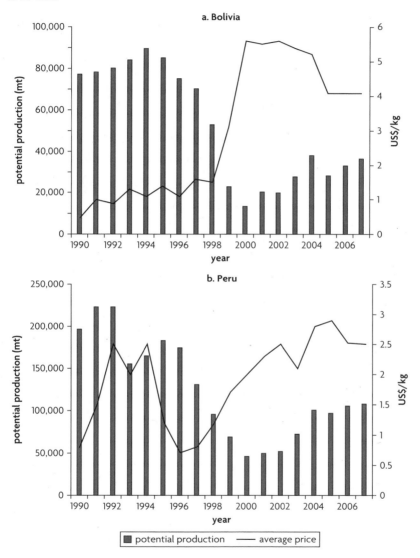

Source: UNODC 2008 and 2009.

According to UNODC (2008), the price of coca base increased between 2001 and 2003. That increase, however, is only nominal. The price of coca base has been stable (as calculated in dollars) or decreasing (as calculated in real pesos) ever since the beginning of the implementation

Figure 7.5. Coca Base Production and Prices in Colombia, 2000–07

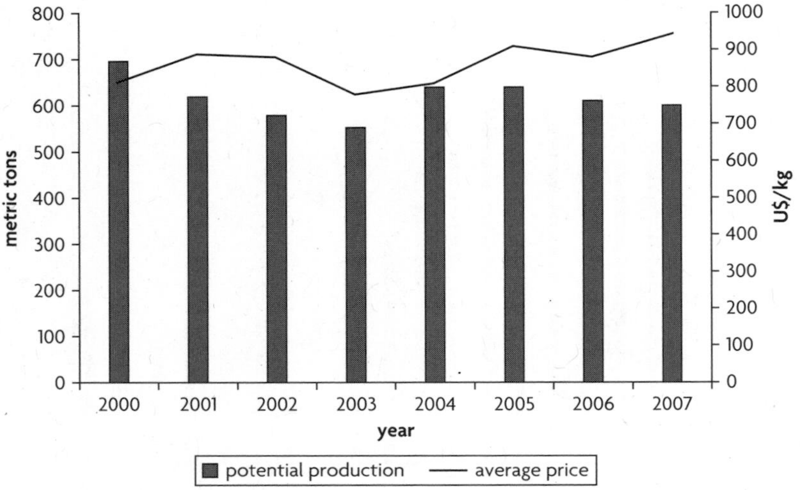

Source: UNODC 2008 and 2009.

of Plan Colombia in 2001, precisely the moment when coca cultivation started to decrease rapidly. According to some sources, this apparent puzzle—of lower cultivation of coca and lower prices of coca base—can be partially explained by the offsetting effects of larger imports of coca paste from Peru and the large increases in productivity per hectare in the production of coca base.[15] The next section will elaborate on this question and on a "twin puzzle," namely, the stability of cocaine prices in the U.S. market despite the large decrease in coca cultivation between 2000 and 2003 in the three producer countries and a relatively stable demand for cocaine in the consumer countries.

Potential Cocaine Production
Using yields per hectare as well as technical coefficients of transformation for each of the main links in the cocaine production chain, UNODC produces an estimate of the potential manufacture of cocaine for each one of the three producer countries in the Andean region. Until 2004, UNODC's estimates relied on other sources for information on technical coefficients, the main source being Operation Breakthrough, a U.S. Drug Enforcement Administration (DEA) project designed to estimate

the amount of cocaine produced in the Andean region by examining the yield and alkaloid content of coca crops and the efficiency of clandestine cocaine-producing laboratories.

In 2004, however, UNODC began a series of field studies to complement its crop-monitoring system that estimated coca leaf yields per hectare, average weight loss for sun-dried and oven-dried leaves, and conversion rates from coca leaf to cocaine, among others (see the Coca Cultivation Surveys for the three producer countries published by UNODC 2005 through 2008). The implementation of those surveys, however, is often hampered by the social tensions prevailing in the coca-producing regions and by the farmers' reluctance to cooperate with the interviewers. Despite the difficulties in carrying out these studies, however, they are of the greatest importance not only in helping us better understand coca and its derivatives' markets but also in allowing us to evaluate the efficiency of antidrug programs more accurately and monitor changes in each link of the cocaine production process.[16]

Not surprisingly, according to UNODC the main trend in potential cocaine production is very similar to that for coca cultivation, that is, a relatively stable total potential production from 1990 to 1999 (about 860 metric tons) and then a decrease between 2000 and 2003. By 2003, cocaine production had reached a minimum level of about 800 metric tons caused, almost completely, by the large decrease in potential production in Colombia (see figure 7.6a). For 2004 to 2006, however, new estimates of coca leaf yields per hectare obtained by UNODC and the Colombian government point to worrisome results, namely, that productivity per hectare has increased from 4.7 to 7.7 kilograms per hectare per year (a 63 percent increase).[17] This new estimate—as well as the sustained high prices of coca leaf in Bolivia, (above $5/kilogram) and Peru (above $2.5/kilogram), which likely created an incentive for farmers in these two countries to increase coca cultivation—is based on a large increase in the estimated potential cocaine production between 2003 and 2004. While in Bolivia, potential cocaine production increased by 35 percent in 2004 and in Peru by 23 percent in the same year, in Colombia it increased by 16 percent, despite the reduction in the number of coca-cultivated hectares.

Using the most recent estimates of cultivation by the CNC, along with the DEA's data on coca yields and laboratory efficiency, the U.S. State

Figure 7.6. UNODC and ONDCP Estimates of Potential Cocaine Production in Bolivia, Colombia, and Peru, 1996–2006

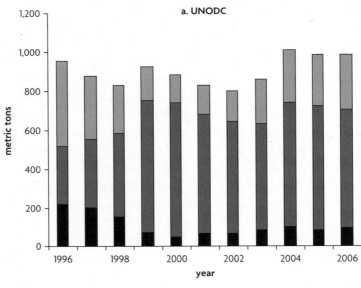

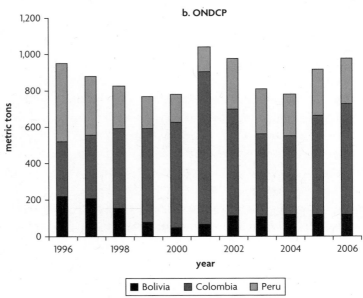

Sources: UNODC 2009; ONDCP 2009.

Department also produces an estimate of potential cocaine production. According to this source, after reaching a peak of more than 1,000 metric tons in 2001, total cocaine production in the Andean countries declined between 2001 and 2004 (see figure 7.6b). For 2005, potential cocaine production is not comparable to prior years because ONDCP includes in its calculation those newly surveyed fields that were not included in previous years. In fact, our own calculations suggest that potential cocaine production would have been 431 metric tons (the same as in 2004) if the newly surveyed areas were omitted. Although potential cocaine production in Bolivia and Peru, according to this source, remained relatively stable during the past five years surveyed (at 110 metric tons and 250 metric tons per year, respectively), in Colombia it decreased very rapidly until 2004 and then increased rapidly again. By 2004 and 2005, potential cocaine production in Colombia (430 metric tons) was about 50 percent of what it had been in 2001 (840 metric tons).[18]

According to an ONDCP report (2005), potential cocaine production declined more rapidly than coca bush cultivation because, since intense aerial spraying started in Colombia in 2001, the proportion of newly planted coca fields is increasing and these fields are less productive than more mature fields. Although it might be true that aerial spraying decreases the average age of coca fields and hence lowers the yields, new evidence suggests that illegal groups engaged in cocaine production are responding to intensified eradication measures with strategies that increase coca yields. As a result, ONDCP estimates that potential cocaine production in Colombia has increased since 2004.

Average Purity

UNODC and ONDCP also gather statistics on the average purity of cocaine by using information from laboratories and seizures of cocaine shipments in producer and transit countries, as well as retail information from street seizures in consumer countries. On the one hand, between 2002 and 2004 the average purity of cocaine in the producer countries ranged between 82 percent and 95 percent (UNODC 2006). On the other hand, because data on purity levels in consumer countries are obtained from drug seizures, many times done at the retail level, the average purity of cocaine varies widely, even for a given transaction size in a given city and year (Caulkins 1994). In addition, the spread in expected purity does not decrease as the quantities transacted increase, and, as a result, the interpretation of simple averages should be treated with care (ONDCP 2009). According to ONDCP, the average expected purity of cocaine[19] in the U.S. market increased rapidly throughout the 1980s for all quantities being transacted; it then decreased during the first few years of the 1990s and remained relatively stable during the 1990s. Finally, in the past few years, expected purity of powder cocaine has increased, reaching levels of about 70 percent for purchases of less than 2 grams in 2006, and 74 percent for purchases of 10 to 50 grams (see figure 7.7).

Although one would expect increasing purity levels as the quantities transacted increase (as occurred in the 1980s), purity differences across quantity levels had almost disappeared in the 1990s, mainly because purity levels at the highest quantities transacted fell. According to ONDCP (2004), those data suggest that diluting cocaine was not as common a practice in the 1990s as it was in the 1980s. In fact, after 1998 higher purity levels prevail for the lowest-quantity purchases. The same pattern is observed when information on purity levels obtained through seizures and other enforcement activities is also included (see figure 7.8).

Figure 7.7. Average Expected Purity of Powder Cocaine in the United States, 1981–2007

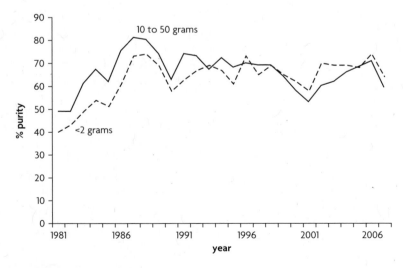

Source: ONDCP 2009, based on STRIDE.
Note: Information from purchases only.

According to evidence cited by Caulkins and Reuter (1998), purity levels do not seem to affect retail transaction prices in consumer countries. The authors explain this apparent mystery, however, by observing that illegal drugs are "experience" goods, for which the price paid is determined partly by the purity the buyer expects at the time of purchase according to information such as the size of the purchase, its location, and other observable characteristics. Given the lack of official regulation in illegal drug markets, sellers can deceive consumers about the purity of the product. At the same time, buyers can later argue that the product was of lower quality than agreed at the time of the transaction. These disputes, not surprisingly, many times end up generating violence.[20]

A Brief Look at Consumption Trends

Although this chapter concentrates on cocaine production and trafficking, to say anything meaningful about the price of cocaine in world markets, we must briefly review demand.

The United States, where cocaine is the second most consumed illegal drug after marijuana, is the main consumer country in the world.

Figure 7.8. Average Purity of Powder Cocaine in the United States, 1981–2007

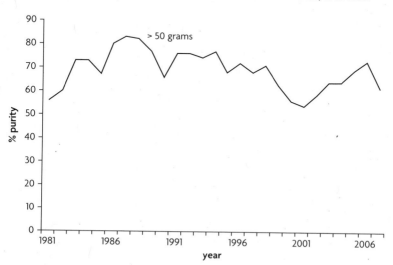

Source: ONDCP 2009, based on STRIDE.
Note: Information from purchases, seizures, and other enforcement activities.

In most European countries, cocaine is the third illegal drug consumed, after marijuana and heroin.[21] While in the United States,
the annual prevalence rate of abuse in the 15- to 64-year-old population is about 2.8 percent; the rate is 2.7 percent in Spain; 2.4 percent
in the United Kingdom;[22] 1.1 percent in Ireland, Italy, and the
Netherlands; and less than 0.3 percent in countries such as France,
Poland, and Sweden.

Cocaine consumption in the United States decreased rapidly between
1985 and 1993; since then, it has remained relatively stable. While in
1985 the annual prevalence rate among 12-year-olds and older in the
general population was about 5.1 percent, by 1993 this rate had decreased
to about 2 percent. Among high school students, prevalence rates
also decreased rapidly between 1985 and 1992: from 13.1 percent to 3.1
percent. In the second half of the 1990s, the prevalence rate among 12th
graders in the United States fluctuated between 3 and 6 percent
(UNODC, *World Drug Report* 2005, using information from the Substance Abuse and Mental Health Services Administration, SAMHSA).
The percentage of the population reporting current (that is, during the
month before the interview) and occasional (1 to 11 times during the
12 months before the interview) use of cocaine also shows the same pattern (see figure 7.9). Other indicators, such as the trend in hospital
admissions for cocaine treatment, also show a decrease in cocaine use
between 1992 and 2002 (the last year recorded). While the primary
admission rate[23] for cocaine per 100,000 inhabitants (age 12 or older)
was about 125 in 1992, by 2002 it had decreased by approximately 24
percent to about 100 (SAMHSA 2005).[24]

Among high school students, the evidence on cocaine consumption
trends is somewhat mixed. Although measures of 30-day prevalence
rates for cocaine use among 12th graders began to increase, next peaked
in 1999, and then remained relatively stable until 2003, for the past three
years recorded it has increased, reaching in 2006 almost the same level
observed at the peak of 1999 (see figure 7.10): 12th graders' perceptions
of the harmfulness of cocaine consumption seem to have declined in the
past few years recorded[25] (University of Michigan 2006).

In Europe, however, cocaine consumption, according to most estimates, has been on the rise in recent years.[26] For instance, in Spain, the
country that shows the highest rates of cocaine consumption in Europe,

Figure 7.9. Percentage of U.S. Population Age 12 and Older Reporting Use of Cocaine, 1985–2007

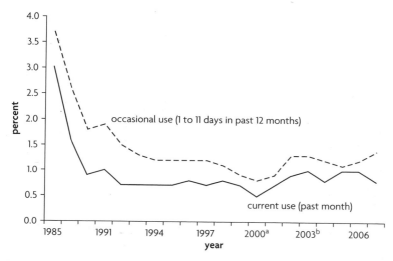

Source: ONDCP 2009.
Note: Results prior to 1999 and the ones after 2002 are not comparable to other years.
a. Change occurred in methodology: in 2000 from paper-and-pencil to computer-assisted interviews.
b. Methodological changed in 2003 in the survey.

Figure 7.10. Cocaine Use in the Past 30 Days among 12th Graders in the United States, 1991–2006

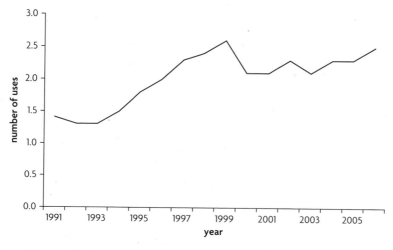

Source: University of Michigan 2006.

the prevalence of cocaine use among the general population (age 15–64) increased from 1.5 percent in 1995 to 2.7 percent in 2003. In the Netherlands, it increased from 0.7 percent in 1997 to 1.1 percent in 2001. In Switzerland, cocaine use among 15- and 16-year-olds increased from 0.9 percent in 1994 to 2.5 percent in 2002. Germany experienced an increase in cocaine use in people between 18 and 64 years of age from 0.2 percent in 1990 to 1 percent in 2003 (UNODC 2004).

Cocaine Prices

According to ONDCP (2009), the price per gram of pure cocaine fell from more than $600 for purchases of 2 grams or less and $320 for purchases of more than 50 grams in 1981 to about $121 and about $48, respectively, in 2007 (figure 7.11).[27] A similar long-term trend in cocaine prices shows up in UNODC estimates (figure 7.12).

Figure 7.11. Average Price of 1 Gram of Pure Powder Cocaine in the United States, 1981–2007

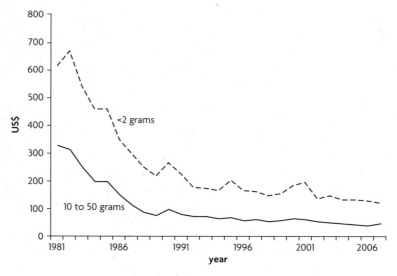

Source: ONDCP 2009.

Figure 7.12. Price of Cocaine in the United States and Europe at Street Purity, 1990–2007

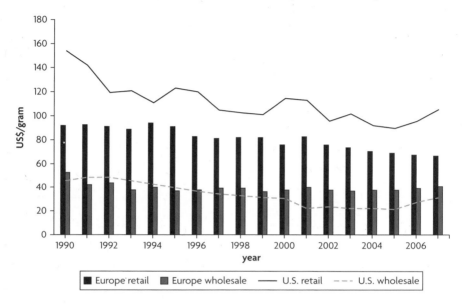

Sources: UNODC 2009; ONDCP 2009.

The Main Puzzle—and Its Resolution

According to most measures available, potential cocaine production decreased about 30 percent or more between 2000 and 2004, while demand in the consumer countries, if anything, remained relatively stable. Yet prices of intermediate inputs (coca leaf and coca base) in producer countries and of cocaine in the consumer countries had been stable or decreasing until then.[28] With a roughly stable demand for the product, lower production estimates, mounting seizures, and increasing interception of drug shipments and destruction of cocaine processing laboratories, cocaine prices would have been expected to rise or remain stable, not fall, as seems, in fact, to have been the case. Or, as Reuter (2001, 18) puts it, "If thorough enforcement did not raise drug prices, then it might still claim success if it lowered availability. But the data, mostly from surveys of high school seniors, show no decrease."

Recent estimates by UNODC found a large increase in estimates of productivity. In particular, the UNODC found that, on average, the number of kilograms produced by 1 hectare of coca in one year increased from 4.7 to 7.7 (UNODC 2006). This rise corresponds to a 40 percent increase in the yield per hectare. When this new estimate of productivity is used to calculate potential cocaine production, UNODC finds that, although the number of coca-cultivated hectares in Colombia decreased more than 40 percent between 2001 and 2008, each hectare is now more productive. As a result of those two factors, potential cocaine production in Colombia has not decreased as much as earlier thought.

Figure 7.13a summarizes the main changes in the market for cocaine between 1980 and 2008, and figure 7.13b summarizes the two opposing forces that kept cocaine supply relatively stable between 2000 and 2008: first, eradication measures tend to decrease cocaine supply by destroying

Figure 7.13. The Market for Cocaine (1980–2008) and the Stability of Cocaine Supply (2000–08)

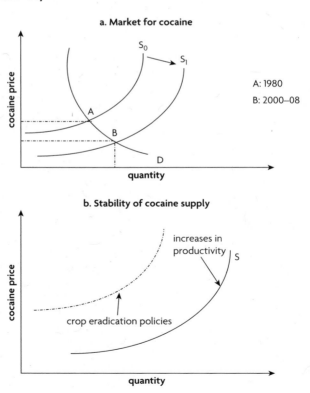

a. Market for cocaine

A: 1980
B: 2000–08

b. Stability of cocaine supply

Source: Authors.

coca crops; and, second, increases in productivity in the production of coca leaf and cocaine have counteracted antidrug policies in producer countries, rendering those policies ineffective in reducing the amount of cocaine produced. Despite the extensive resources spent in the war on drugs, a relatively stable demand and the stability of the cocaine supply kept quantities and prices of cocaine about constant between 2000 and 2007.

The next three sections elaborate on possible sources of bias in the data and draw attention to how the data on cocaine production and consumption should be read and analyzed.

Possible Biases on the Supply-Side Estimates

Although neither UNODC nor ONDCP has any evidence of large-scale coca cultivation or cocaine production in countries other than the traditional three Andean nations, some evidence suggests that cocaine-producing organizations and individuals have tried to counteract the effects of antidrug policies (such as aerial and manual eradication) in producer countries. For instance, peasants intermingle coca crops with legal crops to prevent coca from being detected by satellite imagery, thus avoiding both monitoring and eradication. Such efforts also introduce a bias in the figures on coca cultivation gathered by UNODC and ONDCP as well as in their estimates of potential cocaine production. Another source of bias derives from the assumptions on yields and technical coefficients of transformation that UNODC and ONDCP use to estimate potential cocaine production. Those coefficients of transformation are used to convert quantities of coca leaf into quantities of cocaine through the different stages of processing. The potential biases could result from a higher density of coca crops, more efficient planting techniques, the use of more efficient fertilizers and chemical precursors, and the development of genetically modified coca plants with much higher yields. For instance, Colombian authorities have recently argued that coca yields have increased as a result of the introduction of a new, genetically modified coca variety, which is supposedly much taller and of a much higher quality with a higher percentage of hydrochloride (that is, more cocaine and cocaine of higher purity can be extracted from each leaf); it is also said to be glyphosate resistant (McDermott 2004).[29]

The implementation of more efficient planting techniques and the introduction of new fertilizers and chemicals in the manufacturing process would also lead to the production of more cocaine from fewer coca fields. For instance, after the successful operations to stop the diversion of potassium permanganate (a precursor used in the manufacture of cocaine) in Colombia at the end of the 1990s, drug producers adapted and began using an alternative chemical (sodium hypochlorite), which may have resulted in higher rates of extraction and yields (UNODC 2009). Although the possible sources of bias in the estimation of coca cultivation and potential production are hard to verify, the current efforts of UNODC to conduct field studies in each of the producer countries to come up with better estimates of coca yields—and, in general, technical coefficients associated with the cocaine production process—are headed in the right direction. Because profit margins are extremely high, cocaine producers respond and adapt to antidrug policies in different and, many times, smart ways. Monitoring the responses through field studies is crucial, not only to keep track of the numbers on the supply side but also to evaluate the effectiveness of antidrug policies.

Trends in the Composition of the Demand for Cocaine

Although aggregate figures show that cocaine consumption has, if anything, remained relatively stable in the past few years in the United States and is on the rise in Europe, the long-term trends in the composition of demand may shed some light on understanding the patterns of illegal drug use. In fact, "while the general population surveys have shown very stable prevalence figures throughout the 1990s, aggregate stability masks a great deal of change in patterns of drug use" (Reuter 1999).

As was the case with opium in the past, patterns of cocaine consumption may exhibit a life cycle. There are many reasons to expect a life cycle for drug consumption. Among the most obvious ones are fashion and learning. As Levitt and Dubner (2005, 109) put it when they analyze the financial structure of drug gangs in the United States, "In the 1970s, if you were the sort of person who did drugs, there was no classier drug than cocaine. Beloved by rock stars, moviemakers, ballplayers, and even the occasional politician, cocaine was a drug of power and panache." According to Reuter, the low prices of cocaine have not led to a new epidemic of cocaine consumption because cocaine is no longer a fashionable drug. Cocaine consumption is seen now as dangerous, and "there are enough miserable looking cocaine addicts on the streets of bad neighborhoods to make the case for the drug's perils to any moderately rational youth" (Reuter 2001, 18). Statistics such as the average age of cocaine users in the United States favor this explanation. In addition, hospital and coroner data show the aging of cocaine users. And trends in the Arrestee Drug Abuse Monitoring (ADAM) data show that the average cocaine-using offender is not only getting older but also getting sicker. This evidence, together with increasing incarceration rates, has led to a slowly declining number of cocaine (and heroin) addicts.[30]

Additional evidence also suggests that "a greater proportion of the cocaine-using population is dependent—a finding consistent with the observation that cocaine users developed their habits over time and are now experiencing the problems that stem from long-term use" (Reuter 1999). What this evidence—the composition of cocaine demand by age groups and by occasional versus dependent users—suggests is that the problem of cocaine use, at least in the United States, is "increasingly a problem of long-term users who developed their habits in the early stages of the epidemic" (Reuter 1999). It should be noted, however, that the relatively low prices for cocaine might induce new users to try it and could spur its consumption once again in the near future. The latest available indicators of cocaine consumption among 8th–12th graders in the United States show a worrisome picture: trends in 30-day and annual prevalence of cocaine and crack use have increased for 10th and 12th graders since 2003 (see figure 7.10 above), and the disapproval among 12th graders of people using cocaine occasionally or regularly, as well as their perception of risks in the drug, has decreased (University of Michigan 2006).

The long-term trends in the composition of cocaine demand by age group and by occasional versus dependent consumers illustrate an impor-tant issue: the consumption of cocaine, as observed in the past for other drugs such as opium, may exhibit a life cycle. Furthermore, if the life cycle hypothesis is true, the relative stability of the aggregate figures for cocaine demand, as well as the aging of cocaine consumers, at least in the United States, might indicate future declines in U.S. consumption of cocaine.

Other Sources of Bias in the Numbers

After the demise of the Medellín and Cali cartels during the 1990s, new players entered the cocaine production and commercialization busi-ness in Colombia (when Colombia was already the largest producer of cocaine). The new cartels—such as the Norte del Valle cartel, the Costa cartel, and the different guerrilla and paramilitary fronts—are typically smaller and have a relatively more widespread command structure. In other words, the production and commercialization of cocaine are no longer controlled by a few drug lords such as Pablo Escobar or the Rodriguez Orejuela brothers. Instead, one can argue (drawing on "informed" anecdotal evidence) that after the demise of the Medellín and Cali cartels, a larger group of less visible organizations now controls cocaine production and commercialization. This change in the drug cartel's industrial organization, in turn, may have induced greater competition among the new groups in control of the cocaine trade, lowered (still huge) profit margins, and reduced prices. Greater competition in the initial stages of the cocaine-trafficking chain may have counteracted the effects of antidrug policies implemented in producer countries and, as a result, may have prevented cocaine wholesale prices (that is, prices recorded at the borders of consumer countries) from going up.

Yet another, perhaps related, explanation (UNODC 2005) is the use of cocaine stocks to fuel drug markets while the surge in antidrug policies lasts. In other words, organizations involved in cocaine commercialization have been running down their stocks of cocaine with the expectation that the current intensity of antidrug policies cannot last much longer. However, no significant evidence suggests this explanation. In any case, if it were true, the stocks "should be soon exhausted and a contraction of the market should then become visible" (UNODC 2009).

Although it is very hard, if not impossible, to verify some of these explanations directly for obvious reasons—including lack of price records and transaction quantities at each of the different commercialization stages (or the lack of access to the drug traffickers' accounting books)—the availability of better and more reliable data on coca cultivation, yields, consumption, and the like as it becomes available will help clarify the validity of other possible explanations. Field studies in coca-growing regions such as the ones currently being conducted by UNODC will continue to help clarify whether yields have increased or whether better planting techniques are being used. In other words, better assessments of productivity factors (and how they change over time) are key to understanding the cocaine market. And, going back one step in the cocaine production chain, field studies would be very helpful for comparing the measures of coca cultivation obtained from satellite images with those obtained directly in the fields. As noted earlier, anecdotal evidence suggests that coca growers have found ways to avoid detection by satellite imaging and, therefore, that the measures obtained from satellite pictures might be biased downward. Random, in-the-field measures will provide an estimate of that bias. Also crucial for the analysis of the cocaine market is the understanding of the response of drug producers to antidrug policies. The following section elaborates this point.

Antidrug Policies in Producer Countries

Antidrug policies in the three producer countries have had different emphases in the past few years. In Colombia, those policies have focused on a combination of strategies: from attempting to prevent coca cultivation (using aerial spraying of herbicides over coca fields and alternative development and crop substitution programs) to disrupting the chain of cocaine manufacture and commercialization (by interdicting drug shipments and by destroying the production and transportation infrastructure such as laboratories, landing strips, and small airplanes). In Bolivia and Peru, where aerial spraying of herbicides is forbidden by law, antidrug policies have focused mainly on alternative development programs and manual (forced or voluntary) eradication campaigns. Interdiction of drug shipments, especially of coca paste, has been an important component in the fight against cocaine production in Peru and Bolivia, particularly in the past few years when interdiction has increased rapidly, probably because of the increased cultivation triggered by higher prices for coca leaf in those two countries. Peru also made enormous efforts at the end of the 1990s to disrupt the air bridge between coca base producers and Colombian manufacturers of cocaine. According to most sources, it was the combination of those policies, together with a set of well-targeted alternative livelihood programs in coca-growing regions, that reduced coca cultivation in Peru from 115,000 hectares in 1995 to about 56,000 in 2007.

In Bolivia and Peru, where the livelihoods of many farmers depend on coca cultivation, the government has implemented alternative development programs in well-defined coca-growing regions. Those programs seek to provide the necessary incentives so that farmers abandon coca cultivation and engage in the cultivation of legal crops. Those incentives take the form of monthly payments for not engaging in coca cultivation or assistance in the development of new (legal) agricultural activities. Although the programs have been relatively successful locally, their dependence on continuing national and international funding undermines their potential for success in the long run. Governments in the three producer countries often rely on funding from developed countries to finance alternative livelihood programs and have to decide how to allocate the funding among regions, at the expense of encouraging increases in coca cultivation in those regions not reached by such programs (UNODC 2009). For instance, after the implementation of alternative development programs in Aguatya and Bajo Huallaga (the two regions in Peru with the largest proportion of coca cultivation during the 1990s), coca cultivation had almost disappeared by 2004.

Nevertheless, the high prices for coca leaf induced growers in those regions without any government attention (in the form of alternative programs or services in health and education) to increase coca cultivation. As a result, coca cultivation, if anything, has remained relatively stable in Peru during the past six years.

UNODC, together with government agencies in producer countries, collects statistics on the number of eradicated hectares of coca crops. As mentioned earlier, in Peru and Bolivia eradication is manual, whereas in Colombia it is usually performed by aerial spraying.[31] This difference accounts for the disparity between the average number of eradicated hectares per year in Bolivia (about 8,500 hectares per year between 1999 and 2008) and Peru (about 10,336 hectares per year) and the average number for Colombia (close to 144,000 hectares per year). Eradication in the three countries is undertaken by governmental entities (DIRECO in Bolivia; DIRAN, or the antinarcotics police, in Colombia; and CORAH and DEVIDA for forced and voluntary eradication, respectively, in Peru) with technical and financial support from the U.S. government. Figures 7.14 (a, b, c) show the number of eradicated hectares, as reported by each of the governmental entities in charge of eradication in the three countries, together with the estimated number of hectares cultivated with coca bush for the each of the three producer countries, as reported by UNODC (2009).

Figure 7.14. Coca Bush Cultivation and Eradication in Bolivia, Colombia, and Peru, 1993–2008

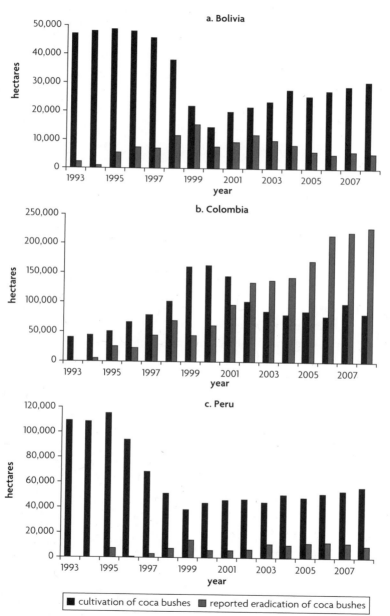

Source: UNODC 2009.

As the aerial eradication campaigns in Colombia intensified after the implementation of Plan Colombia, those individuals and organizations that benefit from coca cultivation and cocaine production have figured out ways of counteracting these campaigns. Because spraying with aerial herbicides is prohibited in national parks in Colombia, for example, coca cultivation has increased rapidly in those areas. The same pattern has occurred in Bolivia and Peru, where farmers have sought remote or protected areas for coca cultivation as a result of government pressure to reduce cultivation in the existing locations. Between 2003 and 2004, cultivation in national parks in Bolivia increased by more than 70 percent, and it increased by 53 percent in protected and forest areas in Peru (UNODC 2005).

Individuals involved in the cocaine production business have created many other ways of counteracting eradication campaigns: (a) conducting pruning operations immediately after aerial spraying (so that the coca plant, cut at 1 foot above the ground, then grows rapidly), (b) intermingling coca crops with legal crops to avoid detection, (c) spraying coca plants with substances such as molasses to prevent the herbicide from destroying the leaves, and (d) developing genetically modified plants that are supposedly resistant to the herbicides currently used.

But aerial spraying, forced eradication, and alternative development programs are not the only measures taken by producer countries to fight illegal drug production and trafficking. Other policies include, but are not limited to, the following:

- curtailing the flow of raw materials used in the cultivation of coca and the processing of cocaine
- discovering and destroying the small local workshops and laboratories where coca base is processed
- destroying the landing strips used by trafficking organizations to ship drugs
- interdicting drug shipments
- dismantling the drug cartels, the networks, and (many times fake) firms that are created to launder the proceeds obtained from illegal drug trafficking.

An increasing number of operations have targeted the different links in the chain of cocaine production and trafficking. For instance, coca base and cocaine seizures have increased in the past few years in all the producer countries (see figure 7.15a and 7.15b for coca base and cocaine seizures in Bolivia and Colombia). Other measures, such as the number of destroyed illegal laboratories used for processing coca paste and

Figure 7.15. Seizures of Coca Base and Cocaine in Bolivia and Colombia, 1997–2007

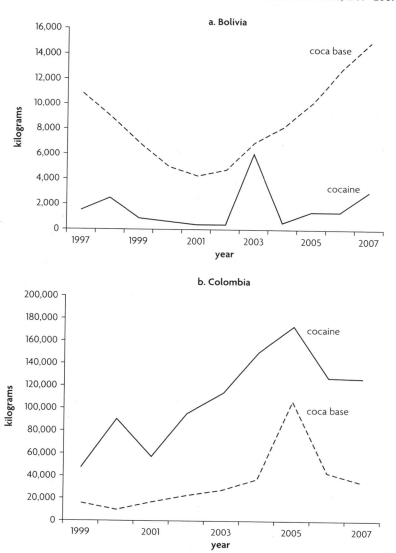

Source: UNODC 2009.

cocaine, also show increasing efforts to combat illegal drug production[32] (see figures 7.16 for Bolivia and Colombia).[33] Cocaine seizures have increased rapidly in the three producer countries, and cocaine seizures in the United States increased rapidly between 2002 and 2005. Ever since then, they have shown a decreasing tendency (figure 7.17).

Side Effects of Antidrug Policies

The implementation of antidrug policies has important side effects in producer countries. Forced eradication measures target, by definition, the first link in the chain of cocaine production. But one can argue, perhaps convincingly, that of all those involved in cocaine production and commercialization, the peasants are perhaps the ones who receive the fewest benefits. Most coca cultivation in the three producer countries takes place in remote and isolated areas that lack any form of government infrastructure, public education, or health services.[34] In other words, eradication measures target those who are most vulnerable to negative income shocks and, as a result, have created a backlash of social pressure against them; such pressure has resulted many times in uprisings

Figure 7.16. Destroyed Illegal Cocaine Laboratories in Bolivia and Colombia, 1997–2007

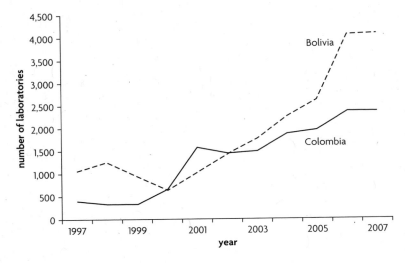

Source: UNODC 2009.

Figure 7.17. Seizures of Cocaine in the United States, 1989–2007

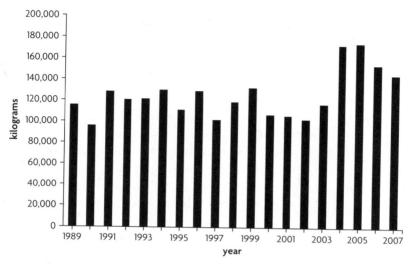

Source: UNDCP and DEA 2009.

and riots such as the ones observed in Bolivia.[35] As Sherret (2005) suggests, the lack of coordination between aerial spraying campaigns (or any form of forced eradication), alternative development programs, and state-financed development infrastructure in the coca-growing areas evidences "a larger pattern of neglect and disregard for those affected by centrally directed policies" (Sherret 2005, 164).

One of the most debated issues related to the side effects of antidrug policies concerns the environmental effects of the aerial spraying in Colombia. As Laurel Sherret has noted,

> The controversy over the health effects of the use of glyphosate herbicides often centers on anecdotal evidence gathered from people living in the areas subject to fumigation versus the scientific evidence obtained from laboratory experimentation . . . and when the political agendas are taken into account, the layers of complexity around this problem are only exacerbated. (Sherret 2005, 157)

The antinarcotics police in Colombia have used aerial fumigation for more than a decade, but since the implementation of Plan Colombia (with considerable funding from the United States), aerial spraying campaigns have intensified, especially in the southern part of the country where most of the coca is produced. The antinarcotics police use a formula known as Roundup (a mixture of glyphosate, the active ingredient in the herbicide, and Cosmo-Flux, a surfactant used to aid the herbicide in penetrating the waxy cuticle of coca leaves). The chemical affects the leaves of the coca plants but not its roots or the soil; as a result, "the bush can be subject to a prune operation at about one foot over the ground to obtain a renewal of the bush in about six months" (UNODC 2005). With an herbicide concentration of 10.4 liters per hectare of coca approved by the Colombian Anti-Narcotics Council, the spraying effectiveness is estimated to be above 90 percent. Common effects on humans, as reported by those people affected, are fever, eye irritation, gastrointestinal irritation, diarrhea, skin irritation, and dizziness.

The available evidence on the effect of aerial spraying of Roundup, however, is quite diverse. A study by the Organization of American States (OEA 2005) argues that the health effects on people from the use of glyphosate and Cosmo-Flux are minimal and that the degree and frequency of exposure are very low. The same study also argues that the effects on wildlife, mammals, and birds are negligible. This study finds evidence of only a moderate adverse effect on some aquatic animals in those localities where coca is grown and where still water is present. Yet another report, prepared by the Center for International Policy (CIP) and nongovernmental organizations from Colombia and Ecuador, argues against the use of the Roundup formula for aerial eradication of coca crops because it "has not been subject to scientific studies to determine its effects on the environment and human health, which goes against the principle of environmental precaution" (CIP 2004, 139).

The study cites evidence from peasants who claim to have been affected by aerial spraying campaigns in different ways: skin irritation; allergies; eye, nose, and throat irritations; nausea; and diarrhea.[36] The study also repeatedly argues that the aerial campaigns in Putumayo and Caqueta, the departments in southern Colombia with the highest density of coca cultivation in the peak years of 2000 and 2001, have been indiscriminate and that the spraying has destroyed legal crops, such as yucca, sugar cane, and plantains, which, according to anecdotal evidence from the peasants cited in the report, leaves them without any means of subsistence. Although CIP's report extensively describes the effects of aerial fumigation with glyphosate on human health and the environment, it barely mentions the negative environmental effects that coca cultivation and cocaine production themselves have on the environment.

A thorough review of the environmental and health effects of aerial spraying of glyphosate is that of Sherret (2005), which explains the crucial distinction between the active herbicide (glyphosate) and its commercially available formulations. The distinction is important because the formula (which, as explained before, is a combination of glyphosate and surfactants) exhibits *synergism*—that is, when the effects of two chemicals used together are greater than the effects of those chemicals used individually. Many times the instructions for use of glyphosate and its formulations are violated, a point that is shared by most of the studies (see, for instance, Sherret 2005; Solomon and others 2005; CIP 2004); and it is precisely the misuse of the herbicide that causes harmful health and environmental effects. For instance, among the many instructions issued by the manufacturer is that Roundup should be applied at distances not greater than 2–3 meters from the tallest plant. That recommendation is not often followed, not only because the topographic conditions are difficult but also because the pilots need to avoid gunfire from the illegal organizations that benefit from the cocaine production and trafficking business. As a result of being unable to spray coca crops from the recommended height, the herbicides often affect legal crop plantations, water sources, and other sites not targeted by the aerial eradication campaigns.

The study by Sherret (2005) also emphasizes that the most harmful environmental effects so far identified by scientific evidence are on aquatic organisms and amphibians, when glyphosate formulations are, perhaps mistakenly, applied to aquatic ecosystems.

The environmental costs of cocaine production are also an important side effect of antidrug policies, because the criminalization of coca cultivation and cocaine production also create environmental costs. Because cocaine production is illegal, it is not subject to government environmental regulations. According to John Walters, director of ONDCP,

> 600 million liters of so-called precursor chemicals are used annually in South America for cocaine production. To increase yields, coca growers use highly poisonous herbicides and pesticides, including paraquat. Processors also indiscriminately discard enormous amounts of gasoline, kerosene, sulfuric acid, ammonia, sodium bicarbonate, potassium

carbonate, acetone, ether, and lime onto the ground and into nearby waterways.[37] (Walters 2002)

Although Walters uses this evidence to answer those who criticize the aerial eradication campaigns, both the environmental costs of aerial eradication and those of coca cultivation and cocaine production have a more fundamental root: the illegal nature of these activities. If cocaine production were legalized, the cultivation of coca and the production of cocaine would be managed as any other crop. They would be regulated, and no chemicals would have to be sprayed to destroy them. Further research is needed to estimate and understand better not only the environmental effects of aerial spraying of glyphosate but also the environmental costs of cocaine production. Together, they will provide a fuller picture of the environmental costs of the criminalization of coca cultivation and cocaine production.

But eradication measures are not the only measures that generate resistance and controversy because of their side effects. Policies such as those implemented by the Peruvian government during the second half of the 1990s, which aimed at closing the air bridge used to transport unrefined coca paste from Peru to Colombia, did not escape fatal accidents. Closing the air bridge involved not only destroying landing strips (which were easily constructed somewhere else at a relatively low cost) but also shooting down small airplanes suspected of carrying illegal drugs. The airplanes that were shot down by the Peruvian Air Force (using information provided by U.S. surveillance planes), however, were not always carrying illegal drugs, and such incidents sometimes resulted in deadly accidents involving innocent people.[38]

The Sustainability and Future Prospects of Antidrug Policies in Producer Countries

Issues relating to the sustainability of antidrug policies in producer countries are perhaps too numerous to be discussed in this chapter. It is worth mentioning a few, however. First, there is the question of who should bear the costs of alternative livelihood programs and eradication activities—producer or consumer countries? While governments in the producer countries face internal pressure from farmers who claim, perhaps sincerely, that their only path to subsistence is the cultivation of coca,[39] they also face external pressure from the consumer countries to fight the production of illegal drugs. That pressure may be, for instance, the threat of being labeled a "narco-state" by the international community or not being "certified" by the U. S. government each year. But besides being an illegal activity, cocaine production and trafficking have had direct links with terrorist and insurgent activities, especially in the case of Colombia. Most probably, if producer countries stop fighting the drug trade and consumer countries do not penalize them, the price of cocaine would drop dramatically, and the drug business would no longer be a source of financial resources for illegal armed groups in producer countries. There is convincing evidence that the involvement of guerrilla and paramilitary groups in illegal drug production and trafficking is sufficiently lucrative to finance their war against each other and against the Colombian state.[40]

The funds to fight against the production of illegal drugs are limited, and many times the governments in producer countries have to sacrifice other, perhaps more productive, investments to finance the war on drugs. Moreover, funds provided by consumer countries (mostly developed economies) are often earmarked for predetermined activities and leave little or no room for governments to allocate the funds to their most productive use. In Colombia, for instance, most of the support provided by the U.S. government comes in the form of small airplanes that can be used only for the spraying of herbicides in coca fields, in training programs for the pilots, and for technical support in identifying coca fields. These imposed political constraints create inefficiencies in the allocation of funds, as well as environmental and social problems in the producer countries—issues not taken into account by the consumer countries at the time of earmarking the aid for specific antidrug policies.[41]

The chapter has posed some questions about the side effects or costs of antidrug policies on health, the environment, and fiscal sustainability, but any analysis of their sustainability should also evaluate their results. The fact that cocaine is an addictive drug is perhaps the crucial determinant of how effective the reduction of cocaine supply is in decreasing the availability of illegal drugs in the consumer countries. As Echeverry (2004) argues, "The efficacy [of the war on drugs] lies on a variable that measures consumer's responsiveness to price increases, i.e., the price elasticity of demand."[42] The rationale for this argument is very simple: if the elasticity of demand for illegal drugs—which captures the percentage increase in demand caused by a 1 percent decrease in the price—is so low that any decrease in the supply translates into a large increase in the price for illegal drugs, then policies aimed at reducing illegal drug production may be self-defeating, as they make the drug business even more profitable and create a greater incentive for producing (and trafficking) illicit drugs. In other words, the very policies that aim to reduce the supply of illegal drugs can induce further increases in the price and drive more production and lead to more violence.[43]

The scarcity of data on prices and quantities of cocaine transacted, however, makes available estimates of the price elasticity of demand unreliable. While most available empirical studies have found a short-run elasticity of demand less than 1 in absolute value (Saffer and Chaloupka 1999; Chaloupka, Grossman, and Tauras 1999; DeSimone and Farrelly 2003; Mejía and Restrepo 2008; Mejía 2008), other studies have found evidence of more responsiveness of cocaine demand to price changes (Caulkins 1996). Using a rational addiction framework (where, in addition to the addictive nature of the drugs, peer pressure plays an important role and current consumption depends not only on past but also on future consumption),[44] Grossman and Chaloupka (1998) estimate a long-run price elasticity of demand for cocaine of about −1.35.[45] Whether the price elasticity of demand for cocaine is higher than 1 in absolute value or whether this is true in the short or in the long run should be on the agenda for future research as better data become available.

Still, the question remains whether producer countries will be able to sustain the high expenditures on eradication programs, alternative development projects, and interdiction efforts, among others, of the past few years to reduce cocaine production and trafficking.[46] It is also important to evaluate the results and to gain a better understanding of how drug producers and traffickers are attempting to counteract antidrug policies (see Mejía and Restrepo 2008; Mejía 2008, 2009). As we saw before, although eradication measures undertaken under Plan Colombia have decreased the number of cultivated hectares, drug producers have responded with better planting techniques, have moved to new territories, and have developed coca plants that have a much higher yield. The reason for those responses is very simple: because cocaine production and trafficking are illegal, the profit margins are huge: the price of 1 gram of cocaine in producer countries is approximately one-tenth of its weight in gold, and that same gram on the streets of Chicago or New York sells for as much as 10 times its weight in gold. The resources that drug producers are willing to invest in counteracting antidrug policies, therefore, are also immense.

Yet another perspective on supply-side controls that focus on eradication of illicit crops is that such policies are doomed from the beginning, because prices of coca leaf are just a negligible fraction of retail prices in consumer countries (the cost of coca leaf required to produce 1 kilogram of cocaine is between $300 and $500, whereas that kilogram at retail could sell for $150,000 in the United States at average street purity levels).[47] The argument is that even if refiners had to pay twice or three times as much to purchase the coca leaf required to produce 1 kilogram of cocaine and if this extra cost is passed along on an additive basis, the increase in retail prices would be negligible. As a result, even "if retail prices do not rise, then total consumption in the United States will not decline as a consequence of eradication" (Reuter 2001, 19). According to that researcher, alternative development programs are also subject to the same incompleteness as eradication, because they assume that cocaine refiners will not increase the price sufficiently to tempt farmers back to coca growing.

On the one hand, any sound and sustainable policy that aims at reducing cocaine production and trafficking by attacking the first link in the chain (coca cultivation) should at least coordinate strategies between the carrots (incentives to farmers to abandon coca cultivation such as alternative livelihood opportunities and better education and health services) and the sticks (the ability and credible commitment of the government to take measures such as forced eradication and interdiction to raise the costs substantially of engaging in the production of cocaine). On the other hand, if consumer countries are unwilling to take measures such as legalizing the use of hard drugs (as seems to be the case) but at the same time want to reduce the inflow of these illegal drugs, they will need to step up their funding not only to finance the implementation of antidrug policies to curtail production and trafficking in producer countries but also to reduce the demand for illicit drugs. Educating potential cocaine users about the dangers of cocaine and treating hard-core cocaine users seem to be much more cost effective than trying to cut off the supply of cocaine at its source. A study by Caulkins and others (2005) finds that consumption can be reduced more cheaply in the United States by treating heavy users than by three alternative enforcement measures usually carried out: control of supply in the producer countries, drug seizures and interdiction of drug shipments, and conventional enforcement measures.

Demand-reduction programs have a wide range of possible action. Among others, they seek to prevent and reduce the use of illicit drugs, treat the addicted, to reduce the consequences of drug abuse, and to increase the public's awareness of the vulnerability and risk associated with drug consumption by disseminating information in local communities and schools on the harmful effects of drugs. Policies aimed at reducing consumption also make it less likely that drug users switch to alternative drugs when the one they are using is not available.

If the legalization of drugs is not possible—perhaps because of political agendas in consumer and producer countries—efforts to reduce the supply and the demand should be taken together. One approach carried out in isolation will not work because the two are complementary. For instance, in times of supply shortages, drug prices may increase and purity levels decline, making it more likely, first, that chronic users will seek treatment and, second, that potential new users will have less opportunity to obtain drugs. As the demand for cocaine goes down as a result of programs to reduce consumption, there will be fewer addicts, and the criminal networks in charge of selling drugs might weaken, in turn making it more costly for drug traffickers to smuggle illicit drugs and to make them available to consumers. Drug substitution therapies and personalized therapeutic programs decrease the cost to drug addicts of seeking treatment and decrease the number of users under the influence of criminal organizations, which has implications for the cost to criminal organizations of supplying drugs.[48]

Conclusion

"Many tens of billions" is probably the right figure for cocaine expenditures each year in consumer countries.[49] Close to 14 million people worldwide are cocaine consumers. Two-thirds of them are in the Americas. Only three countries in the world produce cocaine: Bolivia, Colombia, and

Peru. Potential cocaine production in 2004 was estimated to be about 650 metric tons. A gram of pure cocaine is worth as much as 10 times its weight in gold at retail in consumer countries. In producer countries, the same gram is worth, on average, slightly more than one-tenth of that value. While these figures might be striking enough by themselves to generate interest in the topic, they hide huge complexities. Clearly, a thorough understanding requires accurate data and relevant information about the market for cocaine.

The main purpose of this chapter is to provide a broad review of what we know (and what we do not) about cocaine production and trafficking. By describing the available data on cocaine production and trafficking, the collection methodologies, and some of the possible biases (and what may cause them), we have taken an important step toward understanding the complexities that should drive our future research on illegal drug production and trafficking. In addition, the chapter describes some apparent contradictions that arise from the available data and explored some of the hypotheses that may help explain them. The chapter also examines the efforts to fight cocaine production and trafficking in producer countries, the results of those attempts, and the role of consumer countries. Finally, the chapter reviews and studies the side effects, sustainability, and future prospects of antidrug policies.

Notes

1. See Reuter (2001) and Thoumi (2005a).
2. The purpose of this chapter is not to explain why illegal drug production takes place in some countries while not in others. Francisco Thoumi has extensively examined this topic (see Thoumi 2003, 2005a, 2005c).
3. The cocaine alkaloid was first isolated in the West in 1855 by German chemist Friedrich Gaedcke. Five years later, Albert Niemann described an improved isolation process of the cocaine alkaloid for his Ph.D. thesis and named it "cocaine" (see http://cocaine.org/ and the references there cited).
4. See Thoumi (2005b) for a detailed explanation of how antidrug policies create a cultural clash between government agencies interested in fighting cocaine production and local native populations that have grown and used coca in traditional cultural and religious ceremonies for a long time.
5. These are the Huanuco coca (in Bolivia and Peru), the Amazonian coca (in the Amazon River Basin), and Colombian coca (in Colombia, primarily) (https://www.cia.gov/saynotodrugs/cocaine_b.html).

6. Those yields numbers were taken from different reports (CIA 2004; UNODC 2005). The number used by UNODC to calculate potential production of cocaine in Colombia was 4.7 kilograms of cocaine per hectare per year until 2004, which, according to the source, is taken from a study undertaken by the U.S. government under the name of Operation Breakthrough. However, recent field research carried out by UNODC in Colombia has found a large increase in this productivity estimate. In fact, for the 2006 report, UNODC uses a productivity estimate of 7.7 kilograms of cocaine per hectare per year. We will elaborate on this later.

7. Commonly used street terms for cocaine are: *blow, coke, snow, nose candy, flake, big C, lady, snowbirds,* and *wicky stick* (see http://www.dea.gov/concern/cocaine_factsheet.html and http://www.streetdrugs.org).

8, The stimulation produced by cocaine consumption comes from its interference with the reabsorption process of dopamine, which is a chemical messenger that is associated with pleasure and movement (National Institute of Drug Abuse).

9. More information on the mandate of UNODC, as well as its main goals, can be obtained at http://www.unodc.org/unodc/en/illicit-drugs/index.html.

10. Jensema and Thoumi (2004) argue that UNODC's large proportion of earmarked funding from a few donor countries biases the type of projects on which the funds are spent, hampers its policy evaluation efforts as criticisms can easily translate into a fund shortage, and prevents the organization from experimenting with programs that are not in line with the donor countries' positions on illegal drug issues. Available at http://www.drug-policy.org/documents/Thoumi_Jensema_paper.

11. The analysis of such images includes a number of corrections for cloud cover, spraying, dates of acquisition, and so forth. For a detailed explanation, see the methodological description available in the Survey Reports for each of the Andean countries available at http://www.unodc.org/unodc/en/crop_monitoring.html).

12. Thoumi argues that UNODC does not have enough personnel and claims that "it simply does not have the capability to conduct significant critical studies and to evaluate in detail the quality of the data it collects" (Thoumi 2005a, 189). This claim, however, is backed up only by a specific criticism on a figure of the size of the illegal drug business ($500 billion, which was a clear overestimation) produced by UNODC back in 1997 when this organization was first established. The author also asserts that for the production of UNODC's main substantial product, *The World Drug Report,* the organization relies on several consultants who are hired to write chapters and sections for the report, which, in some sense, contradicts the claim that UNODC lacks the human resources to produce significant quality statistics and analysis.

13. See Rangel (2000) and Grossman and Mejía (2008).

14. Figures 7.1 and 7.2b present ONDCP's estimates of total coca cultivation preserving the sample fixed; that is, they do not take into account for 2005 the 81 percent increase in the fields surveyed.

15. Despite the successful closure of the air bridge between Peru and Colombia, the organizations involved in coca cultivation and cocaine production figured out

other ways (perhaps less efficient but still profitable, such as transportation by river, or using mules to travel jungle paths) to move coca paste from Peru to Colombia (see Kawell 2001).

16. For instance, in 2004 the media reported the discovery, in the Sierra Nevada (in the northern part of Colombia), of a new coca variety that supposedly had higher cocaine content and a higher level of purity and was also resistant to glyphosate. This new variety was seen as the response of drug traffickers to the intensive aerial spraying efforts by the Colombian government, with strong financial and technical support from the United States (see McDermott 2004). However, the Transnational Institute has questioned the validity of this report, arguing that "a few scientific facts provide grounds for questioning the credibility of this report about the cocaine alkaloid content of the coca leaf.... The report's claim that the plant is resistant to glyphosate is equally ambiguous" (see TNI 2004).

17. See UNODC (2006).

18. Again, the calculations excluded the 39,000 hectares of new fields surveyed in 2005 to make the data comparable to previous years.

19. Expected purity levels are based on observations obtained through purchases only and do not include observations from seizures and other enforcement activities (ONDCP 2004).

20. This is not the only link in the trafficking chain where violence arises as a method to resolve disputes. In fact, the recourse to violence is one prominent characteristic of organizations involved in illegal drug trafficking.

21. According to the *World Drug Report* (UNODC 2005), there are approximately 13.4 million cocaine users in the world. Two-thirds are in the Americas (about 6.5 million in the United States and 1.9 million in South America).

22. This percentage is of the population between 16 and 59 years of age.

23. The primary substance is the main substance reported at the time of admission.

24. Cocaine admissions as a percentage of all admissions also declined from about 17.5 percent in 1992 to about 13 percent in 2002.

25. When they respond to this question: How much do you think people risk harming themselves (physically or in other ways) if they try cocaine powder once or twice and occasionally?

26. European countries, probably with the exception of Spain, show prevalence rates of consumption much lower than those in the United States.

27. Caulkins and Reuter (1998) study the relative importance of the cost components in determining retail cocaine prices. According to their estimates, a little more than 50 percent of the cost can be attributed to risk (for incarceration about 24 percent, and for death about 30 percent), whereas (a) import costs account for only about 12 percent of the retail value of cocaine, (b) labor costs for about 13 percent, and (c) costs of product and assets seizures for about 10 percent. The same study also highlights the huge variability of prices across time and market levels and explains why enforcement interventions create only temporary spikes in prices, as a result of the response (in their words, *adaptation*) of suppliers.

28. A very small increase in the retail price of cocaine in consumer countries (at "street purity") is perceivable in the past few years recorded by UNODC (see figure 7.12).

29. Transnational Institute (TNI 2004) quickly responded to this information by questioning its scientific validity.

30. See the analysis in Reuter (2001).

31. See González (2006) for a thorough description of aerial eradication programs in Colombia.

32. For Peru, the numbers of illegal laboratories destroyed are 964 in 2003 and 861 in 2004.

33. See the *World Drug Report* (UNODC 2005, Coca Cultivation Surveys for each of the producer countries) for other measures of recent success in the war against cocaine production and trafficking. For the case of Colombia, the Dirección Nacional de Estupefacientes (DNE) publishes every year a summary of results in the war against illegal drug production in Colombia (see DNE 2004).

34. See Contraloría General de la República (2001).

35. See Stoner (2004) and Lindsay (2003).

36. According to Sherret (2005), "The governments of Colombia and the U.S. have claimed on numerous occasions that supporters of the insurgent and counter-insurgent groups, who derive much of their income from the narcotics industry, are responsible for most of the health complaints that have received so much attention."

37. See Solomon and others (2005).

38. See, for instance, Kawell (2001).

39. See CIP (2004).

40. See, among others, Rangel (2000), Rabasa and Chalk (2001), Thoumi (2003), Bottía (2003), and Diaz and Sanchez (2004).

41. See Grossman and Mejía (2008) and Mejía and Restrepo (2008).

42. See Becker, Murphy, and Grossman (2006) and Mejía (2009).

43. See the framework developed in Becker, Murphy, and Grossman (2006) for the case of consumer countries, Mejía and Restrepo (2008) for the case of producer countries, and Mejía (2008) for a unified framework that combines the interactions and effects of antidrug policies in consumer and producer countries.

44. See Becker and Murphy (1988).

45. However, when individual-specific fixed effects are included, this elasticity reduces to about −0.67. See also a related explanation in DeSimone and Farrelly (2003).

46. See Echeverry (2004).

47. See Reuter (2001).

48. See INCB (2004).

49. The low-end estimate is $35 billion, and the high-end estimate is $115 billion (see Reuter and Greenfield 2001).

References

Becker, G., and M. Grossman. 2004. "The Economic Theory of Illegal Goods: The Case of Drugs." Working Paper 10976. Cambridge, MA: National Bureau of Economic Research.

Becker, G., and K. Murphy. 1988. "A Theory of Rational Addiction." *Journal of Political Economy* 96: 675–700.

Becker, G., K. Murphy, and M. Grossman. 2006. "The Market for Illegal Goods: The Case of Drugs. *Journal of Political Economy* 114 (1): 38–60.

Bottía, M. 2003. "La presencia y expansión municipal de las FARC: Es avaricia y contagio, más que ausencia estatal." Working Paper 2003-03. CEDE, Universidad de los Andes, Bogotá, Colombia.

Caulkins, J. 1994. *Developing Price Series for Cocaine.* Santa Monica, CA: RAND.

———. 1996. "Estimating Elasticities of Demand for Cocaine and Heroin with DUF Data." Working Paper, Carnegie Mellon University, Pittsburgh, PA.

Caulkins, J., and P. Reuter. 1998. "What Price Data Tell Us about Drug Markets." *Journal of Drug Issues* 28 (3): 593–613.

Caulkins, J., P. Reuter, M. Iguchi, and J. Chiesa. 2005. "How Goes the 'War on Drugs'? An Assessment of U.S. Drug Problems and Policy." RAND Occasional Paper, Santa Monica, CA.

CIP (Center for International Policy), and others. 2004. "Informe de la misión de observación sobre los efectos del Plan Colombia en los departamentos de Nariño y Putumayo."

Central Intelligence Agency (CIA). 2004. "Coca Fact Paper: A Primer." Langley, VA: CIA.

Chaloupka, F., M. Grossman, and J. Tauras. 1999. "The Demand for Cocaine and Marijuana by Youth." In *The Economic Analysis of Substance Use and Abuse: An Integration of Econometric and Behavioral Economic Research*, ed. F. Chaloupka, M. Grossman, W. Bickel, and H. Saff, 133–55. Chicago: University of Chicago Press.

Contraloría General de la República. 2001. *Plan Colombia. Primer informe de evaluación.* Bogotá.

DeSimone, J., and M. Farrelly. 2003. "Price and Enforcement Effects on Cocaine and Marihuana Demand." *Economic Inquiry* 41 (1): 98–115.

Díaz, A. M., and F. Sanchez. 2004. "Geography of Illicit Crops and Armed Conflict in Colombia." Working Paper 2004-18. CEDE, Universidad de los Andes, Bogotá, Colombia.

Dirección Nacional de Estupefacientes (DNE). 2004. "Acciones y Resultados 2003." Bogotá, Colombia. http://www.cultivosilicitoscolombia.gov.co/documentos/lb 2003.pdf.

Echeverry, J. C. 2004. "Colombia and the War on Drugs: How Short Is the Short Run?" Working Paper 2004-13, CEDE, Universidad de los Andes, Bogotá, Colombia.

González, S. 2006. "El Programa de Erradicación de Cultivos Ilícitos Mediante Aspersión Aérea de Glifosato: Hacia la clarificación de la política y su debate." Occasional Paper, CEODD, Facultad de Economía, Universidad del Rosario, Bogotá, Colombia.

Grossman, M., and F. Chaloupka. 1998. "The Demand for Cocaine by Young Adults: A Rational Addiction Approach." *Journal of Health Economics* 17 (August): 427–74.

Grossman, H., and D. Mejía. 2008. "The War against Drug Producers." *Economics of Governance* 9 (1): 5–23.

International Narcotics Control Board (INCB). 2004. "Integration of Supply and Demand Reduction Strategies: Moving beyond a Balanced Approach." http://www.incb.org/pdf/e/ar/2004/incb_report_2004_1.pdf.

Jensema, E., and F. Thoumi. 2004. "Drug Policies and the Funding of the United Nations Office on Drugs and Crime." Occasional Paper, CEODD, Facultad de Economía, Universidad del Rosario, Bogotá, Colombia. http://www.drug-policy.org/documents/Thoumi_Jensema_paper.

Kawell, J. 2001. "Closing the Latin American Air-Bridge: A Disturbing History." *Foreign Policy*, "Info Focus" (May 1–2).

Levitt, S., and S. Dubner. 2005. *Freakonomics: A Rogue Economist Explores the Hidden Side of Everything.* New York: Harper Collins Publishers.

Lindsay, R. 2003. "Bolivia Coca Growers Fight Eradication." *Washington Times.* March 25.

McDermott, J. 2004. "New Super Strain of Coca Plant Stuns Anti-Drug Officials." *The Scotsman* (Scotland). August 27. http://www.mindfully.org/GE/2004/Roundup Ready-Coca27aug04.htm.

Mejía, D. 2008. "The War on Illegal Drugs: The Interaction of Anti-Drug Policies in Producer and Consumer Countries." CESifo Working Paper 2459, Munich.

———. 2009. "Evaluating Plan Colombia." In *Innocent Bystanders: Developing Countries and the War on Drugs*, ed. Philip Keefer and Norman Loayza. Washington, DC: World Bank.

Mejía D., and P. Restrepo. 2008. "The War on Illegal Drug Production and Trafficking: An Economic Evaluation of *Plan Colombia*." Working Paper 2008-19. CEDE, Universidad de los Andes, Bogotá, Colombia.

National Institute of Drug Abuse (NIDA). 2005. "Cocaine." NIDA Info Facts. Washington, DC: NIDA. http://www.nida.nih.gov/infofacts/cocaine.html.

ONDCP (Office of National Drug Control Policy). 2002. *Estimation of Cocaine Availability, 1996–2000.* Washington, DC: ONDCP.

———. 2004. *National Drug Control Strategy.* Washington, DC: ONDCP.

———. 2005. "2004 Coca and Opium Poppy Estimates for Colombia and the Andes." Press Release. March 25. http://www.whitehousedrugpolicy.gov/news/press05/032505.html.

———. 2009. "National Drug Control Strategy. Data Supplement 2009." Press Release. January. http://www.whitehousedrugpolicy.gov/publications/policy/ndcs09/ndcs09_data_supl/index.html.

OEA (Organización de los Estados Americanos). 2005. "Estudio de los Efectos del Programa de Erradicación de Cultivos Ilícitos Mediante la Aspersión Aérea con el Herbicida Glifosato (PECIG) y de los Cultivos Ilícitos en la Salud Humana y en el Medio Ambiente." Washington, DC: OEA.

Rabassa, Angel, and Peter Chalk. 2001. *Colombian Labyrinth.* Santa Monica, CA: RAND.

Rangel, A. 2000. "Parasites and Predators: Guerrillas and the Insurrection Economy of Colombia." *Journal of International Affairs* 53 (2): 577–601.

Reuter, P. 1999. "Drug Use Measures: What Are They Really Telling Us?" *National Institute of Justice Journal* (April): 12–19.

———. 2001. "The Limits of Supply-Side Drug Control." *The Milken Institute Review* (First Quarter).

Reuter, P., and V. Greenfield. 2001. "Measuring Global Drug Markets: How Good Are the Numbers and Why Should We Care about Them?" *World Economics* 2 (4): 159–74.

Saffer, H., and F. Chaloupka. 1999. "The Demand for Illicit Drugs." *Economic Inquiry* 37 (3): 401–11.

Sherret, L. 2005. "Futility in Action: Coca Fumigation in Colombia." *Journal of Drug Issues* (Winter): 151–68.

Solomon, K., A. Anadon, A. L. Cerdeira, J. Marshall, and L. Sanin. 2005. *Environmental and Human Health Assessment of the Aerial Spray Program for Coca and Poppy Control in Colombia.* Report prepared for the Inter-American Drug Abuse Control Commission (CICAD), Organization of American States. Washington, DC: CICAD.

Substance Abuse and Mental Health Services Administration (SAMHSA). 2005. *The DASIS Report.* Washington, DC. http://oas.samhsa.gov/2k5/CocaineTX/Cocaine TX.pdf.

Stoner, E. 2004. "Bolivia: An Early Goodbye for President Mesa?" Center for International Policy, Policy Brief, February 13, Washington, DC. http://www.ciponline .org/colombia/040213ston.htm.

Thoumi, F. 2003. *Illegal Drugs, Economy, and Society in the Andes.* Washington, DC: Woodrow Wilson Center Press; Baltimore: Johns Hopkins University Press.

———. 2005a. "The Numbers Game: Let's All Guess the Size of the Illegal Drug Industry!" *Journal of Drug Issues* (Winter): 185–200.

———. 2005b. "Introduction." *Journal of Drug Issues* (Winter): 1–6.

———. 2005c. "Ventajas competitivas ilegales, el desarrollo de la industria de drogas ilegales y el fracaso de las políticas contra las drogas en Afganistán y Colombia." Facultad de Economía Borradores de Investigación Bogotá, Universidad del Rosario.

Transnational Institute (TNI). 2004. "Super Coca?" Drug Policy Briefing 8, Amsterdam. http://www.mindfully.org/Reform/2004/Super-Coca-TNI8sep04.htm.

UNODC (United Nations Office of Drugs and Crime). 2005–2008. *Coca Cultivation Surveys for Bolivia, Peru, and Colombia.* Vienna: United Nations. http://www .unodc.org/unodc/en/crop-monitoring/index.html.

————. 2004. *World Drug Report.* Volume 1, *Analysis;* volume 2, Statistics. Vienna: United Nations. http://www.unodc.org/unodc/en/data-and-analysis/WDR.html.

————. 2005. *World Drug Report.* Volume 1, *Analysis;* volume 2, *Statistics.* Vienna: United Nations. http://www.unodc.org/unodc/en/data-and-analysis/WDR.html.

————. 2006. *World Drug Report.* Volume 1, *Analysis;* volume 2, *Statistics.* Vienna: United Nations. http://www.unodc.org/unodc/en/data-and-analysis/WDR.html.

————. 2007. *World Drug Report.* Volume 1, *Analysis;* volume 2, *Statistics.* Vienna: United Nations. http://www.unodc.org/unodc/en/data-and-analysis/WDR.html.

————. 2008. *World Drug Report.* Volume 1, *Analysis;* volume 2, *Statistics.* Vienna: United Nations. http://www.unodc.org/unodc/en/data-and-analysis/WDR.html.

————. 2009. *World Drug Report.* Volume 1, *Analysis;* volume 2 *Statistics.* Vienna: United Nations. http://www.unodc.org/unodc/en/data-and-analysis/WDR.html.

University of Michigan. 2006. *Monitoring the Future.* Ann Arbor: University of Michigan. Institute for Social Research. http://www.monitoringthefuture.org/new.html.

U.S. Department of State. 2005. *International Narcotics Control Strategy Report: Remarks at Special Briefing.* Washington, DC: U.S. Department of State.

U.S. General Accounting Office (GAO). 2003. *Drug Control: Coca Cultivation and Eradication Estimates in Colombia, Draft Report.* GAO-03-319R. Washington, DC: GAO.

Walters, J. 2002. "The Other Drug War." Op-Ed. *The Oregonian* (Portland). April 22. http://www.state.gov/p/inl/rls/op/2001/9637.htm.

8

Responding to the Challenge of Afghanistan's Opium Economy: Development Lessons and Policy Implications

William A. Byrd

Accounting for about a quarter of total economic activity in Afghanistan, the opium economy lies at the heart of the challenges that country faces in state building, governance, security, and development: its magnitude and importance are virtually unprecedented in global experience. Since 2002, efforts to reduce the size or even limit the expansion of the opium economy have failed. Annual opium production burgeoned especially in 2006 and 2007 and, despite moderate declines subsequently due largely to market factors, was the third largest in Afghanistan's history in 2009, remaining well above the peak level of the 1990s. In the meantime, the drug industry has evolved in directions that further increase the threat it poses to the country's entire state-building and development agenda. Counternarcotics measures—designed largely in isolation from other interventions, often implemented piecemeal or inconsistently, and suffering by all accounts from widespread corruption during implementation—contained the seeds of their own failure.

Comments from David Mansfield, Alastair McKechnie, Adam Pain, Philip Keefer, and an anonymous reviewer are gratefully acknowledged. Responsibility for any remaining errors or oversights rests solely with the author.

Introduction, Background, and Strategic Overview

This chapter reviews the experience with counternarcotics efforts in post-Taliban Afghanistan, derives some lessons from that experience, and spells out implications for policy. The main finding is that there are no "silver bullets" (easy or single-dimensional solutions) and that counternarcotics instruments must be deployed in an intelligent way—with modest expectations, a long time horizon, a strong and sustained commitment, and adequate resources—to improve prospects for success. This chapter explores the broad principles and approaches that underlie a "smart strategy" for responding to the drug industry in Afghanistan.

Because the chapter deals with the opium economy in Afghanistan, it focuses very much on the supply side of the narcotics equation. Although the growing use of illicit narcotics in Afghanistan raises concerns (see MacDonald 2007), which this chapter touches on, the main threat to the country's development emanates from the cultivation, trade, and processing of opium and associated criminality and corruption. The difficulties in curbing the opium economy in Afghanistan, however, are orders of magnitude greater because of high world and regional demand for illicit opiates. Moreover, with their narrow law enforcement focus and limited recognition of development, security, and political implications, current global counternarcotics policies impose a heavy burden on Afghanistan. Even if the country were able to make progress in reducing opium production, unless broader changes take place on the demand side, production would most likely shift elsewhere, as past international experience has demonstrated.

The rest of this introductory section provides some historical background, summarizes Afghanistan's opium economy from a development perspective, and highlights its strategic importance. The next section outlines the structure of the opium economy and recent trends, followed by an analysis of the determinants of opium poppy cultivation and the dynamic evolution of the drug industry. The final sections review the experience with counternarcotics activities in Afghanistan since 2001 and highlight some key lessons and policy implications.

Historical Background

The genesis and subsequent history of large-scale opium production in Afghanistan have been intimately linked with the wars and upheavals in the country and in the surrounding region during the past two decades of the 20th century. Opium has been produced for a very long time in Afghanistan, but until the end of the 1970s, the production was on a small scale for traditional purposes, was limited mainly to a few areas, and was produced primarily for local or regional consumption.

The Soviet Union's occupation of Afghanistan at the end of 1979, the emergence of a theocratic regime in Iran in the same year, and the development of the opium-processing industry in Pakistan, as well as developments farther away (for example, in Turkey), together created the enabling conditions for massive expansion of opium poppy cultivation in Afghanistan. Opium became a lucrative source of financing for the Mujahideen resistance forces fighting against the Soviet occupation, and the links to processing facilities in Pakistan paralleled those between Afghan resistance forces and Afghan political parties in Pakistan that were sponsoring and supporting the resistance. Iran's abrupt elimination of opium poppy cultivation at the beginning of the Khomeini regime, Turkey's shift to licit production, and Pakistan's more gradual phaseout of opium poppy cultivation (while remaining a very important location for opium processing and the narcotics trade) provided "space" in the world market for Afghanistan to emerge as a major exporter of opium, including exports to meet Iran's domestic consumption requirements. Although reliable data are not available, Afghanistan had clearly become a very significant opium producer by the mid-1980s.

After the departure of Soviet forces in 1989 and especially after the collapse of the Najibullah regime in 1992, international financing for armed groups in Afghanistan was sharply reduced, further increasing the relative importance of opium in providing funding for factions in the civil conflict that ensued. The Taliban regime—which took over Kandahar and much of the south in 1994, conquered Kabul in 1996, and controlled some 90 percent of Afghanistan's territory by the end of the decade—provided an environment in which opium production and trade could flourish. Treating it essentially as a legal crop, the Taliban collected tax (*ushr*) on opium at a low rate, as in the case of other agricultural products. Estimates of opium poppy cultivation, which were made on a more systematic basis by the United Nations Office on Drugs and Crime (UNDCP, subsequently UNODC) beginning in 1994, showed continuing increases to a peak of more than 90,000 hectares in the 1998–99 season, when Afghanistan accounted for close to 80 percent of total global illicit opium production.

Before the 2000–01 growing season, in what turned out to be its final year in power, the Taliban regime effectively banned opium poppy cultivation (but not trade) in the territories it controlled. While the motivation for the ban is subject to speculation—and major drug industry actors may have gone along with it because of oversupply and large stocks from previous bumper harvests—that ban was unquestionably the most successful and cost-effective short-run reduction in production of illicit narcotics achieved in history. The sustainability of this blanket ban was very doubtful, however, although the Taliban were overthrown before the question could be answered definitively. Evidence suggests that the ban hurt the Taliban politically, and planting of opium poppy resumed in the second half of 2001 in many places even before the end of the Taliban regime. Moreover, during the ban, opium poppy cultivation in the one province completely outside the Taliban's control (Badakhshan) increased by an estimated 160 percent, with some heroin-processing facilities reportedly also moving there.

Thus, in the immediate aftermath of the Taliban regime, extensive planting of opium poppy, which had been almost completely eliminated, resumed. As a result, within two years, poppy cultivation and opium output were back to "normal" levels similar to those of the 1990s. The high farm-gate price of opium created by the ban persisted for several years. Those prices, as well as efforts by the drug industry to diversify beyond the main production areas in the south, led to extensive opium poppy cultivation in nontraditional growing areas in other parts of the country.

Strategic Importance and Development Perspective

The opium economy is one of several critical issues facing Afghanistan. It relates closely and in complex ways not only to the agenda for economic growth and poverty reduction but also to state building, the political process, governance, security, and counterinsurgency. The strategic integration of all those issues is essential if Afghanistan is to make substantial and sustained progress in the face of a complex and closely linked set of development challenges.

The close relationships among drug traders, warlords-turned-politicians, and corrupt officials in government agencies that have been partly compromised by the drug industry (for example the police and the Ministry of Interior) are good examples of the strategic links associated with the drug industry, discussed further in the section titled "The Dynamics of the Opium Economy." The opium economy and the insurgency both thrive in an insecure environment with a weak and corruptible state that is not capable of imposing the rule of law. Thus, even though their purposes do not always converge, the Taliban and the drug interests often work synergistically in ways that damage Afghanistan's state-building agenda.

The opium economy provides substantial incomes to segments of the rural population, stimulates aggregate demand, and supports the balance of payments, although it has only secondary and indirect benefits for government revenue. As argued by Martin and Symansky (2006), however, the macroeconomic impact of the opium economy is less than might be expected from its sheer size, because much income beyond the farm level never enters Afghanistan in the first place and some goes right out again in the form of capital flight or import financing.

The opium economy is also contributing to possible "Dutch disease" effects in Afghanistan by providing an influx of money and driving up rural wages.[1] Opium harvesting as well as opium trading earns such high returns that labor is discouraged from shifting to legal activities. Moreover, as the opium economy has become entrenched in some areas and has been a major economic activity for more than two decades, it has affected prices for agricultural land in and around opium-producing areas and rates for rentals and sharecropping. Opium poppy, however, takes up only a small proportion of Afghanistan's total agricultural land.

In sum, the opium economy poses a complex development challenge. On the one hand, it contributes heavily to local incomes; on the other hand, its illegality and associated corrupt and criminal activities weaken the basic institutions of the state. In this context, poorly designed and implemented counternarcotics measures can adversely affect development to the same degree as the opium economy itself, possibly even more. The poverty impact of such measures—resulting from reductions in the incomes of farmers cultivating opium poppy (most of them sharecroppers or tenants on others' land) and of wage laborers employed in opium poppy cultivation and harvesting—can be very significant. Both the Taliban ban of 2000 and the 96 percent reduction in the cultivated area for opium poppy in Nangarhar Province in 2005 deepened poverty, both directly and indirectly through opium-related debt and through coping strategies like asset sales, as well as through ripple effects on the rest of the local economy. Thus, the development and poverty implications of the opium economy and of actions taken against it need to be fully taken into account in both the development and the counternarcotics strategy.

Overall Patterns and Trends in the Opium Economy

After looking briefly at data and research issues, this section summarizes our knowledge of Afghanistan's opium economy and recent trends. Cultivation and production, trade and processing, opium prices, drug-related financial flows, and what little is known about the structure of the drug industry are touched on.

Data and Research Issues

That quantitative information on Afghanistan's opium economy is limited and of varying quality and reliability is not surprising, given its illicit and informal nature, as well as the weaknesses of the country's statistical system in general. Moreover, logistical and security constraints seriously hinder the collection of primary data on the opium economy. In addition, there are technical issues, for instance, related to the coverage and interpretation of satellite imagery. And the varying reliability of data and the changing collection and estimation methodology over time complicate the identification and assessment of trends.

Nevertheless, data on the opium economy are generally no worse—and in many respects are better—than the data available on the rest of Afghanistan's economy. Estimates of the area under opium poppy cultivation are produced annually by UNODC[2] using remote sensing supplemented by a survey, although estimates of yields (and, therefore, of opium production) are less reliable. Opium price data also are collected monthly in an increasing number of provinces. Moreover rural households, smaller drug traders, and *hawala* (informal money transfer) dealers have been accessible for careful interviewing and information collection.

Thus, overall, data issues have not prevented meaningful research on Afghanistan's opium economy (see Byrd and Buddenberg 2006, 4).

Cultivation and Production

With data limitations in mind, summary information on opium in Afghanistan is presented in table 8.1. Among the various estimates, those of the total area under opium poppy cultivation are the most reliable but still have significant margins of error.[3] Yield estimates have a greater margin of error, particularly when disaggregated to the provincial level. Compilation of the estimated farm-gate opium price introduces a further, although likely smaller, margin of error, with the result that the estimated farm-gate income has a considerably larger margin of error than the estimate of the cultivated area. Assumptions about border prices, from which the total potential export value and (as a residual) the gross income beyond the farm level are calculated, introduce substantial further unreliability into these numbers.

Amid annual fluctuations, the total national area under opium poppy cultivation has shown a generally rising trend since the early to mid-1990s, which was interrupted by the Taliban ban that almost wiped out the 2001 harvest. Cultivation reached new peaks in 2006 and 2007, following which there were significant declines in 2008 and 2009. Estimated opium production shows broadly similar trends, although percentage changes differ, reflecting fluctuations in estimated opium yields. Despite modest reductions over the past two years, opium production in 2009 stood third highest in Afghanistan's history and remained well above the peak level of the 1990s. Estimated gross income per hectare rose very sharply after the Taliban ban (reflecting a supply shock–induced spike in prices, shown in figure 8.1), and gross farm income increased greatly in subsequent years as production burgeoned, before subsiding in 2008 and 2009 as a result of price and output declines.

National cultivation trends mask major diversity across provinces, selected examples of which are shown in figure 8.2. Cultivation estimates for some provinces tend to move together (at least fluctuating in the same direction), often with somewhat offsetting changes from year to year. In other cases, fluctuations across provinces are partially offsetting within a year. In 2005, for example, the year in which cultivation in Nangarhar Province declined by 96 percent because of a largely effective

Table 8.1. Summary Statistics on Afghanistan's Opium Economy, 1995 and 2000–09

Indicator	1995	2000	2001	2002	2003	2004	2005	2006	2007	2008	2009
						Year					
Production (tons)	2,300	3,300	185	3,400	3,600	4,200	4,100	6,100	8,200	7,700	6,900
World market share (%)	−52	70	11	74	76	87	87	92	93	93	n.a.
Number of provinces producing opium	8	22	11	24	28	34	26	28	21	16	14
Area under opium poppy (thousands of hectares)	54	82	8	74	80	131	104	165	193	157	123
As % of total agricultural land	n.a.	n.a.	n.a.	n.a.	1.6	2.9	2.3	3.65	2.5	2.1	1.6
Area under poppy/area under cereals (%)	2.0	3.2	n.a.	3.2	2.8	5.9	n.a.	n.a.	n.a.	n.a.	n.a.
Gross farm income per ha. (US$)	1,000	1,100	7,400	16,200	12,700	4,600	5,400	4,600	5,200	4,662	3,562
Gross potential value of opiate exports (US$ millions)	n.a.	850	n.a.	2,500	2,300	2,800	2,700	3,100	4,000	3,400	n.a.
Gross farm income from opium (US$ millions)	50	90	60	1,200	1,000	600	560	760	1,000	730	438
Downstream income in Afghanistan (US$ millions)	n.a.	760	n.a.	1,300	1,300	2,200	2,140	2,340	3,000	2,670	n.a.

Source: UNODC (2003); UNODC and Government of Afghanistan (2004, 2006, 2007, 2008, 2009).

Note: The estimate of total agricultural land was sharply adjusted starting in 2007, so the figures for percentage of agricultural land are not comparable as between 2007–09 and earlier years.

Figure 8.1. Dry Opium Prices in Kandahar and Nangarhar, 1997–2006

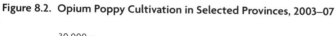

Source: Byrd and Jonglez 2006, 120.

Figure 8.2. Opium Poppy Cultivation in Selected Provinces, 2003–07

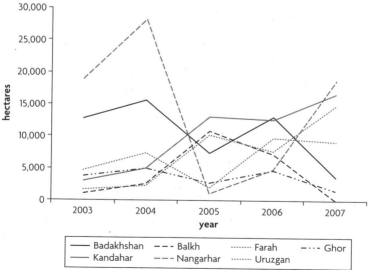

Source: UNODC 2003; UNODC and Government of Afghanistan 2004, 2006, 2007.

ban on cultivation imposed by the provincial authorities, cultivation in Kandahar, Balkh, and Farah rose sharply, largely offsetting the impressive decline in Nangarhar. Great diversity also prevails at the local or district level and, as demonstrated by extensive fieldwork, across households, although there are common factors influencing their decisions on opium poppy cultivation. In recent years, opium production has become increasingly concentrated in the southern part of Afghanistan.

Trade and Processing

Less is known about the trade in opium in and around Afghanistan, its conversion into refined products (morphine and heroin), and trade in those products. Nevertheless, a rough picture can be gleaned from field research and interviews with (mostly smaller) opium traders (see Pain 2006b), reinforced by information on drug seizures in neighboring countries. It is worth emphasizing that unlike many other agricultural products, opium is a durable good, with a shelf life of several years— longer than heroin powder.[4] Therefore, sizable inventories of opium can be and are maintained, opium can be and is used as a form of saving and even as "currency," and speculation in and sizable capital gains and losses on opium inventories can occur with fluctuations in prices. In fact, opium inventories appear to be adjusted to offset, at least partly, the large fluctuations in production and to help smooth supplies in the major consuming countries.

The many thousands of smaller opium traders typically operate on a part-time and seasonal basis (for example, shopkeepers). At this level, frequent entry and exit characterize opium markets, and higher opium prices following the Taliban ban in the year 2000 attracted more small traders to the opium business. Trade margins for smaller traders are relatively low, except when proximity to borders or crossing of those borders allows them to earn a premium for facing increased risks of interdiction. Research suggests that drug traders often have a background in trading legal goods and that they respond to financial incentives and risks in deciding whether and how much to trade in opium and opiates. According to fieldwork, the most important source of risk for traders has been price fluctuations, although more recently the risk of seizure or theft by authorities appears to have increased (Pain 2006b).

Moving up the "pyramid" of the drug trade in Afghanistan, fewer and fewer, and individually more important, actors are involved, culminating with no more than several dozen key traffickers at the top (see Shaw 2006, 204). Higher-level elements in the drug industry have close links to some warlords and their militias, as well as to government officials and some of the figures active in the conflict-affected politics of Afghanistan.

Nothing indicates that the drug industry is a monolithic cartel or that it functions like a cartel in pricing or other behavior; but entry into the middle and upper levels, and increasingly even into the lower levels, is becoming more difficult (Pain 2006b; Shaw 2006). In addition, some signs of cooperation and "regulation" suggest that when it is in their interests, different elements of the drug industry can work together effectively, including across ethnic lines. By the same token, although some of the fighting in the south as well as elsewhere may be drug related, all-out "drug wars" between criminal gangs of the kind seen in some other countries appear not to have been the norm in Afghanistan.

Finally, the activities of even the major Afghan drug traders do not appear to extend very far beyond the borders of Afghanistan. Before the early 1990s, the bulk of opium produced in Afghanistan was processed into morphine or heroin in neighboring countries, mainly Pakistan. In recent years, however, most Afghan opium has been processed in-country. This major transformation reflects in large part Pakistan's efforts to drive out heroin-processing labs from its territory, which culminated in the mid-1990s (see MacDonald 2007). As in the case of opium poppy cultivation itself, heroin-processing activities have gravitated toward Afghanistan where the "enabling environment"—insecurity, lack of rule of law, and protection by armed militias—remains conducive to such activities. After drug shipments cross the border, though, other trafficking groups, which are associated with the neighboring countries or with transnational organizations, appear to take over.

Price Patterns and Trends

Considerable data on opium prices are available (see UNODC 2003; UNODC and Government of Afghanistan 2006–09) and can be analyzed, albeit with caution. It should be noted that the farm-gate opium price composes only a small part of the price of opiates at Afghanistan's borders and a truly minuscule percentage of the wholesale or retail price in the consuming countries of the Organisation for Economic Co-operation and Development (Byrd and Jonglez 2006).

As shown in figure 8.1, prices of raw opium have fluctuated widely, most notably the sharp spike in prices associated with the Taliban ban,[5] a period followed by persistent high prices for several years. This finding suggests that the "risk premium" associated with opium poppy cultivation rose considerably after 2001, probably reflecting criminalization along with significant, although patchy and haphazard, enforcement efforts, including eradication, and likely greater extortion of "protection money" from farmers by various authorities as well as by Taliban insurgents. Prices have been pushed down in recent years, however, by the very large increases in output in 2006 and 2007 and an apparently sizable overhang of inventories of opium. This overhang seems to have carried over into 2008 and 2009, when, despite moderate declines in production, prices fell substantially to levels approaching those prevailing in the 1990s.

Quantitative analysis of farm-gate opium prices, which makes use of several instruments ranging from simple correlation coefficients to linear regression and more sophisticated co-integration techniques (see Byrd and Jonglez 2006), indicates that opium markets in Afghanistan have several features that should be taken into account in policy formulation:

- Opium markets are flexible and mobile; while actions against the opium economy can be effective locally in the short run, they encourage shifts of production and trade to other areas.
- Regional and cross-border price differentials in particular suggest that interdiction of opium, especially at borders, can have a significant impact.
- According to available price data, internal opium markets appear to have been more "integrated" during the 1990s than in recent years, perhaps reflecting the disruptive effects of counternarcotics actions on opium markets.
- Price data for recent years suggest that the Helmand and Kandahar region in the south is functioning as a "central market" for opium in Afghanistan.

Drug-Related Financial Flows

Most of drug-related financial flows within Afghanistan, as well as to and from neighboring countries (primarily Pakistan), pass through the ubiquitous *hawala,* the informal financial transfer system referred to earlier. *Hawala* is based on very solid networks of trust and business relationships, under which money transfers in opposite directions are offset against each other and any remaining imbalances are settled through transfers between dealers (see Maimbo 2003). Very little physical transfer of money needs to occur, *hawala* dealers can operate effectively with small cash reserves, and the system is remarkably efficient (as evidenced by the small spreads in quoted exchange rates).

Analysis based on extensive interviews with *hawala* dealers (Thompson 2006) provides insights into the nexus between the drug industry and *hawala* and the considerable variation across different parts of the country. In the economically less developed province of Badakhshan, for example, field research indicates that at certain times of the year close to 100 percent of the liquidity in the *hawala* system is derived from drugs. In a much more developed province like Herat, however, only 30 percent of the *hawala* market's overall transaction volume appears to be linked to drugs, although the analysis of such links is complicated by use of drug money in legitimate import businesses. In addition to being a center of opium production and trade, the southern region is a focal point for money laundering: apparently about 60 percent of *hawala* flows are drug related, and 80–90 percent of *hawala* dealers are involved in drug-related money transfers.

Beyond Afghanistan's borders, Dubai appears to be a central clearing point for international *hawala* activities, and various cities in Pakistan are also major transaction centers. Even payments for drug shipments to Iran reportedly enter Afghanistan from Pakistan. Transfers of funds from major drug-consuming countries to regional countries like Dubai and Pakistan appear to occur largely through the formal banking system; *hawala* becomes dominant in the onward transfers of funds into and within Afghanistan.

The *hawala* system plays other important roles in addition to the laundering of drug money. Its positive contributions include serving as an efficient vehicle for remittances and providing money transfer services in the many parts of Afghanistan without banks, participating in foreign exchange and nascent treasury bill markets, and playing an instrumental role in the successful introduction of a new, stable currency for Afghanistan in 2002–03.

Dynamics of the Opium Economy

More important than a static picture of the opium economy are the evolutionary trends and structural changes that it has undergone, reflecting its own internal dynamics and the drug industry's response to changing counternarcotics policies and measures. This section argues that, partly as a result of counternarcotics policies that have been implemented unevenly and in a corrupt manner, Afghanistan's drug industry has become more consolidated and has compromised parts of some government agencies, with serious adverse effects on the state-building and development agenda.

Determinants of Household Decisions

Because opium poppy is an annual crop, rural households in Afghanistan make decisions every year on whether to plant opium poppy, how much to plant, and how to organize the required labor and other inputs, as well as when and how to sell (or store) the output. Relative to its high value, opium poppy economizes on land and water use (although it requires decent, nonwaterlogged soils and adequate water at the right times). It is highly labor intensive, however, and skilled labor is at a premium during harvest time. Market links for sale of the raw harvested opium are very strong, especially as compared with those for licit agricultural products, and drug traders also can make available key inputs—in particular credit and seeds—as necessary.

Extensive fieldwork conducted during the past decade has provided valuable insights into the various factors influencing rural households' decisions on cultivation of opium poppy. The best of this research (notably by Mansfield and Pain 2005), undertaken at great personal risk, has built up a significant degree of longitudinal knowledge—of provinces, localities, and even some households—as well as a wealth of cross-sectional information.

The research reveals that, although farm-gate prices of opium provide signals for producers and are a major determinant of incomes (see Byrd and Jonglez 2006), a one-dimensional, price-based model of farm-level decision making with respect to opium poppy cultivation does not fit the facts found in fieldwork, or even the broad trends seen in aggregate data. Changes in cultivation patterns in households and localities respond to many factors, of which the farm-gate price of opium, although very important, is only one. These factors are intimately related to the development challenges confronting Afghanistan, and they highlight the fact that a counternarcotics strategy can succeed only if it is embedded in and consistent with a broader development strategy.

Eradication efforts and enforced reductions in production, sometimes have major price effects that can significantly affect cultivation decisions in a perverse direction. Particularly if the reduction in cultivation is very large, the associated increase in farm-gate opium prices can be quite sharp (more than 1,000 percent in the short run at the time of the Taliban ban). Such a rise in price sends a very strong market signal for expansion of opium poppy cultivation in areas where the ban does not apply (non–Taliban-controlled areas in the case of the Taliban ban) or is not enforced. High prices also encourage areas with more marginal potential to engage in cultivation, as occurred in the case of Ghor after the Taliban ban (Pain 2006b; Mansfield 2006).

Household assets play a key role in guiding cultivation decisions, as argued by Mansfield (2006; United Kingdom 2007). Those assets, broadly understood, include the number of able-bodied males and their labor skills, agricultural land, irrigation water, proximity to labor markets, and jobs that pay regular salaries (such as in government), as well as more conventionally defined physical assets like livestock and vehicles. Households with relatively few such broadly defined assets have fewer (if any) viable alternatives to opium poppy cultivation or engaging in wage labor in the opium economy. More asset-rich households, in contrast, have more choices and opportunities for viable licit livelihoods and hence will tend to be much less dependent on opium, even though they may cultivate poppy opportunistically to increase their incomes. The implication is that law enforcement efforts as well as political and moral pressure can encourage better-off households to eschew involvement in the opium economy.

Access to commodity markets also can be viewed as an "asset" that reduces households' dependence on opium. The growth and extension of local vegetable markets in areas of Nangarhar close to Jalalabad City provide a good example of how improved access to markets can lead to sustainable reductions in opium cultivation. Such factors may also be at work near other provincial capitals, cities, and transport routes.

Another broadly defined asset, which is important but affects a locality or area rather than households individually, is a modicum of security for persons and property, at least sufficient to conduct small-scale economic activities and transport agricultural produce. The massive expansion of opium poppy cultivation in southern Helmand Province occurred when the Taliban insurgency there was intensifying, and other examples demonstrate the link between insecurity and opium at a more micro level (see GTZ/AKDN 2007 for a study of two districts in Badakhshan Province in this regard).

Mansfield (2006; United Kingdom 2007) finds evidence of the importance of such assets in the initially successful effort to reduce cultivation of opium poppy sharply in Nangarhar Province in 2004–05. The Nangarhar opium ban has turned out to be largely sustainable in more central localities where most households are higher up along the asset spectrum and in particular have relatively good access to commodity and labor markets. They have shifted successfully to licit—and sustainable—economic activities. In fact, after an adjustment period of usually not more than two to three years, such households can actually become better off than when they had been cultivating opium poppy, in particular when household labor is freed up from labor-intensive opium production.

More remote areas, where households have fewer assets, suffered severely from the ban and by the third year had been reverting to opium poppy cultivation. In the worst-off areas, the ban was not fully implemented from the beginning. Forcing households and localities with fewer assists to forgo cultivating opium poppy has led to drastic coping responses like asset sales and migration, which increase rather than reduce their underlying dependence on opium. Given their very meager assets and limited alternatives, the opportunity cost of engaging in opium poppy cultivation for such households is very low, and their decisions in this regard may not be affected by law enforcement actions or pressures. Viewed in this light, the subsequent re-imposition of the ban against opium poppy cultivation in Nangarhar, which again has brought production down to negligible levels in the past couple of years, will not necessarily prove sustainable in the more remote areas and, according to several reports, has resulted in increasing poverty, discontent, and insecurity.

Erosion or loss of some of the assets discussed above often constitutes an important "push" factor for households to engage in the opium economy. For example, in studying the main opium-producing areas in the northern province of Balkh, Pain (2006a, 2007) points to local population growth (including through return of displaced persons) and degradation of irrigation systems, which reduces water availability, as causes for making opium poppy cultivation a more attractive alternative in comparison with other crops. In the case of Ghor Province, loss of livestock caused by the severe drought of the late 1990s was an important factor for both traders and farmers in becoming involved in the opium economy. Declining security in southern Helmand Province since 2005 appears to have contributed to massive expansion of opium poppy cultivation there.

Historical and social factors also play a significant role in cultivation decisions. Pain (2007) argues that basic structures (agro-ecology, settlement history, and ethnicity), social positions of individuals within a locality (including ethnicity within the local context and socioeconomic position), and intermediary factors (community, markets, institutions, and behavior) together influence decisions on opium poppy cultivation (see Pain 2007, fig. 1). Although recognizing that market price signals can encourage wider diffusion of opium poppy cultivation, as appears to have occurred in Balkh Province post-2001, he argues that informal "regulation" of markets and ethnic or other links with the drug trade play an important role. In particular, the ethnic or other ties that facilitate the drug trade and the transfer of labor techniques constitute another enabling factor. For example, ethnic Pashtuns transplanted to Balkh decades earlier had retained ties with their tribes and ethnic groups in the southern opium-cultivating provinces, relationships that facilitated the spread of opium poppy cultivation to Balkh (see Pain 2006a). Moreover, existing trading networks for other goods, irrespective of ethnic connections, can help promote the opium trade when conditions are right. Pain (2006b) documents how many opium traders in Ghor had their origins in the livestock trade, which dried up as the severe and protracted drought decimated their herds in the late 1990s.

Broader Drug Industry Dynamics: Changing "Vicious Circles"

We now turn to dynamic patterns and trends in the drug industry as a whole.[6] Figure 8.3 depicts a vicious circle involving the opium economy, warlords, and insecurity—broadly reflecting the situation as opium

Figure 8.3. The Vicious Circle of the Drug Industry in Afghanistan

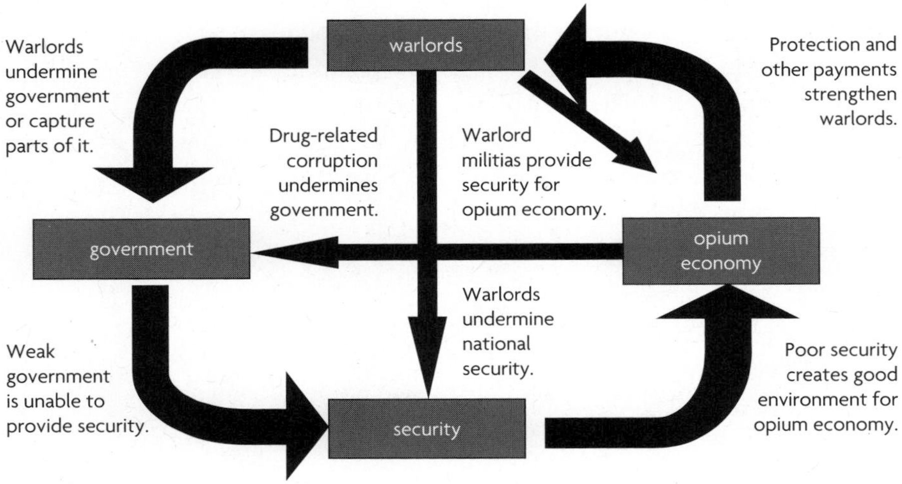

Warlords undermine government or capture parts of it.

Protection and other payments strengthen warlords.

Drug-related corruption undermines government.

Warlord militias provide security for opium economy.

warlords

government

opium economy

Warlords undermine national security.

Weak government is unable to provide security.

Poor security creates good environment for opium economy.

security

Source: Adapted from World Bank 2005, 120.

production rebounded in the first two years after the downfall of the Taliban. In this situation, payments from the opium economy strengthened warlords, who, in turn, undermined the state while drug-related corruption also undermined the state. In return for payments, warlord militias helped provide the enabling environment (often including armed protection) for the operation of the opium economy. The weak government was unable to provide genuine security or rule of law, and this void created an environment that allowed the opium economy to thrive. Thus, the dynamic tendencies at work perpetuated a large opium economy and a weak, ineffective state, particularly its inability to provide security.

This vicious circle suggested that a multifaceted strategic framework would be needed to address the opium economy effectively and the problems it causes for Afghanistan's development agenda. In addition to reducing the size of the drug economy through effective counternarcotics measures more narrowly construed, this framework would need to include several additional elements:

- curbing warlords' powers by stopping payments and other support to them by disarmaing, demobilizing, and reintegrating to take away their militias; and by co-opting them into the government as appropriate;

- building government capacity and effectiveness as well as resources;
- reforming and building capacity in the security sector (see World Bank 2005, fig. 7.4).

A strategic framework along these lines appeared attractive, and several of the key elements were put in place to some extent or were at least initiated. Improvements at the broader strategic level, however, fell far short of what was needed. As a result, the opium economy has further expanded, and both the opium problem and its adverse impacts on the state-building and development agenda have become worse.

As depicted in figure 8.4, the transformation of warlords into politicians has been accompanied by compromising parts of some government agencies like the Ministry of Interior and the police by drug industry interests. The strengthening triangle among drug interests, their sponsors, and parts of the government is symptomatic of the way counternarcotics efforts have inadvertently contributed to consolidation of the drug industry, primarily through widespread corruption in their implementation (see Shaw 2006). Security forces—most notably

Figure 8.4. Consolidation of the Drug Industry in Afghanistan

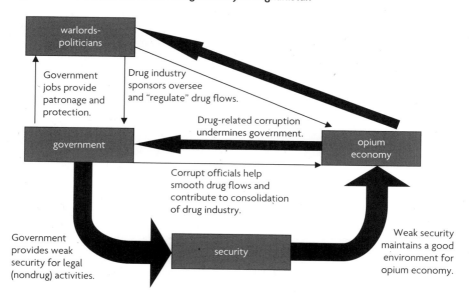

Source: Author.

the police—are, in part, facilitating the activities of the drug industry rather than countering it.

Overall, this dynamic evolution of the drug industry constitutes a profound threat to Afghanistan's state-building and development agenda. And the fundamental equation between a weak state (partly compromised by drug interests) and a thriving opium economy remains. Moreover, the expanding Taliban insurgency in the south (not depicted in figure 8.4) adds complexity to the picture and helps provide an enabling environment of insecurity for the drug industry, further heightening the associated risks.

Counternarcotics Experience in Afghanistan

Afghanistan has a National Drug Control Strategy (NDCS), first prepared in 2003 and subsequently updated and refined several times. The goal, priorities, and pillars of the NDCS are outlined in box 8.1. The NDCS has much to commend it, including its explicit emphasis (a) on the

---

Box 8.1 National Drug Control Strategy—Objective, Priorities, Pillars

The NDCS, which has gone through several versions, puts forward a credible multidimensional approach, which is briefly summarized below.

Overall Policy Goal

To secure a sustainable decrease in cultivation, production, trafficking, and consumption of illicit drugs with a view to complete and sustainable elimination.

National Priorities

- Disrupt the drug trade by targeting traffickers and their backers and eliminating the basis for the trade.
- Strengthen and diversify legal rural livelihoods.
- Reduce the demand for illicit drugs, and treatment of problem drug users.
- Strengthen state institutions both at the center and in the provinces.

Pillars of Activity

(a) Public awareness, (b) International and regional cooperation, (c) Alternative livelihoods, (d) Demand reduction, (e) Law enforcement, (f) Criminal justice, (g) Eradication, and (h) Institution building

Source: Afghanistan Government (2006).

need for a multiyear time horizon and for sustainable progress against drugs, (b) on the importance of alternative livelihoods in supporting the role of eradication, and (c) on the rejection of aerial and chemical spraying, among others. The NDCS, however, is not specific on short-run prioritization and sequencing, on regional targeting, or on the lessons learned from earlier experience with counternarcotics efforts. Nor have adequate resources been allocated (or even estimated) for proper implementation. Annual detailed counternarcotics implementation plans, which provide short-term operational guidance and are organized around the pillars of the NDCS, lack the strategic links, synergies, response to diversity, prioritization, and sequencing necessary for making the counternarcotics strategy work effectively.

Experience with Different Counternarcotics Instruments

Until the Taliban's comprehensive and highly successful ban on opium poppy cultivation, counternarcotics efforts in Afghanistan were marginal, consisting primarily of some small pilot alternative development projects. Before their ban, the Taliban treated opium de facto as a legal commodity and taxed it at moderate rates accordingly. The ban in 2000 applied to opium poppy cultivation but not to trade in opium and opiates, and no actions were taken at the time against opium inventories or their holders.

Efforts to shrink the size of the opium economy in the post-Taliban era have been significant but fragmented, detached from the development agenda, and unevenly applied over time and across the country. Given the entrenched nature of the opium economy, it is no surprise that counternarcotics efforts failed to prevent large increases in opium production in 2006 and 2007. Although output has subsequently declined, this appears to reflect market factors to a large extent, in particular lower opium prices and substantially higher prices of wheat. Afghanistan's experience with the main counternarcotics instruments deployed so far, briefly summarized next, provides useful lessons for the future.

Eradication and Enforced Cultivation Reductions. This category includes reductions in opium poppy cultivation achieved through pressure, persuasion, and threat of eradication, as well as from outright eradication of crops in the field. In fact, where sharp reductions in cultivation have been achieved, physical eradication accounted for only a very small proportion of the decrease in cultivated area.

The two main instruments for physical eradication of opium poppy fields have been the Central Poppy Eradication Force (CPEF) and the so-called "governor-led eradication" implemented by police and other forces in the provinces. The CPEF has limited capacity, often faces local resistance, and has to rely on local guidance on where to focus its eradication efforts. As a consequence, most of the limited physical eradication of poppy crops that has occurred has been under the leadership of provincial governors. There are serious concerns, however, that because of the close ties between many local officials and drug interests, governor-led eradication is especially vulnerable to corruption in implementation.

By far, pressure and persuasion are responsible for most of the reductions in opium poppy cultivation that have been achieved, including passing orders down through the provincial and district administrations of the government, as well as traditional village and higher-level committees of elders (*shuras*). Religious arguments, building on the widespread popular perception that opium as a narcotic drug is "against Islam," have played an important part in such campaigns. The credible threat of eradication, though, has been used in efforts to achieve reductions through pressure and persuasion.

Overall, eradication has generally not had a sustainable impact. Within two to three years after the nearly complete cessation of cultivation under the Taliban in 2000–01 and in Nangarhar Province in 2004, poppy cultivation in both cases rebounded. Moreover, even at the time of the bans, cultivation increased sharply in other areas—in areas controlled by the Northern Alliance in the case of the earlier ban and in other provinces at the time of the dramatic reduction in Nangarhar.

Three main reasons explain the limited success of eradication:

- First, eradication is technically difficult. The opium economy has amply demonstrated that it is "footloose" both across space and over time, with impressive reductions in opium poppy cultivation being offset by increases in other areas or in subsequent years.[7] Because opium poppy is an annual crop, cultivated on well under 10 percent of Afghanistan's irrigated area, it can easily shift locations—opium traders, wage laborers, and even farmers are quite mobile in response to the changing geographical focus of counternarcotics measures.[8]

- The second reason is political resistance to and corruption in the implementation of eradication programs. Their unpopular ban undermined political support for the Taliban in key Pashtun areas, possibly making it easier for the regime to be overthrown in late 2001. The government's campaign against drugs in 2004–05—led by President Hamid Karzai, which achieved by far its greatest success in Nangarhar Province—also carried significant political costs for the government, especially in that province. Adverse popular sentiments on eradication can lead to a political reaction, which the antigovernment interests and the drug industry itself can exploit. Corruption in implementation aggravates such political repercussions, thus undermining the credibility and perceived legitimacy of the government among the rural populace.[9] Moreover, such corruption tends to result in eradication that disproportionately affects the poor, because the poor lack the political connections or resources to bribe the authorities not to destroy their crops.

- The third reason is that eradication does not address the deeper determinants of opium poppy cultivation. More sustained success with eradication and enforced reductions in cultivation has occurred in localities or provinces that were relatively new to opium poppy cultivation (for example, Wardak Province in 2004) or that had more access to resources, assets, and opportunities (central areas of Nangarhar, for example). According to experience in Afghanistan, eradication and enforced reductions in cultivation are economically unsustainable, except in better-off localities where people already have viable alternative livelihoods—including access to water, land, and commodity and labor markets. When imposed on poorer areas and households that lack opportunities for other economic activities, eradication can worsen poverty and can increase the dependence on opium. Individual households can suffer reduced incomes, forced asset sales, and opium-related debt (see Zia and others 2005), which weaken coping capacities and resilience, thereby making it more likely that farmers will subsequently return to opium poppy cultivation. According to reports, for example, farmers whose opium poppy fields have been eradicated several times have, nevertheless, continued to cultivate opium poppy as long as market conditions justify doing so, because that is the only way they can manage (and have any hope of reducing) their opium-related debts.

Thus, although eradication attacks the most visible part of the opium economy and can achieve sizable and quantifiable results in the short run, experience indicates that those results are not sustainable. Moreover, eradication often has adverse consequences, perversely increasing the underlying dependence of many rural households on the opium economy and undermining the credibility of the government and others involved in eradication.

The shortcomings of eradication would be multiplied were chemical spraying to be involved—especially aerial spraying—as opposed to manual or mechanical eradication as used up to now in Afghanistan. Patterns of human settlement and intercropping mean that avoiding impact on people, livestock, and other crops from chemical spraying would be very difficult. Even if the actual health and other effects are not significantly harmful, chemical spraying provides a propaganda victory for antigovernment interests. In a context where infant and child mortality rates are extraordinarily high, where there are frequent crop failures, and where livestock suffer from numerous diseases, all such problems encountered for many years to come could be blamed on chemical spraying. The insurgency would undoubtedly take advantage of what the affected rural population would widely perceive as a hostile act against it, driving a further wedge between the people and the government.

Interdiction. Interdiction efforts in Afghanistan were limited at first.[10] From 2003 onward, however, there has been increasing emphasis on interdiction, including law enforcement actions against drug traders, raiding and closure of opium marketplaces, seizure of stockpiles, and destruction of heroin-processing facilities. Strong efforts have been made to build up police forces, to train judges for special counternarcotics courts, and to set up prison facilities for drug traffickers. These activities are having some impact, although it has been much more difficult to go after the larger actors in the drug industry. However, corruption in the implementation of some interdiction activities has been a serious issue. According to some reports, some drug traders have been arrested and then released in return for a bribe, and their drug shipments have been confiscated, not for destruction but for onward sale by corrupt local authorities—including the possibility that part of the shipment is returned to the trader for an additional bribe (Pain 2006b). Implemented in a corrupt manner, both interdiction actions and eradication have inadvertently contributed to consolidation of the drug industry around fewer, more powerful, and better politically connected actors (see Shaw 2006). Clearly, some local and regional power holders have used enforcement activities to favor their own (if they are directly involved in the drug industry) or allied drug industry interests.

Alternative Livelihoods. Alternative livelihoods programs aim to assist farmers in shifting from opium poppy cultivation to alternative sources of income (see Mansfield 2007 for a review). The earliest efforts involved simple "crop substitution" projects, which subsequently gave way to "alternative development" approaches. Although somewhat broader, these efforts still focused on substituting other crops for opium, concretely involving relatively small-scale, localized rural projects. Given the economic and social forces that led to opium poppy cultivation, such projects were grossly inadequate. Even in cases where they were successful in narrow terms, they tended merely to displace illicit drug cultivation elsewhere. The shift to an "alternative livelihoods" concept was meant to encompass the broader factors, including access to assets like land, water, and credit, as well as markets. But this conceptual improvement has not been translated into practice, because such programs have continued to focus on discrete projects that mainly involve other crops.[11]

Many recent efforts to attack the development roots of opium poppy cultivation have been not only narrow but also far too short term in their orientation. They have been used to try to (partly) mitigate the immediate income declines suffered by rural households that exit from the opium economy. Key examples include cash-for-work programs and provision of agricultural inputs (typically seeds and fertilizer). Focused on short-run incomes rather than on markets, assets, and financing, such programs do not change the long-run and deeper conditions that contribute to households' decisions to cultivate opium poppy. Indeed, abundant research since the 1990s has demonstrated that a short-run "quid pro quo" approach does not work (Mansfield 2002); nevertheless, it continues to be widely used. Moreover, the approaches taken have been counterproductive, because promises have been made and popular perceptions have been that those programs would deliver immediate results. The inevitable failure to meet such unrealistic expectations has discredited the government, donors, and the counternarcotics strategy more generally.

Initiatives to articulate and implement a broader, longer-run development approach as part of a counternarcotics strategy have continued through "mainstreaming" the counternarcotics dimension within development activities, national development programs in particular. The hope is that in this way development programs can have an enhanced and scaled up counternarcotics impact, while avoiding "doing harm" (that is, inadvertently supporting expansion of the opium economy). For example, as defined by the World Bank (2006) in its mainstreaming guideline note for Afghanistan, the process involves factoring opium considerations into all aspects of the World Bank's engagement with Afghanistan, including analytical work and policy dialogue. More recently, a joint report by the United Kingdom's Department for International Development and the World Bank recommended a multifaceted set of development programs and economic interventions to support sustainable reductions in opium production (see World Bank and United Kingdom 2008).

Demand-side Interventions in Afghanistan. Although high demand along with criminalization constitutes a critical enabling factor for the illicit narcotics industry worldwide and although countries near Afghanistan generate a large regional demand for opiates, domestic demand within Afghanistan has been very small relative to the size of the opium economy, which is predominantly an export-oriented activity. Nevertheless, drug use is becoming a significant and increasing problem in Afghanistan, spurred by chronic insecurity and conflict, as well as by returning refugees who became drug users in neighboring countries.

Demand-side issues have been neglected in Afghanistan, although recently more attention has been devoted to them, including concerns about HIV/AIDS transmitted by intravenous drug users. Resources devoted to reducing demand in Afghanistan have been minuscule in comparison with efforts devoted to eradication and interdiction. Although demand measures will not have a significant effect on the size and importance of the opium economy, because it is overwhelmingly an export activity, they will be important in reducing the adverse impact on problem drug use in the country.

Communications and Education. Communications and education have been another neglected area, despite some successes in reducing opium poppy cultivation through pressure and persuasion, communications down the line within government, and interactions between local administrations and village *shuras* (groups of elders). There are also widespread indications from fieldwork that communications by radio and through mosques have been effective in informing the rural population that opium poppy cultivation is illegal and may be subject to eradication. However, communication efforts have failed to manage expectations about delivery of development assistance and, on the contrary, have tended to fuel such expectations.

Moreover, according to anecdotal evidence, it appears that other communications efforts have at least sometimes gone far off the mark, reflecting a lack of sensitivity to the local cultural context, language issues, and aspects related to the target population (for example, that most of the rural population is illiterate). A striking example is discussed by Mansfield (GTZ/AKDN 2007), where, being unable to read, people who looked at a counternarcotics poster gave widely varying interpretations unrelated to the intended message. For example, no one saw an armed, turbaned young man in the poster as a terrorist or insurgent (which was the intended depiction), because people with such clothing and carrying a weapon would be a normal part of the local scene.

Lessons and Policy Implications

As discussed earlier, eradication and enforced reductions in cultivation, as well as hasty and fragmented alternative livelihoods projects, have been major elements of the counternarcotics effort in Afghanistan in recent years. Long experience provides ample evidence that those problematic instruments carry significant adverse side effects. The key lesson is that there is no substitute for effective rural development over the longer term in weaning rural populations away from dependence on opium poppy cultivation. This finding has major implications for the design, time horizon, funding, and sequencing (in relation to eradication) of development activities intended to contribute to counternarcotics objectives.

Knowledge that Even "Better" Counternarcotics Instruments Are Not Easy Solutions

In addition to the hard-learned lessons about eradication and alternative livelihoods, experience in Afghanistan has also demonstrated that other counternarcotics instruments, which appear far more attractive for valid reasons, are not in and of themselves solutions to the opium problem.

Emphasizing Interdiction rather than Eradication. Interdiction, which has recently been emphasized by the U.S. government and other members of the international community, is attractive on a number of grounds. First, the number of "targets" is several orders of magnitude smaller than the number of farmers who cultivate opium poppy. If interdiction actions against a relatively small number of drug traffickers can have an impact equivalent to an eradication campaign, interdiction would be much more cost effective from a technical perspective. Second, rather than criminalizing farmers, this option could target the elements of the drug industry that constitute the major threat to Afghanistan's state-building, governance, and development agenda. Third, interdiction is likely to increase the "wedge" between farm-gate and downstream prices, potentially even reducing farm-gate prices in the short run and thereby discouraging cultivation.[12] In contrast, eradication tends to increase farm-gate prices. Finally, interdiction, if effectively implemented in an even-handed way, can enhance the government's credibility by going after criminal elements rather than farmers and wage laborers.

Despite those attractive features, interdiction is far from a panacea. Significant figures involved in politics and government may be involved in or beneficiaries of the drug industry. A serious interdiction effort is, therefore, likely to provoke political resistance by powerful actors. Institutional development and capacity building in the concerned law enforcement agencies are essential but will take time. And sustained resources, albeit of a much lower magnitude than required for the other instruments, are needed. Moreover, as seen from the experience of other countries such as Iran, interdiction can elicit strong and effective responses by the drug industry, ranging from armed resistance against police to assassinations, bribery and corruption, and political manipulations. Thus, although it can reap important benefits in the short run—not least by sending strong signals of the government's commitment to confronting the drug industry—a counternarcotics strategy driven by interdiction can trigger an increasing spiral of drug-related violence. And finally, as in the case of eradication, implementation of interdiction measures in an uneven and corrupt way not only harms the credibility and perceived legitimacy of the government but also can be a vehicle for consolidating and strengthening the drug industry.

Interception of Precursor Chemicals. Although transforming opium into morphine is a straightforward technical process with fairly simple requirements, processing opium into heroin is more sophisticated and requires precursor chemicals, in particular substantial amounts of acetic anhydride. Because most opium produced in Afghanistan is currently being processed in-country unlike the situation in the 1990s and earlier, interdicting and disrupting the flow of precursor chemicals into Afghanistan is often advocated, and some may see it as a relatively straightforward solution. However, Afghanistan's porous borders and the inability of the international community to stem cross-border flows of arms, insurgents, and illicit drugs themselves suggest grounds for caution. Moreover, acetic anhydride is used for other purposes in many countries. And finally, because precursor chemicals account for a very small proportion of the price of heroin at Afghanistan's borders, even successful efforts to disrupt their supply and sharp increases in their prices will not necessarily curb heroin processing. Recent fieldwork suggests that, with the unprecedentedly large opium harvests in 2006 and 2007 and with the possibly more effective controls in some key source countries, prices of acetic anhydride have risen dramatically, but those higher prices do not appear to have had a dramatic impact on its availability or on heroin processing.

Untried Proposals

A number of other proposals for dealing with Afghanistan's opium problem have not yet been tried in the country. Unfortunately, none of the approaches is a "silver bullet" either.

Licensing Production. Not yet tried in Afghanistan, although strongly advocated in some quarters, is the idea of licensing the country's opium production for sale and processing in the legal market for pharmaceuticals. Licensed production of opiates occurs in several other countries, most notably Australia, France, India, and Turkey. However, only India produces licensed opium by labor-intensive techniques similar to those currently used in Afghanistan; the other countries grow poppy straw rich in pharmaceutical ingredients using capital-intensive modern agricultural techniques. Clear international rules govern licensed production of opiates, including monopsony purchase by the government and stringent controls to prevent leakages into the illicit market. Opportunities for engaging in licensed production are supposed to be open to "traditional" producers of opium, a status for which Afghanistan would appear to qualify, but that would need to be confirmed.

Unfortunately, although superficially attractive, the proposal for licensed production of opium in Afghanistan founders on several basic practicalities:

- The security, rule of law, and governance situation in Afghanistan is inadequate for licensed and effectively controlled production of opium. India, with a much better situation and internationally accepted control mechanisms in place, suffers from substantial leakages of opium from the licensed into the illicit market, which is estimated by some observers at around 30 percent (see United Kingdom 2001). In Afghanistan, leakages could be expected to be even larger.
- With under 10 percent of Afghanistan's good agricultural land now devoted to opium poppy cultivation, if the current level of production is licensed, the same amount of illicit production could spring up within a couple of years, and total opium output could very easily double in a fairly short time.
- The licensed price would inevitably be far lower than the price of illicit opium, reinforcing incentives for leakages and parallel production for the illicit market.

Even if such problems could be resolved, which does not appear feasible in the foreseeable future, equally daunting obstacles originate from the international side:

- Stocks of licensed opium produced by India with labor-intensive techniques are building up. Moreover, Afghanistan and indeed India do not appear to have a comparative advantage in licit cultivation (see figures cited in Mansfield 2007). Thus, the scope for large licensed production by Afghanistan using current techniques would appear to be limited.

- More generally, although some have argued that there is a worldwide shortage of opiates for licit purposes like pain management in developing countries, that claim is subject to debate. Any shortage would not appear to be at all near the magnitude that could accommodate Afghanistan's recent or current production of illicit opium. Thus, existing licensed producers would need to reduce their output sharply to accommodate a shift by Afghanistan to licensed opium production. But there is no sign of any willingness on their part to do so.

Buying Up the Opium Crop. A somewhat similar proposal is that the international community, rather than putting large amounts of money into counternarcotics measures of doubtful effectiveness, should simply buy up the opium crop for one or two years as an interim solution. In addition to avoiding problems associated with eradication and other enforcement measures against the opium economy, this measure is seen as temporarily disrupting the drug trade and sharply reducing funding available for criminal and anti-state interests, as well as buying some time for development of sustainable alternative livelihoods to wean farmers away from poppy. A crash program for developing viable legal livelihoods in opium poppy–cultivating areas would need to accompany any program for buying up the opium crop.

Although in some respects attractive, this proposal is problematic because, as discussed earlier, strengthening and diversifying legal livelihoods take a long time and buying the crop for only one or a few years would not do much good. Moreover, it would provide incentives for stimulating further growth of opium poppy cultivation, as in the case of licensed production. If it involves a commitment to buy all the opium produced, costs would likely mount from year to year, or otherwise increasing amounts of opium would go back into illicit channels. And there are a host of technical issues such as pricing that would not be easily resolved and would affect production incentives and potential for leakages. Finally, the public sector apparatus, presence, capacity, and level of governance required for this approach to be administratively feasible are not in place. Thus, this proposal would not have lasting benefits. Moreover, by setting a precedent for engagement of the government and the international community in the purchase of opium, buying up the opium crop would send very mixed signals to farmers and would generate problematic incentives.

Blanket Agricultural Subsidies or Price Supports. Another "silver bullet" that has not been tried in Afghanistan but is sometimes proposed is a subsidy or price-support scheme for crops planted to replace poppy. This option is seen as stimulating the development of licit crops to substitute for opium and also as a way of providing income support for former poppy farmers during a transitional period until their new cropping patterns get firmly established on a financially sound basis.

This proposal also raises a number of very serious issues. As has been amply demonstrated by Afghanistan's experience, opium cultivation is footloose, so that a subsidy or price-support system would need to cover the entire country to be effective. This scale would add greatly to its cost and, moreover, would involve putting in place a national subsidy or price-support system that Afghanistan would be unable to afford any time in the foreseeable future. In addition, as shown through international experience, agricultural subsidies and price-support systems tend to be self-perpetuating because they become politically difficult to terminate once in place. Given the shortage of domestic revenue in Afghanistan and other development priorities, how long could the international community credibly commit to providing blanket subsidies or financing price supports?

Another important question is what crops would be subsidized and how they would fit into Afghanistan's development agenda. Wheat is by far the most important agricultural product and tends to be the crop of choice for farmers who stop cultivating opium poppy, but wheat is not the crop of Afghanistan's future. As a low-value, relatively land- and water-intensive crop—and not labor intensive—wheat does not mesh well with Afghanistan's resource endowment. Moreover, in good years Afghanistan already comes close to meeting domestic demand for food grains from its own production, and there are no export prospects for wheat in the region given that several neighboring countries are themselves sizable producers and exporters. What Afghanistan needs to develop instead is high-value, labor-intensive licit crops with good export potential, including through agro-processing.

Finally, Afghanistan's porous borders—and the same kinds of governance and security issues that affect some of the other proposals discussed earlier—would make a blanket subsidy or price-support scheme virtually impossible to implement. The large production of wheat in neighboring countries, most notably Pakistan (where there is a subsidy on wheat flour) and Kazakhstan, would add further complications and risks. Costs would likely increase, and trade patterns would be further distorted.

Toward a "Smart Strategy" Against Drugs in Afghanistan

The lessons from experience with different counternarcotics instruments in Afghanistan and elsewhere, and the discussion earlier of other proposed solutions to the opium problem, clearly demonstrate that there are no easy answers. On the demand side, high global demand for illicit opiates shows no sign of diminishing. On the supply side, the conditions that lead farmers to cultivate opium are deep-seated and not possible to change rapidly or inexpensively. Moreover, many of the commonly proposed "solutions" could actually worsen the situation. Calling for modest expectations in the short run and for exercise of caution, however, is *not* a recipe for inaction. As emphasized earlier, the opium economy is simply too important and too harmful to Afghanistan to neglect or downplay. Even though the illegality of the opium economy and the high global demand for illicit opiates are likely to persist in the foreseeable future, experience provides some grounds for hope that strategies exist that can reduce opium cultivation in Afghanistan.

Experience in Afghanistan and elsewhere suggests the following principles as a guide to development of a "smart strategy" against drugs in Afghanistan (see Byrd and Buddenberg 2006). One is to focus on those parts of the drug industry that pose the greatest danger to the nation and its development agenda—that is, the larger drug traffickers and their sponsors, who threaten to undermine state building through political corruption and through compromising state agencies such as the police and Ministry of Interior. Those actors, not the farm households engaged in opium poppy cultivation or wage labor in the opium economy, constitute the real threat.

A second principle is to take fully into account the adverse side effects and distortions induced by counternarcotics instruments, which could undermine or even negate any beneficial effects. A prime example is corruption in the implementation of counternarcotics policies. There is no point in designing a plan that may work well but only in the absence of corruption, when it is obvious beforehand that corruption is an inevitable factor in implementation.

A third principle is to minimize perverse incentives. If, for example, counternarcotics assistance (especially support for alternative livelihoods) is concentrated in the major opium-producing areas, other (noncultivating) areas are likely to resent that attention and may even weaken their efforts to avoid the opium economy.[13] More generally, experience suggests that counternarcotics efforts should not focus excessively on the major *current* opium-producing areas but should instead consider strong measures to discourage the spread of the opium economy to currently nondependent provinces and localities.

A fourth principle is to respond to diversity in the rural opium economy, based on the expanding body of knowledge, and to exploit opportunities offered by local resources, accessibility of markets, and improvements in security and governance. In areas where people have some assets, where there are land and water resources, where commodity and labor markets are accessible, and where there is a modicum of security and somewhat effective governance, it is possible to get away from dependence on the opium economy. Moreover, when these ingredients are in place, the shift from opium to sustainable licit livelihoods can occur within a few years. Without such essential resources, assets, and opportunities in a locality, there is no alternative to longer-term rural development, which inevitably will take much time to achieve.

Finally, it is essential to continue to monitor and build knowledge about the evolving opium economy, to engage in sound and careful policy analysis, and to use the findings of research and the lessons from experience to inform the design and implementation of counternarcotics measures.

Based on those principles, a smart strategy against drugs in Afghanistan could include the following key elements:

- *Eradication* and *enforced reductions* in poppy cultivation should be focused on the better-off and new opium-producing areas. Experience in such areas (for example, with eradication in Wardak Province, a new opium-producing area, several years ago) suggests that those measures can be successful and have a sustained impact. When a locality is targeted for eradication on such a basis, the goal should be virtually complete elimination of opium poppy cultivation in that locality rather than partial reduction; this approach will minimize the risk of corruption in implementation and associated distortions. Chemical spraying, especially aerial spraying, must be avoided for reasons explained earlier.

- With respect to *interdiction,* and recognizing the political difficulties involved, all efforts should be focused against medium and larger drug traffickers and their sponsors. In addition to causing disruption of the drug trade in the short run, this approach will set a very positive example for counternarcotics efforts at lower levels. Given the weakness of the judiciary and the difficulties in successfully prosecuting major drug figures (although some progress has been made in operationalizing special counternarcotics courts and in training personnel), extradition may be called for in some cases. Moreover, actors associated with the drug industry should at least be removed from their positions in government, which can have a significant impact in the Afghan context. Aside from the direct benefits, such action will also send a strong signal of credibility for the counternarcotics strategy.

- With respect to *alternative livelihoods,* do not throw money at short-term alternative livelihoods programs but rather support sensible rural development, thereby fully understanding that it will take time. Resources for effective rural development will need to be scaled up as sound programs are developed and refined through field experience. Lessons from international experience should be brought to bear in this regard. Part of the rural development effort could involve support for promising high-value horticultural products, such as almonds, raisins, pistachios, and others, as well as livestock products. Many of those goods would need to be exported, and innovative approaches to developing exports using the international and Afghan private sector could be explored for this purpose.

- *Mainstreaming* of the counternarcotics dimension in development programs is very important and will help in scaling up meaningful efforts on the development side. Mainstreaming should not be approached mechanically but rather in a flexible and results-oriented manner. And while moving forward expeditiously with necessary technical and support work to make mainstreaming a reality, expectations about progress in the short run should be kept modest.

- As emphasized earlier, efforts and resources should not be concentrated only in the main opium producing areas; rather a kind of *"containment" strategy* could be considered to close off increasingly large parts of the country from vulnerability to dependence on opium. Over time, this progressive approach will help narrow the geographical scope and range of the drug industry and restrict its options for opposing counternarcotics measures.

- Finally, and more generally, just as the counternarcotics dimension needs to be mainstreamed in development programs, there is also a need to mainstream the *development dimension* in counternarcotics strategy and actions. Given the importance of the opium economy in Afghanistan, this kind of "reverse mainstreaming" of development and governance considerations in decisions, policies, and instruments for fighting drugs is essential. In particular, it could help avoid problems like those encountered in the past when counternarcotics measures have been designed and implemented in isolation from the broader development and state-building agenda.

Notes

1. The "Dutch disease" refers to the adverse macroeconomic and development impacts of a large inflow of funds to a country, whether this inflow results from natural resource exploitation; a sharp price increase in existing natural resource exports; a surge of development assistance or direct foreign investment; or, as in the case of Afghanistan, income from illicit narcotics production and exports. By raising the real exchange rate and prices of nontradables, the resource inflow weakens the competitiveness of other sectors, in particular manufacturing. The

"Dutch disease" can also entail adverse effects on governance and accountability (for example, through the corrosive effects of large inflows of resources in terms of corruption and other manifestations of poor governance).

2. The United States also produces annual estimates of the total area devoted to opium poppy cultivation, which in recent years have been fairly similar to UNODC's estimates. However, there are wide discrepancies between U.S. and UNODC estimates of the opium poppy cultivated area in individual provinces. For convenience and consistency, UNODC estimates are used throughout this chapter.

3. For example, in the case of the 2004 estimate of 131,000 hectares of opium poppy cultivation, UNODC and Government of Afghanistan (2004, 21) indicated that the range of possible estimates was from 109,000 to 152,000 hectares, implying a margin of error (a 90 percent confidence interval) of around plus or minus 16–17 percent. In 2006, the range of estimates was somewhat smaller, between 150,000 and 180,000 hectares, for a margin of error of plus or minus 9 percent (UNODC and Government of Afghanistan 2006, 115).

4. Opium dries out over time, which reduces the weight, but there is a well-established price differential between stored "dry" opium and freshly-harvested "wet" opium, so that any loss in value is minimal, especially in relation to the large observed fluctuations in opium prices.

5. It should also be noted that there are large short-run fluctuations in local opium prices—lasting hours or at most days—that are not captured in the monthly price data. Those fluctuations reflect entry and exit of major buyers in local markets and substantially increase short-run trading risks for small traders (see Pain 2006b).

6. See also the discussion in chapter 5 on vicious circles and dynamics of illegal narcotics production in several countries.

7. It should also be noted that like other crops, opium poppy is best rotated from time to time to maintain soil quality and high yields. Thus, a "stop-go" pattern whereby there are sharp reductions in a province or locality in one year followed by a rebound in subsequent years often makes agronomic sense. The widespread reports of an excellent opium harvest in Nangarhar Province, in the third year after the near-complete ban imposed in 2004, provide a striking example.

8. Illegal narcotics production is also mobile across countries, as noted in chapter 3. This characteristic poses major difficulties for efforts to reduce global supply, which, as argued in that chapter, can shift the location but not necessarily reduce the volume of production.

9. See Anderson (2007) for an interesting account of a particular case where political or corruption considerations influenced and constrained eradication efforts with adverse consequences.

10. This general category encompasses the full range of law enforcement measures beyond the farm level, including arrest of drug traders, seizure of drug shipments, closing of opium bazaars, and destruction of heroin-processing

facilities, as well as actions against drug industry sponsors whether inside or outside the government. Internationally, the term *interdiction* is often reserved for law enforcement efforts against movements of illicit narcotics across borders, in particular, interception of drug shipments on their way to or in consuming countries, whereas actions against all levels of the drug industry in producing countries may be lumped together as production and refining controls. In this chapter, interdiction refers to law enforcement actions against drugs beyond the farm level. See Ward and Byrd (2004, 57–60) for a summary discussion on interdiction up until 2004.

11. See Mansfield and Pain (2005) for an extensive discussion on the use and misuse of the term *alternative livelihoods*.
12. There is some evidence of such a negative effect on farm-gate prices from threatened or actual interdiction measures (see Ward and Byrd 2004).
13. Some provincial governors have publicly complained that their provinces, which are not significant opium producers and do not face major security problems, are not getting much development assistance.

References

Afghanistan Government. 2006. *National Drug Control Strategy: An Updated Five-Year Strategy for Tackling the Illicit Drug Problem.* Kabul: Ministry of Counter-Narcotics.

Anderson, Jon Lee. 2007. "The Taliban's Opium War: The Difficulties and Dangers of the Eradication Program." *New Yorker.* July 9.

Buddenberg, Doris, and William A. Byrd, eds. 2006. *Afghanistan's Drug Industry: Structure, Functioning, Dynamics, and Implications for Counter-Narcotics Policy.* Vienna: UNODC, and Washington, DC: World Bank.

Byrd, William A., and Doris Buddenberg. 2006. "Introduction and Overview." In *Afghanistan's Drug Industry: Structure, Functioning, Dynamics, and Implications for Counter-Narcotics Policy,* ed. Doris Buddenberg and William A. Byrd, 1–23. Vienna: UNODC, and Washington, DC: World Bank.

Byrd, William A., and Olivier Jonglez. 2006. "Prices and Market Interactions in the Opium Economy." In *Afghanistan's Drug Industry: Structure, Functioning, Dynamics, and Implications for Counter-Narcotics Policy,* ed. Doris Buddenberg and William A. Byrd, 117–54. Vienna: UNODC, and Washington, DC: World Bank.

Byrd, William, and Christopher Ward. 2004. "Drugs and Development in Afghanistan." World Bank Social Development Papers, Conflict Prevention and Reconstruction 18. Washington, DC: World Bank.

GTZ (German Technical Corporation)/AKDN (Agha Khan Development Network). 2007. *Governance, Security, and Economic Growth: The Determinants of Opium Poppy Cultivation in the Districts of Jurm and Baharak in Badakhshan.* By David Mansfield. Consultant report.

Macdonald, David. 2007. *Drugs in Afghanistan: Opium, Outlaws, and Scorpion Tales.* London: Pluto Press.

Maimbo, Samuel Munzele. 2003. "The Money Exchange Dealers of Kabul." World Bank Working Paper 13. Washington, DC: World Bank.

Mansfield, David. 2002. "The Failure of Quid Pro Quo: Alternative Development in Afghanistan." Paper prepared for the International Conference on Alternative Development in Drug Control and Cooperation, Feldafing, Germany, January 7–12.

———. 2006. "Opium Poppy Cultivation in Nangarhar and Ghor." Afghanistan Research and Evaluation Unit (AREU) Case Study Series on Water Management, Livestock, and the Opium Economy. Kabul: AREU.

———. 2007. "Counter-Narcotics Mainstreaming in ADB's Activities in Afghanistan, 2002–2006." Manila: Asian Development Bank (ADB).

Mansfield, David, and Adam Pain. 2005. "Alternative Livelihoods: Substance or Slogan." Afghanistan Research and Evaluation Unit (AREU) Briefing Paper. Kabul: AREU.

Martin, Edouard, and Steven Symansky. 2006. "Macroeconomic Impact of the Drug Economy and Counter-Narcotics Efforts." In *Afghanistan's Drug Industry: Structure, Functioning, Dynamics, and Implications for Counter-Narcotics Policy,* ed. Doris Buddenberg and William A. Byrd, 25–46. Vienna: UNODC, and Washington, DC: World Bank.

Pain, Adam. 2006a. "Opium Poppy Cultivation in Kunduz and Balkh." Afghanistan Research and Evaluation Unit (AREU) Case Study Series on Water Management, Livestock and the Opium Economy. Kabul: AREU.

———. 2006b. "Opium Trading Systems in Helmand and Ghor Provinces." In *Afghanistan's Drug Industry: Structure, Functioning, Dynamics, and Implications for Counter-Narcotics Policy,* ed. Doris Buddenberg and William A. Byrd, 77–115. Vienna: UNODC, and Washington, DC: World Bank.

———. 2007. "The Spread of Opium Poppy Cultivation in Balkh." Afghanistan Research and Evaluation Unit (AREU) Case Study Series on Water Management, Livestock and the Opium Economy. Kabul: AREU.

Shaw, Mark. 2006. "Drug Trafficking and the Development of Organized Crime in Post-Taliban Afghanistan." In *Afghanistan's Drug Industry: Structure, Functioning, Dynamics, and Implications for Counter-Narcotics Policy,* ed. Doris Buddenberg and William A. Byrd, 189–214. Vienna: UNODC, and Washington, DC: World Bank.

Thompson, Edwina A. 2006. "The Nexus of Drug Trafficking and Hawala in Afghanistan." In *Afghanistan's Drug Industry: Structure, Functioning, Dynamics, and Implications for Counter-Narcotics Policy,* ed. Doris Buddenberg and William A. Byrd, 155–88. Vienna: UNODC, and Washington, DC: World Bank.

United Kingdom, Afghan Drugs Inter Departmental Unit. 2007. *Beyond the Metrics: Understanding the Nature of Change in the Rural Livelihoods of Opium Poppy*

Growing Households in the 2006/07 Growing Season. By David Mansfield. Consultant report.

United Kingdom, Foreign and Commonwealth Office. 2001. *An Analysis of Licit Opium Poppy Cultivation in India and Turkey.* By David Mansfield. Consultant report.

UNODC (United Nations Office on Drugs and Crime). (2003). *The Opium Economy in Afghanistan: An International Problem.* 2nd ed. New York: UNODC.

UNODC and Government of Afghanistan. 2004, 2006, 2007, 2008, 2009. *Afghanistan Opium Survey.* Kabul: UNODC and Government of Afghanistan.

Ward, Christopher, and William Byrd. 2004. "Afghanistan's Opium Drug Economy." World Bank South Asia PREM Working Paper Series, Report SASPR-5. Washington, DC: World Bank.

World Bank. 2005. *Afghanistan—State Building, Sustaining Growth, and Reducing Poverty.* World Bank Country Study. Washington, DC: World Bank.

———. 2006. "Treating the Opium Problem in World Bank Operations in Afghanistan: Guideline Note." Washington, DC: World Bank.

World Bank and United Kingdom, Department for International Development. 2008. "Afghanistan: Economic Incentives and Development Initiatives to Reduce Opium Production". By Christopher Ward, David Mansfield, Peter Oldham, and William Byrd.

Zia, M. E., D. Radcliffe, C. Ward, W. Byrd, K. Goeldner, R. Kloeppinger-Todd, S. Maimbo, D. Mansfield, D. Pearce, S. Rasmussen, and E. Zeballos. 2005. "Rural Finance in Afghanistan and the Challenge of the Opium Economy." World Bank South Asia Region PREM Working Paper Series, Report SASPR-9. Washington, DC: World Bank.

Index

Boxes, figures, notes, and tables are indicated by italic b, f, n, and t following page numbers.

A

acetic anhydride, 329
adolescents and drug use, 28,
    270, 271*f*, 277
Advisory Committee on the Traffic in
    Opium and Other Dangerous
    Drugs (Opium Advisory
    Committee), 75
aerial spraying, 279, 280, 282,
    285–88, 324. *See also*
    eradication
Afghanistan, 7–8, 301–40.
    See also Taliban
    alternative development and
        livelihoods, 323, 325–26
    shift from opium to sustainable
        licit livelihoods, 322–24, 334
    "smart strategy" including,
        335–36
    asset-rich households and opium
        cultivation, 315–16, 323
    case study, 201–5

Central Poppy Eradication Force
    (CPEF), 322
conditions favoring opium-related
    activities, 201–3, 303, 311, 315
consequences of illegal drug industry,
    242, 302, 334
corruption, 319, 322, 324–25,
    337*n*9
counternarcotics policies, 321–27
    acetic anhydride, interception
        of, 329
    blanket agricultural subsidies or
        price supports, 332–33
    buying up of crop, 120–21,
        331–32
    containment strategy to close off
        parts of country, 336
    effectiveness of, 301, 302
    emphasizing interdiction over
        eradication, 328–29
    eradication. *See* eradication
    interdiction. *See* interdiction
    licensing production, 330–31

mainstreaming development
dimension in counternarcotics
policies, 336
mainstreaming of counternarcotics
dimension in development
programs, 336
"smart strategy," 8, 302, 333–36
data and research issues,
306–7, 334–35
demand-side interventions, 326–27
economic and political impact
of opium, 304–6
dynamics of opium economy,
314–20
financial flows, drug-related,
313–14
hawala system, 306, 313–14
political and government officials
involved in trade, 311, 319,
323, 328
weak government and
insecurity, 318
eradication initiatives, 8, 315, 321–24
interdiction preferred over, 328–29
"smart strategy" including, 335
governor-led eradication, 322
historical background, 302–4, 317
interception of chemicals for
processing, 329
interdiction, 324–25
preferred over eradication, 328–29
seizure levels, 102, 102*t*
"smart strategy" including, 335
lessons learned and policy
implications, 327–33
loss of assets as reason for opium
cultivation, 317
narco-state status, 122–23
National Drug Control Strategy
(NDCS), 320–21, 320*b*
opium pricing, 311–12
data available on, 306, 309*f*
farm-gate prices, 312, 328, 338*n*12

high prices as encouraging
cultivation, 315
not dependent on consumption
destination, 99
variations, 128*n*15, 309*f*, 312,
337*nn*4–5
opium production levels, 29, 30*f*,
244*n*5, 307–10, 308*f*, 308*t*
crop rotation to maintain soil
quality and high yields, 337*n*7
dominance of market, 100,
195, 244
household decision on
participating in opium
cultivation, 314–17
inventories, maintenance of, 310
overview, 196–97, 301
provincial variations, 308,
309*f*, 310
under Taliban, 31, 100,
204–5, 303–4
opium trade and processing, 310–11
routes for trafficking, 15, 204
security issues of opium
cultivation, 316
smuggling on borders, 118, 204, 333
social factors in decision to
cultivate opium, 317
Soviet invasion, 203, 303
structure of illegal drug industry,
241, 310–11, 319–20, 319*f*
Taliban. *See* Taliban
trends in opium economy, 306–14
vicious circle involving warlords
and insecurity, 317–20, 318*f*
tribal composition, 202
U.S. invasion, 205
Agrarian Federation of the Selva
Maestra (Peru), 236
Agreement Concerning the
Manufacture of, Internal
Trade in, and Use of Prepared
Opium (1926), 76

agricultural crops, shift in. *See* alternative development programs (ADPs)

AIDS. *See* HIV/AIDS

Akram, Q. Farooq, 23

alcohol
considered in U.S. as more pressing problem than drugs, 68
prohibition in U.S., 35, 81

Alegría, Ciro, 228

alternative development programs (ADPs)
in Afghanistan, 322–26, 334–36
blanket agricultural subsidies or price supports, 332–33
in Bolivia, 221, 279–80
countermeasures to eradication, 7, 112, 113–15, 130n31, 282
education, prevention, and treatment, 3
illegality as bar to, 15–16
policy changes to emphasize, 48–49, 127n1, 291, 327
European emphasis on, 90
evaluation of, 11, 149–50, 285
financing of, 280
in Peru, 279–80
types of programs, 150
unanswered questions about, 4, 23–28

Alvarez, Elena, 238

amphetamines, 97

Anderson, Jon Lee, 337n9

Anslinger, Harry J., 79, 80

anti-Chinese policies in U.S., 69

Anti-Drug Abuse Act (U.S. 1986), 87

Anti-Drug Abuse Amendment Act (U.S. 1988), 87

antidrug policies. *See specific countries and drugs*

Arciniega-Huby, Alberto, 235

Arrestee Drug Abuse Monitoring, 277

arrests and drug offenses, 166

assassins for hire, 206

Australia and legal opium production, 103, 330

B

Banzer Suárez, Hugo, 223, 225, 239

Barber, Klaus, 223

Bayer, 63

Becker, Gary S., 41, 171

Belaúnde, Fernando, 231, 232

Ben-Haim, Yakov, 23

Bewley, Truman F., 23

Bhattacharya, Jay, 54n8

biopsychological theories of addiction, 54n8

Bird, William, 205

blanket agricultural subsidies or price supports, 332–33

body-packing, 108, 129n22, 129n24

Bolivia
alternative development, 113, 114, 279–80
amnesty period, 224
case study, 218–27
cocaine interdiction, 140–41
cocaine pricing, 261–64, 263f
cocaine production, 7, 99–100, 99t, 140, 140f, 196
history of, 220, 224–26, 258, 259f
cocalero movement, 200–201
consequences of illegal drug industry, 242
cultural divide, 218–19
destruction of illegal cocaine laboratories, 284, 284f
eradication incentives, 112, 113, 225, 226, 282
gas export, 226
history of, 219

illegal drug industry, characteristics
of, 222–23, 241–42
indigenous population and coca
cultivation, 17
land reform, 219
Ley del Regimen de la Coca y
Substancias Controladas
(Law 1008), 221–22,
225, 246*n*23
military, 218, 223–24
Plan Dignidad, 225
political upheavals, 226–27
secession movement, 227
seizure levels, 283–84, 283*f*
sindicatos, 221–22
social structure of, 219
violence, 219, 242
Boyum, David, 111
Brazil
cocaine production, 99
organized crime linked to drug
trafficking, 21
violence associated with drug
trade, 19
Brent, Charles H., 70, 71
bribery. *See* corruption
British Dangerous Drugs Act
(U.S. 1920), 80
British East India Company, 66
British Empire and drug trade,
66–67, 72
British Home Office study on costs
of drug use, 24–25
British Royal Opium Commission, 71
Bush, George W., 127*n*1
Buxton, Julia, 4, 61
Byrd, William, 7–8, 301

C

Cabieses, Hugo, 232
Cabral, Sérgio, 19
Calderón, Felipe, 20, 116

Cali cartel, 118, 211, 212, 213,
222, 238, 277
cannabis. *See* marijuana
Cardoso, Henrique, 50
cartels, 278. *See also* Colombia; Mexico;
specific cartels by name
cash-for-work programs. *See* alternative
development programs (ADPs)
Catholic Church, 208
Caulkins, Jonathan P., 54*n*11, 127,
130*n*33, 292, 295*n*27
Cave, Jonathan, 118
Center for International Policy, 286
Center for Strategic and International
Studies, 246*n*29
Central Asia. *See also specific countries*
drug consumption increase, 15, 98
drug production, 107
organized crime and drug
trafficking, 22
Central Poppy Eradication Force
(CPEF; Afghanistan), 322
Chaloupka, F., 290
Chapare region, Bolivia, 113–14,
130*n*32, 220, 221–22, 225,
245*n*14, 246*n*21, 262
Chavas, J., 167
chemicals
cocaine production and, 275–76
opium processing and, 329
children
drug use and, 28, 87, 270, 271*f,* 277
in military, 206
China
historical opium use in, 65, 67
opening of treaty ports in, 67
opiate use in, 98, 128*n*6
opium production, 67, 103
seizure levels, 102, 102*t,* 128*n*13
Chirac, Jacques, 130*n*40
Christian-based anti-opium campaigns,
68, 70–73, 78
Chumacero, Rómulo, 5–6, 165

civil liability of drug dealers, 87
classification schedules, 85, 87, 227
Clawson, Patrick L., 234
CNC. *See* Crime and
  Narcotics Center
coca chewing, 64, 228–29, 243, 254
Coca-Cola, 64
cocaine
  antidrug policies in producer
    countries, 279–84. *See also*
    Bolivia; Peru; Plan Colombia
  side effect of, 284–88
  sustainability and future prospects
    of, 288–92
  consumption trends, 136,
    137*f*, 162*n*3, 191*n*2,
    269–72, 271*f*, 276–77
  aging of users, 276–77
  composition of demand for
    cocaine, 276–77
  high school students, 270, 271*f*
  policy tailored to, 49
  prevalence of consumption
    by country/regions, 42,
    43*f*, 44–45, 44*t*, 96,
    97–98, 98*t*, 162*n*3,
    256, 295*n*26
  psychological addiction, 96, 277
  data sources on, 256–58
  ONDCP, 257–58. *See also*
    Office of National Drug
    Control Policy
  possible biases in, 275–79
  UNODC, 256–57. *See also* UN
    Office on Drugs and Crime
  destruction of illegal
    cocaine laboratories,
    284, 284*f*
  duration of "high" from, 256
  equilibrium analysis of
    market, 175–79
  history of, 64
  interdiction in Europe, 34

international agreements to
  regulate, 84. *See also*
  historical foundations of
  drug control regime
overview, 254–56
pricing
  components of, 295*n*27
  data collection on, 261–64
  at different points in distribution
    system, 104, 105*t*, 106,
    108, 130*n*33
  elasticity of demand in consuming
    countries, effect of, 46–47,
    152–53, 158, 290
  enforcement impact on, 6–7, 31,
    35–40, 36*t*, 38*f*
  in Europe, 272, 273*f*
  in game theory model of war
    on drugs, 147–49
  Peru production and trafficking,
    effect on, 237–39
  puzzle of decreased production,
    yet falling price, 273–79, 274*f*
  ratio of consumer price and base
    price, 189, 190*t*
  seizure rates, effect on, 118
  trends during Plan Colombia,
    136, 137*f*
  in U.S., 272, 272–73*f*
processing steps, 235
production, 99–101, 99*t*,
  253–300. *See also* Bolivia;
  Colombia; Peru;
  producing countries
  coca cultivation and yields,
    255, 258–61
  genetically modified plants
    and, 275, 282
  history of, 67–68
  intermediate prices, 261–64
  levels of, 29, 30–31, 30*f*
  new fertilizers and chemicals
    and, 275–76

patterns of, 103–11
potential production, 264–67,
    266f, 293, 294n6
productivity increases, 137–42,
    139f, 273–74
puzzle of decrease, yet falling price,
    273–79, 274f
stability of dominant countries,
    125–26, 195
supply-side estimates, 275–76
purity levels, 267–69, 268f, 295n19
seizure levels, 101–2, 102t,
    283–84, 283f, 285f
seriousness of problem of
    addiction, 27
side effects of use, 256
trafficking, 14–15, 101–2, 102t
    compared to heroin
        trafficking, 108
    flow to U.S., 142, 143f
cocaine hydrochloride, 255
cocalero movement, 200–201
coca plants, 255, 295n16
    new, genetically modified plants,
        275, 282
Colombia. See also Plan Colombia;
    Revolutionary Armed Forces of
    Colombia (FARC)
antidrug policies, 279
Anti-Narcotics Council, 286
cartels, history of, 211–13. See also
    Cali cartel; Medellín cartel;
    North Valle cartel
case study, 205–10
civil war (La Violencia), 209–10
cocaine pricing, 261–64, 263f
cocaine production
    dominance of market, 99, 99t, 125,
        195, 214, 243, 258–59, 259f
    history of, 210–14
    new, genetically modified
        plants, 275
    overview, 196–97

Plan Colombia and, 137, 138–40,
    140f, 259, 260
reduction due to spraying, 113
taxing to support civil war,
    123, 214
consequences of illegal drug
    industry, 242
Constitution, 208, 214
costs of fighting drug trafficking, 13
destruction of illegal cocaine
    laboratories, 284, 284f
economy of, 208
enforcement efforts. See also
    Plan Colombia
    aerial fumigation, 285–86
    corruption and, 116
    organized crime's challenge to
        law and order, 21, 22
    seizure levels, 101, 102t, 140–42,
        141f, 283–84, 283f
equilibrium analysis of market
    and, 175, 177
guerillas and paramilitary
    groups, 212, 214–15,
    216–18, 258, 289
history and geography of, 206–8
"justice and peace" law, 216–17
marijuana production, 210–11
migration within, 207,
    209–10, 214
military, 210
opium production, 100, 100t,
    109, 126
politics in, 208–9, 215–16
revenues, 244–45n8
social structure of, 206, 245n10
terrorism and, 156, 216, 240
trafficking, 213–15, 241
    platform to U.S., 108, 109
tribal composition, 207
violence, 209–10
    associated with drug trade, 19
    intradrug trade wars, 212

Comfort, Gary, 118
Commission on Narcotic Drugs,
    83, 89, 89t
Committees in a Defense Front against
    Coca Eradication in the Upper
    Huallaga, 236
communications as way to reduce
    opium production, 327
comparative advantage for a nation's
    production and trafficking, 125
competition in illegal drug industry, 278
Comprehensive Crime Control Act
    (U.S. 1984), 87
Conservative Party (Colombia), 208–9
consuming countries. See also
    specific countries
    costs of prohibition to, 12–13
    enforcement policies, effectiveness
        of, 160, 291
    pricing, effect of antidrug policies
        on, 29, 31, 46–47
    quality of drugs, 15
    trends, 97–99, 97t, 191n2, 256, 292
containment strategy to close off
    parts of country, 336
contemporary drug control regime,
    81–90, 82t
Controlled Substances Act
    (U.S. 1970), 86
Convention against Illicit Traffic
    in Narcotic Drugs and
    Psychotropic Substances (1988),
    61, 82t, 88–90, 247n32
Convention for Limiting the
    Manufacture and Regulating
    the Distribution of Narcotic
    Drugs (1931), 74t, 76–77
Convention for Suppression of the
    Illicit Traffic in Dangerous
    Drugs (1936), 74t, 77, 79
Convention on Psychotropic
    Substances (1971), 61,
    82t, 86–88, 247n32

CORAH. See Special Coca Control
    and Eradication Project in the
    Upper Huallaga
corruption
    in Afghanistan, 7, 319, 322, 323,
        324–25, 337n9
    in Colombia, 116
    in counternarcotics
        implementation, 334
    de facto legalization's effect on, 119
    as distribution chain entry barrier, 17
    in Mexico, 116
    in Myanmar, 106
    organized crime and, 10, 18–23
    in Peru, 239
    producer countries and, 125
Costa cartel, 278
costs of prohibition, 10
    ability to sustain, 290
    Plan Colombia, 150–52, 153–54
    social costs. See Social and
        political consequences of
        war on drugs
    unfairness as to who bears the
        cost, 55n19
    U.S. expenditures on government
        enforcement of war on drugs,
        12, 88, 166, 189t. See also
        foreign aid, U.S.
Cotler, Julio, 231
counterfeiting, 206
counternarcotics policies. See specific
    countries and drugs
CPEF (Central Poppy Eradication
    Force; Afghanistan), 322
crack, 255–56
Crafts, Wilbur, 70, 71
Crane, Barry, 118
Crawford, Gordon, 118
Crime and Narcotics Center (CNC),
    257, 265
criminalization policies, effect of,
    54n16, 200–201

crop eradication. *See* eradication
crop substitution projects. *See*
    alternative development
    programs (ADPs)
Cuánto S.A., 231
Cuban criminal organizations, 211
cultural diversity. *See* ethnicity

D

Dammert-Ego-Aguirre, Manuel, 239
DARE (Drug Abuse Resistance
    Education) program in
    schools, 87
DEA. *See* Drug Enforcement
    Administration, U.S.
Deas, Malcolm, 245*n*9
death penalty for drug "kingpins," 87
death rate. *See* violence associated with
    drug trafficking
decriminalization. *See* legalization
de facto legalization of production or
    trafficking, 119–20
demand for drugs. *See* drug
    consumption
Deobandi Isalmic tradition, 203
De Soto, Hernando, 235, 236
destruction of illegal cocaine
    laboratories, 284, 284*f*
developing countries
    antidrug policies, effect on, 2–3,
        9–59, 96–102
    costs of prohibition on, 12–13, 50
    opportunity costs, 13, 106
development programs. *See also*
    foreign aid, U.S.
    mainstreaming of counternarcotics
        and, 326, 336
diacetylmorphine, 63
displaced citizens, 206
Division of Narcotic Drugs, 83, 89
Drug Abuse Resistance Education
    (DARE) program in schools, 87

drug consumption. *See also* consuming
    countries; *specific drugs
    and countries*
    analysis of market for illegal drugs,
        165–94
    choice of drug by users, 27–28
    consuming countries and regions,
        97–98*t*, 97–99
    historical overview, 63–65
    history of, 63–65
    social costs of, 26
    time inconsistency and
        addiction, 54*n*8
    in trafficking countries, 14–15
    uncertain costs of, 23–28
    uncertain response of demand
        for drugs to prohibition
        policies, 41–47, 122
    wealthy consuming countries' change
        of policies, effect of, 2, 5
Drug Dealer Liability Act
    (U.S. 1999), 87
Drug Dependence Expert
    Committee (WHO), 83
Drug Enforcement Administration,
    U.S., 87, 88, 214
    Operation Breakthrough,
        264–65, 294*n*6
Drug Free Workplace Act
    (U.S. 1988), 87
drug industry. *See* drug trade, generally
drug policies, design of, 27–28
    "carrot and stick" components,
        5, 149–50
    criminalization as focus, 54*n*16, 165
    demand-reduction programs, 292
    differentiation among types of
        drugs, 49
    education, treatment, and public
        health issues, 48–49, 127*n*1, 291
    emotional factors in, 53*n*1
    increasing legalization, 184–87,
        185*t*, 193*n*22

increasing penalties, 182–84,
    183t, 193n19
increasing riskiness of activity,
    179–82, 181t, 190, 191t
uncertain efficacy of, 22, 28–41, 47–48
drug production. *See* producing
    countries; *specific drugs
    and countries*
Drug Supervisory Board, 77, 81, 83, 85
drug testing of federal employees and
    contractors under Executive
    Order 12564 (1986), 87
drug trade, generally. *See also specific
    drugs and countries*
  comparative advantage for a
    nation's production and
    trafficking, 125
  conditions conducive to,
    197–98, 200–201
  consumption. *See* consuming
    countries
  economic consequences of, 6–7
  equilibrium model of. *See*
    equilibrium model of chain
    of illegal drug trade
  factors in determining location of
    illegal drug activity, 198–200,
    211, 217–18, 243–44
  historical overview, 65–67
  innovations to circumvent
    enforcement, 11, 49,
    160–61, 282
  participants in, used in equilibrium
    model, 167–73
  pattern of national involvement
    in, 103–11
  production. *See* producing countries
  routes to U.S. and Europe, 30–31
  stability of, 126
  structure of international drug
    industry, 104–11
  supply-side controls, 111–19
  trafficking. *See* trafficking countries

drug use. *See* drug consumption
Dubai as financial center for clearing
    hawala activities, 313
Dubner, S., 276
Durrani dynasty (Afghanistan), 202
"Dutch disease" effects in Afghanistan,
    305, 336–37n1
Dutch Opium Act (U.S. 1919), 80

E

E. Merck and Company, 63
Echeverry, J. C., 289
economic consequences of drug trade,
    6–7. *See also specific drugs*
economic theories of rational
    addiction, 27
The Economist
  on corruption and opium in
    Afghanistan, 21
  on costs of containment
    policies, 55n19
Ecuador
  cocaine production, 103–4
  seizure levels, 102, 102t
Eitrheim, Øyvind, 23
elasticity of demand
  cocaine, 152–53, 158, 290
  heroin, 41
Ely Lilly, 232
ENACO (National Coca Enterprise;
    Peru), 229–30
environmental consequences of
    spraying, 7, 112, 285–88
equilibrium model of chain of illegal
    drug trade, 6, 165–94
  assessment of effects of alternative
    policies, 179–87
  competitive equilibrium, 174–75
  crop producer, 167–69
  data, 188–91
  drug consumer, 171–73
  drug producer, 169–70

drug trafficker, 170–71
functional forms and calibration,
    175–79, 176–78t, 178f
general equilibrium model, 167
government, 174
increasing legalization, 184–87,
    185t, 193n22
increasing penalties, 182–84,
    183t, 193n19
increasing risk of illegal activities,
    179–82, 181t, 190, 191t
market-clearing conditions, 174
spending to control illegal
    drugs, 166, 188,
    189t, 191n1
eradication
    in Afghanistan, 8, 315, 321–24,
        328–29, 335
    in Bolivia, 225, 226, 258, 280, 281f
    Colombia, 281f
        aerial spraying, 280, 282
        prioritizing interdiction over, 5
        U.S. aid paying for, 153
    countermeasures to, 7, 112, 113–15
    effectiveness of, 7, 112–13, 291
    effect on developing countries, 3
    loss of farmer income, 10, 16–18,
        305, 323–24
    in Peru, 232–33, 240, 258, 280, 281f
    policy to draw back from, 49
    tebuthiuron (aka Spike), use of,
        232, 246n30
    unintended effects of, 7
Escobar, Pablo, 21, 111, 212, 213
ethnicity
    in Afghanistan, 202, 317
    in Bolivia, 219
    in Colombia, 206
Europe. See also specific countries
    controlled drug use initiatives
        (historical overview), 78–79
    drug consumption patterns, 191n2,
        256, 270, 295n26
    drug pricing and demand,
        32–33f, 32–34
    drug trafficking to, 31, 104, 212, 224
    local production of cocaine or
        heroin, 103
    opiate use, 98
European Monitoring Center for Drugs
    and Drug Addiction, 128n3
Executive Order 12564 (1986), 87
extradition treaty of Colombia and
    U.S., 211–12

F

FARC. See Revolutionary Armed Forces
    of Colombia
farmer losses, 10, 16–18, 305, 323–24.
    See also alternative development
    programs (ADPs); eradication
Farrell, G., 204
Federal Bureau of Investigation
    on number of drug users
        in U.S., 166
Federal Bureau of Narcotics, 80, 81, 87
First Command of the Capital, 21
Food and Agricultural
    Organization, 117
food source, cultivation of drugs
    for, 64–65
foreign aid, U.S.
    for alternative development
        programs, 280
    to Colombia for war on drugs,
        135–36, 136t, 153–54,
        162n2, 289
    termination of assistance to
        countries deemed
        uncooperative in, 88,
        245–46n17
forest areas, coca cultivation in, 282
France and legal opium
    production, 103, 330
Fujimori, Alberto, 235–36

Fujimori Doctrine, 235
fungus, effect on cocaine crop, 237, 238
Fusarium oxysporum fungus, 237, 238

G

Gaedcke, Friedrich, 293n3
game theory model of war on drugs,
    144–52, 148f, 162n7
gangs, 19. *See also* organized crime
GAO. *See* Government
    Accountability Office
García, Alan, 233–34, 241
García-Meza Tejada, Luis, 218, 223–24
Gaviria, César, 50, 213, 224
Geneva Convention (1928), 74t,
    75–76, 79
German Opium Act (U.S. 1929), 80
Germany
    cocaine use, 272
    drug policies and consumption, 35
    seizures, 109
    U.S. introduction of antidrug
        legislation after
        World War II, 83
Global Illicit Drug Trends (UNODC),
    97, 130n39
globalization, effect of, 243
Godfrey, Christine, 25
Gollier, Christian, 23
Gómez-Buendía, Hernando, 206
Gonzales-Manrique, José E., 231
Government Accountability
    Office (GAO)
    on cocaine interdiction levels,
        140–42, 142f
    on Plan Colombia
        aid amounts, 136, 162n2
        efficacy of, 143
government structure and drug
    production, 106–7
Greenfield, Victoria, 17, 127
Grossman, Michael, 41, 290

guerilla movements
    in Bolivia, 214–15, 216–18
    in Colombia, 212, 214–15,
        216–18, 258
    organized crime links to, 20
    in Peru, 233, 242
Guinea-Bissau and drug
    trafficking, 14–15, 18
Gutiérrez Rebollo, José, 22

H

Hague conference of 1911, 73
Harrison Narcotics Tax Act
    (U.S. 1914), 80
Hawaii, U.S. acquisition of, 70
hawala system (Afghanistan),
    306, 313–14
Hazaras, 202
Health and Human Services
    Department, U.S., 26
hemp, 64–65
heroin. *See also* Afghanistan
    consumption trends
        elasticity of demand, 41
        policy tailored to unique
            aspects of consumption, 49
        prevalence of consumption by
            country, 42, 43f, 45–46, 45t, 97,
            97t, 98–99
        seriousness of problem of
            addiction, 27, 96
    economic consequences of
        drug trade, 7–8
    eradication efforts, 112–13
    first sales of, 63
    pricing, 31, 35–40, 37t, 38f
        "buying up the crop" control
            strategy and, 120–21
        at different points in
            distribution system,
            104, 105t, 106
        Taliban ban and, 205

production
    patterns of, 103–11
    stability of dominant countries,
        125–26, 195
    seizure levels, 101, 102, 102t, 116
    trafficking, compared to cocaine, 108
historical foundations of drug control
        regime, 4, 61–93
    contemporary drug control regime,
        81–90, 82t
    Convention against Illicit Traffic
        in Narcotic Drugs and
        Psychotropic Substances
        (1988), 61, 82t, 88–90
    Convention for Limiting the
        Manufacture and Regulating the
        Distribution of Narcotic Drugs
        (1931), 74t, 76–77
    Convention for Suppression of the
        Illicit Traffic in Dangerous
        Drugs (1936), 74t, 77, 79
    Convention on Psychotropic
        Substances (1971), 61,
        82t, 86–88
    drug trade, 65–67
    drug use, 63–65
    evaluation of interwar control
        regime, 77–81
    Geneva Convention (1928),
        74t, 75–76
    International Opium Convention
        (1912), 73–75, 74t
    intoxicating substances, 62–63
    Lake Success protocol (1946), 82t, 83
    Opium Protocol (1953), 82t, 84
    Paris Protocol (1948), 82t, 83–84
    Shanghai Opium Conference (1909),
        4, 62, 71–73
    Single Convention on Narcotic Drugs
        (1961), 61, 82t, 84–86
    U.S. early policies on opium, 68–73
HIV/AIDS, 16, 96, 326
Hobson, Richmond Pearson, 81

Holt, M., 167
Huallaga region, Peru, 231, 232, 233,
        234, 236

I

ideological imperatives, 8
Illicit Crop Monitoring System
        (UNODC), 261
immigration. See migration
incarceration
    costs of, 24, 87
    rates due to drug-related offenses,
        13, 14f, 54n11, 87
    as threat to smugglers, 118
inconsistency of social views on
        drugs, 26
in-country enforcement for producing
        countries, 115–16
India
    historical opium trade
        from, 66, 84
    licensing production of opium,
        330, 331
    opiate use, 98
indigenous population
    coca chewing by, 64, 228–29,
        243, 254
    coca cultivation and, 17, 84
    cult use of drugs, 64
Indonesia and drug trade, 67,
        68, 78, 196
ineffectiveness of drug policies.
        See limited efficacy of
        antidrug policies
infrastructure development, 130n32
injecting syringe, invention of, 65
innovations by drug producers
        and traffickers. See drug
        trade, generally
Inter-American Development Bank
    Chapare region, Bolivia and, 220
    Peru and, 231

interdiction
  Afghanistan, 324–25, 328–29, 335
  cocaine use in Europe and, 34
  Colombia
    Plan Colombia, 140–42,
      141–42f, 154, 155
    prioritizing over eradication, 5
  effect on developing countries, 3
  effect on prices, 118
  level of seizures, 101–2, 102t, 116,
    128n12, 283–84, 283f, 285f
  loss of farmer income, 10
  Peru, 238
  policy to draw back from, 49
  range of activities constituting,
    337–38n10
International Crisis Group report
    on cocaine trafficking, 18
International Narcotic Education
    Association, 81
International Narcotics Control Board,
    85, 89, 89t, 103
International Narcotics Control Strategy
    Report (State Department), 15,
    115–16, 257
International Opium Convention
    (1912), 73–75, 74t
International Police Commission, 77
Iran
  drug consumption trends, 15
  opium production, 103
    ban on, 201, 303
    monopoly and, 84
  as route for trafficking in Afghanistan
    heroin trade, 15, 204
  seizure levels, 102, 102t
  as transshipment country, 109

J

Java and drug exports, 67–68, 103, 196
Jensema, E., 294n10
Johnson, Gary, 26

Juarez cartel, 22
Jullien, Bruno, 23

K

Karzai, Hamid, 323
Kazakhstan
  drug consumption in, 15
  Russian border and, 130n35
Keefer, Philip, 1, 3, 9
Khun Sa, 111
kidnappings, 206
Kilmer, Beau, 127n2
Koch, Christopher, 80

L

Labrousse, Alain, 246n331
La Corporación, 223
Lakdawalla, Darius, 54n8
Lake Success protocol (1946), 82t, 83
land mine victims, 206
Lao People's Democratic Republic and
    opium production, 100, 100t
Latin America. See also specific countries
  drug consumption patterns, 191n2
  populist governments, 209
laudanum, 63
laundering of drug money, 313
League of Nations, 75, 83, 220
Ledebur, Kathryn, 246n24
Lee, Rensselaer, III, 234
legal compliance as norm, 244n2
legalization
  Brazil, 19
  de facto legalization of
    production or
    trafficking, 119–20
  drug use after, 54n13
  health care costs of, 16
  increasing legalization, effect of,
    184–87, 185t, 193n22
  Netherlands, 34, 120
  Peru, 17, 236, 240

rents to traffickers, 18
U.S., medical marijuana in states, 26
legislative history. *See* historical
    foundations of drug
    control regime
Lehder, Carlos, 111, 212
Levine, Michael, 222
Levitt, S., 276
Liberal Party (Colombia), 208–9
licensing production of opium, 330–31.
    See also legalization
limited efficacy of antidrug policies,
    5, 8, 95–96
    equilibrium analysis of market
        and, 187
    historical foundations of drug
        control regime, 4, 49, 61–93
    Plan Colombia and, 5, 136–37, 143,
        154–55, 161
Loayza, Norman, 1, 3, 9, 129n17
local production of cocaine or heroin
    in U.S. or Europe, 103
Los Zetas, 21

M

MacCoun, Robert J., 1, 12, 41, 48
Macroconsult S.A., 231
mainstreaming
    counternarcotics dimension in
        development programs, 336
    development dimension in
        counternarcotics policies, 336
Mansfield, David, 315, 316, 327
marijuana
    in Colombia, 210–11
    legalization
        of medical marijuana in
            U.S. states, 26
        in Netherlands, 34, 120
    medicinal use of, 63
    Mexican drug trade and, 28
    prevalence of consumption of, 97

production levels, 100–101, 128n11
seriousness of problem of
    addiction, 27
Marijuana Taxation Act (U.S. 1937), 80
Martin, Edouard, 305
May, Herbert, 79
Medellín cartel, 21, 118, 211,
    212, 222, 224, 277
medical (licit) use of drugs, 26,
    63, 80, 84, 196
Mejía, Daniel, 5, 6–7, 135, 143, 144,
    148–49, 150, 158, 163n8, 253
Merck, 63, 64
Mesa, Carlos, 226
Mexican migrants and antidrug
    legislation, 81
Mexico
    drug cartels, 21, 28, 213
    enforcement efforts
        army combating drug gangs, 20
        corruption and, 116
        costs of fighting drug trafficking,
            12–13, 53–54n6
    eradication of poppies, 112–13
    links with Bolivian traffickers, 225
    links with Colombian traffickers,
        213, 238
    marijuana production levels,
        101, 129n18
    opium production, 100, 100t, 107
    trafficking platform to U.S., 108, 109
migration
    within Bolivia, 221
    within Colombia, 207, 209–10,
        214, 245n16
    Mexico to U.S., 81
    from producing and trafficking
        countries, 110–11
military
    in Bolivia, 218, 223–24
    children in, 206
    in Colombia, 210
    in Peru, 228, 229

monopoly, 84, 122–23
Montesinos, Vladimiro, 239
Morales, Edmundo, 232
Morales, Evo, 17, 193n21, 201, 221,
    226, 227, 246n21
Morales-Bermúdez Cerruti,
    Francisco, 229
Morphine, 63, 69
Movement toward Socialism
    (MAS; Bolivia), 227
MRTA. See Tupac Amaru
    Revolutionary Movement
Mujahideen, 204, 303
Mullah Omar, 204
Multisectoral Drug Control
    Committee (Peru), 229
Murphy, Kevin M., 41, 171
Myanmar and opium
    production, 29, 30f
  corruption and, 106
  de facto legalization, 120
  dominance of market, 100

N

narco-state status, 122–23,
    130n40, 224, 289
National Agrarian Confederation
    (Peru), 236
National Confederation of Farmers
    in the Coca-Growing Valleys
    of Peru, 240
National Drug Control Strategy
    (NDCS; Afghanistan),
    320–21, 320b
National Narcotics Leadership Act
    (U.S. 1988), 87
national parks, coca cultivation in, 282
National Planning Department
    (DNP; Colombia), 135
NATO's International Security
    Assistance Force, 21
needle exchange programs, 54n16

Netherlands
  Chirac calling narco-state, 130n40
  cocaine use, 272
  history of Dutch trade in opium and
    cocaine, 66, 67, 68, 196
  marijuana legalization in, 34, 120
  marijuana production levels,
    101, 128n11
  tolerance toward drugs, 26
New Mexico and decriminalization of
    medical marijuana, 26
New York Times racist article on
    cocaine, 80
Niemann, Albert, 293n3
Nigeria and drug trafficking,
    110, 129n22
Nixon, Richard, 86, 242
nontraditional drug control
    methods, 119–24
  blanket agricultural subsidies or
    price supports, 332–33
  buying up the crop, 120–21, 331–32
  de facto legalization, 119–20
  licensing production, 330–31
  "smart strategy," 8, 302, 333–36
  strategic location, 122–24
North, Douglass C., 244n2
North Valle cartel, 214, 278

O

Ocampo, José Antonio, 245n8
Office of National Drug Control Policy
    (ONDCP)
  on Andean cocaine production,
    258–59, 259f, 260f, 261, 262f
  on cocaine pricing, 261, 262f, 272, 272f
  on cocaine purity, 267–69, 268–69f
  on Colombian cocaine production,
    137, 139, 157
  compared with UNODC, 257–58
  on economic costs of drug
    abuse, 24, 25

overview, 257–58
possible biases in data, 87, 275–76
on potential cocaine production,
    264–67, 266f
on self-reported use of drugs, 31
on U.S. spending to control illegal
    drugs, 166
Operation Breakthrough (U.S. DEA
    project), 264–65, 294n6
opiates. See heroin; morphine; opium
opium. See also Afghanistan
agreements and conventions on,
    73–77, 74t
Chinese recreational use of, 65
evaluating interwar control
    regime, 77–81
global production levels, 100, 100t
historical trade in, 1, 62–63, 65–67
interception of chemicals for
    processing, 329
medicinal use of, 63
minimizing spread of opium
    economy as goal, 334
monopoly, creation of, 84,
    122–23, 195
shift from Thailand and
    Turkey to Myanmar
    and Afghanistan,
    29–30, 30f
U.S. early policy on, 1–2, 68–73
Opium Advisory Committee, 75,
    76, 77, 83
Opium Control Board, 75
Opium Protocol (1953), 82t, 84
Opium Wars, 1, 67
opportunity costs in developing
    countries, 13, 106
Organization of American States on
    environmental effects of
    spraying, 286
organized crime, 3, 10, 17, 18–23
Orphanides, A., 171
overdoses, 15

P

Pacula, Rosalie Liccardo, 12, 127n2
Pain, Adam, 317
Pakistan
    Inter Services Intelligence, 203
    opium processing, 311
    opium production, 100,
        100t, 201, 303
    as route for trafficking in Afghanistan
        heroin trade, 204
    seizure levels, 102, 102t
Palmer, David Scout, 244n8
Palomino, Nelson, 240
Paoli, Letizia, 127
paramilitary in Colombia, 212,
    214–15, 216–18
Paris Protocol (1948), 82t, 83–84
Parke Davis, 63, 64
Pastrana Arango, Andrés, 215, 216
Paz-Zamora, Jaime, 224
PEAH (Special Upper Huallaga Project;
    Peru), 232
People's Democratic Party of
    Afghanistan (PDPA), 203
Permanent Central Opium Board, 76,
    77, 81, 83, 85
Peru. See also Shining Path
    "air bridge denial" policy, 237, 237t,
        239, 258, 279, 288, 294n15
    alternative development, 113, 279–80
    antidrug policies, 279
    case study, 227–41
    civil dictatorship, 236
    cocaine interdiction, 140–41
    cocaine pricing, 261–64, 263f
    cocaine production, 7, 99–100, 99t,
        140, 140f, 196
        abandonment due to infestation
            and low prices, 237
        history of, 228–29, 258, 259f
    consequences of illegal
        drug industry, 242

corruption, 239
Decreto Ley 22,095, 229
eradication initiatives, 232–33,
    240, 258, 282
Fujimori presidency, 235–36
geography of, 227–28
illegal drug industry, characteristics
    of, 231–32, 236–39, 241–42
indigenous population and coca
    cultivation, 17
Law 27,436 (2002), 229–30
legalization
    of coca cultivation, 17, 236, 240
    de facto legalization, 120
military, 228, 229
Multisectoral Drug Control
    Committee, 229
National Confederation of Farmers
    in the Coca-Growing Valleys of
    Peru, 240
National Strategy against Drugs
    2002–7, 229
politics in, 229–31
social structure of, 228, 246n26
Special Coca Control and
    Eradication Project in the
    Upper Huallaga
    (CORAH), 232
peyote, 64
Pharmacy Act (U.K. 1868), 69
Philippines, 1–2, 70
Philippines Opium Commission, 70–71
physical stimulation, drug use for, 64
Pizarro, William "Pato," 222–23
Plan Colombia, 5, 135–64
    calibration of costs, 150–52, 153–54
    cocaine production levels, 137,
        138–40, 140f, 259, 260
    control of land vs. control of
        traffickers, 154–56, 159–61
    defined, 162n1
    drug routes as most factor in cocaine
        trafficking, 153
    goals of, 136, 162nn5–6, 216, 259
        U.S. vs. Colombia, 155–56
    interdiction, 140–42, 141–42f, 154–55
    land as unimportant factor in
        cocaine production, 153, 159–60
    limited efficacy of, 5, 136–37, 143,
        154–55, 161
        high costs vs., 158–61
    main findings, 152–56
    motivation for research agenda,
        136–42, 162n1
    price elasticity of demand in
        consuming countries, effect of,
        152–53, 158
    research agenda to evaluate,
        142–44, 161
    response of drug producers to, 290
    simulation (game theory model of
        war on drugs), 144–52,
        148f, 162n7
        results and robustness of,
            156–58, 163n9
    U.S. financial aid for, 135–36,
        136t, 153–54
        allocation of U.S. subsidies, 154–56
Plan Dignidad (Bolivia), 225
policy implications. See drug policies,
    design of
Popular Democratic Unity (UDP;
    Bolivia), 224
Portuguese traders of opium, 66
Posada, Carlos Esteban, 6–7, 253
potassium permangante, 276
preemptive purchase of drug
    crops, 120–21
pricing. See specific drugs
private benefits of drug use, 26–27
producing countries, 99–100t, 99–101,
    196–201. See also Bolivia;
    Colombia; Peru
    antidrug policies in, 279–88
        limited efficacy of, 29
        post–World War II, 83

side effect of, 284–88
sustainability and future prospects
of, 5, 288–92
compensation mechanisms, 123–24
control model and historical
background, 62
in-country enforcement, 115–16
legislation in, 119–20
location choices, 109, 122, 123,
129n17, 198–200
number of countries, 122–23
patterns of, 103–11
stability of industry in, 123
supply-side controls targeted
at, 111–16
productivity increases in cocaine
production, 137–42, 139f, 273–74
genetically modified plants and, 275
new fertilizers and chemicals
and, 275–76
productivity losses due to drug-related
offenses, 13, 25
profitability of drug trade
changes in, as factor in smaller
organizations, 278
cocaine and heroin, 104, 105t, 106
compared to agricultural and
industrial commodities,
117, 117t
compared to alternative
development, 115
concentration at top of distribution
chain, 17, 18t
in developing countries, 10
effectiveness of war on
drugs and, 160
opium traders, 310
retail prices and, 29–30
prohibition, consequences of, 3–4,
9–59, 284–88
definitions and sources of
variables, 51–53
measurement of enforcement, 39–41

negative consequences, 10, 12–23,
54n7, 166, 334
in Afghanistan, 327–28
farmer losses and rents to
traffickers, 10, 16–18,
305, 323–24
organized crime, 3, 10, 18–23
public health, 11, 14–16, 32, 34f
policy implications, 47–50
uncertain efficacy of policies,
28–41, 47–48
uncertain response of demand for
drugs, 41–47
prostitution, 206
protected areas, coca cultivation
in, 282
Protecting Our Children from Drugs
Act (U.S. 2000), 87
psilocybin, 64
public health consequences of
prohibition, 11, 14–16, 32, 34f
Pudney, Stephen, 53n1
Puka Llacta (Red City; Peru), 233
punitive approach to drug trade and
consumption
death penalty for drug "kingpins," 87
increasing penalties, 182–84,
183t, 193n19
past ineffectiveness of, 165–66
U.S. emphasis on, 72, 78, 79
Pure Food and Drug Act
(U.S., 1906), 72
purity of drugs in consuming
countries, 15

Q

quality of drugs in consuming
countries, 15
cocaine purity levels, 267–69,
268f, 295n19
quantity of drugs consumed, 99. See
also consuming countries

R

racism, 80
Ramírez, Noe, 22
Reagan, Ronald, 87, 242
recreational use of drugs, 65
Red Command (CV), 21
refining facilities, crackdown on, 116
religion
    opposition of Islam to drugs, 322
    use of drugs in, 64, 255
remittances, 313
Restrepo, P., 143, 144, 148–49,
    150, 158, 163n8
Reuter, Peter, 1, 5, 12, 17, 41, 48, 95, 111,
    118, 127, 273, 276, 295n27
Revolutionary Armed Forces of
    Colombia (FARC), 20, 123, 155,
    215–16, 258
Rivolo, Rex, 118
Roca-Suárez, Jorge, 224
Rodas, Hugo, 222
Rodriguez, Eduardo, 227
Rospigliosi, Fernando, 239
Roundup, 286
Ruggiero, V., 109
Ruiz-Hernández, Hernando, 211
Russia
    border accessibility, 130n35
    seizure levels of heroin, 101

S

Samper, Ernesto, 213
Sánchez de Lozada, Gonzalo, 17, 226
seizure. See interdiction
Sevigny, Eric, 54n11
Shanghai Opium Conference (1909),
    4, 62, 71–73
Sherret, Laurel, 285, 287, 296n36
Shiites in Afghanistan, 202
Shining Path, 20, 232–36, 239,
    240, 246nn28–31
Sinaloa drug cartel, 22

Sindicatos (Bolivia), 221–22
Single Convention on Narcotic Drugs
    (1961), 61, 82t, 84–86,
    242–43, 247n32
"smart strategy," 8, 302, 333–36
Smith, Peter H., 17
Smoking Opium Exclusion Act
    (U.S., 1909), 73
smuggling. See trafficking countries
Soares, Rodrigo, 3, 9
social and political consequences of
    war on drugs, 4–5, 6
    harm reduction, social costs of, 12
    private benefits of drug use, 26–27
    social costs, 10, 13, 24, 25, 50
    social unrest, 7, 9
    uncertainty of social benefits of
        alternative policies, 23–28
social changes needed as solution to
    drug problem, 242
sodium hypochlorite, 276
South, N., 109
Southeast Asia and cocaine
    production, 196, 243
Soviet invasion of Afghanistan, 203, 303
Spain
    cocaine use, 98, 270, 272
    colonization of Colombia, 207–8
    commercialization of coca in
        Andes by, 65
    legal opium production, 103
    opium trade and, 67
    permissive policies and drug
        consumption, 34–35
    seizure levels, 101–2, 102t
Spanish-American War of 1898, 70
Special Coca Control and Eradication
    Project in the Upper Huallaga
    (CORAH; Peru), 232, 233
Special Upper Huallaga Project
    (PEAH; Peru), 232
spraying. See aerial spraying;
    eradication

stability of drug trade, 126
State Department, U.S.
    on opium production in
        Afghanistan, 244n5
    on potential cocaine production,
        265, 267
Stephens, Bret, 53–54n6
Suárez, Roberto, 223, 224
Sumatra and drug exports, 196
Sunni in Afghanistan, 202
supply-side controls, 71, 86, 111–19
    alternative development. See
        alternative development
        programs (ADPs)
    enforcement. See interdiction
    eradication. See eradication
    global supply reduction, 126–27
    production and refining
        controls, 111–12
Symansky, Steven, 305
synergism, 287
System to Retrieve Information from
    Drug Evidence (STRIDE), 157

T

Taft, William Howard, 70
Taiwan and cocaine production, 103
Tajikistan
    drug production, 107
    as transshipment country, 109, 118,
        130n35, 204
Taliban, 7–8, 20–21, 203–5, 303–4, 320
    curtail of poppy production, 31, 100,
        204–5, 304, 306, 321
Taraki, Nur Mohammed, 202
taxation
    Taliban collection of tax on
        opium, 303, 321
    tax-based legislation in U.S., 80
tebuthiuron (aka Spike), use of,
        232, 246n30
Terazona-Sevillano, Gabriela, 246n29

terrorism, 20, 156, 216, 240
Thailand
    alternative development, 114
    government campaign against drug
        trafficking, 20
    opium production, consumption,
        and trafficking, 29, 100,
        100t, 103, 128n7
Thorne, J., 204
Thoumi, Francisco, 6, 53n6, 106, 107,
        125, 130n31, 195, 244n1, 293n4,
        294n10, 294n12
Toledo Manrique, Alejandro Celestino,
        239–40
trafficking countries, 101–2, 102t.
        See also Afghanistan;
        specific countries
    cartels and, 118–19, 223, 224
    comparative advantage and, 125
    enforcement controls, 111, 116–19.
        See also interdiction
    focus on larger traffickers and
        sponsors, 334
    heroin vs. cocaine smuggling, 108
    increase in drug consumption
        in, 14–15
    legislation in, 119–20
    patterns of, 103–11, 142, 143f
    rents to traffickers, 16–18
Transnational Institute, 295n16
transshipment, 103–4, 109
treatment
    expenditures on, 12
    higher cocaine prices
        increasing, 130n38
    illegality as bar to, 15–16
    in international agreements, 85–86
Treaty of Paris (1898), 70
Treich, Nicolas, 23
trends. See specific drugs
Tupac Amaru Revolutionary
    Movement (MRTA),
        234, 246n331

Turkey
  opium production, 29, 129n28, 303
    ban on, 201
    licensed production, 330
    monopoly, 84
  seizure levels, 102, 102t

U

uncertain costs of drug consumption,
    4, 23–28
uncertain efficacy of policies, 22, 28–41
uncertain response of demand for
    drugs, 41–47
UN Drug Control Program, 89
UN Economic and Social Council,
    83, 89t
UN General Assembly Special
    Session (1998), 89
United Kingdom. *See also* British
    Empire and drug trade
  cocaine use, 98
  Department for International
    Development on factoring
    opium considerations into
    all engagement with
    Afghanistan, 326
  regulation of drugs, 69
United States
  alcohol prohibition, 35
  anti-drug legislation, 69, 72
  cocaine use, 98, 256, 269–72, 271f
  costs of war on drugs, 12, 13, 22
  drug consumption patterns, 26,
    31, 33f, 191n2
  drug pricing in, 31, 32–33f
  drug trade route to, 30–31
  early policies on opium, 1–2, 62,
    68–73, 78
  empire building debate, 70
  import amounts of cocaine, 49
  incarceration rates due to drug-
    related offenses, 13, 14f

invasion of Afghanistan, 205
local production of cocaine or
    heroin, 103
number of drug users in, 166
opiate use, 98
seizure levels, 101, 102t, 284, 285f
spending to control illegal drugs, 166,
    188, 189t, 191n1. *See also*
    foreign aid, U.S.
UN Office on Drugs and Crime
    (UNODC)
  on alternative development, 114, 237
  on cocaine pricing, 261, 262f,
    272, 273f
  cocaine production estimates by, 99,
    136–37, 139, 157, 237, 239, 259,
    260f, 261, 262f, 264–65, 266f
  on cocaine productivity, 273–74
  on cocaine purity, 267–69
  compared with ONDCP, 256–57
  criticism of, 294n12
  on drug prices and qualities, 37
  on eradication efforts, 280
  establishment of, 89, 89t
  funding from, 294n10
  Illicit Crop Monitoring System, 261
  on opium production in Afghanistan,
    196, 205, 244n5, 303–4, 306,
    337nn2–3
  overview, 256–57
  possible biases in data, 275–76
  on potential cocaine production,
    264–67, 266f, 294n6
  reporting of prevalence of illicit drug
    use, 97, 127n2
  on seizures, 128n12, 130n34, 140, 142f
Uribe, Álvaro, 216
Uribe, M., 150
U.S. Agency for International
    Development (USAID) and
    Bolivia, 220, 221
Uzbekistan as transshipment
    country, 109

V

Van Ours, Jan C., 53n1
Venezuela
  cocaine production, 99, 103–4
  seizure levels, 102, 102t
Vereenigde Oost-Indische
    Compagnie (VOC), 66
Versailles Peace Agreement (1919), 75
vicious circle
  of illegal drug activity and
    political organizations,
    197, 199–200
  of opium economy involving
    warlords and insecurity,
    317–20, 318f
victim costs of property crimes related
    to drug use, 24–25
Vietnam's opium production, 100, 100t
violence associated with drug
    trafficking, 13, 17, 18–23,
    295n20. *See also specific cartels*
  in Afghanistan, 311, 329
  in Bolivia, 219, 242
  in Colombia, 209–10

W

Wall Street Journal on
    drug policies, 50
Walters, John, 287–88
Ward, Christopher, 205
War of the Pacific (1879–83),
    196, 226, 228

war on drugs. *See also* Plan Colombia;
    prohibition, consequences of
  detrimental effects of, 8
  game theory model of, 144–52,
    148f, 162n7
  history of, 86, 87–88, 242
  termination of assistance to countries
    deemed uncooperative
    in, 88, 245–46n17
White House Office of National Drug
    Control Policy. *See* Office of
    National Drug Control Policy
    (ONDCP)
Williams, Edward Huntington, 80
Wilson, Suzanne, 17
women and opiate addiction in U.S., 69
World Bank
  on colonization of Chapare region,
    Bolivia, 220
  on factoring opium considerations
    into all engagement with
    Afghanistan, 326
World Drug Report (UNODC), 127n2,
    294n12, 295n21
World Health Organization, 83
World War I, 74–75
Wright, Hamilton, 73

Z

Zambrano, Marta, 17
Zedillo, Ernesto, 50
Zervos, D., 171

ECO-AUDIT
Environmental Benefits Statement

The World Bank is committed to preserving endangered forests and natural resources. The Office of the Publisher has chosen to print *Innocent Bystanders* on recycled paper with 30 percent postconsumer fiber in accordance with the recommended standards for paper usage set by the Green Press Initiative, a nonprofit program supporting publishers in using fiber that is not sourced from endangered forests. For more information, visit www.greenpressinitiative.org.

Saved:
- 19 trees
- 6 million Btu of total energy
- 1,826 lb. of net greenhouse gases
- 8,797 gal. of waste water
- 534 lb. of solid waste